The Feminine Symptom

The Feminine Symptom

ALEATORY MATTER IN
THE ARISTOTELIAN COSMOS

Emanuela Bianchi

FORDHAM UNIVERSITY PRESS *New York* 2014

the
modern language
initiative

THIS BOOK IS MADE POSSIBLE BY A COLLABORATIVE GRANT
FROM THE ANDREW W. MELLON FOUNDATION.

Library of Congress Cataloging-in-Publication Data

Bianchi, Emanuela.
  The feminine symptom : aleatory matter in the
Aristotelian cosmos / Emanuela Bianchi.
    pages cm
  Includes bibliographical references and index.
  ISBN 978-0-8232-6218-2 (cloth : alk. paper)—
  ISBN 978-0-8232-6219-9 (pbk. : alk. paper)
  1. Aristotle. 2. Teleology. I. Title.
B485.B525 2014
185—dc23
                                    2014014676

Printed in the United States of America

17 16 15   5 4 3 2 1

First edition

For David

CONTENTS

ACKNOWLEDGMENTS

This project has had such a long gestation that it is impossible to acknowledge adequately all those who have contributed one way or another to its genesis. At the very least, I should say that I am profoundly grateful to a bevy of brilliant and generous interlocutors, mentors, readers, and friends for their support and feedback, as well as for the invaluable institutional backing, without which this work could not have been accomplished.

Thank you to Richard Bernstein, Judith Butler, and Dmitri Nikulin for their immensely helpful critiques when this project was in its early stages. In particular, Judith Butler and Kaja Silverman's seminars in the Rhetoric Department at UC Berkeley were formative for my thinking in this book. I am grateful to the UNC Charlotte Department of Philosophy, in particular Michael Kelly, Marvin Croy, and Nancy Gutierrez for granting me space and time for research and writing, including sponsoring my stay at the University of Dundee. A semester spent at the University of Dundee as a Humanities Research Fellow enabled great progress on the manuscript, and I thank the School of Humanities and the Philosophy faculty, especially Rachel Jones, for providing a rich and productive intellectual environment. At New York University I owe Jacques Lezra, chair of the Comparative Literature Department, Joy Connolly, Dean of Humanities, and the Humanities Initiative many thanks for both moral and financial support throughout the publication process, and Susan Protheroe for all kinds of material assistance. I am also deeply grateful for the unstinting support and mentorship over the years of Judith Butler, Drucilla Cornell, Kaja Silverman, and Walter Brogan.

Earlier versions of parts of this book were delivered as papers at meetings of the Ancient Philosophy Society, the Society for Phenomenology and Existential Philosophy, the Society for Ancient Greek Philosophy, philoSOPHIA: A Feminist Society, the Irigaray Circle, the Society for Women in Philosophy, the American Philosophical Association, and the Society for Literature, Science, and Arts; I am grateful to these organizations for hosting me, and to the many invaluable conversations that ensued in the fertile contexts they offered. I am especially thankful to the members of the Ancient Philosophy Society, a remarkable scholarly community whose erudition, feedback, support, and companionship have contributed to this book in immeasurable ways. In particular I would like to thank Sara Brill, Walter Brogan, Ryan Drake, Jill Gordon, Josh Hayes, Sean Kirkland, Aryeh Kosman, David Farrell Krell, Christopher Long, Jessica Mayock, Holly Moore, Michael Naas, Eric Sanday, Michael Shaw, and Adriel Trott, without whose insights this work would be a mere shadow of itself.

I have been exceptionally lucky that these chapters have at various stages found fine and careful readers in Sara Brill, Rachel Jones, Homay King, Katherine Stephenson, David Kazanjian, and members of the UNC Charlotte Philosophy faculty reading group, all of whom gave unsparingly of their time and provided enormously enriching feedback for which I am hugely grateful. I particularly thank Mike Shaw, Kate Thomas, Rebecca Hill, and two anonymous readers for their unprecedented generosity in reading and commenting on the entire manuscript. I only hope I have done justice to their suggestions as the book evolved. Any errors or failures of analysis remain my own, of course.

I thank my editors Helen Tartar and Tom Lay at Fordham University Press, Laura Helper-Ferris for vital editorial guidance, Tim Roberts at the Modern Language Initiative for shepherding the book into print, Michael Koch for painstaking copyedits, Andrew Joron for a fine index, Jonathan Eburne for an important file, Sammy Cucher and Anthony Aziz for the stunning cover image, and Elizabeth Benninger for invaluable research assistance.

In addition to these more formal kinds of engagement, this book has been vastly strengthened by the wisdom, conversation, friendship, kinship, support, love, comradeship, and community of many people in many contexts, more than I could ever hope to mention, including Dina Al-Kassim, Paula Austin, Anthony Aziz, Ellen Babcock, Sara Beardsworth, Cristina Beltrán, Pearl Brilmeyer, Shay Brawn, Eric Butler, Naveen Chandra, Zahid Chaudhary, Ed Cohen, Simon Critchley, Sammy Cucher, Chris Cuomo, Alison Dell, Josh Dubler, Ronald Duculan, Lisa Duggan, Melissa Ehn, David Eng, Tony Freitas,

Raelyn Gallina, Nish Gera, Gina Glennon, Gayatri Gopinath, Amy Greenstadt, Elizabeth Grosz, Gillian Harkins, Brooke Holmes, Donna Hunter, Robin James, Leigh Johnson, Nina Katchadourian, Homay King, Kent Klaudt, David Landau, Kyoo Lee, Carla Loomis, Babs Lornie, Moira McNamara, Will McNeill, Rob Miotke, Christina Morus, Roopali Mukherjee, Patrick O'Donnell, Tei Okamoto, Johanna Oksala, Mariana Ortega, Katrin Pahl, Ann Pellegrini, Jennie Portnof, Sara Pursley, Josh Ramey, Mary Rawlinson, Avital Ronell, Teemu Ruskola, Liam Ryan, Josie Saldaña, Gayle Salamon, Heron Saline, Catherine Sameh, Nic Sammond, Bethany Schneider, Erin Small, Fanny Söderbäck, Amanda Staab, Gus Stadler, Kate Stark, Jeff Stark, Sheila Stark, Jill Stauffer, Nicolai Stern, Kate Thomas, Susan Thompson, Rosemarie Tong, Karen Tongson, Neon Weiss, Mike Witmore, Damon Young, and Catherine Zimmer. José Esteban Muñoz, who welcomed me into the queer community he helped to build at NYU with open arms, shockingly left this world far too soon, just as the book is going to press. His queer utopian philosophical vision infuses the sensibility of this book. I thank Christopher Long in particular for a long philosophical friendship and extended shared agonizings with Aristotle's highly elliptical Greek. I thank my mother, Lorenza Bianchi, for her unflinching fierceness and her unwavering faith in me, and Kyra Grosman for making life surpassingly sweet. David Kazanjian has been there over the years in a way that no language I know, ancient or modern, really has any words for, and my thanks to him are expressed in the dedication of this book.

Chapter 4 was published in a different version as "Sexual Topologies in the Aristotelian Cosmos: Revisiting Irigaray's Physics of Sexual Difference," *Continental Philosophy Review* 43, no. 3 (August 2010): 373–89, and appears with kind permission from Springer Science+Business Media B. V. Chapter 3 previously appeared in modified form as "Receptacle/*Chōra*: Figuring the Errant Feminine in Plato's *Timaeus*," *Hypatia* 21, no. 4 (2006): 124–46. Small portions of chapters 2 and 6 were previously published in "Material Vicissitudes and Technical Wonders: The Ambiguous Figure of Automaton in Aristotle's Metaphysics of Sexual Difference," *Epochē* 11, no. 1 (2006): 109–39. A previous version of a section of chapter 6 also appeared as "Aristotelian *dunamis* and sexual difference: An analysis of *adunamia* and *dunamis meta logou* in *Metaphysics* Theta," *Philosophy Today* 51 (Supplement 2007): 89–97. A brief passage in the Coda previously appeared in "The Interruptive Feminine: Aleatory Time and Feminist Politics," in *Undutiful Daughters: New Directions in Feminist Thought and Practice*, ed. Henriette Gunkel, Chrysanthi Nigianni, and Fanny Söderbäck (New York: Palgrave Macmillan, 2012).

A NOTE ON THE TRANSLATIONS

I have consulted a variety of translations for the Greek texts, sometimes preferring the formulations of one translator over another, and sometimes offering my own translations, always with the overall aims of clarity, fidelity, and consistency. To this end, I have sometimes modified a given translation to highlight the presence or force of a particular word, often just reverting it to the Greek. I have marked these instances with the notation "translation modified" in the notes. I have used Latin transliterations of the Greek throughout for readability.

Introduction

Nature's aim, then, is to measure the generations and endings [*teleutas*] of things by the measure of these [heavenly] bodies, but she cannot bring this about exactly on account of the indeterminateness [*aoristian*] of matter and the existence of a plurality of principles which impede the processes of generation in nature and destruction, and so often are the causes of things occurring contrary to Nature [*para phusin sumpiptontōn*].

ARISTOTLE, Generation of Animals

And revolutions also come into being from a coincidence [*sumptōmatos*].

ARISTOTLE, Politics

By exhibiting this "symptom," this crisis point in metaphysics where we find exposed that sexual "indifference" that had assured metaphysical coherence and "closure," Freud offers it up for our analysis.

LUCE IRIGARAY, Speculum of the Other Woman

The notion of *telos*—the end, or the "for the sake of which" things exist or happen—is a famously intractable keystone in the architecture of Western metaphysics and science. Originating in Aristotle's philosophical system, it structures nature and human action: through *telos* they are ultimately understood, and by *telos* they are ultimately caused. The Aristotelian *telos*, the good or what is best (*to beltion*), therefore dominates and provides the justification for a rigorously hierarchical cosmological system encompassing the physical world, the biological world, and the human world of ethics and politics.

Sexual difference and the phenomena of sexual reproduction turn out to be decisive matters for Aristotelian teleology. Teleological processes are, after all, most self-evidently given in biological phenomena, and are found at the level of organs and behaviors, as well as in organisms as a whole, which are readily understood functionally as aiming toward certain ends. And Aristotle's biological investigations cover numerous volumes, comprising about a quarter of his extant corpus. It is not too much of a stretch, to my mind, to characterize him as first and foremost a biological thinker, and it is no accident that one of the greatest expositions of his teleological thinking is found in chapter 1 of *Parts of Animals*. Furthermore, the division into male and female, although by no means universal, is nonetheless an endemic structural feature of both natural and human worlds, and accordingly Aristotle thematizes this distinction in texts as diverse as *Generation of Animals*, *Politics*, and *Poetics*. Indeed in *Generation of Animals* he undertakes a detailed examination of the biology of sexual reproduction that both enables and necessitates this division.[1] Just as Heidegger designated Aristotle's *Physics* as the "hidden, and therefore never adequately studied, foundational book of Western philosophy," for its focus on the problem of motion, so this study looks to Aristotle's *Generation of Animals* and its study of natural coming-to-be as the hidden and therefore never adequately studied foundational book of Western patriarchal metaphysics.[2] This central problem of motion and that of gender are profoundly connected: Aristotle identifies the female as the source of matter for the offspring, while the male provides the principle of motion, generation, soul-principle, *logos*, and form.[3] In an extended technical analogy, he writes, "it is the shape [*morphē*] and form [*eidos*] which pass from the carpenter, and they come into being by means of the movement in the material [*hulē*] . . . his hands move his tools and his tools move the material. In a similar way to this, nature acting in the male of semen-emitting animals uses the semen as a tool."[4] Aristotle in this way installs a technicity, a scene of artifactual production, at the heart of natural generation, which is thereby ineluctably marked as an operation of the masculine upon the feminine, the active upon the passive. Aristotle's male-female distinction and the difficulties it raises—in particular the key problematic of the female offspring—provide a uniquely revelatory set of lenses through which to view the production and sustenance of Aristotelian teleology, whether in nature, in human life, or in relation to the central questions of the *Metaphysics* concerning causation, the being of substance, and the nature of becoming.

Through an examination of Aristotle's explicit theories of sexual difference, as well as psychoanalytic and deconstructive analyses of figures and tropes of sex and gender in his texts, this book explores the role of sexual difference in the constitution of the Aristotelian cosmos—from the biological, through the physical, cosmological, divine, and metaphysical, and into the human world. Sexual difference, according to this analysis, not only provides a kind of structural scaffold for the cosmos, but also is repeatedly and insistently a site of its aporias, and its unraveling. The investigations shed light not only on the persistence and pervasiveness of the question of gender for Aristotle, but on the very cohesion of the Aristotelian text in its structure, movement, and forces, and in the complexities of its unfolding. What is thereby disclosed is a constitutive tension in Aristotle's writings between, on the one hand, his push to systematize, classify, hierarchize, and subject the multiplicity of phenomena both natural and artificial to an overarching teleology, and on the other his painstaking attention to saving the same phenomena, his attunement to the very texture of becoming in its singular and irreducible contexts. Making central the problematic of sexual difference and sexual reproduction within Aristotle's texts, a symptomatic scene appears that draws into sharpest possible focus an aporetic turbulence resulting from this confluence of these two philosophical vectors, the systematic and the phenomenological. The primary symptom is the female figure itself, exemplified *par excellence* by the female offspring.

If the male provides the *logos,* the formal principle, and the source of motion, the problem immediately arises—whence the female offspring? Aristotle tells us that the female appears as the result of a material mishap—there may be too much bulk and coldness at the scene of conception because of innumerable factors, for instance the youth or old age of the parents, an excess of fluid or femininity in the body, or simply due to winds in the south during copulation.[5] If these deviations are large, there will be an obvious deformity in the offspring, a "monstrosity," but if they are small a female will result—a situation that is also, for Aristotle, teleologically necessitated because the species is such that it can only be perpetuated through sexual difference.[6] Here, then, unpredictable exigencies in the material conditions of reproduction give rise to a fault, a misstep, a deviation in the teleological transmission from father to son. The female offspring arises because of the unpredictable and unaccountable, the aleatory motions of matter. And yet it—quite inexplicably—also plays a necessary part in the teleological unfolding of nature. It is exactly this inexplicable *confluence* of the aleatory and the teleological that I am calling "the feminine symptom." Aleatory matter—that is, matter that is apparently self-moving, disruptive, exterior to any teleological unfolding, indeed that acts *against nature*—poses continual

difficulties for the Aristotelian cosmos. But it is insofar as this wayward and disobedient matter acts in concert with, at the same time
as, and to the same ends as the teleology, that it appears as precisely
symptomatic. In short, the feminine symptom is the inexplicable
coincidence (*sumptōma*) of causal orders, and aleatory matter is the
site at which the symptom arises.

The notion of symptom, however, deserves closer investigation. In
the first instance, one might say a symptom is a surface manifestation of a deeper dysfunction. Difficulties, aporias, contradictions, surface phenomena we encounter in the text show us that something is
wrong, indicate a need for investigation, and call us to excavate the
workings of the text to seek the source of the problem. The symptom
discloses dysfunction, but also, as a sign, points beyond itself, telling us to look elsewhere for its cause. In the case of Aristotle, however, it is not always easy to distinguish a problem on the surface
from a more fundamental and indeed perhaps constitutive dysfunction. While Aristotle is often praised for his detailed attention to phenomena of all kinds, and for his genuine attempt to do justice to their
multiplicity and complexity, it is not at all difficult to see—and many
authors, especially feminists, have pointed it out—that insofar as he
is also a system builder on a grand scale, his metaphysical system is
explicitly patriarchal, dominative, hierarchical, and oppressive. In the
teleological ordering, each kind of being takes its place in an inescapable hierarchy, and participates in the perpetuation of that hierarchy.

Instead of anachronistically castigating Aristotle for his nonpro-
gressive, nonmodern, or nonliberal views, or indeed trying to rescue
him through "charitable" readings (which like the questionable virtue
after which they are named tend to paper over difficulties and salve
the philanthropist's bad conscience rather than attend appropriately
to complexities), this book proceeds instead through what Gayatri
Chakravorty Spivak has termed a "critical intimacy" with the writings at hand.[7] The endeavor of such affirmative deconstruction is to
read Aristotle as closely, as intimately, indeed as generously as possible, all the while maintaining a rigorous critical eye. This double
strategy of reading calls us at once to listen to the Greek assiduously,
to attend to the textuality of the text, the philological nuance, the
rhetorical trope, and especially the resonance of its figures, but also
refuses to forget that it is always today that we read or reread Aristotle. Reading takes place in a sense both here *and* there, and a responsible, responsive reading practice, one which not only reads but also

responds, is a Janus-faced one in which we ask both what the text means *for Aristotle* in his own terms and context, and what the text also might mean *for us*. This hermeneutic is by no means perfectly circular but rather punctuated, disjunctive, abyssal, risky, and uneven. It assumes that no reading is uninterested or ahistorical—each reading brings the reader's place, time, and social location, interests, and critical concerns to the table. It is therefore incumbent upon the scholar to make his or her investments in the work (intellectual, political, affective, cultural, and so on) as explicit as possible, all the while striving for rigor and precision throughout the interpretation. A certain creativity is at work in these readings, to be sure, in some places more than others, and at the same time so is a certain practice of listening and of letting be: one may *allow* an interpretation to emerge and at the same time take responsibility for finding particular elements in the text more germane than others, given one's guiding questions. Eve Kosofsky Sedgwick in her later work drew a hugely influential distinction between *paranoid* and *reparative* reading strategies, one driven by critical suspicion and the other driven by an impulse to repair the world and the texts from which our worlds emerge.[8] For Sedgwick, a symptomatic reading would be the kind of paranoid reading that puts critical faith in gestures of unveiling and exposure, while reparative readings accrete and assemble the perhaps minor positive moments or happy contingencies of a text, visible in the interstices of the toxicities of hegemony, knitting them into a texture that might enable and magnify possibilities for living on, and even living well. Both of these impulses or strategies animate this book to some extent, and I find no grounds for their incompatibility. Though it must be said that one does not need to dig very deep to find the hierarchical violence of classical antiquity enshrined in the texts of Aristotle, not least in his character0ization of slaves and women as naturally lacking or deformed. Alongside paranoid and reparative reading strategies are no doubt many other affective stances at work in what follows (possibly involving the full range of transferential feelings one might normally associate with fathers, mothers, or lovers real and symbolic: rage, love, frustration, forbearance, hatred, wonder, and so on), and any claim on my part to be fully conscious of them all would be necessarily disingenuous.[9]

This book, then, explicitly takes up the question of gender and in foregrounding that question asks about the legacy of Aristotle's hierarchical system for us. In paying attention to the sexed and gendered

symptoms produced in and by the systematicity of these texts, the
teleological and hierarchical system may be unsettled from within, or
rather, it may be shown to be unsettled in advance, constitutively and
incessantly unsettled, and unsettling. The symptom not only reveals
the system's dysfunction; by violating the constituting boundary of
the system, both internal and external, it also discloses that boundary
as continually called into question, and consequently also in continual
need of fortification—a fortification that will itself inevitably give rise
to more symptoms, as demonstrated so beautifully in Derrida's elaboration of the logic of autoimmunity.[10] The project therefore becomes
not so much identifying and curing the underlying problem or cause
that generates the symptom, but rather tracing *how* the text produces
both system and symptom in concert, and then, asking further, if and
how the text itself may be productively rethought or understood gen-
eratively in light of its symptomaticity. Indeed, we might speak of a
symptomatic reading precisely along Althusserian lines, in which a
particular attentiveness to a text's *lacunae*, the "failures in its rigour,
or the outer limits of its effort," may also *open a space* for reading.[11]
The operation of the symptom as traversing both the interior and the
exterior of the teleological system is well expressed by Judith Butler
in the following formulation: "A constitutive or relative outside is, of
course, composed of a set of exclusions that are nevertheless *internal*
to that system as its own nonthematizable necessity. It emerges within
that system as incoherence, disruption, a threat to its own systematicity."[12] The feminine symptoms we encounter in what follows will
appear in many guises—as contradictions or aporias in the texts, as
unruly forces capable of waylaying teleological processes, as multiple
overdetermined figures that articulate and disarticulate boundaries,
as means through which fault lines in the system may be disclosed
and constitutive assumptions uncovered; they also act as vehicles that
offer openings and possibilities for rereading and refiguration. Tracing the appearance and operation of the feminine symptom throughout Aristotle's corpus will, I hope, yield a progressively compelling
account of the Aristotelian cosmos as both constituted by and threatened by that symptom, a cosmos and indeed a metaphysics that can
ultimately no longer be meaningfully sustained with any stability or
claims to self-same unity.

   If this notion of symptom as nonthematizable necessity, or as that
which both exceeds and founds a system, is deconstructively expedi-
ent, then the Greek meaning and etymology of symptom, *sumptōma*,

exponentially multiplies this serendipity. *Sumptōma* is literally a falling together (from *sum-*, together + *piptō*, to fall), anything that befalls one, a chance, a mischance, or a calamity. Coincidence (*co-* + *in-* + *cadere*) is the most literal Latinate cognate. The falling together of the *sumptōma* suggests both an unexpected, unchosen, and forceful downward motion and an irreducible plurality, the falling of more than one thing together, at the same time. *Sumptōma* is not, however, one of Aristotle's most usual words for chance or aleatory phenomena—in the chapters dealing with chance in *Physics* II he primarily uses *tuchē* (meaning chance in the human sphere, or luck) and *automaton* (chance or spontaneous occurrences in the natural sphere), though in one important passage he conjoins *sumptōma* with these terms in the service of decisively severing them both from *telos* or final cause, establishing the latter as properly natural and nonsymptomatic.[13] Nonetheless *sumptōma*, and the related verb *sumpiptō* (to coincide or to occur), do appear with some regularity throughout the corpus, and in several cases the word occurs in conjunction with the mention of women or the sphere of the feminine.[14] Certain instances are especially illuminating and it will be worthwhile to devote some time to them. The first appears in *On Sophistical Refutations*, the second in the *Rhetoric*, and a couple more in the *Politics*. Taken together, they offer a glimpse into the profound significance of the *sumptōma*'s operation in Aristotle's texts.

In *On Sophistical Refutations*, *sumptō ma* occurs in a discussion of how linguistic gender may be the occasion for solecism or grammatical error, with the goal of forcing a sophistic opponent into commiting such an error. The overall theme is thus errancy in language, slips of the tongue that lead one to mistaken formulations: these are the very parapraxes—due to what Lacan calls "an incessant sliding of the signified under the signifier"[15]—that psychoanalysis will later find meaningful and indeed symptomatic. Aristotle, having noted the ambiguities inherent in gendered language in its relation with the world, especially pronouns, says one can happen (*sumpiptei*) to err in both names and things.[16] Just three lines earlier, he has given an example of a feminine noun, *klinē*—a bed, that is, an object of use that would normally take an -*on* ending but does not, and which therefore may easily lead us into error. *Klinē*'s primary meaning may be a bed, but it also signifies what inclines, declines, and deviates from the orthogonal.[17] This word will reappear in the discussion of the slant (*enklisis*) of the sun's path along the ecliptic in

chapter 5. It also forms the root of that most controversial and enig-
matic concept of ancient aleatory materialism, the Lucretian *clinamen*, the almost imperceptible, uncaused and unpredictable atomic
swerve.[18] In this passage Aristotle is saying, in so many words, that
both words and things that deviate and decline along gendered lines
may give rise to symptoms, in particular on account of their unex-
pectedly feminine valence. The aleatory, the feminine, and the symptomatic strikingly emerge here together, in concert with one another.

The second instance of *sumptōma*, at *Rhetoric* I.9, occurs in the
context of a discussion on how to assess moral worthiness. Aristotle says that coincidences and strokes of luck (*kai ta sumptōmata kai
ta apo tuchēs*) must be counted as valid and included when assess-
ing a man's virtue, because *repeated* acts of virtue show a man to be
praiseworthy, and presumably even lucky chances must count in such
a calculation.[19] But Aristotle has just given a quote from Simonides to
illustrate the point that virtue is more noble when it goes beyond what
one might reasonably expect from a person. The woman referred to
in the quote, Archedice, is all the more virtuous because she is not
proud, even though she hails from a family of tyrants according to
the inscription on her tomb given by Thucydides: "Daughter, wife,
and sister of tyrants."[20] Intensifying the contradiction, the previous
section tells us that, "virtues and actions are nobler when they proceed from those who are naturally worthier, for instance, from a man
rather than from a woman."[21] According to these examples, then, a
woman may be deemed worthy if she manages to exceed her chance
circumstances, the accidents of her birth, but never as worthy as a
man, who may in fact be deemed virtuous precisely because of strokes
of luck or accident! Aristotle's bias here is far from implicit, and in its
blatant inconsistency this argument's symptomaticity is simply undeniable. The tropes of gender and chance folded together here seem to
occasion a kind of hyperbolic aporia, a quite glaring illustration of
the feminine symptom.

Finally, there are several revealing appearances of *sumptōma* in the
Politics. In Book V, the *sumptōma* appears as an unspecified coincidence interpreted by a bridegroom as a bad omen when he comes to
fetch his bride. Because of this *sumptōma* he leaves without her, and
her family puts him to death during a sacrificial ritual, all of which
ends up giving rise to extensive factionalism at Delphi.[22] The very next
example attributes factionalism at Mitylene (a location, like Delphi,
long associated with female power) to a problem with heiresses. The

entire passage concerns the domestic, feminine roots of factional conflicts in kinship disputes, where symptoms in the sphere of the household or *oikos* lead to widespread disruptions in the *polis*. Additional uses of *sumptōma* at *Politics* II.12 and V.5 are unrelated to the theme of sexual difference, but are worth mentioning as they highlight the extraordinary political significance of the Aristotelian *sumptōma* for contemporary readers. The first relates to the founding of Athenian democracy as initiated by Solon. Solon had constituted the jury courts from all citizens, which finally led to rule by the people in what is widely understood as the first democratic political system (with participation limited to male citizens). Aristotle argues that this democracy arose not at all by the intention of Solon, who bestowed minimal power on the people and actually appointed all government officers from the wealthy, but rather as a result of a coincidence, a *sumptōma*: a historical contingency in which the common people adopted bad (*phaulous*—mean, low in rank, common) leaders against the wishes of the respectable classes, in a chain of events leading eventually to a democratic government.[23] The second usage tells us that revolutions may also come into being as a result of a *sumptōma*.[24] Appearing at the source of both democracy *and* revolutions, the *sumptōma* signifies a fundamental disruption of hierarchy and teleology.

Although in this book the female or feminine is a privileged locus of symptomatic material activity in the Aristotelian cosmos, clearly it is not the only one. Just as feminine matter may be disruptive and disobedient in the natural sphere, and women in the *oikos* may disrupt the political sphere, so, importantly, the people more generally may disrupt and undermine existing systems of rule in ways that are unpredictable and unknowable in advance. Here, then, Aristotle foreshadows Althusser's aleatory materialism of the historical encounter—a theme to which I will return in the coda.[25]

Although *sumptōma* is the term with the most intimate etymological tie to the notion of symptom that guides this investigation, Aristotle also invokes a series of important terms to designate the generalized field of the aleatory, the chancy or random. Perhaps most well-known is his notion of accident (*kata sumbebēkos*) that appears as an attribute of substance (Socrates is musical by accident) and as opposed to the essential or in-itself (*kath' auto*) (Socrates is a man, and therefore a rational animal, *zōon logon echon*, essentially). So in the *Physics* the famous four causes are essential causes, causes *kath' auto*, while the supplementary causes are accidental, *kata sumbebēkos*. And these supplementary causes are not just the accidental as incidental, but also constitute a field of what for him may indeed act *against nature* (*para phusin*) rather than according to nature (*kata phusin*).

Among these supplementary causes, then, are *tuchē*, signifying luck or chance in the human world of choice; and *automaton*, indicating random or spontaneous occurrences in nature. It is specifically due to such *automaton* that the female arises in reproduction, as well as the monstrosities of which the female is just a mild form, and the spontaneous generation (*genesis automatos*) of certain lowly life forms such as shellfish. The feminine thus appears as *both for and against* nature: the female disrupts or breaks down the reproductive process, but her appearance is of course necessary to nature's continuance. Nature itself, it should be noted, is a fully teleological system for Aristotle, and despite the feminine gender of the Greek *phusis* that leads translators to personify it as a "she," in a precise illustration of the very Aristotelian solecism encountered a few moments ago, it is not at all associated with the feminine as it may be for us.[26] And perhaps counterintuitively, necessity, *anankē*, is also found in the field of the aleatory, of what disrupts or acts against nature. Plato's *Timaeus* introduces the "third kind" or "errant cause" as what comes about through necessity (*di' anankēs*), and therefore places necessity on the side of *chōra*, the feminine, and that which is beyond the reach of reason.[27] Aristotle, by contrast, reclaims necessity for the side of teleology and reason, and argues that for the most part it issues from final causes. Thus the prime mover and perfect circular motions of the heavens are necessary *par excellence* because they cannot be otherwise. There is also another type of necessity for Aristotle, a "disagreeable" force or compulsion (*bia*) that is shown when natural teleology is disrupted, when a stone, for example, is thrown upward rather than moving downward according to its natural inclination. Such *bia* remains for him on the side of the aleatory.[28] Generally, then, we find the aleatory at work in phenomena involving matter qua its indeterminacy, plurality, and self-motion, and in things that somehow occur "at the same time" (*hama*). The feminine symptom shows itself in phenomena as wide-ranging as monstrosities (*terata*) and in what is deformed or mutilated (*anapēros*) (in the sphere of biology), as the involuntary in the sphere of animal movement, in the slant (*enklisis*) of the sun's trajectory, and most generally as what falls or moves in a downward direction, or what occurs exceptionally, in the sublunar realm. Textual phenomena too, moments of contradiction and aporia in and between Aristotle's texts, appear as symptomatic no less insistently than his own explicit examples.

The feminine resonances of *sumptōmata*—of chance, mischance, coincidence, misdirection, deviation, monstrosity, inclination, obliquity, plurality, falling, and most specifically *falling together*—will therefore echo throughout the various readings that follow. Here Irigaray's figure of the two lips also comes into play. Irigaray's two lips are a pivotal topological and embodied intervention into a masculine philosophical imaginary dominated by the phallus, an alternate figure for imagining feminine sexual difference, language, and desire.[29] This figure also has a surprising etymological connection with the symptom. The common etymological root of lip, labia, and labile is, after all, the Latin verb *labi* (to slip or fall). In their restless indeterminate plurality, their simultaneous materiality and figurality, and their unmistakable femininity, the two lips also have an intimate relation to, and may be said to fall together with, the symptom. The figure of the lips helps us read various sites of boundary and articulation in Aristotle's cosmos, and its Platonic precursor, as feminine, chiasmatic, and labile.

This association of the symptom with Irigaray's topological figuration of feminine sexuality as labial and labile raises the question of the relation of this study to Irigaray's project of feminine philosophical reading more generally. By noting this association, I do not mean to claim too strongly that reading Aristotle symptomatically or through the feminine symptom holds the promise of yielding up or uncovering a lost feminine imaginary, or indeed a feminine philosophical imaginary to come: a way of thinking, knowing, experiencing or desiring that would claim to represent anything like "feminine sexual difference" as such, although Irigaray's own investigations into "the Greeks," as well as her elemental investigations of Nietzsche and Heidegger, may well be regarded as doing so.[30] The present study of Aristotle is rather one that takes up an already fully realized metaphysics, in which no unadulterated trace of "the feminine" might be detected, but rather in which "the feminine" always signifies the scene of a certain adulteration. Hence the designation of the feminine symptom: the symptom is precisely an effect within a constituted system, functioning to point beyond itself with no necessity of arriving at a ground. And while it is true that Plato's *Timaeus* can be understood along with John Sallis as a critical turning point in which the elemental discourses of the Presocratics are taken up and decisively

transformed for metaphysics,[31] it is strictly within the terms of the
Platonic and Aristotelian philosophies that this investigation is situated rather than in relation to their shadowy and perhaps more suggestive precursors. The lure and promise of the project is thus less a
prephilosophical, elemental, or chthonic feminine sexual difference
as such, than one of making visible and tangible the necessarily unsettling and unsettled place of the feminine in Aristotelian metaphysics, and alerting us to disruptions that may, perhaps, be productively
seized at the right time and place. But the relation between the feminine symptom and the two lips is also fortuitous, and perhaps itself
symptomatic rather than determinative, seizing on a rather different
aspiration than that of Irigaray for the form, function, and being of
the feminine in Greek philosophy, namely what is aleatory, symptomatic, unassimilable, and disruptive.

Insofar as the symptom is said to arise out of and in concert with
a philosophical system, the question of the unity of the Aristotelian corpus inevitably arises. Is there indeed a single, unified "system" at work, elaborated variously in the many domains of Aristotle's
inquiry? What of the significant philosophical differences and distinctions that may emerge in different domains and different contexts?
This project assiduously avoids any claim of substantive unity, but
rather proceeds according to an antisystematic, symptomatic methodology. Tropological insights thus emerge at key textual moments
throughout Aristotle's writings on natural philosophy and metaphysics, and through juxtapositions and overlayerings such moments connect and accrete, weaving text to text in sometimes unexpected ways.
Attending to the symptomaticity of the feminine in this way, according to what we might call along with Plato a kind of "bastard reasoning," allows a rather different sort of Aristotle to emerge.[32] This figure
is neither that of traditional Aristotelianism nor the misogynist figure
characterized by some feminist readings, nor even the more polyvocal Aristotle that appears in reparative phenomenological readings in
the Heideggerian vein, although elements of all these approaches have
contributed immeasurably to the present undertaking. My emphasis
on the systematic teleologism of Aristotle clearly echoes a medieval
Aristotelianist tradition whose most luminous figure is perhaps Aquinas,[33] while building on a twentieth-century history of strong feminist
readings that have drawn our attention to the fundamental, structural role of gender—alongside matter and form, passivity, and activity—in Aristotle's thinking.[34] Recent phenomenological readings, on

the other hand, have downplayed systemic factors and have attended instead to important countercurrents in Aristotle's texts, in particular his abiding push toward the singular, specific, and the wondrous, his desire to do justice not simply to his own experience of the phenomena but to how others have spoken of them, in a practice that Christopher Long has called a "legomenology . . . oriented by and attentive to the saying of things."[35] Such approaches are certainly exemplary in their attunement to Aristotle's words, but however richly they complexify his legacy, they do not entirely vitiate the overarching teleological and hierarchical architecture with which I am grappling.

In what follows, I do not seek to minimize what I see as Aristotle's systematic aspirations, and when there are contradictions within or between texts I am disinclined to explain them as the result of, for example, developmental shifts in Aristotle's thinking, nor do I find it useful to pass them over lightly. Insofar as they violate Aristotle's own injunction to noncontradiction they are clearly untenable, but I also seek to treat them as generative and productive sites that shed light on the unstable and uneven field of forces falling under the rubric of the Aristotelian corpus. And this is the crux: the Aristotelian corpus is precisely a field of vectors that constantly work both with and against one another. Zones of stability certainly can be found. Themes certainly repeat, echo, and are magnified. There are moments for reading generously, and also moments that necessitate refusal. And some parts simply cannot be reconciled with others. Pushing on these tensive junctures can be tricky: no justice is done to the works if we apply our own desire for compatibility and unification to them, but equally, throwing mud without inquiring as to the meaning of such contradictions—and symptoms are nothing if not meaningful—would violate the spirit of critical intimacy. Critical intimacy demands that the aporias arising from these crosscurrent and undertows must be read for their local and global significance, sensitively, critically, and without compromise.

It should not go unmentioned that the organic unity implicit in the very notions of corpus and symptom (or the phallus if not the two lips) echoes Aristotle's own concern with the animal organism—a unified system whose ideal state is one of health—as the primary object of philosophical inquiry and the privileged site of teleological activity. Medical analogies involving doctoring and health are endemic in Aristotle's works, and are themselves key sites for the appearance of the feminine symptom. In her unparalleled study of the medical symptom in Ancient Greece, *The Symptom and the Subject*, Brooke Holmes traces carefully the role played by medical symptoms in the formation of the understanding of the physical body. She points out that *sumptōma* was not yet even a medical term in fourth-century Greece. Rather, the doctors of the time—much like Aristotle, the doctor's son—use demonstrative pronouns (*tode, tade, touto,* etc.) to refer to the phenomena that interest them. Nonetheless, the Aristotelian text, the corpus, gives rise relentlessly to the inexplicable coincidings and aporias indicated by the term *sumptōma*. Like Holmes, I understand these symptoms less, "as windows onto hidden worlds . . . but as phenomena that help to generate and sustain worldviews."[36] Philosophical system, the Aristotelian corpus, the animal organism alike are constituted thusly by those who seek to read, understand, and diagnose them: on the one hand, aspirations to unity and consistency are at work, including the clarification of functional relationships between parts and wholes, and on the other, the appearance of symptoms manifest fault lines, breakdowns, dysfunctions, and precarities, even as they also open the way to more profound analyses of their constitution.

Another way we might think of a symptom is as a manifestation of a truth that remains hidden, of something that keeps itself concealed or in abeyance. According to Heidegger in the Introduction to *Being and Time:* "One speaks of 'appearances or symptoms of illness.' . . . Appearance, as the appearance 'of something,' thus precisely does *not* mean that something shows itself, rather, it means that something makes itself known which does not show itself."[37] Heidegger is discussing how the phenomenon, what "shows itself" (from *phainesthai,* the middle voiced form of "to show or shine forth"), may be distinguished from mere semblance, and thus he carefully differentiates the symptom from what dissembles, noting that the privative "not" of that which does not show itself is distinct from the privation of truth that is semblance or "mere appearance." The question of the truth of what is concealed, however, comes into radical doubt in the field of the feminine, and the feminine symptom has a more complex relation to the notion of privation or what remains concealed than these remarks would betray. First, it should be noted that, as Irigaray and others have insisted, the othering of the feminine in the texts of Western philosophy associates it invariably with semblance, with "mere appearance" (and of course we are familiar with the theme of woman as the figure for the deceptive lure of Truth itself from

Nietzsche). This means, as Margaret Whitford puts it, that, "femininity, then, *qua* appearance, is thus an integral if unacknowledged part of the economy of truth."[38] And further, the classic "feminine symptom" is that of hysteria, the symptom for which there is no identifiable, physiological "material" cause, the very condition out of which psychoanalysis and psychoanalytic thinking, the talking cure and the working through, developed in the late nineteenth century. Behind all of these, and ever-present, are the texts of Plato, and in particular the passage from semblance to truth in the allegory of the cave in Book VII of the *Republic* so thoroughly investigated for its feminine resonances by Irigaray in the latter part of *Speculum of the Other Woman*, and the final passages of the *Timaeus*, in which the wandering womb (*hustera*), an errant cause much like the receptacle/*chōra* itself, creates so much trouble for the female constitution. Cave, womb, privation, nontruth, semblance, deception, errancy; the feminine symptom's relationship with truth, and therefore the truth claims of the current study, are compromised at best. And yet in Aristotle's treatment of ontological becoming privation plays a central role that is not reducible to truth function or logical negation: a particular formation thus emerges at the site of the female, involving *both* matter *and* privation.

Any student of dialectic is aware that dynamic becoming, any ontological movement or progress, necessitates a passage through the negative. However, the relationship among the three terms *form, matter*, and *privation (sterēsis)*, as Aristotle outlines it at *Physics* I.8–9, ought not to be understood under an anachronistic Hegelian rubric of dialectical logic as a movement of spirit, a dynamic relationship between A and not-A. Aristotle is concerned to show that while it is impossible for something to arise out of nothing, there is indeed a sense in which the coming-to-be of a given form supplants its opposite or lack, as A supplants not-A, but matter nonetheless abides through this supplanting as a constant substrate. The form of the bed emerges from the wood, which is such that it embraces both the initial lack of form, and also enables the bed's form to emerge (in a way that water, for example, would not). The privation here, then, the lack, is precisely a lack of completion; the condition of a thing that has not attained its telos, its *entelecheia* or holding-itself-at-its-end. Privation, then, in this conception signifies less a simple not-A than a not-yet-A, with A always already foreseen, already determined and destined in advance. In a formulation unique to this passage, Aristotle tells us here that matter actually *desires* (*oregesthai*) form, "like the female which desires the male and the ugly which desires the beautiful."[39] What lacks perfection is necessarily oriented toward that perfection, seeking the completion it signifies, if not actively then at least in the Greek middle voice, neither actively nor passively. Privation is thus central to the form-matter schema, but also suggests an incipient and already oriented movement *within* matter, a capacity or potency for form that shows that here we are to understand being not simply as substance, *ousia*, but rather according to *dunamis* (potentiality, potency) and *energeia*.

The final chapter of this book thus analyzes the *dunamis-energeia* schema according to its sexed and gendered valences. I argue that the female or feminine is not simply on the side of matter and passivity with respect to form and what is active, but that she also represents lack or incompletion. Furthermore, this lack is characterized not only by the *dunamis* or capacity inherent in matter, but by a determinate *powerlessness*, a lack or privation not just of completion, but of *dunamis* itself, namely *a-dunamia*. Matter can easily be understood as *potential*, as *dunamis*, and sometimes Aristotle makes this very determination.[40] The extraordinary thing about matter as site of potential is that it is not simply the potential to become A, but also the potential *not* to become A, as Aristotle makes clear in key passages in both the *Metaphysics* and *De Generatione et Corruptione*.[41] Read according to the feminine symptom, then, the matter that obediently desires and stretches out toward form also harbors a threat of indeterminacy, a threat of impotency, a threat that the being in question may not come to be in quite the way envisioned by the teleology, or not come to be at all.

Feminist readings of Aristotle's biology typically begin from the observation that in sexual reproduction the complex of formal cause, the source of motion (efficient cause), and final cause—*telos*—is marked as masculine (conveyed by the male sperm), while matter, that which is moved, what is passive, is aligned with the feminine. This is undeniably the case. However, reading for the feminine symptom, this book finds that these alignments are themselves also unsettled by an alternate, subterranean understanding of matter that emerges throughout these readings of Aristotle's texts not just as pure passivity, nor as simply participating in teleology, but as harboring opaque and unpredictable motions that have the capacity to disrupt and derail the unfoldings of teleological processes. What the following chapters show is that femininity is not for Aristotle characterized merely by passivity and obedience, which amount in a sense to the same thing, but is also freighted by the phenomena of chance, coincidence, plurality, and force, by an indispensable and irreducible capacity to err, obstruct, deflect, and indeed move, though not necessarily in ways that are easily predictable or accessible to knowledge. I will construe feminine matter, then, as symptomatic, as not simply acted on by form, but as itself an obscure site of unaccountable movements, as a site of the possibility that A *as such* might not come to be exactly as expected, but that A', A+, A-, or perhaps even B, C, Q, or X might emerge, that is, as a site with potentials for all sorts of unforeseen monstrosities, deformations, and creative revolutions. This analysis therefore also brings into focus Aristotle's engagement in a polemic not simply or principally with Plato, but also, and perhaps more critically, against Empedocleanism and the atomism of Leucippus and Democritus. Indeed, the Aristotle brought into relief here, the Aristotle on the side of form—whether immanent or transcendent—has perhaps more in common with Plato than is generally acknowledged, especially in his continual resistance to the atomist specter of a world without form or end.

The project of addressing the traditional questions of first philosophy—being, substance, cause, the divine, the one—in relation to sexed and gendered beings—particularized, historicized, and politicized—insists not only the central philosophical relevance of sex and gender, but also that it is through this particularizing violation of philosophy's self-constitution as such that philosophy can be at its most decisively illuminating. So while Heidegger, especially in his exemplary readings of Aristotle, and Derrida in his deconstructive engagement with the philosophical tradition, have been models and primary interlocutors for this project, it is to Luce Irigaray that I owe the most overarching philosophical debt. Despite the differences already discussed between our two approaches, Irigaray has insistently foregrounded the issue of feminine sexual difference in the philosophical texts of the Western tradition, and without her example this book would not even be conceivable. Irigaray brings a feminist psychoanalytic understanding to the texts of Western philosophy, and interprets its concepts, structures, and figures according to topologies of sexed and gendered bodies in a fashion enabled, strictly speaking, by the categories, structures, and dynamics of psychoanalytic theory. The readings I undertake here are therefore necessarily informed by psychoanalytic theory which, I think it is fair to claim, uniquely made possible in the twentieth century the appearance of questions of sex and gender at the center of the philosophical stage. Psychoanalysis in this context appears not only as a kind of phenomenology of early life, but as a phenomenology of the lived body, a register in which sex, sexuality, and gender are always already in play and at issue in the orders of the imaginary and the symbolic, and in the psychical and political topographies of bodies, texts, not to mention in the very construction and elaboration of philosophical systems.

Nonetheless, approaching classical texts through a psychoanalytic lens is not without its own hermeneutic difficulties. Along with Page duBois, I agree that psychoanalytic interpretations of ancient cultures often rest on an assumption of the universal applicability of psychoanalytic categories and that they therefore may participate in a kind of circularity that seeks to guarantee that very universality, while in fact enacting colonizing and appropriative gestures. However, as duBois also points out, "psychoanalysis supports, is produced by, and is compatible with metaphysical, hierarchical, Western thought; it is the heir of Aristotelianism, of the logic of the great chain of being in which God emanates forth a series of beings arranged on a ladder of diminishing value and quality, from god to philosopher to master to husband to wife to slave to animal down through the oysters."[42] If we accept that psychoanalysis is indeed an heir to Aristotelianism, then mining psychoanalysis for its capacity to diagnose and unsettle the foundations of the very metaphysical tradition which conditioned its possibility does not simply impose an alien theoretical framework upon a set of culturally and historically removed object texts, but also sets in motion a kind of immanent critique. Here, differently situated texts arising from the same tradition may be read against one another in new ways, and in so doing, it is hoped, the assumptions and limitations of both discourses and the tradition in which they participate may be exposed, while offering new openings and possibilities for thinking through and beyond that tradition. The work here, then, is in a strong sense a psychoanalytic, deconstructive, and feminist *working through*. It does not deal with Aristotle summarily so as to leap beyond him into brand new territory, for such negation inevitably remains haunted by that which it repudiates. Nor is it a work of retrieval or reanimation. It rather tarries within Aristotle's terms, inhabiting them, revealing lines of interconnection and fission, disclosing their rhythms and falterings, the ways and means through which they interrupt themselves and therefore the apertures they might offer for living with, on, and beyond them.

Along with Irigaray, I understand the texts of Western philosophy to be fundamentally informed by the morphology of sexed bodies. And by paying attention in an Irigarayan spirit to the particularities of the sexed and gendered figures by which philosophy has sought to convey its concern with the abstractions of truth, substance, being, causality, matter, form, the good, freedom, space, place, motion, time, and so on, we can continue to ask these questions on a genuinely philosophical footing. The feminine within sexual difference thus encompasses the following denotations: a subject position, a political constituency, a phenomenological and corporeal facticity, and a structural element for metaphysics, revealed in what follows as fundamentally symptomatic in the Aristotelian text.[43] In training our focus on the manner and contexts in which feminine figures are deployed, then, we will discover that they do not always quite fit their designated place, but act in a self-displacing fashion to signify beyond themselves with profoundly consequential reverberations. Instances that appear at first sight to be mere examples, ornaments, figures, or analogies turn out to be constitutive. Indeed, this methodological strategy finds an uncanny echo at the very heart of the notion of "cosmos" that is the object of the inquiry. While the primary meaning of *kosmos* in Greek is order, a word that comes to be used by the philosophers (starting reputedly with Pythagoras but certainly used by Parmenides and Heraclitus, Plato, and Aristotle) to indicate the order of the whole universe, another, older meaning of *kosmos* found in Homer and Hesiod is ornament or adornment, particularly the adornments worn by women.[44] The root here is the verb *kosmeō*, to arrange or set in an order, to marshal armies as well as to beautify women. *Kosmos*, then, involves the bringing of order or perfection to that which—prior to this bringing (if it indeed makes sense to talk of anything properly knowable prior to such ordering)—is presumably in a kind of disarray: a morass of soldiers, the body of a woman.[45] Indeed anything that is ordered cannot be so immanently but *has been brought to order by another*, and in so doing its lack, its impropriety, its inadequacy as such, is made manifest. These multiple meanings of *kosmos* are at work in the very dynamic of Plato's *Timaeus*—in which the ideal city is shown in all its perfection by being at war, and where in the cosmogony the demiurge brings the "third kind," the disorderly feminine receptacle/*chōra*, into a state of order. *Kosmos*—underlying world order or furbelow, sign of excess vanity, necessary supplement, and deceitful cosmetic—the feminine symptom is laid bare here in its very articulation.[46] The fundamental terms and concepts in play thus already unsettle themselves, are unsettled even in advance of any interpretation, and cannot remain consistent or achieve the stable and harmonious systematicity that is their explicit aspiration. This feminist deconstruction assumes that nothing of femininity or woman is essential either in language or in nature, but rather traces the textual threads of the female and the feminine and in so doing finds them always already unweaving themselves. Here harmony is disclosed as conflict, equilibrium as disequilibration, and order as errancy.

Chapter 1 introduces Aristotle's four causes in the *Physics*, and emphasizes the central role of *logos* in the Aristotelian notion of cause. Aristotle's word for cause, *aitia*, means both cause and explanation, that is, it refers to both something independently operating *in nature* and something being explained in such a way that is satisfactory *for us*. As these two registers (which could anachronistically be allied with fact and value) are inseparable for him, I argue that the sex/gender distinction also to some extent loses its meaning in this territory. This means that throughout the analysis it is possible to use the *female*, the *feminine*, and *women* more or less interchangeably to indicate a structural pole in the field of sexual difference. I then turn to the account of sexual reproduction in *Generation of Animals*, showing how it paradigmatically illustrates Aristotle's theory of cause, but also how the problem of the female offspring constitutes a central difficulty. If the form is provided by the male, and the matter by the female, how can a female offspring result? The female offspring is produced at the confluence of two fundamentally separate and, for Aristotle, conflictual forces—the vicissitudes of matter and the teleology of nature. The female offspring thus appears as the feminine symptom *par excellence*—and here symptom is understood in its Greek sense of coincidence, or falling together, as well as in the sense of a surface phenomenon that discloses a deeper dysfunction. In order to gain some clarity on the problem, I explicate Aristotle's notion of accident (*kata sumbebēkos*) in the *Metaphysics*, and chance (*tuchē* and *automaton*) in the central chapters of *Physics* II, seeking to tease out their definition and mechanisms, and whether they can be reconciled with the account of the four essential causes. What is at stake is how matter might play a role that is not simply passive but in which it rather harbors its own, unruly, hard-to-perceive motions.

Chapter 2 continues this pursuit of aleatory matter by turning initially to the problem of necessity addressed by Aristotle at the end of *Physics* II. I first consider Aristotle's contrast between hypothetical and simple necessity, tracing his typologies of necessity in the *Metaphysics* and elsewhere, and showing that it is a mistake to understand simple necessity as the kind of physical, billiard ball–type necessity inhering in matter we are familiar with in modern discourses. Simple necessity, for Aristotle, refers rather to the metaphysical necessity of the prime mover and the heavens which cannot be otherwise. Insofar as Aristotle does recognize such a thing as "material necessity" it rather appears as supplementary and disagreeable in relation to both hypothetical and simple necessity correctly understood. However, if such material necessity remains largely unacknowledged in his theoretical texts, it returns quite insistently in the biological writings. In the biology of reproduction, such material necessity is connected with *automaton*, that is, chance or spontaneity in the natural sphere. I thus examine the various resonances of *automaton* in Aristotle's theory of cause and generation: *automaton* as a kind of chance or spontaneity in nature, the analogy with the wondrous automatic puppets (*automata*) as an explanation for embryonic development, as well as the phenomena of spontaneous generation in natural world, *genesis automatos*. *Automaton*'s etymology and the resonances of sexual difference in Aristotle's various accounts of *automaton*, I argue, turn out to be decisive both in relation to reproduction and to the wonder that is for him the source of the philosophical enterprise. Finally, in the account of *automaton* in *Metaphysics* VII, we find unequivocal confirmation that matter, at least sometimes, has the capacity to move itself in a way that is quite independent from any teleologically necessitated situation.

In chapter 3, I provide a philosophical context for Aristotle's account of motion, and find feminist tools by which to understand it, by returning to the cosmology and cosmogony of Plato's *Timaeus*. In the middle section of the dialogue, aptly termed the "chorology" by John Sallis, Plato describes the creation of the world of Becoming as the imprinting of a maternal receptacle by the paternal realm of Being. In a close reading of this section I investigate how the maternal-feminine receptacle/*chōra* is conceived by Plato as multiple, restless, and multivalent. The receptacle's insistent refiguration (as mother, nurse,

ointment, gold, wax tablet, and finally as *chōra* [space]), provides
an unstable field that persists between the two realms of Being and
Becoming, articulating them and disarticulating them, and knowable
only through a kind of bastard reasoning. A discussion of the example of the *ekmageion*—the wax tablet or stamp—explores how figurality itself is at stake in the dialogue, while the complexity of the
relationship between the realms of Being and Becoming is also examined through a discussion of necessity and persuasion. Indeterminate
and also multiply determining, the receptacle/*chōra* signifies, aporeti-
cally, the compresence of both containing and spacing. In dialogue
with other philosophical and feminist readings I explore the potential for engaging the notion of *chōra* as a tool for a feminist analysis
of Aristotle. These accounts have largely omitted the significance of
the receptacle/*chōra* as the source of cosmic motion, the shaking and
wandering (*planōmenon*) motion that is also, more famously, attributed to the womb at the close of the dialogue. I read the receptacle/
chōra in relation to the Irigarayan figure of the two lips—the two lips
show a way out of Plato's inescapably maternal figuring of femininity
in the receptacle/*chōra*, while the *chōra*'s errant motions foreground
the moving, and therefore temporal, dimension of the two lips. These
wandering, feminine movements found in the *Timaeus* may, furthermore, be seen as reappearing or persisting in the Aristotelian system
as the submerged and marginalized motions of aleatory matter.

Chapter 4 continues the Irigarayan investigation of ancient natural
philosophy, turning now to Aristotle's notion of place. In the *Physics*,
Aristotle explicitly reduces Plato's receptacle/*chōra* to matter (*hulē*)
on the one hand, and to place (*topos*) on the other.[47] The Aristotelian
account of place as container, and as proper (*oikeios*) place as telos in
the sublunary realm, is examined through Irigaray's understanding
of gendered topologies in which women provide containership to men
but have no "place" of their own. I analyze the distinction between
sublunary and cosmological dimensions of place in Aristotle through
the Freudian distinction between anaclitic and identificatory attachment, in which desire for the mother is superseded by love for the
father and resolved in the Oedipus complex. Other elements in the
Aristotelian text further complicate this narrative, in particular the
aporia involving the very boundary of the cosmos and the relationship
between space and time: here I read Aristotle's use of the word *hama*
(together or at the same time) as a "falling together" (*sumptōma*), and
therefore as another instance of the feminine symptom. Such feminine

symptomaticity once again gives grounds for disrupting this teleology of gender, opening onto not merely an ethics of sexual difference, but providing both space and place for a proliferation of non-normative, queer, transgender, and intersex modes of sexed and gendered subjectivity.

The conception of motion or *kinēsis*, so central to Aristotle's philosophy, is dealt with in chapter 5. Following the trajectory of falling inherent to the meaning of the symptom, the investigation begins at the highest level, with the celestial motion of the heavenly spheres and their relationship to the prime mover, followed by an inquiry into the very being and constitution of the prime mover. While the prime mover is proffered as pure *energeia*, complete and perfect, I argue that its transcendent status is secured only insofar as it represents the *aporetic* and thus the *symptomatic as such*. Moving downward from the heavens toward earth, I treat the boundary between the heavens and the sublunary realm in terms of the inclination (*enklisis*) of the sun's ecliptic, also read as an overdetermined feminine symptom that affords a passage between the masculine perfection of the heavens and the feminine mutability of the earth. The sun's slanting disruption of the heavens' circular perfection provides a passage to the temporal dimension of cyclicity, occasioning a discussion of the Epicurean *clinamen* in relation to Aristotelian cosmology.

The sublunar movements of the simple bodies—the elements of earth, air, fire, and water—are treated in the next section. In the discussion of elemental movement toward *proper place* in the *Physics* and *De Caelo* we see Aristotle forging a remarkable equivalence of place and form, instituting a vertical hierarchy that corresponds to the teleological hierarchy of the cosmos. Matter here is indeed seen to be self-moving, but this movement is cast as natural and proper (*oikeios*) or selfsame (*autos*) and is folded into a broader teleology of potentiality and actuality, whereas disorderly movements *against nature* (*para phusin*) are simply acknowledged but are otherwise left unexplained.

Following this I consider animal motion, focusing on Aristotle's small text *De Motu Animalium*. Here, I highlight the contrast between motion that is primarily structured by telic desire with the disturbances introduced by *phantasia*, involuntary motions, and corporeal vicissitudes, reading the latter once again according to the logic of the feminine symptom. The chapter closes with an excursus on Aristotle's notoriously difficult definition of motion in the *Physics* in terms of *dunamis* and *entelecheia*, suggesting, with the help of Iris Young, the possibility of a feminist account of nonteleological motion inherent in the notion of *energeia*. This serves as an apt introduction to the themes of the final chapter.

Chapter 6 considers Aristotle's turn in *Metaphysics* IX to a new twofold schema for being: that of *dunamis*, or potentiality, capability, power, and possibility; and *energeia/entelecheia*, or actuality, activity, or being-at-completion. First, I consider what is at stake in the shift from the language of matter to the language of *dunamis*, arguing that the aleatory dimensions of materiality so productive for a feminist analysis are thereby covered over. I suggest a way to reconceive *dunamis* that would preserve rather than erase a field of disruptive possibilities in the unfolding of being. Next, I consider the definition of *dunamis* as it is developed in *Metaphysics* IX in relation to sexual difference, and consider passive *dunamis*, *dunamis tou pathein*, as a possible locus of feminine power. In dialogue with feminist appropriations of Heidegger such as those of Carol Bigwood and Patricia Huntington, I trace usages of *dunamis* in *Generation of Animals* as well as in the *Metaphysics*. I find that ultimately for Aristotle the feminine appears less as a receptive power or malleability, than as a simple absence or evacuation of *dunamis*, namely *adunamia*. As it does for Lacan, the feminine appears to simply signify lack, and portends impotence or castration. Turning finally to *energeia* and *entelecheia*, I read these concepts against their aspiration to masculine and telic self-sufficiency, emphasizing their necessary relationship to potentiality, impotentiality, and the aleatory materiality and figurality of the feminine symptom.

In the coda I suggest some consequences of my reading of Aristotle for contemporary feminist political theorizing. While Aristotle qua architect of patriarchal metaphysics arguably represents everything that political philosophies of liberation are up against, Aristotle's refractive approach to the many levels of discourse, whether metaphysical, physical, biological, cosmological, or political, also meshes—oddly—with a new materialist and nonhumanist political sensibility found in authors like William Connolly, Manuel de Landa, Jane Bennett, and Elizabeth Grosz, for whom processes discerned at the level of material and ontological becoming may also be found to be operative at the level of politics (and vice versa). Reading Althusser's notion of aleatory materialism as a philosophy of the encounter alongside Derrida's *a-venir*, the future as the radically unexpected to come, shows that aleatory materialism opens onto a radical understanding of the ethico-political as the unforeseen historical encounter, occurring among unpredictable social and political aggregations. The primary claim developed in this book—that Aristotle constructs a profound association between the aleatory and the feminine that reverberates throughout the Western philosophical tradition—is given a brief genealogical treatment that in turn opens up the possibility of thinking contemporary materialist politics specifically as feminist politics: aleatory feminism. A strategic and nonessential alliance between aleatory materialism and feminist politics, aleatory feminism intervenes into every conception of the feminine as passive, mute, and powerless. It does this not by claiming the space of agency, articulation, mastery, or subjectivity that has been the traditional preserve of (some) men, but by interrupting the political scene from nowhere and at no particular time through impertinent, inappropriate, and evental interventions such as those of Pussy Riot, the Occupy movement, and the Arab Spring. Whether such interventions "take hold" is hardly the test of their potency. Rather, the ineliminable persistence of aleatory feminism as a mobilizing of the feminine symptom represents a utopian possibility *immanent to* both patriarchal metaphysics and hierarchical regimes, that of undermining those gendered oppositions that do so much work to structure and uphold them: subject and object, agent and patient, ruler and ruled.

CHAPTER ONE

Aristotelian Causation, Reproduction, and Accident and Chance

In *Generation of Animals* Aristotle famously states, "we should look upon the female state as being as it were a deformity [*anapērian*], though one which occurs in the ordinary course of nature [*phusikēn*]."[1] This pronouncement, extraordinary to the twenty-first–century eye, reveals in its short formulation the barest outlines of a grand scheme, at once metaphysical, physical, biological, ethical, and political. Let us sketch out its features. The first thing to note is a hierarchy in nature: some things are deformed, while others are more perfect and complete, and the female state deviates from an assuredly masculine perfection. Secondly, the word *anapēros*, a deformity, signifies a being that is maimed or incapacitated, and is derived from the verb *pēroō* (to maim, to mutilate, to castrate)—indeed the Aristotelian author of *History of Animals* X uses the word frequently in the latter sense.[2] So the female is, as it were, a mutilated, castrated male. Something is certainly missing—in Lacanian parlance, she is defined by lack. This deformity and deviation from perfection, however, is not a detraction from nature. It is a part of nature, occurring *by* nature (*phusikēn*). Nature therefore admits deformity, lack, nonbeing within being, and here its name and mark is female. Nature is thus characterized by a hierarchy of value in which the more perfect, the more complete, the masculine is *better*, and the less than complete, the deviant or deformed, is necessarily something less than good, of less worth, if not outright malign. In Aristotle's medieval legacy, the Christian God, God the Father, stands at the metaphysical center of the cosmos, embodying all that is good, perfect, eternal, and complete while woman—standing for corruption, imperfection and mutability—is located firmly in the temporal world of fate, fortune, worldly temptation and pleasures.[3] Although it would be unjust to treat Aristotle simply in terms of an entrenched Aristotelianism, gender hierarchy is nonetheless a fundamental and irreducible feature of Aristotle's world. This is true not only of his cultural context or his political views, but is thoroughly intertwined with and inseparable from his natural philosophy and teleological metaphysics. In this light, recent scholarly attempts to defend Aristotle's biology against feminist charges of sexism, or that try to parse out what is rational and philosophic from what is ideological in his writings, appear misguided and anachronistic.[4] The presence of gender hierarchy or sexism here is not detachable, any more than hierarchy is detachable from teleology, or "fact" is detachable from "value" in antiquity, indeed in any premodern philosophical worldview. It is rather utterly systemic and constitutive.

Aristotle's masculinist biases have been widely documented and have typically focused upon his form/matter distinction, in which the male is aligned with form, and the female with the material cause.[5] Indeed, in *Generation of Animals* Aristotle clearly states that in reproduction the male contributes the principle of movement and generation, and the female contributes the matter.[6] While Aristotle famously identifies four essential causes—formal, final, moving, and material—in all situations of coming-to-be, in reproduction the first three (formal, final, and moving), "often amount to one," and may thus be understood together as forming a complex that is paternal and masculine.[7] Matter, on the other hand, is the passive feminine recipient of any given form. And insofar as in "man" the principle of rational soul is transmitted via the male sperm, the rational faculty also resides on the side of the male. Very schematically, the groupings form/male/active/rational on the one hand and matter/female/passive/irrational on the other give a natural hierarchy of value that we find repeated and elaborated elsewhere, notably in *Politics*, Book I, where he asserts that men are the natural rulers of women.[8] In this way, Aristotle reiterates a simple and dogmatic declaration of the subordination of female to male, and of women to men, throughout the various subject areas he addresses.

Upon closer examination, however, a different, more complex picture of the way that sex and gender plays out in the biology, physics, and metaphysics can be discerned. More fundamental than the

male's alliance with active form versus the female's with passive matter is the alignment of the feminine with luck and chance—a lability
and unpredictability *in matter* that is opaque to reason and at odds
with natural teleology, which as a whole bears a masculine sign. In
what follows, then, I will pursue Aristotle's various reckonings with
aleatory phenomena. Luck or fortune (*tuchē*), chance or spontaneity (*automaton*), and necessity (*anankē*) appear in the *Physics* as secondary and supplemental to the four essential causes—formal, final,
moving, and material. These phenomena, and the feminine sign they
carry, function *symptomatically* in Aristotle's philosophy; they disrupt the oppositional symmetry of the pairings form/matter and
activity/passivity that form the basis of both traditional and feminist
accounts of the theory of causation and of Aristotle's entelechial system more generally.

As outlined in the introduction, the notion of the symptom bears
multiple significations. In the first instance one can point to the every-
day modern meaning, common to medical and psychoanalytic usage,
of an observable phenomenon that indicates or discloses an underlying condition of dysfunction or disease. While not the core of the
breakdown itself, it is a corollary or secondary manifestation functioning as a sign pointing to the real problem, and constituting a
demand that the problem be addressed. In this textual and hermeneutic context, it refers to something recurrently problematic in the text,
apparently peripheral to its main concerns, indicative of an underlying dysfunction and intimating a disruption of the philosophical system at hand. The symptom—and this is the deconstructive point—is
generated by and native to the system (as Aristotle says, the female is
that which generates in itself),[9] and at the same time it gives a sign of
dis-ease, posing a threat that may lead to the unraveling of the very
systematicity of the system. Beyond and anterior to the modern sense
of symptom lies the Greek *sumptōma*, the "falling together" of the
coincidence, chance, or mischance. The symptom in this sense discloses the chance confluence of two (or more) separate causal paths,
something we might rightly characterize in a contemporary framework as the *event:* something truly new and unpredictable that necessarily escapes and exceeds the logic of a teleological system.[10]

Before turning to a discussion of Aristotle's theory of biological
reproduction, I will introduce the physical and metaphysical context
by examining Aristotle's theory of causation in *Physics* II. Rather
than approaching Aristotelian metaphysics through the discussion of

primary substance (*ousia*) in the central books of the *Metaphysics*, I will foreground the theory of causes, returning to the question of substance only in the final chapter. This tack is supported by certain of Aristotle's own claims, and it also allows us to foreground the complexly intertwined kinetic processes of natural coming-to-be, *genesis*, and technical production, *poiēsis*, and their inherent directedness toward final cause, as well as to trace the intricacies of the relationship of sex and gender to that teleology. Concentrating on Aristotle's own understanding of aleatory phenomena, and uncovering the role of matter therein, will allow a rather different conception of the operation of the feminine to emerge—one that is less passive, more unpredictable, and more dangerous than previously imagined.

THE FOUR CAUSES, *LOGOS*, AND SEX AND GENDER

To understand a *thing*, according to Aristotle, is to discover the *why* of it (*to dia ti*), that through which it is or has come to be. And this is to acquire the *first causes*, principles, essential factors or beginnings (*archai*) of things.[11] In the *Metaphysics* he says we can only claim to know a particular thing when we have understood its primary causes.[12] Furthermore, we are told that such causes cannot be unlimited, neither in their nature nor in their number, for then all knowledge would be impossible.[13] Aristotle's argument for this bounded and limited reality has both logical and ethical dimensions. He first rejects the possibility of an infinite regress of causes in every direction on logical grounds, asserting that a first cause is the necessary condition of all other causes. But then, more forcefully, he states that, "those who introduce infinity do not realize they are abolishing the nature of the good."[14] "No-one," he goes on to say, "would attempt to do anything if he were not likely to reach some limit, nor would there be any intelligence in the world, because the man who has intelligence always acts for the sake of something, and this is a limit because the end [*telos*] is a limit."[15] It is thus axiomatic for Aristotle that the good is that for the sake of which (*hou heneka*) something is done, and vice versa: things occur and are done, always or for the most part, for the sake of the good. The possibility of understanding, of scientific knowledge, and ultimately of wisdom, depends, for Aristotle, upon the existence of a bounded cosmos. Its limit terms may thus be discovered in an inquiry into the nature of primary causes, and which are at once physical, metaphysical, and ethical.

Furthermore, the existence of these first causes and our knowledge of them cannot be effectively separated. This is first of all because first causes are of several kinds:

> It is a common property, then, of all "beginnings" to be the first thing from which something either exists or comes into being or becomes known; and some beginnings are originally inherent in things, while others are not. Hence "nature" is a beginning, and so is "element" and "understanding" and "choice" and "essence" and "final cause" for in many cases the Good and the Beautiful are the beginning both of knowledge and of motion.[16]

As this passage indicates, first causes and beginnings can be physical, metaphysical, ethical, aesthetic, and so on. They can be inherent in things, they can be inherent in us and in our actions, and they also transcend this distinction, residing in the divine actuality of the Good or the Beautiful. This rich, plural account of causation stands in sharp contrast to at least one version of a modern physicalist notion of causation, in which "action at a distance" has no place, and in which the attribution of cause is modeled upon the example of billiard balls, of matter involved in an economic exchange of motive force, determinate, quantifiable, predictable, and expressible in terms of mathematical laws.[17]

Second, causes for Aristotle are *both* identifiable factors-in-the-world contributing to motion, change, and coming-to-be, *and* explanations of these processes. The Greek *aitia* means both cause *and* explanation—that which satisfies our desire for a meaningful *account* of what is responsible for a given phenomenon. The *why* of something is not to be given necessarily in terms purely of an independent, objective, separable realm of nature, but is to have explanatory value *for us*.[18] Such explanations might indeed posit an irreducible exteriority in the course of their elaboration, but they are not strictly separable from criteria of our own satisfaction arising from the field of *logos*, of what is said, of account, statement, reason, formula, that is, from a human world of ethical, political, or indeed aesthetic discourse. The ambiguity of *aitia*, as well as the multivalence of *archai*—that beginnings can be physical, metaphysical, ethical, aesthetic, and so on—means that any account that would try and treat these dimensions as strictly separate and separable would be misguided. In the same way, in tracing the figurations of femininity through these ancient texts, I am not concerned to separate a natural, biological notion of sex from social, political, cultural or linguistic categories of gender. Such modern distinctions cannot retain their meaning in an ancient context. Rather, feminine and masculine figures in the Aristotelian and Platonic corpuses traverse these designations and have structural significance as such, whether they are manifest in the context of natural or metaphysical cause, of social role, or of cosmic order.

As is well known, Aristotle gives us four senses of the notion of cause: the material cause (the matter or substrate of a thing; the moving or efficient cause), the proximate motive cause of a thing, the final cause (the goal or end of an entity or action), and the formal cause (the essence of a thing, what it is to be that thing). In the following review of the causes, we will see how the notions of form and *logos* are intertwined, further illuminating the intimate relationship between language and being signified by the notion of *aitia*:

> *The material cause.* The material cause is the matter (*hulē*) or substrate (*hupokeimenon*, that which lies under) out of which something is generated. This may be identified as being the particular material constituent(s) of a particular thing, a "this something" (*tode ti*), such as this bronze of a particular statue; the bronze in general of which bronze statues are made; or the generic material of which a statue in general may be made.[19] The components of a whole, such as elements or parts of bodies, or premises of a syllogistic conclusion, are all causes in this sense.[20] The fact that the material cause is an irreducible substrate (*hupokeimenon*) that underlies all concrete things leads Aristotle to consider it as a candidate for primary substance (*ousia*); however, he concludes it is only a "this something" potentially and is not *in fact* separable from a shape or form or *logos*, so it cannot be primary substance tout court, though it is said to be a kind of substance or nature.

> *The motive cause.* This cause, the proximate moving cause or "efficient cause," has often been identified as that closest to our modern, physicalist sense of cause.[21] Aristotle defines it as that from which change, motion, or coming to rest occurs. It most often denotes the proximate source of alteration or motion in any given circumstance, but as Aristotle's examples show it is a

far cry from the kind of physical cause we associate
with the action of billiard balls upon one another. In
Physics II.3 he identifies an advisor or a father of a
child as motive causes, and in *Metaphysics* III.2 he
gives both the art and the architect as the motive causes
of a house (not the action of hammer on wood). This
cause seems to be what discloses itself to us as the
salient and most *knowable* thing that *acts* to bring
something into being, or to cause an event. Initiation
and paternity are united in the figure of the masculine
actor—not the billiard ball, but the man holding the
pool cue and his skill in the art of billiards. There is
thus an individual being identifiable as a moving cause
(in art, the architect; in nature, the father), alongside
a *logos* in virtue of which the motion is conveyed
(the art itself, or *logos* transmitted in the male seed).
This paternal cause is what *shows itself* as the most
significant proximal agent of creation or motion in a
given circumstance.[22]

The final cause. This is the end (*telos*), the purpose for the
sake of which (*hou heneka*) something is done, or the
"good" (*to agathon*) toward which it works. It is the
answer to the question "Why is something done?" and
can be either a real or apparent good. According to
the example in *Physics* II.3, in answer to the question
"Why does he walk?" the response "In order to be
healthy" gives the final cause. It does not need to be the
walker's explicit reason to be true—the walker might
be interested in whatever is going on in the park—but
it must be a good knowable by reason in order to
count as a legitimate final cause. This example once
again demonstrates the comprehence of fact and value,
being and *logos*, the melding of cause and explanation
denoted by *aitia*. It is the *reason* behind the action, one
that must satisfy us as the ultimate explanation for the
action. In thus satisfying our reason, it appears as the
most substantial cause, a good not merely apparent
but also metaphysical. The final cause, says Aristotle,
"tends to be the greatest good and *end* of the rest [of
the causes]."[23] The final cause, then, is that toward

which the other causes work; in a sense it determines and dominates the other causal processes by structuring their actions both temporally and logically. The final cause on the level of particular events and instances can be understood as a small-scale reflection of Aristotle's broader metaphysical and macrocosmic entelechy, in which change driven by essential causes for the most part (if not always) unfolds unidirectionally, from potentiality to actuality. This movement is ultimately driven by the divine Prime Mover, that figure of pure actuality and activity: the good as such.[24] The distinction between, and connections among, local *teloi* and the ultimate *telos* are not however simply described, and they will be further explored in the discussion of motion in chapter 5.[25]

The formal cause. In Aristotle's explanation of the formal cause in the *Physics*, his invocation of both *logos* and essence (*to ti ēn einai*, what it is to be a thing) are instructive in understanding the indeterminability of the sex/gender distinction in this context. Aristotle's use of the notion of form differs profoundly from the Platonic use of the concept (*eidos* or *idea*), against which Aristotle argues vehemently at *Metaphysics* I.6–9. For Aristotle the form inheres in the thing, resides within it as its immanent essence, while for Plato (according to Aristotle) the individual thing is radically different from the form in which it participates; the form resides in a transcendent, ideal realm. Aristotle describes formal cause as, "the form [*eidos*] or the pattern [*paradeigma*], this being the formula [*logos*] of the essence [*to ti ēn einai*], and also the genera of this; for example, in the case of the octave, the ratio 2:1, and, in general, a number and the parts in the formula [*logos*]."[26] In the *Metaphysics*, he defines this cause as "the substance [*ousia*] or essential nature [*to ti ēn einai*] of the thing (since the 'reason why' [*to dia ti*] of a thing is ultimately reducible to its formula [*logos*], and the ultimate 'reason why' is a cause [*aitia*] and a principle [*archē*])."[27] These notoriously complex definitions seem at first to raise more difficulties than they resolve. It is at least clear that

> while Aristotelian form can be abstract, "generic," as
> well as applying to particulars, for Aristotle the form is
> primarily the *logos* or formula of "what it is to be" (*to
> ti ēn einai*) of a this, a *tode ti*, the thing which tells us
> what differentiates it from other things, makes it that
> particular thing and no other thing.[28]

Logos is once again central to Aristotle's presentation of the concept of form. Apostle renders this word as "formula," yet it is a difficult word to translate, covering as it does our concepts of word, saying, story, speech, account, and thought and reason, as well as esteem, calculation, proportion, or condition. What is the force of Aristotle's inclusion of *logos* in the description of formal cause? A modern interpretation might confer the sense of an epistemological, as opposed to an ontological, meaning upon this aspect of form. As Apostle writes in his commentary: "If by 'formula of the essence' he means what is in the thing, this would be the form, or what we might call the 'structure,' like the soul of a man; but if he means what is in the mind as signifying what is in the thing, then this is the *knowledge* of that form."[29] However, such a rigid and delimited distinction between the intelligible and the intellect—between what intelligible objects exist independently of us on the one hand and our rational knowledge of those objects on the other—is not articulated with any clarity in Aristotle's philosophy. Indeed the coincidence of these two is arguably the cornerstone of Platonic rationalism and it is of course in the divine prime mover, rendered as "thought thinking itself" (*noēsis noēseōs noēsis*) at the culmination of the *Metaphysics*, that their coincidence most eminently occurs for Aristotle.

Perhaps the Heideggerian rendering of *logos* as "the laying that gathers" is more suggestive. *Logos*, from the verb *legein* (laying, or letting-lie-before), thus gathers into presence, letting being lie before.[30] The *logos* here indicates a more primordial relationship between knower and known than even that diremption allows or can convey. I want to suggest, then, that *logos* articulates *both* our knowledge or concept of a thing, *and* whatever resides in the thing that provides the ground through which we apprehend that, for example, a horse is a horse. It is a precondition for our understanding; the *logos* reveals form to us, the essence of a thing, what it is named and what it truly is, in one and the same movement.[31] The distinction between *to ti ēn einai*, the "what it is to be" an individual thing, and the *logos*, the "formula of the essence," is not therefore a distinction between ontological and epistemological aspects of essence, but rather may be understood as one of particular and genus, the kind of thing it is. The genus, for Aristotle, never takes ontological precedence over the particular; he clearly characterizes them in *Categories* V as second and first substance, respectively. But neither does he enlist the *logos*, which he counts as an intrinsic part of the definition of formal cause, as a secondary component of form in service to the essence. The important point is that formal cause is to be understood both as the essence or "what it is to be" inhering in a thing (for example, the shape and being of the statue), and as a conceptual entity (for example, the statue inhering in a sculptor's art, or in his artistic intention) without demanding a decisive, anachronistic, distinction be drawn between ontological and epistemological dimensions of *logos*, between object and subject, between what is "out there" and "in the head." Instead, it is what is—and can be—articulated; the condition of possibility of articulation, and the articulation, all at once.[32]

While *logos* itself, in its opposition to matter, is a category that itself may be understood in relation to sexual difference (as the Derridean formulation "phallogocentrism" suggests), I want to reiterate that according to this conception of *logos* in Aristotle it is impossible to successfully sustain a separation between an empirical entity such as biological sex, understood as inherent or independently existing in the materiality of nature, and the *logos* of gender, or the set of cultural and social meanings discursively circulating and accreting around, indeed discursively producing, a material substratum of sex.[33]

According to Aristotle, then, male and female differ in both form (*eidos*) and *logos*. As he goes on to explain, "in those animals in which these two faculties are separate [*kechōrismenas echousi tas dunameis*], the bodies [*ta sōmata*] and nature [*phusin*] of the active partner and passive partner must be different [*heteran*]."[34] Male is defined as that which generates in another, and female as that which generates in itself.[35] The active and passive parties, male and female, thus differ in body, nature, essence, and *logos*. And the main assumption buried in the "generates in another, generates in itself" distinction is less that the female possesses some sort of completion or self-sufficiency that is lacking in the male, but rather that the female principle, as passive matter, lacks the efficient or moving cause, the transitive *archē kinēseōs* or source of motion requisite in all coming-to-be. Returning to the formula at the start of this chapter, the female state is as it were a deformed male, but she nonetheless has her own *logos* and essence. This *logos* and essence are thus constituted and defined by a certain lack. In *Generation of Animals*, Aristotle lays bare the causal elements of natural coming-to-be in sexual reproduction in an exemplary way. As we will see, his rendering of the female or feminine raises fundamental questions for the metaphysical account of causation that underpins Aristotle's entelechial system.

CONCEIVING OF A GIRL

Sexual reproduction as described in *Generation of Animals* stands out as an object illustration of Aristotle's causal theory. The male's semen, he says, contributes the *form* of the offspring, and the menstrual blood the *matter* out of which it is to be made. More than that he designates the female's menstrual blood, or *katamenia* (literally, the monthly), as "prime matter" (*protē hulē*),[36] a rare claim indeed, since he also insists that matter cannot exist apart from some form, cannot be spoken of by itself, and is unknowable in itself.[37] But this notion of prime matter in Aristotle is somewhat tricky, and indeed, as the discussion of heredity in chapter 6 will show, the properties of the menstrual blood are indeed difficult to determine (in part because it is in the very nature of matter to be "indeterminate").[38] At *Met.* V.4 he makes a potentially helpful distinction between two senses of *protē hulē*: relational and general. So bronze might be said to be primary *in relation to* the statue, in so far as it is the nearest and most relevant material cause out of which the statue is made, but one might further resolve bronze into its elements, and ultimately find that it is water, insofar as it is something that melts.[39] Most commentators have found that while the elements—earth, air, fire, and water—may be designated as *protē hulē* in the general sense, the menstrual blood is thus only *protē hulē* in the relational sense.[40] This is supported by a passage at *Met.* VIII.4 where Aristotle programmatically gives all four causes of a man as the menstrual blood (material), the semen (moving), the essence (formal), and the end (final). He follows with, "We must, however, state the *nearest* (*engutata*) cause. What is the matter? Not fire or earth, but the matter proper to man."[41] However, in *Generation of Animals* I.20, Aristotle introduces the claim about the menstrual blood thus: "although the female does not contribute any semen to generation, yet contributes something, that is, what constitutes the menstrual fluid [*hē tōn katamēniōn sustasis*]. But the same is true if we consider this generally from the theoretical standpoint. . . . Thus, if the male is the moving and active (or productive) partner [*kinoun kai poioun*], and the female, *qua* female, the passive [*pathētikon*], surely what the female contributes to the semen of the male will not be semen [*gonē*] but matter [*hulē*]."[42] His highly programmatic statement follows: "And this is what appears to be the case; for the nature of the menstrual blood is that of prime matter [*kata gar tēn prōtēn hulēn estin hē tōn katamēniōn phusis*]."[43] The shift here from the biological to the metaphysical, and back to the biological, is seamless, with the menstrual blood clearly standing in here as a perceptible representation of the theoretical substance, of *matter as such and in general.*

This diremption of form and matter in the reproductive scene therefore accomplishes a radical separation between active and passive components of generation. Of the two "residues," female and male, one approaches as closely as possible the impossible state of formlessness, and the other approaches as closely as possible pure form, consisting only of *pneuma* or soul heat (of which more later) and water, its materiality virtually erased.[44] The relative formlessness of menstrual blood is necessitated in that it is thereby readied for "enformation" by the male principle, and thus cooked or "concocted" in the womb, according to Aristotle's culinary theory of embryogenesis. Here we can see the relevance of Luce Irigaray's question, "how can a girl be conceived?" For if the form is always provided by the male, the masculine principle, it remains a mystery how a female child may result.[45]

Aristotle in fact provides a wonderfully comprehensive explanation of the perplexing phenomenon of female offspring, which deserves to be quoted at length:

> Males take after their father more than their mother, females after their mother. Some take after none of their kindred, although they take after some human being at any rate; others do not take after a human being at all in their appearance, but have gone so far that they resemble a monstrosity, and, for the matter of that, anyone who does not take after his parents is really in a way a monstrosity, since in these cases Nature has in a way strayed [*parekbebēke*] from the generic type. The first beginning of this deviation is when a female is formed instead of a male, though (a) this indeed is a necessity required by Nature, since the race of creatures which are separated into male and female has got to be kept in being; and (b) since it is possible for the male sometimes not to gain the mastery [*kratein*] either on account of youth or age or

some other such cause, female offspring must of necessity be produced by animals. As for monstrosities [*teras*], they are not necessary so far as the purposive or final cause is concerned, yet they are accidentally [*kata sumbebēkos*] necessary, since we must take it that their origin at any rate is located here.[46]

This passage gives two different, and opposed, explanations for the existence of female offspring. First, any species in which sexual reproduction takes place relies on the existence of females for its perpetuation. Females exist by natural necessity (*anankaia tē phusei*), that is, by *teleological* necessity, in order to safekeep (*sōzesthai*) the kind (*to genos*) that is separated into male and female. This explanation invokes an overarching final cause: the imperative of life, of nature itself. The second explanation, by contrast, involves a kind of error in the mechanism of reproduction: nature *strays* from kind, and the male fails to "gain the mastery" (*kratein* is a concept familiar from political contexts, carrying the sense of seizing control and ruling that may also be understood as an establishment of sovereignty). Proper heat is required to create males, while a deficiency will result in a female. The factors and circumstances that may contribute to such deficiency are numerous, and may be internal or external: the parents may be too young, too old, too fluid or feminine of body, or the wind may be in the south, or copulating animals may simply be facing the south.[47] "Such a small thing may tip the scale and be the cause of heat and cold," says Aristotle: the feminine symptom as downward weight issues from unpredictable and indeterminable material circumstances—aleatory matter as such.[48] But again, such accidents will *necessarily* happen. A small deviation from the ideal temperature, then, will create the required female; a larger deviation will create occasional "monstrosities" (*terata*): calves with two heads, babies with six fingers, and the like. In this way, femininity can be seen to function as a sign of, and a figure for, masculine failure. An error in concocting the offspring reveals a susceptibility of the natural, telic unfolding to another kind of necessity, namely accidental necessity, a necessity inherent in the forces or compulsions of matter. Aside from noting the deep misogyny of theorizing femaleness as a mild form of monstrosity, and indeed the profound *normativity* inherent in the Aristotelian cosmos, the following question demands an answer: How are we to understand this strange confluence, this *necessary* coinciding—note the echo of *sumptōma* as coincidence here—of these two different regimes of necessity or causality in the reproduction of a female offspring, in the conception of a girl?

If the creation of female offspring is an accident necessary to the continuance of reproduction, it is also true more generally that accidental and chance phenomena are necessary to a plural, material world. Nature is in a fundamental sense oriented toward teleological sustenance of beings, but as Aristotle concedes later in *Generation of Animals*, in a discussion of certain monstrous phenomena that seem to occur fairly regularly, "the result seems to be less of a monstrosity because even that which is contrary to nature [*para phusin*] is, in a way, in accordance with nature [*kata phusin*], that is, when the nature according to form has not gained mastery over what accords with matter."[49] So here, we glimpse the notion that there are forces at work that may exert themselves against nature, and these are in accordance with the matter. Matter here is set in an agonic, rather than a passive, harmonious or desiring relationship with form. Aristotle has here just reiterated the position elaborated in *Physics* II, that what is natural (*kata phusin*) occurs either *always* (that is, as in the heavens), or *for the most part* (in the sublunar realm); in other words *unnatural* things, accidents that are against nature (*para phusin*) and in accordance with matter, occur as exceptions to what is for the most part the case. However, the *aporia*, the *symptom*, still remains: how do female offspring arise exactly half the time in sexually differentiated beings?[50] Simply put, there is no explanation. But to investigate the broader context that allows for the emergence of this feminine symptom, one has to ask how the notion of accident fits into Aristotle's account of causation. And further, how does he account for the multiplicity of causal accounts or explanations by which the inquirer might make sense of the provenance of multiple beings and events in this plural world? Before clarifying the roles of accident, chance and necessity and their relation to the female in the scene of reproduction, it will be necessary to examine their roles in Aristotle's account of causation. Turning again to *Physics* II, we will see that Aristotle clearly distinguishes between the primary causes, the causes "per se" (*kath' hauto*) and accidental (*kata sumbebēkos*) causes.

THE ALEATORY CAUSES: ACCIDENT, *TUCHĒ*, *AUTOMATON*

After his delineation of the four essential causes in *Physics* II, Aristotle goes on to state that "it happens [*sumbainei*] that, as causes are

spoken of in many ways [*pollachōs legomenon*], there may be many
non-accidental causes of the same thing."[51] This *legetai pollachōs*,
"said in many ways" is more famously used in relation to being itself
(*to on*), indeed Heidegger calls it a "constant refrain." In the typology of the four principal ways that being is spoken in *Metaphysics*
VI.2, the first is *kata sumbebēkos*, being according to accident (the
other three are being according to the true and false, according to the
categories, and according to potentiality and actuality).[52] Cause, like
being, is thus also always spoken of multiply. It is not just accidental contexts, then, that introduce multiplicity into an otherwise univocal discourse—a manifold way of speaking is present at the most
fundamental levels of analysis, and accident is encompassed in this
manifold. Heidegger understands Aristotle's *legetai pollachōs*, "said
in many ways," not as indicating a system, or a need for a system, but
as a task. It is thus the task of Aristotle's philosophy to work through,
analyze, and interpret the question of being in all its polyvocality,
and in its relationship to the multifariousness of phenomenal beings.
And the task in this section is to inquire how Aristotle sets about
separating what is essential yet not univocal from what is accidental,
supplementary, indefinite, and inherently plural. From the *Categories* onward, Aristotle insists upon the primariness of the *tode ti*, the
"this something" that one may deictically point to, as a fundamental
object of philosophical inquiry. The centrality of the *tode ti*, along
with his desire to do justice to the complexity and multiplicity he sees
in the world, to "save the phenomena" as the famous formulation has
it, leads him inevitably to an extensive engagement with the notion
of accident.[53] In order to give any account of things that exist that
does justice to their multiplicity, their alterability and their being in
time and motion, and which gives an account of beings that does not
seek to reduce them to a unity and avoids the Parmenidean reduction
of being to the one, of *to on* to *to hen*,[54] there must be consideration
given to the ontological status of accident, of happenstance, of what
"just happens to be the case."

Kata sumbebēkos, the usual translation of which is "accidental," is given by Heidegger as, "with respect to being co-present."
Kata: according to, with respect to; and *sumbebēkos*, from *sun*: with,
together, and *bainō*: to go, to step, to walk; thus, "walking together,
walking alongside." The relation is contrasted to one of intrinsical-
ity or self-sameness, the *kath' hauto* that by contrast signifies a cause
with respect to itself, according to itself, indicating an internal link

with its effects.[55] A builder builds a house in virtue of his art of building, not in virtue of his musicality; his musicality just happens to be there, alongside his art of building. It is only as a matter of accident that the efficient cause of the house is a musical man.

How, then, is the *kata sumbebēkos* to be understood?[56] Accident (*sumbebēkos*), is the thirtieth and last of all the definitions of *Metaphysics* V, and Aristotle gives it here as "that which applies to something and is truly stated, but neither necessarily nor usually."[57] Thus, he says, if a man engages in planting and finds a buried treasure, this is an accident, since it neither follows of necessity nor usually. And in a rather pleasing, if surprising, example he says that if a cultured man is white, that is also an accident, since that is neither necessary nor usual. (Here, it is the coexistence of culturedness and whiteness that is called accidental, since it is in virtue of the copresence of two unrelated accidents or attributes, culture and whiteness, which bear no internal causal relation to each another, that the accident occurs.) Any attribute, then, that applies to a subject, except those that apply in virtue of the nature or substance or essential cause of that subject (such as its matter or its definition), is an accident. Thus Socrates is accidentally white, cultured, and wearing sandals today, but he is essentially a man (form), a rational animal (*logos*, definition), made of flesh and blood (matter), and fathered by a man (moving cause). His end or telos qua man is living well and *eudaimonia*, which may be achieved—according to the ethical and political treatises—by cultivating contemplation, practical wisdom, right action, and politics.

Notably, the very notion of matter emerges in *Physics* I on the basis of a consideration of the relationship between a subject and its accidental predicates. Having taken us through the doxographic tradition, Aristotle finds himself in agreement with the Eleatic position that it is impossible for something to come from nothing: A cannot come from not-A tout court. Nonetheless, contra the Eleatics, he believes that change exists, and seeks to give an account of ontological coming-to-be. In I.7 he turns to an example involving accidental attributes, arguing that A may emerge from not-A in the sense that a man may change from being not cultured (not-A) to being cultured (A). Something, in this case a specific man, must be posited that underlies and persists throughout the change. Turning to the unqualified coming-to-be of substances, then, he argues that the same model applies. There must be something that underlies and persists throughout the change, a substrate or *hupokeimenon* (thing that underlies), and this is the *matter*. The bronze underlies and persists as the statue comes to be, and in natural contexts plants and animals come from seeds.[58] Form comes to be installed one way or another from a prior state in which that form was not there, while matter is there, abiding all along. Aristotle's absolutely innovative threefold model of ontological coming-to-be, involving matter, privation, and form (the former as underlying substrate, the latter two as primary contraries, not-A and A) is thus developed on the basis of accidental change. The subject, in the subject-predicate structure (Socrates is/is not cultured), is recrafted as the substrate, or matter, in the scene of ontological coming-to-be. Noteworthy here is that it is *form* that takes the place of the accidental predicate, while *matter* takes the place of the subject. This homology of matter and subject will form part of the impetus for Aristotle's inquiry into whether matter is primary substance (*ousia*) in the *Metaphysics* VII.3 (but it cannot be because it fails to be a primary object of knowledge, and is not individual, unified, or separable in the way that a "this" is). So while at the level of accidental change, the substrate that underlies such change is unified and a "this," and the accidents move in and out of the substrate in a way that is strictly unknowable and unpredictable, when we move to the ontological level a strange reversal takes place: form as the "definition" or "formula" is closely allied with essence and becomes the telos, the unshakable destiny, as it were, of coming-to-be, and at the same time the notion of the substrate as matter as such becomes elusive, the site of an irreducible indeterminacy, and, as I am arguing, is also the site of opaque aleatory activity—the accidental as such.

Returning to the definition of accident in *Metaphysics* V.30, we are told that accidents arise from no definite cause; they arise by indefinite (*aoriston*) causes, or else by luck (*tuchē*). A man's arrival in Aegina, is by accident if it was not intended but if instead his ship was carried from its course by a storm, or if he was captured by pirates.[59] Something definite, the storm, was the cause of his arrival, but it itself was accidental since it was neither necessary nor usual. This unforeseen occurrence, then, created a disjuncture between the man's intended destination and his actual destination, such that we say he arrived in Aegina "by accident." The final instance of accident offered in this section is that which later in the tradition is named a "property," namely, it is that which arises in a thing as a result of itself, but which is not contained in its essence or definition, such as the fact that the sum of a triangle's internal angles is equal to two right angles. These accidents differ from the others in that they may be "eternal." They arise in fact from the essence of a thing, but do not partake in its definition, and are therefore thought of as "being alongside" rather than essential in themselves.[60]

Aristotle also distinguishes the accidental from the *kath' hauto* on explicitly epistemological grounds. He states that there is no *science* (*epistēmē*)—whether practical, productive, or speculative—that concerns itself with accidents, and there can be no observation (*theōria*) about what comes to be accidentally.[61] Accidents are fundamentally opaque to our vision, for the only things that can be taught and learned and thus be part of science or knowledge are things that happen either always and by necessity, as is the case in the heavens, or at least usually and for the most part, as is the case in the sublunary realm. Accident, says Aristotle, "is only, as it were, a sort of a name . . . something closely akin to the non-existent."[62] This name thus appears to give a positive determination for that which in fact can only be negatively defined: "Since, then, there are among existing things some which are invariable and of necessity (not necessity in the sense of force, but that by which we mean that it cannot be otherwise), and some which are not necessarily so, nor always, but usually: this is the principle and this the cause of the accidental. For whatever is neither always nor usually so, we call an accident."[63] The separation of the *kath' hauto* and the *kata sumbebēkos* relies, then, on a prior separation of science (*epistēmē*) and that which does not conform to, but rather exceeds, any expectation or pattern. To the extent that *epistēmē* is teachable and learnable, it relies on repeatable formulae (*logoi*), on instances of the *logos* that correspond to events occurring always or for the most part, observable again and again. Accident, then, is the name for the indefinite and indefinable set of phenomena that escape knowledge and science, escape the *technē*, *theōria*, and *praxis* which characterize science, and which instead inhere in the particularity and multifariousness of events and existing things.[64]

While accident is to be determined negatively as unknowable and inexplicable, in the discourse on cause in *Physics* II Aristotle must still give an account of the things we attribute to chance, which he divides into *tuchē* (typically translated either as fortune, luck, or chance) and *automaton* (typically translated as chance or spontaneity; due to this confusion I leave them mostly untranslated).[65] These are commonly given as explanations of events and phenomena, and are spoken of as causes—"many things are said to exist and to come to be through *tuchē* or *automaton*,"[66] but they are not causes per se in any straightforward way. In the central books of *Physics* II he begins the inquiry by raising the question of whether they actually exist at all, citing an "old argument" that really all things that seem to happen by luck and chance can actually be attributed to some definite or essential cause.[67] Thus, if a man comes to market and meets by chance someone whom he wished to but did not expect to meet, each man's trajectory can be fully accounted for by his own set of definite causes (that is, each went to market in certain definite circumstances for certain definite reasons). But it is a testament to Aristotle's sensitivity to how things are said that he seeks a more accurate account, because, as he puts it, "all speak of some of these things as being by *tuchē* and others as being not by *tuchē* . . . and this fact should have been touched upon by them in some way or other."[68] Having thus made the chance encounter at the marketplace the model for *tuchē*, Aristotle goes on to inquire into the nature of *tuchē* and *automaton*, and to outline the distinction between them.

As with the definition of accident, Aristotle first observes that *tuchē* and *automaton* are neither necessary, nor eternal, nor what happens for the most part, but are rather exceptional. Further, it is when such exceptional things seem to come to be "for the sake of something," that is, they accidentally fulfill a final cause or telos, that *tuchē* is invoked. He reiterates that there are accidental causes (such as the builder of a house also being musical), and that these are indefinite and numerous, but returns once again to the scene of the chance encounter to make the point about luck or chance and final cause. Thus, someone engaged in collecting contributions, with that as his general goal or final cause, may have gone to a particular location without this goal in mind, not knowing that he was likely to receive payment there, but in fact when he went there received the money he desired. So a preexisting goal or telos was fulfilled, but incidentally, accidentally, by, as we say, luck or chance. These themes have a surprisingly contemporary currency. For instance, in the spate of films released around the turn of the millennium featuring chance encounters, such as *Run Lola Run* (1998), *Sliding Doors* (1998), and *Happenstance* (2000), random and trivial events, such as whether someone catches a particular train or not, gain significance *as such*, and *appear* as lucky chances, insofar as major consequences in the characters' lives may be attributed to them, consequences relating to the characters' final causes (such as Lola's need to get a considerable sum of money to save her boyfriend's life). And Aristotle himself in the *Poetics* argues that while chance events do not have particular narrative potential just in themselves, we nonetheless find it most wondrous when chance events seem (*dokei*) to have happened by design.[69]

Aristotle, as in the passages on accident, is again concerned to forge a separation between cause and effect in cases of luck and chance, showing that the causes of the latter are necessarily indefinite, *aoriston* (the man who ended up getting his money may have been on his way out to do any number of incidental things such as seeing a play or following someone).[70] *Tuchē*, then, does not exist simply, without qualification (*haplōs*), but only in relation to final causes knowable through reason or thought. *Tuchē* may be in the realm of choice and thought, but it is contrary to reason, says Aristotle, since reason can only address that which is either always or for the most part, while *tuchē* appears as a rarity or an exception.

Tuchē turns out to be a special case of chance for Aristotle. It involves thought (*dianoia*), action (*praxis*), and above all choice (*prohairesis*), that is, the valuations and activities of the human world. Thus good fortune, *eutuchē*, seems close to happiness, *eudaimonia*.[71] Hence the sense of the translation "luck" with its desirable evaluative connotation, and chance as the wider predicate indicating aleatory phenomena more generally. *Tuchē* strictly speaking does not apply to inanimate things, nor beasts, nor children, because they do not—for Aristotle—act out of choice. *Automaton*, rather, implies action without choice, but Aristotle initially does not articulate it in a way that separates it fully from final cause. The first two examples Aristotle gives are: a horse whose arrival at a particular place happened to save him (from an unspecified danger), and a tripod that happens to land on its feet. In the first case, the final cause is the preservation of the horse's life, a final cause inherent in nature but nonetheless a good, the preservation and continuance of life. And in the second, the inherent final cause of the tripod, as a human artifact, is to be sat on by a person—if it were not for this its landing upright would not appear as a lucky chance. Note that while there is nothing capable of choice or action here, there are still evaluative and normative *teloi* at work in the appearance of these aleatory phenomena, and this is why we can speak of them as lucky. The causes of these telos-fulfilling effects are external to their fulfillment, however, and did not come about for any particular purpose—they just *happened to* fulfill a telos.

There is also a privative aspect of *automaton*, in which rather than a final cause being accidentally fulfilled, it is accidentally vitiated. An action is thus said to have been undertaken "in vain" (Aristotle notes that "as a sign" the root of the word *matēn*, "in vain," appears in the word *automaton*, an etymology examined more closely in chapter 2). Thus, he says, one may take a walk for the sake of a bowel movement, but the desired movement might not come, in which case walking would have been in vain.[72] And one might say (though somewhat awkwardly) that a stone fell in vain, to no purpose, if it were not deliberately thrown by someone (even if both ended up striking a man).[73] It is at this textual moment, then, that we get the first clue that within nonhuman, material contexts (here the body and the earth) there are certain forces at work that might resist or obstruct the operations of final cause. And finally, Aristotle tells us that *automaton* may most clearly be distinguished from *tuchē* in natural coming-to-be, that is, in cases when something is generated contrary to nature (*para phusin*).[74] So here, finally, we are in the territory of monstrosities, the aleatory within nature itself that gives rise to its opposite, what is against nature: the very scene of the feminine symptom. But does Aristotle attribute such *automaton* to the material cause? Is this where we might uncover an Aristotelian account of aleatory matter?

The next question, decisive for our inquiry, is thus how *tuchē* and *automaton* may be characterized in terms of causes *kath' hauto*. And what Aristotle says here is that "each of them is an *archē tēs kinēseōs*"—a principle or source of motion, that is, a kind of motive cause or efficient cause—"for they are always among causes either by nature or by thought, but their multiplicity is indefinite [*to plēthos aoriston*]."[75] And by way of concluding the inquiry into the nature of cause in *Phys.* II.6, he reasserts that such causes cannot be prior to essential causes. Indeed, they are always in a certain way supplementary to them and parasitical upon them for their appearance. Moving deftly to the macrocosmic level, he asserts this very supplementarity as evidence that "intellect or nature [*noun kai phusin*] is of necessity a prior cause . . . of this whole universe."[76]

What are we to make of this claim that *tuchē* and *automaton* are to be described as efficient or moving causes? We may recall from the discourse on the four essential causes that the moving cause or *archē kinēseōs* is paradigmatically *paternal* and demiurgic—a maker, a father or an advisor. But in this context, these unaccountable motions, these aleatory deviations and errancies, do not come from a unitary paternal source, but arise from obscure sources of motion that are, rather, multiple and indeterminate. In the case of the craftsman or the advisor, such failures are indeed an ever-present possibility that Aristotle calls *hamartia*—a kind of mistaken or errant conduct that falls short of evil or depravity, indeed in the *Poetics* he famously attributes this "flaw" to the greatest of tragic figures, namely Oedipus and Thyestes.[77] In nature, however, such errancy can only be attributed to the vagaries of matter, as indicated by the examples of the recalcitrant body that resists healthy practice and the falling stone given earlier. Aristotle seems to notice the problem with attributing motion simply to a moving cause understood on a paternal model, and goes on to grapple with this in the next two chapters of *Physics* II. He argues in chapter 8 that just as an error (*hamartia*) may occur in matters of art (a grammarian might not have written correctly; a doctor may not have given the right medicine) so a similar situation—one might gloss here a slip, an omission, or a swerve—may pertain in nature, thus giving rise to monstrosities as failures of final cause.[78] But his acknowledgment of the plural and indeterminate nature of aleatory phenomena precisely as *sources of motion* raises the question of the persistence of a different order of motion, indeed a different order of necessity. Here, the final cause and the moving cause cannot be the same, either numerically *or* generically; and this order of material necessity and its nonpaternal moving cause seems to impose itself in certain situations as the very source of those failures.

To be clear: in *technē*, in artifactual coming-to-be, the four causes are all easily separable: the bed's matter is the wood, the matter (*hulē*) out of which it is made; the bed's form (*eidos*) is its *logos* in the mind of the sculptor and also its shape or *morphē*; the bed's moving cause (*archē kinēseōs*) is the carpenter, the craftsman; and the bed's final cause, its *telos*, or "for the sake of which" (*hou heneka*), is to be slept on. In *phusis*, natural coming-to-be, however, the three latter, nonmaterial causes are in effect the same. The formal cause is the form inherent in the creature, most fully realized as the healthy adult horse, for example. This formal cause is also the final cause, since foals grow toward adulthood, and the adult (male) horse, as the father, is also the moving cause, since, as Aristotle puts it, "man begets man."[79] So while the moving cause is not numerically identical with the form and the telos, it is identical in kind—they are both adult male horses. The formal cause and final cause must therefore also be present in some respect in the seed, the sperm that is the vehicle for reproduction. The intercession of the female in reproduction is here invisible; she merely provides the matter, the substrate to be enformed, and this may be counterposed to the other three causes.

The problem, then, is evident. If the four essential causes provide a full account of generation, what is the second source of physical motion that acts to obstruct or intercede? What is the provenance of this accidental, random, aleatory force that intervenes to disrupt and deform teleological processes? Aristotle does indeed aver here that "the principles that cause physical motion are two,"[80] but we should not take this as an acknowledgment of any movements inherent in matter. Rather, he is telling us that motion is to be understood as issuing both from formal/final causes (causes that are not themselves moved, in so far as they represent "the for the sake of which" as "the good"—the form of a horse), *and* following from a particular something, that is, from that particular seed from a particular father. Indeed, in *De Gen. et Corr.*, in a polemic with both Plato and with unnamed materialist thinkers (presumably the atomists) he is particularly clear that matter cannot be a source of motion: "If one were to say that matter generates by means of its movement, he would speak more in accordance with the facts of nature . . . However these thinkers are also wrong; for to be acted upon, that is to be moved, is characteristic of matter [*tēs men gar hulēs to paschein esti kai to kineisthai*], but to move, that is to act, is the function of another power."[81]

Now, one might say that aleatory phenomena in part arise from the multiplicity of formal and final causes in the world; so that when a man with the goal of planting a tree instead finds treasure, this is a lucky chance only in so far as the prior *telos* of financial gain is understood as good or desirable. But they also arise from the vagaries or vicissitudes of matter: the unexpected storm sending the ship off course, the child born with six fingers, the unforthcoming bowel movement: here any identifiable final cause is vitiated by the inherent aleatory unpredictability, *automaton*, whose only possible site and provenance is matter itself. Indeed, he writes in the *Metaphysics*: "Therefore the cause of the accidental is the matter, which admits of variation from the usual."[82] And in an extraordinary passage in *Generation of Animals* Aristotle puts in this way: "Nature's aim, then, is to measure the generations and endings [*teleutas*] of things by the measure of these [heavenly] bodies, but she cannot bring this about exactly on account of the indeterminateness [*aoristian*] of matter and the existence of a plurality of principles which impede the processes of generation in nature and destruction, and so often are the causes of things occurring contrary to Nature [*para phusin sumpiptontōn*]."[83]

Here Aristotle clearly and unequivocally charges the multiplicity of things occasioned by matter in the sublunar world, and indeed the indeterminacy of matter itself, with the obstructions and deviations that occur against nature and according to coincidence (*sumpiptontōn* is a form of the verb from which *sumptōma* is derived). But in the *Physics* he seems reluctant to make such a determination. In II.8, in a polemic with Empedocles, he addresses "how necessity exists in natural things"[84]—how, for example, rain seems to fall not *in order to* grow corn, but because "what goes up must be cooled, and the resulting water comes down, and when this takes place, the growth of corn happens [*sumbainei*]."[85] At last, it seems, Aristotle is preparing to grapple with what we understand in modernity as disenchanted physicalist causation on the model of billiard balls. Such rain may indeed also spoil the wheat on the threshing floor, and here we see it act to vitiate final cause; but the point is that it acts anyway, of necessity, utterly indifferent to whether the crops succeed or fail, and indeed the corn itself happens to grow by accident (*sumbainei*) whether its function is to feed us or not. Nonetheless, Aristotle prefers not to linger here but moves straightaway to organismic examples in which the blind necessity of physical things, in other words "chance," seems to be an entirely unreasonable explanation for the structure of functional biological parts. He highlights the absurdity of the claim that this kind of necessity could give rise to animal dentition—"the front teeth of necessity coming out sharp and so fit for tearing but the molars broad and useful for grinding food, not however for the sake of this but by coincidence [*sumpesein*, again the verb from which *sumptōma* is derived],"[86]—and throws disdain on Empedocles's nascent theory of evolution: "whenever all the parts came together as if generated for the sake of something, the wholes which by *automaton* were fitfully composed survived, but those which came together not in this manner, like the man-face offspring of oxen mentioned by Empedocles, perished and still do so."[87] He makes short work of this apparently reasonable argument with his familiar stochastic claim, that what occurs by nature does so either always or for the most part, whereas that which occurs by chance is infrequent and exceptional, thus: "It is not during the winter that frequent rain is thought to occur by *tuchē* or coincidence [*sumptōmatos*], but during the summer, nor frequent heat during the summer, but during the winter."[88] As for biological coming-to-be, the thrust of his argument is familiar: things evidently grow, are structured in certain ways, and engage in certain behaviors for the sake of an end, whether for survival or for reproduction. And while matter is a part of nature as is form, it is form "that may be an end while all the rest are for the sake of an end," and which is therefore determinative in the last instance.[89]

Aristotle in these passages thus acknowledges, albeit just barely, an order of necessity wherein material or physical factors such as hot and cold interact in determinative and nonteleological ways (although the elements in turn behave teleologically insofar as they move toward their proper places, up for fire and air, down for water and earth). He falls short, however, of acknowledging in this causal context that matter itself may therefore be the site or source of such subterranean, nonteleological, aleatory motions. Though secondary, deviating, disruptive, and obstructing, accident and chance are also *necessary* to the sublunary world of coming-to-be and passing away, forming the excess beyond "for the most part," and constituting their own, resistive, order of necessity. If there were no accident, everything would be, as it is in the superlunary realm of the heavens, moving in perfect circles, eternally and fully predictably. We might say then that accident, luck, and chance *must* exist independently as causal factors, since they are irreducible and necessary forces in nature, even though they seem to make their appearance only retroactively, in relief against the essential causes. And, though Aristotle barely admits it, they are indeed a kind of source of motion, though plural and indefinite, and certainly not assimilable to the *archē kinēseōs* as essential, paternal cause.

In the very last chapter of *Physics* II, then, Aristotle turns to the problem of necessity itself, starting off with what seems to be a promising question for this pursuit of the aleatory matter that produces the feminine symptom: Does what is necessary exist by hypothesis (that is, in relation to a final cause), or does it exist simply or absolutely?[90] But this is more complex than it looks, because simple or absolute necessity turns out for Aristotle to have nothing to do with matter whatsoever.

CHAPTER TWO

Necessity and *Automaton*

Aleatory Matter and the Feminine Symptom

Necessity, *anankē*—often figured as a goddess in Greek mythology and tragedy—is discussed by Aristotle in multiple contexts, including the final chapter of *Physics* II, in *Parts of Animal, Generation of Animals, De Generatione et Corruptione, Posterior Analytics*, and the *Metaphysics*.[1] Aristotle in these texts gives us various typologies of necessity, but often reduces the types to just two: teleological or hypothetical (*ex hupothēseōs*) necessity and simple or absolute (*haplōs*) necessity. At first sight, simple necessity may appear as a promising description for how an order of matter *separate from teleology* might operate in Aristotle's physical and metaphysical universe. But things are not so straightforward, because simple necessity turns out not to be opposed to teleology at all, although another kind of necessity, force or compulsion (*bia*), steps in to perform this role. If we are to shed any more light on the opaque activity of aleatory matter, the feminine symptom and its operation in Aristotelian cosmos, a detailed investigation of Aristotle's understanding of necessity and its complex normative character in the philosophical and biological treatises will be in order first. This will clear the way for a consideration of *automaton,* or chance and spontaneity in nature, and in particular *genesis automatos,* or spontaneous generation, in Aristotle's theory of reproduction. Aristotle's treatments of necessity and *automaton* will arguably provide the most potent site in his causal theory for understanding the agonic split between teleological nature and what deviates from it, and thus for laying bare the workings of the feminine symptom. In exploring the ontological and textual operation of these key concepts, this chapter completes the discussion of Aristotelian causation begun in chapter 1.

ARISTOTLE'S TYPOLOGIES OF NECESSITY

Physics II.9 begins with this very question: "As for that which is necessary, does it exist by hypothesis or also simply?"[2] Hypothetical necessity, at least, is relatively clear. It is teleological necessity, that is it describes what must pertain in order that a given *telos* may be fulfilled (to get *this* result, *these things* are required, for example, for a house to be built, we *need* these materials, assembled in this order according to the builder's art). But what of simple necessity? At first sight we might be tempted to understand it as the necessity inhering in matter and its motions, the "physical necessity" that gives rise to rainfall and unexpected storms and creates deformities and females: the necessity of *automaton*, which we might also want to identify as the material necessity of the atomists. Recall Aristotle's question from *Physics* II.8: "What prevents nature from acting, not for the sake of something or for what is better, but by necessity, as in the case of rain, which does not fall in order that wheat may grow."[3] Indeed Peck, in his extended introduction to *Generation of Animals*, indicates that this is precisely Aristotle's meaning, describing necessity as it is opposed to "the better," and then describing simple or absolute necessity as that "involved in the Material and Motive Causes—as a reassertion of themselves by these Causes against the Final cause and against nature as she advances toward her achievement of it."[4] However, *pace* Peck and other commentators, Aristotle is actually very careful to avoid any such formulation of simple or absolute necessity. This deserves further investigation.

In *Metaphysics* XII Aristotle gives a threefold account of necessity, adding to hypothetical and simple necessity a third category: force, compulsion, or constraint (*bia*): "For necessity has all these meanings: that which is by constraint [*bia*] because it is contrary to impulse; and that without which excellence [*to eu*] is impossible; and that which cannot be otherwise, but is absolutely necessary."[5] The second meaning, "that without which excellence is impossible," would seem to correspond to hypothetical necessity: that which is necessary for, or the *sine qua non* of, a desirable or excellent result. First, then, we have *bia*, force or compulsion that acts against nature, and last we have what seems like a general definition of simple or absolute necessity:

"that which cannot be otherwise." This does not shed much light on the problem of what Aristotle means in the *Physics* by "simple necessity." The most extended account of necessity, however, is offered in the philosophical dictionary, *Metaphysics* V, in which it is defined in six ways and which culminates in a definition of simple necessity.

Aristotle begins his definition of *necessary* (*anankaion*) in *Metaphysics* V.5 with the observation that in the first instance it applies to those things without which a life cannot be sustained; thus certain things are said to be necessary for existence, such as respiration or nutrition. Second, *necessary* refers to that without which some desired good or telos cannot be or come to be, or without which some evil cannot be escaped: necessary for the sake of something else. Here he gives two familiar examples: it is necessary to sail to Aegina to recover one's money, and taking medicine is necessary in order to get rid of disease. This is also the sense in which bricks and stones are necessary to building a house. These first two definitions correspond to what Aristotle calls hypothetical necessity—they indicate the way that things may be *necessary for* some final cause or another. The first refers to sustaining natural being as such, to the necessity of *phusis* as teleological, while the second apparently refers to the coming about of *chosen* goals: necessity in the realm of *technē*. Aristotle defines the third kind of necessity as force or compulsion, *bia*, which hinders, prevents, and disrupts the teleological vectors of impulse (*hormē*), choice (*prohairesis*), and calculation (*logismos*). And this sense of necessity as compulsion, he tells us, "is disagreeable."[6] By way of illustration, he quotes both Evenus: "For every necessary thing is by nature grievous," and, notably, Sophocles's *Electra*: "Compulsion [*bia*] makes me do this of necessity."[7] Why, though, is Electra's compulsion disagreeable? Electra is defending her own relentless mourning, and her concomitant desire to avenge the murder of her father, Agamemnon, by her mother, Clytemnestra, and her stepfather, Aegisthus. The chorus is admonishing her, pleading with her to let it go. But Electra is driven by passionate, terrible (*deinos*) necessity (221) to grieve for her dead father and to seek vengeance, calling on the furies or Erinyes (110), among other deities, for assistance in her endeavors. Here, the order of necessity may be found "disagreeable" insofar as it involves mourning, grief, and rage, and gives rise to tragic consequences: it is in essence a tragic compulsion, or in another register we might quite precisely call it a death drive.

But we should observe that the necessary compulsion of vengeance also carries a feminine sign in this context, and not only

because Electra is the one lamenting, or because the work of mourning is traditionally women's labor. It does so also because throughout the *Oresteia*'s tragic cycle the very order of vengeance is marked
as feminine. The abject, grotesque, feminine Erinyes or Furies are
the very figures for vengeance, blood paying for blood, called up by
Electra in her passion. Recall from Aeschylus's *Eumenides* that following Orestes's act of matricide the Erinyes are subsequently roused
to avenge that murder in turn, and that Apollo, defending Orestes,
makes the winning argument against them (with Athena casting the
deciding vote). Apollo invokes the exact claim later made by Aristotle: the mother contributes nothing essential in reproduction. At the
trial, Apollo asserts that, "the so-called 'mother' is not a parent of
the child, only the nurse of the newly-begotten embryo. The parent
is he who mounts; the female keeps the offspring safe, like a stranger
on behalf of a stranger."[8] He then offers the example of Athena herself, born of no woman and sprung fully formed from the head of
Zeus, as proof of the irrelevance of the mother in procreation, conveniently forgetting that Zeus's act of childbirth was only made possible
because he had previously swallowed and incorporated his pregnant
consort, Metis.

Aristotle adds at the close of his discussion of compulsive necessity
that it "seems rightly to be something inexorable; for it is opposed to
motion which is in accordance with choice and calculation."[9] Here,
then, choice and calculation, the masculine operations of intellect,
are clearly separated from the disagreeable, passionate, inexorable,
feminine compulsions of vengeance that serve to vitiate them. Aristotle, like Athena, votes on the side of Apollo and Orestes against such
compulsion. We might also, not wrongly I think, hear behind this
invocation of compulsive, necessary vengeance, an echo of a polemic
against Anaximander, author of the earliest extant fragment of Western philosophy, which states: "Whence things have their origin, there
they must also pass away according to necessity; for they must pay
penalty and be judged for their injustice, according to the ordinance
of time."[10] Such a worldview, of perpetual payment for perpetual
injustice in cycles of coming-to-be and passing away, is of course profoundly at odds with Aristotelian teleology.[11] Necessity qua compulsion or force is thus associated in Aristotle's text with an older order
of *phusis,* one in which dangerous, chthonic, feminine forces are seen
to operate far beyond the sway of post-Socratic, rational, deliberating
men who above all desire the good and the true.

Having thus described this disagreeable compulsion, Aristotle then turns to what may be his very broadest and most abstract definition of the term: "that which cannot be otherwise [*to mē endechomenon allōs*]."[12] This definition is one from which, he says, all the others may "somehow be derived," since compulsions force things to take place in a certain way, and final causes necessitate things without which they would otherwise be impossible.[13] The language here is worth attending to, because *mē endechomenon allōs* signifies literally that which cannot take on, admit, or receive some other thing. *Endechomenon* is a middle-passive present participle whose root is *dechomai*, to receive or accept. *Dechomai* may also be heard in Plato's formulation of "necessity" or the "errant cause" in the *Timaeus*: the *hupodochē* or receptacle which is also, figured as a mother or nurse.[14] Here, then, the necessary *as such* is articulated as that which by contrast *cannot* receive others—it is impassive, inexorable, unchangeable, nonreceptive, nonfeminine, and therefore certainly masculine. What is more, Aristotle uses precisely this formulation (*to me endechomenon allōs*) in *Metaphysics* XII to delineate simple, *haplōs*, necessity.[15] What in essence cannot be otherwise, simply and without qualification, is eternal, possesses no matter, no potentiality, and enters into no motion or change: the definition of the necessary as such thus reflects the reality of the prime mover itself.

In the next part of the definition of necessity in Book V, Aristotle indeed departs from the world of matter and change, telling us that necessity operates in logical demonstrations such as syllogisms (and also, presumably, mathematics). Then he finally moves to considering directly the "first and most authoritative [*kuriōs*] sense of the necessary,"[16] namely *simple (haplōs)* necessity, saying, "there are certain things which are eternal and immutable, there is nothing in them which is compulsory [*biaion*] or contrary to their nature [*para phusin*]."[17] The prime mover—the unmoved mover of the superlunary sphere, which is pure actuality, form, eternal, unalterable, pure intellection, pleasure, wonder, and good—is thus the very figure of simple necessity. Simple necessity in itself is eternal and unchangeable, but it also causes a certain kind of coming-to-be in nature. As confirmed in *De Generatione et Corruptione* II.11, generation by simple necessity must "be cyclical and return upon itself."[18] Further, "It is in cyclical movement and cyclical coming-to-be that absolute (simple) necessity [*to ex anankēs haplōs*] is present, and if the process is cyclical, each member must necessarily come-to-be and have come-to-be, and if this necessity exists, their coming-to-be is cyclical."[19] In other words, what is mutable and changing may be characterized by simple necessity if the change itself is always and eternally the same, that is, cyclical. Teleological nature always acts *for the sake of* something or for what is better: the temporal cycles of generation and destruction observed in sublunary nature issue from and imitate the necessary cyclical motions of the heavens, which in their perfection and eternity are better, closer to the good, than the vagary-filled cycles of the sub-lunary, into which accident and force can intervene to cause rains in summer, and heat waves in winter.[20]

Simple necessity, the kind of necessity that characterizes the prime mover, the internal necessity that receives nothing into itself and brooks no external compulsion, is thus transmitted to the heavens, and finds its way into the sublunar sphere where it may now be char-acterized as hypothetical necessity, whatever is necessitated by a given telos or final cause (whose ultimate figure is the prime mover). The explanatory distinction Aristotle makes in *Metaphysics* V.5 is that, "some have an external [*heteron*] cause of their necessity, and oth-ers have not, but it is through them that other things are of neces-sity what they are."[21] Thus hypothetical necessity *issues from a telos*, which has a necessitating action upon other things, especially matter, thus in order to be built the house *must* be made of bricks and stones, placed in a certain order. And simple necessity, as we have seen, char-acterizes the ultimate telos itself, the prime mover. However, in the sublunary realm there are plenty of things that hinder a given *telos*, and these represents an order of necessity that comes from outside, but from where? This is utterly unexplained. Aristotle clearly does not want to dignify this *bia* or compulsion—or rather the *motion* in compulsion, in the *para phusin,* and in chance and spontaneity—as having a source or a cause of its own. Such *bia* may have at the high-est level of generality the same incontrovertible character as simple necessity in that it is also "what cannot be otherwise" (Aristotle calls it inexorable, which amounts to the same thing), but it remains unex-plained, and apparently inexplicable. It thus functions, as it were, as simple necessity's contrary—its threatening, uncanny mirror.[22] Aris-totle does tell us, after all, at *Generation of Animals* IV.10, that what occurs contrary to nature may be traced to the "plurality of prin-ciples and indeterminacy of matter," and these presumably give rise to a whole sphere of compulsive and forcible movements. This order of necessity, insofar as it acts against teleology, thus characterizes the field of the aleatory. For who knows if a berry eaten by an animal will be one that provides it with the necessary nourishment for survival or if it will, through force or compulsion, poison and kill the creature?

To be clear: necessity as *compulsion*, as what drives aleatory matter, as the source of monstrosities, as the feminine automatism of forces acting upon us contrary to reason and choice, is far from simple.[23] But how does this compulsion interact with the teleological order that issues from simple necessity and to which it is seemingly fundamentally opposed? Aristotle is obviously both aware of and concerned to refute philosophical arguments (in particular from the atomists) that posit a certain fundamental necessity or even motility operating inherently in matter. Furthermore, he also recognizes the complexity of this interface between the two orders of necessity, especially in his descriptions of biological structures and processes in animal organisms. Here, as discussed in the case of the female off-spring—our exemplar for the feminine symptom—the compulsions of material necessity do not simply conflict with teleological imperatives, one struggling agonistically against the other, but both, inexplicably, are often seen to cooperate. In pursuit of this curious symptomaticity, and of the fugitive source of matter's aleatory compulsions, let us return to the biological writings.

NECESSITY IN ARISTOTLE'S BIOLOGY

The first chapter of *Parts of Animals* is devoted to a discussion of the method of inquiry, including an extended consideration of natural causation and necessity. Aristotle introduces the theme of necessity up front, prompted by the doxographical context: "Almost all philosophers endeavor to carry back their explanations to necessity, but they omit to distinguish the various meanings of necessity."[24] He then distinguishes the now familiar couplet of simple and hypothetical necessity. And he polemicizes briefly against Empedocles's theory of biological formation through chances and accidents, emphasizing the authoritative role of telos and final causation, *hou heneka,* in natural coming-to-be, and therefore the prevalence of hypothetical necessity in nature. Strikingly, Aristotle considers prevalent materialist theories of becoming in turn, citing the Empedoclean principles of strife (*neikous*) and love (*philia*), Anaxagoras's principle of mind (*nous*), and also *automaton* (the reference is obscure but he may possibly mean the atomists), attributing to all these thinkers the idea that within matter itself a certain necessity prevails. This necessity shows itself in the way that principles such as the hot and the cold inhere within elemental matter (as in fire and earth), or in the way that air and water flow upward and downward, and in and out, which necessitates that bodies be structured in certain ways.[25] Similarly, in *Physics* II.9, he starts off with a popular idea of material necessity thus: "Nowadays, it is thought that what exists by necessity does so in generation, as if one were to consider the wall as having been constructed by necessity, since what is heavy travels down by its nature and what is light travels up by its nature,"[26] Although such factors have their role to play as material causes, they are insufficient and subordinate, since necessity in natural things is essentially hypothetical, that is teleological, and final and formal causes must be given first and foremost by the physicist.

Nonetheless, in both texts Aristotle does not *deny* these material necessities in their facticity. In fact in the *Physics* we glimpse yet another claim for matter as a site and perhaps even a source of motion: "It is evident, then, that the necessary in natural things is what we call 'matter' and also the motions therein."[27] He has a few lines earlier admitted that, "if there are no stones, there can be no house, and if there is no iron, there can be no saw."[28] So clearly, matter matters, it is the *sine qua non,* and it may contain its own motions even if an account of these is not explicitly given. And the possibility that appropriate materials may not be available for specified ends haunts the teleological universe as a constant threat. But is Aristotle admitting here that matter actually *moves itself*? If he is, he quickly passes over the question. In the very next line, he writes "We may also add that both [*amphō*] causes must be stated by the physicist, and the final cause more so [*mallon*] than the cause as matter, for it is the former which is the cause of the latter, not the latter of the end."[29] So here the threat that the appropriate matter may not be available is mastered, and the final cause, insofar as it stipulates what kind of matter is needed, is actually said to *cause* the matter! Likewise in *Parts of Animals* he tells us that, "there are more causes than one in natural generation, there is the one for the sake of which the thing is formed, and the one to which the beginning of the motion [*hē archē tēs kinēseōs*] is due."[30] So while these two may seem to be opposed, and it may seem that Aristotle is here offering the possibility that the movements inherent in matter may indeed act independently and causally, even if subordinated to the *telos,* the language of *archē kinēseōs* nonetheless circles us back to the motive cause delineated in the *Physics*. Remember that the motive cause is an essential cause sharply distinguished from the matter: the *archē kinēseōs* is defined as an advisor or father, or as the craftsman's art or *logos*, identical in the natural context with the form and the *telos* generically if not numerically. Material necessity, however, with its compulsions and deviations, remains as a phenomenon to be reckoned with both as part of the doxographical tradition, and as what shows itself in things. In the biological treatises Aristotle is forced to confront it, even if indirectly, and we find that it is mostly revealed through examples rather than in any explicitly theoretical exposition.

A slightly problematic moment occurs a little further on in *Parts of Animals* I.1, where he says, "We have then, these two causes before us, to wit, the "for the sake of which" and also necessity, *for many things come into being owing to necessity.* Perhaps one might ask which "necessity" is meant when it is specified as a cause, since here it can be neither of the two modes which are defined in the philosophical treatises. There is, however, in generation [*genesis*] a third mode; as when we say that nourishment is necessary, we mean it in neither of the two modes, but we mean that without it no animal can be."[31] Once again it looks as if, having dismissed the usual couplet of simple and hypothetical necessity (familiar from the philosophical treatises), Aristotle is about to tell us about material or physical necessity. However the discussion actually devolves once again into a discussion of hypothetical or teleological necessity—*these* conditions are necessary *in order that this* might take place. And this misdirection is instructive because it indicates, once again, the extent of Aristotle's reluctance to dignify matter with any force of its own. There is one possible source, referred to by Balme, for understanding these "two modes which are defined in the philosophical treatises" as teleological and material necessity, and it is found in a passage on cause in the *Posterior Analytics*.[32] Quite unusually, Aristotle there states, "necessity is of two kinds: one acts in accordance with the nature or natural tendency of an object, the other forcibly opposed it (thus both the upward and the downward movements of a stone are due to necessity, but not to the same necessity.)"[33] So here we have an even-handed treatment of the two orders, with compulsion appearing as a simple alternative to teleological necessity, and existing alongside it. This is quite at odds with its treatment in the *Metaphysics* as an afterthought, as disagreeable, and as supplementary to and parasitic

upon both hypothetical and simple kinds of necessity. And though
this apparent elevation of compulsion to equal status with teleological
necessity may well be the referent for this remark in *Parts of Animals,*
it cannot explain the strangeness and symptomaticity of these scenes
where the orders meet, and in which compulsive necessity is continually subordinated to teleology in Aristotle's biology.

At the very end of *Parts of Animals* I.1, he provides the following
illustration:

> Although respiration takes place for such and such a *purpose,* any
> one stage of the process follows upon the others *by necessity.* Neces-
> sity means sometimes (a) that if this or that is to be the "for the sake
> of which" then such and such things must be so [i.e., hypothetical
> necessity]; *but sometimes it means* (b) *that things are as they are
> owing to their very nature,* as the following shows: It is necessary
> that the hot substance should go out and come in again as it offers
> resistance, and that the air should flow in—that is obviously neces-
> sary. And the hot substance within, as the cooling is produced, offers
> resistance, and this brings about the entrance of the air from without
> and also its exit. This example shows how the method works and also
> illustrates the sort of things whose causes we have to discover.[34]

Here, the behavior of hot and cold, and the behavior of matter and
air with respect to inflow and outflow, confront a teleological ordering of things. In certain illuminating situations, then, both in *Parts of
Animals* and *Generation of Animals,* we find that the refrain "on the
one hand for the better, on the other by necessity" becomes almost
familiar. Indeed, sometimes things in biological organisms exist just
because of material necessity and with no purpose at all, as for example in the discussion of the spleen in *Parts of Animals* in which we are
told it is just there by necessity as an incidental component or accident
(*kata sumbebēkos*), while the kidneys are precisely there *not* of necessity but for a good purpose.[35]

Examples proliferate of this kind of aleatory, material necessity
in natural things but not occurring "according to nature." The most
striking, perhaps, is that of the female offspring, already discussed in
chapter 1: the coinciding of two orders of necessity that is the feminine symptom:

> The first beginning [*archē*] of this deviation is when a female is
> formed and not a male though (a) this is indeed a necessity of nature
> [*anankaia tē phusei*], since the kind must be preserved that is sepa-
> rated into male and female, and (b) since it is possible for the male
> not to gain the mastery through youth or age or some other such

cause, female offspring must of necessity [*ananke*] be generated [*gin-esthai*] in animals.[36]

Aristotle has also given a more detailed account of this necessary mechanism: "When the 'principle' is failing to gain the mastery and is unable to effect concoction owing to deficiency of heat, and does not succeed in reducing the material into its own proper form, but instead is worsted in the attempt, then of necessity the material must change over into its opposite condition [*ananke eis tounantion metaballein*]. Now the opposite of the male is the female."[37] It seems here that Aristotle is positing a mechanism that necessarily inheres in matter, that a certain deficiency of heat will give rise to a radical transformation of something into its contrary, although he does not argue for it.[38] In this case, then, the necessity within matter seems to devolve to that required by teleological nature (so that the species can be kept in being), in other words hypothetical necessity—this indeterminacy or undecidability, this sleight or misdirection of reason, is, one might say, a sign of the symptomatic par excellence.

Menstruation in females, too, results from a deficiency in the female: she "cannot effect concoction and therefore of necessity [*ananke*] residue must be formed not only from the useless nourishment, but also in the blood-vessels, and when there is a full complement of it . . . it must overflow. On the other hand, in order to serve the better purpose and end [*heneka de tou beltionos kai tou telous*], nature diverts it to this place and employs it there for the sake of generation."[39] Necessity in material processes is thus taken up by nature, which now begins to emerge as a handy and efficient craftsman. Milk arrives in the breasts in its final stage of readiness *ex anankes*, and it does so *coincidentally* just at the right time for the purpose of nourishing the young.[40] And in the account of embryogenesis we find another such confluence: the embryo "sets" into a solid and sloughs off fluid inevitably, just as rennet curdles milk, creating a membrane (*humēn*) around the new organism: "This is the result of necessity, but also it is to serve a purpose: (a) necessity ordains that the extreme surface of a thing should solidify when heated as when cooled; (b) it is requisite that the young animal should not be situated in fluid but well away from it."[41] Such coincidings, *sumptōmata*, occur not just specifically in the female embryo, and yet all embryonic development of course takes place *in* the female body or *from* the female as in the case of an egg (eggs themselves are said to grow of necessity because they contain a "yeast-like residue" but also for the sake of what is better).[42] The development of the membrane, the *humēn* itself, then, is yet another indication of feminine symptomaticity. Derrida's extended discourse on the hymen in its undecidability and all of its *aporiai* comes to mind: *Humēn* is after all the god of marriage, what paradoxically conjoins the two sexes as well as what separates them.[43] I will return to this theme of the boundary as a site of the undecidable in my discussion of Aristotelian place in chapter 4.

The behavior of fluids and residues in particular is a recurring theme here. In addition to the respiration example, Aristotle refers to the agonic confluence of the two orders of necessity in other fluidic contexts. They appear in the production of the blood and serum (and since menstrual blood is the *protē hulē* for the organism in generation there is an explicit feminine mark here too), and also in relation to the use of ink in squid and octopus. According to Aristotle, these creatures discharge ink in fear as others sometimes expel urine, but here the ink squirt functions as a defensive mechanism that saves (*sōteria*) them from harm.[44] Irigaray has theorized such contexts of organic flow and fluid mechanics as feminine, as opposed to a masculine imaginary of units and solids, in her key essay "The 'Mechanics' of Fluids" in *This Sex Which Is Not One*.[45] And this gendering would seem to be borne out by Aristotle's biology. In the case of horned animals, he tells us that their bodies are said to contain an overabundance of earthly matter, producing a residue that "flows upwards of necessity." Nature then, "makes use of and turns [this] to advantage" by making that flowing residue into horns and providing them with a means of defense.[46] An earthly, but flowing, feminine, bodily residue is thus transformed by nature's opportunism into a preeminent signifier of masculinity. But deer—the only animals with solid horns according to Aristotle—also shed their horns of necessity, because of their weight, and also on purpose to "take advantage of the extra lightness."[47] So the masculine signifier is oddly precarious, readily subject to an unmanning that nature in turn embraces and assimilates to its purpose—perhaps, one might say, prophylactically.

As well as appearing in a subordinate role in feminine fluidic contexts, necessity is also subordinated to teleology in a way that establishes a clear hierarchy in the very structure of the body. The hierarchy that the teleological account gives rise to is starkly demonstrated in the account of the diaphragm or *phrenes* that separates the region around the heart from the region around the stomach.[48] The heart, as seat of sensitive soul (*psuchē aisthētikē*), is according to Aristotle the body's nobler part (*timiōteron*). Nature therefore divides it from the lower and ignoble stomach, which exists of necessity *for the sake of* the upper, by acting as a receptacle for food. Note once again the ambivalence of the use of "necessary" here—it it seems to refer to the brute necessity of matter moving through the system, the stomach functioning as a lowly "receptacle" (*dektikon*) for food, but it is also necessary *hypothetically*, that is, for the sake of nourishing the higher parts. The *phrenes* as separating but once again as also providing a connection—in this case to sensation and thought (*phronein*)—is nicely illustrated a little later on by the phenomenon of laughter as a response to tickling, indicating the intimacy and proximity of upper and lower bodily orders, and their mapping on to the two orders of necessity.

In these examples and others, then, nature seems to appear as a strange kind of actor or craftsman, opportunistically taking up or discarding the offerings of material necessity insofar as they befit teleological purposes. A passage about the formation of flesh and bone at *Generation of Animals* II.6 turns out to be revelatory in this regard. Aristotle is describing how flesh and bone are hardened by heat in fetal development, just as earthenware is baked. He tells us, that, however, the heat, "does not produce [*poiei*] flesh or bone out of any chance thing at a chance place or a chance time, but this happens by nature at a place or time ordained by nature [*to pephukos kai hou pephuke kai hote pephuken*]."[49] He continues, "that which is *potentially* [*dunamei*] will not be brought into being by a motive agent which lacks the appropriate *actuality* [*energeia*]; so, equally, that which possesses the *actuality* will not produce [*poiēsei*] the article out of any casual material. No more could a carpenter produce a chest out of anything but wood; and equally without the carpenter no chest will be produced out of the wood."[50] A few lines after the appearance of the carpenter, nature is compared with a cook, providing the appropriate amount of heat, since the heat resides in the seminal residue. And furthermore, "with those animals that are formed spontaneously [*automatōs*] the cause responsible is the movement and heat of the climatic conditions. Heat and cooling . . . are both *employed by Nature* [*chrētai hē phusis*]. Each has the potential [*dunamis*] of making one thing into this and another into that, but in natural generation heating and cooling happen to be [*sumbainei*] for a purpose [*heneka tinos*]."[51] And, just a little later, a painter analogy: "In the early stages the parts are all traced out in outline; later on they get their various colours and softnesses and hardnesses, for all the world as if a painter were at work on them [*hōsper an hupo zōgraphou tēs phuseōs dēmiourgoumena*]."[52]

On the one hand, then, the hot and cold have their various necessary effects on various materials: setting, melting, hardening to various degrees, pushing fluids this way and that, and so on. We still have no explicit causal or philosophical account of these movements, but Aristotle, the doctor's son, is certainly familiar with the medical tradition, the importance of the hot and the cold in those works now collected under the name of Hippocrates as well as the provenance of hot, cold, moist, and dry in the Presocratic *phusikoi* and as aligned with the four elements in Empedocles. And the more these material operations are explicitly considered, the more a particular conception of Nature (and perhaps here we should follow Peck in capitalizing it) comes into view, that of Nature as *craftsman* or *demiurge* (cook, clay-modeler, painter), *employing* and *making* various products in the active voice.[53] Now the craftsman analogy is familiar from Aristotle's definition of sexual difference in the first book of *Generation of Animals*: "regarding the male as the active producer [*poiētikon*] and mover, and the female as passive [*pathētikon*] and moved, we see that one thing comes to be from them comes to be in the sense that a bed is formed from the carpenter and the wood, or a ball from the wax and the form."[54] So while the feminine gender of *phusis* might tempt us to personify Nature as a female demiurge (as Peck frequently does), the discourse of sexual difference reveals a slippage between the demiurgic male in sexual reproduction, and Nature itself arranging and ordering generation, opportunistically exploiting necessity in things as and when suitable for its purposes.

This formation is even more clearly articulated in an explicitly antiatomist context in the final lines of *Generation of Animals*. Democritus, we are reminded, has no account of final causation, but in a by now familiar move Aristotle counters that animals are naturally constructed for the sake of what is better. The other factors involved in the process he says, "are causes *qua* moving [*kinounta*] and instruments [*organa*] and as matter [*hulē*]," and the image of nature as craftsman employing its instruments is then cemented: "it is likely that Nature makes the majority of its works by means of *pneuma* used as an instrument. *Pneuma* serves many uses in the things constructed by nature, just as certain objects do in the crafts [*technai*], e.g. the hammer and the anvil of the smith."[55] I will address the strange constitution and role of *pneuma* later in this chapter. Of note here is the turn at the close of the text that succeeds quite seamlessly, *pace* Heidegger, in assimilating nature to a scene of technical production and instrumental reason. The final *coup de grâce* for material necessity comes, significantly, in a medical example: "To allege that the causes are of the *necessary* type is like supposing that when the water has been drawn off from a dropsical patient the reason for which it has been done is the knife, and not the patient's health, *for the sake of which* the knife made the incision."[56] Here the duplicity of *aitia* as both cause and reason or explanation becomes manifest. For Aristotle, the scene is far less that of a surgeon's knife slicing skin and releasing fluid in a somatic *katharsis*—a series of forces and flows— nor of the body's native, opaque vagaries in which it may ail, and then respond or fail to respond to treatment, than that of the doctor's art, his masterful, paternal *technē* and *logos* using the instruments at hand, and plying health upon the errant, symptomatic body with health as the ultimate goal or telos, and therefore as the supreme *aitia*. The doctor, then becomes a sort of figure for nature itself, imposing his cuts, less those of a knife than the cuts of decision, of choice or *prohairesis*, sculpting pliant materials into dynamic shape, accepting some and rejecting others, forming them into a fully functional *energeia*, with particularly convenient tools at his disposal, and with a goal identical to that of nature's: health and preservation. Aristotle is usually understood to theorize no demiurgic creator in his cosmos, the divine prime mover of the *Metaphysics* famously impassive and disinterested, certainly not a creator divinity. But perhaps here in the biological texts we find, buried and obscure, the demiurge himself, under the guise of Nature, and *par excellence* in the figure of the doctor.

Now all along my claim has been that there is an opaque order of material necessity, aleatory matter, which Aristotle for the most part acknowledges only negatively, as a *bia* or compulsion that *gets in the way* of teleology, or as symptomatically, as luck or chance coincidentally or uncannily operating in concert with Nature's aims, construed broadly. One might argue on Aristotle's behalf that there is nothing inconsistent in his account, and that teleology goes all the way down. On this view, the plurality of things would mean that different teleological pathways sometimes come into conflict with each other, especially given that the four elements themselves are teleologically driven to find their "proper places": fire and air (to a lesser extent) moving upward, earth and water (to a lesser extent) moving downward.[57] Further, given the plurality of all these various *teloi* (nature's aim of preserving life alongside the propensities of the elements and the cyclicity of the seasons ordained by the heavenly bodies), the necessary motions of material things would be far from aleatory but instead fully calculable, if only one were apprised of all initial conditions. And the metaphysical account itself would not be inconsistent or give rise to symptoms. But recall the key passage from *Generation of Animals* IV.10: "[Nature] cannot bring [regular cyclicity] about exactly on account of the indeterminateness [*aoristian*] of matter and the existence of a plurality of principles [*archai*] which impede the processes of generation in nature and destruction, and so often are the causes of things occurring contrary to Nature [*para phusin sumpiptontōn*]."[58] Alongside the plurality of principles is *also* the indeterminateness of matter. Matter's lack of determinacy (or boundary, *horos*), as well as the multiplicity of the beginnings or principles of motion, appear as the *sumptōmata* of the cosmos, the chance occurrences, falling together where they may.[59]

I have traced throughout these texts an insistence on Aristotle's part that the motive cause or the source of motion is always accounted for in nature by a recourse to some telos or another, the paternal motive cause exemplified by the *logos* in the sperm that is generically identical with the formal and final causes. However this *indeterminacy* of matter hints at a different *archē kinēseōs* or source of motion for compulsion, and for, *tuchē* and *automaton* (the latter are characterized in *Physics* II.6 as accidental, plural and indeterminate moving causes). We can only conclude that these opaque, aleatory sources of motion reside *within matter itself*. And indeed, the very notion of the motive cause as *numerically distinct* from the formal and final causes requires the intervention of the material cause, without which such dispersal or numerical differentiation would not be possible, so the material cause must, too, be the source of plurality as such. Where the atomist doctrine, in order to offset the threat of a fully determined universe, must eventually (in Lucretius's Epicureanism if not in Epicurus himself) posit an atomic swerve (a *clinamen* that comes from nowhere), Aristotle finds the required indeterminacy in the nature of matter itself. Matter thus gives the possibility that things in the sublunary world can *always* be otherwise, can always admit of otherness, that there is a continual restless agonic struggle for and against fulfillment of *teloi*, both in the natural and human worlds. Indeed, matter constitutes the very possibility that a thing might both be and not be, it is the very condition of possibility of coming-to-be and passing away: "Now all things which are generated, whether by nature or by art, have matter; for there is a potentiality for each of them to be, and also not to be, and this potentiality is the matter in each."[60] However, it is precisely as a result of Aristotle's exclusion of disruptive material necessity from the field of proper necessity in the philosophical treatises that this aleatory necessity returns, by accident, by chance, and symptomatically, in the biological treatises, and *par excellence* in the teleological function of giving rise to a female in sexual reproduction.

AUTOMATON AND REPRODUCTION

The term *automaton*, and its meaning for Aristotle as chance or spontaneity in nature, should already be familiar from the discussion of *Physics* II in the previous chapter. In *Generation of Animals* it is also used specifically to refer to a rather remarkable phenomenon: that of spontaneous generation (*genesis automatos*), which Aristotle finds to be common among certain creatures such as shellfish that, to his mind, do not reproduce sexually but rather arise directly out of the environment.[61] Here, Aristotle is addressing the coming-to-be of something in nature that does not, indeed *cannot* have a paternal source of motion that is identifiable with its formal or final cause, as is the way in sexual reproduction, and indeed in nature in general. *Automaton*, then, is a curious term in this context. We are more familiar with it as a term for a self-moving machine or a robot, and indeed this sense of *automaton* was also current for the Greeks, and referred to puppets moved by strings and pulleys, often referred to as the "wondrous automatons" or simply "wonders" (*thaumata*). What, then, is the relation between aleatory movements in nature, and these technical wonders? Remarkably, it turns out that Aristotle deploys the figure of *automaton* not only in relation to chance and to spontaneous generation, but also in this quite different sense as an indispensable trope in his explanation of sexual reproduction and embryonic development.[62] At *Generation of Animals* II.5, Aristotle describes how the male implants the active principle of movement, the *archē kinēseōs* that is sensitive soul, into the matter provided by the female. However, he has also told us that the parts of the animal are present *potentially* (*kata dunamis*) in this matter.[63] After the male supplies the principle of motion, then one event of fetal concoction follows on from the other "just as it does so," he says, "in the wondrous automatons [*hōsper en tois automatois thaumasi*]."[64] The Greek "wondrous automatons" were technically complex mechanisms made up of ropes and pulleys, activated by a small initial motion, leading to a "miraculous" series of movements, apparently spontaneous and self-directed. They are described in detail only much later in antiquity by Galen and Heron of Alexandria (who gives detailed instructions for their construction), but it is indeed these very *thaumata* that are also responsible for creating the famous shadows in Plato's cave.[65] While Plato's wonders lull, captivate, and seduce the prisoners in the cave, the importance of wonder to Aristotle's method cannot be underestimated: the first book of the *Metaphysics* gives the experience of wonder as an incitement to thinking, as the original and continuing *archē* of philosophy itself.[66] And indeed, the automatic puppets themselves are given as the first example of something inspiring investigation by causing wonder in the *Metaphysics*.[67]

How the aleatory motions of the natural world come to bear the same name as complex technical wonders that mimic intentional movement is itself an intriguing question, and the following considerations may help shed light on an old etymological puzzle regarding *automaton*, as well as Aristotle's employment of the term.[68] In the *Physics* Aristotle speculates that *automaton* is derived from *auto*, "self," and *matēn*, "to no purpose, in vain," bolstering his point that what occurs by chance does so in a way that is at odds with any given *telos*, that exceeds or disrupts the pursuit of a goal. However, most—though not all—philological authorities trace the root of -*maton* to the Indo-European *men-*, meaning "to think," with the implication that the *automaton* is self-moving because it appears to be possessed of a mind (also derived from *men-*), and to think for itself.[69] This implication may make a certain sense when applied to the homuncular puppets, though the imputing of something like an already separate and separable "mind" to an inanimate object should strike us as thoroughly un-Greek, and quite modern. The archaic Greeks may have seen all sorts of natural forces and entities as divine or as inhabited or commanded by divinities, but the notion of mind or soul as separate from body or matter only emerges slowly and unevenly in the Greek philosophical tradition, as evidenced by, for example, the thought of Anaxagoras and Plato. Furthermore, it is hard to see how the term *automaton*, when used to refer to the workings of nature and its spontaneous and senseless motions, could mean "driven by intention or will," as such an etymology would imply. In the Aristotelian view, exactly the opposite is meant. *Automaton* is indeterminate, plural, unpredictable, and may actually thwart the will, as I showed in my discussion of *hamartia*. A philological investigation of *automaton* and how it exactly comes to mean both aleatory phenomena *and* machines possessed of illusory self-motion will thus help to illuminate Aristotle's text, and the production and operation of aleatory matter and the feminine symptom within its terms.

Automaton first appears in writing in Hesiod and Homer, both dating from about the eighth century BCE. Hesiod uses it in *Works and Days* in the story of Pandora's box. In order to avenge Prometheus's theft of fire, Zeus fashions Pandora, the first human woman on earth, and she is granted gifts from many other gods (*Pan-dora* means all given). Once Pandora opens the box and releases the gods' gifts upon the land terrible things ensue, including diseases that "of their own accord" (*automatai*) spread among men.[70] Resonances abound here with the Aristotelian account, in which the random motions of *automaton* are pressed into the service of teleological reproduction throught the phenomenon of the female, and the female appears as the crossing zone where the aleatory and the purposeful find their inexplicable conjuncture. In Hesiod, the diseases that multiply are not possessed of any mind or will, but are part of the mute proliferations of nature. However, they are also the means through which the gods' will is carried out—these natural proliferationss are thus haunted by the will of Zeus, the divine fate to which all men are subject. Further, these gifts of the god are promulgated through the body and the being of a woman, and Pandora's own actions and intentions are thus subsumed in the unfolding of that divine will. She is thus, in a sense, a puppet of the gods, a kind of automaton in her own right. A second instance of the term occurs in *Works and Days* shortly thereafter, in which the earth's bearing fruit, enjoyed by the golden race of mortal men living in the time of Cronos, is described as *automatē* (Evelyn-White gives "unforced").[71] The burgeonings of the natural world, of Gaia, the feminine earth, are once again the emphasis here.

Contemporary with Hesiod, three instances of the term appear in Homer's *Iliad*. First, when Agamemnon calls a counsel of elders, Menelaus comes unbidden (*automatos*), because he knows "in his heart" (*kata thumon*) the concerns of his brother; second, when Hera and Athena in full warrior glory, furious with the all-powerful Father Zeus for his support of the Trojans, set out from Olympus in their

chariot: Hera lashes the horses and the gates of heaven open self-bid-
den (*automatoi*); and lastly, when Thetis visits Hephaestus in order
to plea for a shield and armor for Achilles, she finds him at work,
fashioning golden wheeled tripods, which might "of themselves"
(*automatoi*) enter the gathering of the gods and then return to his
house.[72] While Hesiod's examples refer exclusively to the spontaneous motions of nature, Homer's refer instead to mysterious actions at
a distance occurring in and among the world of mortals, gods, and
artifacts. The first two are apparently incited by the strength of emotion and involve transfer of affect: one of a man upon another man
with whom he shares a bond of kinship, the other of goddesses raging
against Zeus's paternal authority. Are thought and will at work here?
Certainly intention is implied, but it is manifested through the force
of powerful emotions, its mode of motion utterly obscure, unconscious, and uncanny. Menelaus travels without knowing why, moved
by something "in his heart" (*kata thumon*) rather than his mind; the
gates are caught up in the motions of Hera's fury against Zeus. The
last example, the self-moving tripods of Hephaestus, inaugurates
the marvelous "automaton" as the product of the craftsman, who,
through his skill and cunning, creates "a wonder to behold [*thauma
idesthai*]."[73]

Homer is also the source for a suggestive essay by nineteenth-century French linguist Michel Bréal, who argued that the core sense
of *automaton* does not involve thought but rather movement. He
believes that the root is from the participle *memaōs*, from *maiomai*,
to desire, to be eager, but he seeks to show that within the Homeric
corpus *memaōs* tends to refer to any kind of rapid motion—a physical force rather than a desire or will of the soul—proposing that an
element of the Indo-European root *men-* signifies "to move, to run,"
and finding counterparts in the Latin composite verbs *im-minere*,
e-minere.[74] This is not quite the same as asserting with Aristotle that
the word is derived from *matē* (folly, fault) or the related *mataō* (to
be idle, to dally), and *matēn* (in vain, at random, without reason,
idly, falsely); but it does, like them, lead us away from imputations of
mind, thought, or will. Looking more closely at this Indo-European
root actually reveals a variety of coexistent meanings, and one source,
the Larousse *Dictionnaire Des Racines Des Langue Européenes*,
gives an overarching definition: "indicating the movements of spirit
(*l'esprit*)."[75] These movements are as varied as *menō*, *memona* (to
desire, to seek, to yearn for); *menos* (might, force); *mnēmē* (memory);

mainō (to madden); *mania* (madness); *mousa* (muse); and *manthanō* (to learn). Watkins defines the root as "to think, with derivatives referring to various qualities and states of mind and thought" and separates these into zero-grade form (mind, willing, madness), full-grade form (love [*minna* in Old High German], memento, comment, mentor), o-grade form (admonish, demonstrate, muse, music), an extended form (memory, mindful), and a suffixed form.

The sources that give an explanation for the -*matos* suffix in *automaton* (Pokorny, Chantraine) tend to stress *memona*, to be furiously eager, but also to purpose or intend, the imperfect and perfect of which is *mematō*, hence -*matos*.[76] Here an echo of the double meaning of *automaton* may be heard: the swift burgeonings of nature *but also* that which moves by design. The related noun is *to menos* (might, force, strength, fierceness, life, spirit, passion, and intent or purpose); the Sanskrit cognate is *manas* (spirit or passion). *Maino-mai* indicates to rage furiously, to be mad as in the Bacchic frenzy of maenads (again the feminine example), but is also used of natural things: Liddell and Scott give an instance in Aristophanes where it indicates a vine that is never done bearing fruit, and one in Asclepius in which it signifies the malignancy of an ulcer (these two examples echo the Hesiodic uses of *automaton* as the proliferations of nature, whether superabundant or malign). *Maiomai* once again means to seek, to search, to strive, to covet. One 1860 British etymological dictionary of Greek suggests that the vanity or folly of *matē* might derive from the idea of seeking without finding, whereas German sources (Pokorny, Hofmann) emphasize the sense of the root *ma-*, meaning to wave with the hand, and the related meanings of duping, fiddling, and conjuring (the relation to the Sanskrit *maya*, illusion, is given by Pokorny).[77] Prellwitz, writing in 1905, is clear that the—*matos* suffix is related to *mōsthai* (to strive), *mōlos*, and *matēn*, noting (as does Chantraine) that the same ending, -*matos*, appears in *elematos*, which also means idle, in vain.

One kind of purpose or will is grounded in reason, in *logos*, in speech, while the other is beyond *logos*: motile, unreasonable, mad, or uncontrolled (Hesiod writes, "of themselves [*automatoi*] diseases came upon men continually, by day and by night, bringing mischief to mortals silently, for wise Zeus took away speech from them"[78]). We are thus in the territory of what psychoanalysis will call the drive, of what Kristeva calls the semiotic as distinct from the symbolic, a theme to which I will return in my consideration of the Platonic *chōra* in chapter 3. Haunting this distinction are the ideas of illusion, of trickery, of sleight of hand, as well as the feminine frenzies of the Bacchae, the antipatriarchal fury of Hera and Athena against Zeus, the diseases of Pandora, and in Homer's *memona* the natural speed of horses, and rocks pushed onward by a torrent. So the etymological considerations reveal *automaton* as motile drive, acting beyond conscious thought, whether in the unstoppable burgeonings of the natural world, in the dancing bodies of women, or through the fierce affect of heroes and goddesses. *Automaton* moves through the world, and moves through us, in a way that exceeds our conscious control or the gatherings of *logos*. It is as such that we can see in it the compulsions and repetitions of what Freud will come to call the death drive. We can clearly see how this threatening force, this drive, becomes tamed and mastered as *automaton* comes to mean a technical artifact, the product of a highly skilled *technē* and *logos*, so much so that the craftsman himself appears as an enchanter or magician as he produces something that seems to *move itself*. *Automaton*, is then moving, burgeoning, natural, fully *alive*, but also that which is only *seemingly* alive, the illusion of life given by the master craftsman.

This uncanny ambiguity has been famously exploited by Descartes in his paranoid suspicion about men seen from his window in the Second Meditation: "what do I see . . . but hats and coats which may cover automatic machines."[79] And it perhaps reached its most significant cultural expression in the aesthetic practices of the surrealists such as automatic writing and automatic drawing, which they saw as a direct expression of unconscious drives. For the surrealists, the figure of the *automaton* is, in the formulation of Hal Foster, that which "assumes our human vitality" while we in turn "take on its deathly facticity."[80] That is, *automaton* figures a chiasmus, a crossing point between life and death, *phusis* and *technē*, as such. So—to risk a vast simplification—*automaton* not unlike woman herself, signifies not only the death drive, semblance, the threat of repetition compulsion, errancy, blindness, castration, and *thanatos*, but also occasions the erotic, Pygmalionesque promise of masculine mastery over life and death.

AUTOMATON IN ARISTOTLE

How does the notion of seeking or striving relate to or give rise to the essential idea in *matēn*, of failure, folly, purposelessness, action carried out in vain? Important to remember is that the Greeks (in contrast to post-Hegelian philosophers) did not construe striving to be a central feature of man's existence. As the tragedies so readily demonstrate, striving is more often than not bound to fail. Furthermore, the insistence of the feminine figure across Greek texts as mantic, as manic, as frenzied, as she through whom unreasoned and chthonic vengeful forces flow, as fecund, as uncontrolled, but also, as developed in Aristotelian thought, as flawed, foolish, and bound to failure, as *lacking capacity or potency*, needs to be emphasized. Aristotle's notion of *automaton* carries with it a schematized rendering of these contradictions—on the one hand that which causes wonder, is marvelous and illusory but nonetheless ultimately designed and therefore reasonable, teleological, and knowable; on the other that which proliferates senselessly, and appears as disruptive, aleatory, and going nowhere.

Physics II.6 gives an instructive illustration of this ambiguity. In demarcating *automaton* and *tuchē*, Aristotle explains that *automaton* is the broader category, describing any event that that isn't directed toward an explicit telos. *Tuchē* appears as a subset of *automaton*, a name for this missing of the mark (or rather hitting it unintentionally) when choice or reason is involved. *Automaton*, he goes on to say, is however most clearly distinguished from chance (*tuchē*) in cases of natural coming-to-be that occur *against nature* (*para phusin*). He then adds, "And there is another distinction, for the one the cause is external, for the other internal."[81] Which then is the external cause, and which the internal? The majority of commentators and translators, including Charlton, Hardie and Gaye, Barthélémy Saint-Hilaire, and Ross who follow Simplicius and Philoponus, specify that *automaton* must be the external cause, acting *against* nature and therefore outside it (Aristotle indeed specifies *automaton* as a cause external to an event a few lines earlier).[82] This leaves open the question of what is *internal*. If *tuchē* is the internal cause, how can it be a subset of an external cause? Simplicius explains that the internal must be what causes things to come to be contrary to nature (*para phusin*), but that this cannot be *automaton*—rather there is a *kath' auto* cause that is something like "pressure or imbalance or excess of matter or shortage or some other such thing."[83] These causes, however, seem to me to be not *kath'auto* but rather the chance vagaries of matter—*automaton* itself. Aquinas, Albertus Magnus, Apostle, and Hope, come down on the other side: *automaton* is internal, and *tuchē* is an external cause. Apostle, in an illuminating but complex note, returns us to the site of biological reproduction and spontaneous generation: "Monstrosity is generated by *chance* [i.e., *automaton*], which is a cause in, let us say, the sperm, and monstrosity is not the usual effect. But, one may say, the cause of a thing generated without a sperm is not in the matter, but outside, and this may be the heat of the Sun or some such thing, although once that heat is inside, it may be viewed as a chance cause."[84] This is rather complicated, indicating that external causes may inexplicably become internalized in nature, especially in the case of *genesis automatos*.

If, however, we set this possibility aside, and assign exteriority and interiority to *tuchē* and *automaton* respectively, I am inclined to read *automaton* along with Aquinas and Apostle as ultimately internal, because what is at issue in Aristotle's passage is a successive determination of *automaton*. So there is a movement from a more general sense of that which is judged *from the outside* as at odds with a presumed telos, and thus deemed a stroke of good luck or bad luck (that is, *tuchē*), to its finer specification as an aleatory force *within* nature that acts *against* nature (note that the evaluative dimension remains here, because what acts against nature acts against teleology in the broadest sense, which aims at the good, but this is not spoken of as bad luck or *dustuchē* because it is not in the realm of choice). *Automaton* cannot be one of the four causes *kath' auto*, and yet it is encrypted within one of these four causes, namely the material or *hulē*. It is inherent within and immanent to the material cause as the ever-present possibility of not being, or rather of being otherwise, the capacity for producing a certain monstrosity that is peculiar to biological life that is ultimately located in the matter and manifests as the female. In short, the ambiguity of interiority and exteriority noted by Apostle is indeed part of matter's very being: the exteriority, the circumstantial "elsewhere" from which *automaton* and chance arise, is strictly speaking found at the heart of *hulē*.

The very ambiguity in interpretation now begins to appears as itself symptomatic. Recall that the female offspring in *Generation of Animals* might be caused by a deficiency of heat in the sperm due to youth or old age, but may also be due to winds in the south or some other environmental circumstance. Matter's indeterminacy is also inevitably an indeterminacy about inside and outside. Aristotle continually avoids granting whatever it is that acts against nature any sort of causal or ontological substantiality, and therefore chance and spontaneity are easily understood as exterior, as a deformation of teleology that always comes from elsewhere, but this elsewhere, this alterity, cannot remain as exterior, but must also be understood as an alterity *within*, that which inheres in matter as its very plurality and aleatory capacity: its symptomaticity.

Returning now to the scene of reproduction, and especially to the role of *ta automata*, the marvelous automatic puppets, we find that Aristotle in *Generation of Animals* gives a quite explicit account of their mechanism: "the parts of these automatons, even while at rest, have in them somehow or other a potentiality [*dunamis*], and when something external sets the first part in movement, then immediately the adjacent part comes to be in actuality [*gignetai energeia*]."[85] The principle of motion is supplied from outside, and then the potential, the *dunamis* secreted in the machinery by technical wizardry, is activated or actualized as a result of an interaction between this *archē* and this *dunamis*. If in sexual reproduction we were not apprised of the presence of the *archē*, the motive force of the semen, fetal development would also appear to be miraculous, like the illusion created by automatic puppets.[86] Similarly, Aristotle ascribes the mysterious chain of events observed in fetal development to a potential or *dunamis*, inherent in the menstrual blood. This matter, called *protē hulē*— with the implication that it is devoid of all motion, all principle, all form (as far as that is possible), and all *logos*—is now imagined to harbor extensive powers akin to those encrypted within the complex structure of automatic puppets: the result of great technical skill and extensive labor. That *protē hulē* should contain the potential for the complex chain of development leading to the generation and growth of all the parts of animals is indeed miraculous, though perhaps all that is meant by such potential is that this matter is "appropriate for" embryogenesis in a way that, say, wood is not. Nonetheless, Aristotle is ascribing to feminine matter a kind of potential here that that demands to be demonstrated, to be made manifest and clear, through an analogy with the wondrous puppets, in that the form, the *energeia*, the being of the final product is *already somehow concealed* in the matter. And it is an index of the profundity of Aristotle's masculinism that he attempts to account for the mysteries of embryogenesis through an analogy with technical feats whose apparent miraculousness is an effect of great expertise, the result of masterful masculine *technē* and *poiēsis*, rather than *phusis* and *genesis* in itself.

Furthermore, of the source of movement for embryonic development, he goes on to say that, "in one way it is the external agency

[i.e., the sperm] which is causing the thing's movement . . . by having at one time been in contact with it." But "in another way, it is the
movement resident within [*hē enousa kinēsis*], just as the building of a
house for a house."[87] What, then, is this internal movement? Again, it
seems he is gesturing toward matter as harboring movement in itself,
but he quickly dispels this impression with the housebuilding analogy.
The movement within is not due to independent, feminine, motions
of matter, but is bookended on the one hand by the efficient kickstart
of the masculine principle, and on the other by the motion inherent in
any coming-to-be, analogized primarily with the productive actions
of *poiēsis*, here the labor of housebuilders, the underlaborers of the
potentiality-actuality schema. The embryo here has now become its
own source of motion in its own substance or being, and its development is governed by the natural motion of *genesis,* the unfolding
of potential into actuality characterized by hypothetical, teleological, necessity, and the only source given for the movement itself here
is that akin to the work of men of action and making. The techni-
cal-productive analogy repositions the ordering and directing motive
force for development on the side of form and telos, allowing Aristotle
to elide the issue of whether the menstrual blood itself provides any
motive force.[88]

GENESIS AUTOMATOS

In the case of spontaneous generation, there is no such easy way for
Aristotle to separate active, motive causes and material components
of the creature. In his discussion at *Generation of Animals* III.11,
Aristotle focuses in particular on a class of creatures called *ostrako-
derma* (literally, animals with earthenware skins), the Testacea, animals with shells including bivalves and gastropods: snails, whelks,
oysters and the like.[89] These creatures pose a problem for Aristotle
because they are clearly animals, and therefore must not only possess nutritive soul, like plants, but also sensitive soul (the third kind
of soul, rational soul, is reserved only for man). However, they are
not divided into male and female and do not reproduce sexually.
Rather, Aristotle classes them as either generating from themselves
like plants, or generating spontaneously (*automatōn*) from the environment. Plants, which according to Aristotle do not reproduce sexually, possess only nutritive soul.[90] Animals are animals by virtue of
possessing sensitive soul, and where sexual reproduction takes place,

this soul *in potentia* is implanted by the male as an aspect of the semen. The female residue, that is, the menstrual blood, lacks the principle of sensitive soul.[91] In sexual reproduction, the semen's soul principle, and thus its capacity as the vehicle of form, is explained by its possessing *pneuma*, translatable as breath, air, or spirit but best left in the original Greek. As described in *Generation of Animals* II.3, the *pneuma* in the sperm causes it to be fertile: it is something hot, but different from fire, which effects no generation. *Pneuma* thus contains in its nature the earthly analogue of *aithēr*, the element of the stars. Its presence is evidenced by the generative power of the heat of animals, and in spontaneous generation by the heat of the sun.[92] This *pneuma* is combined with water as a foamy concentrated mixture to form the residue that is semen, but Aristotle now tells us in III.11 that it is also found in environmental water. "Now it gets enclosed as the corporeal liquids [*sōmatikōn hugrōn*] become heated and form as it were a frothy [*aphrōdēs*] bubble."[93] In the case of the spontaneous generation of the *ostrakodermata*, the soul heat in the frothy slime of putrefying sea water and earth combined with the seasonal heat in the environment causes concoction and congealing, and once a portion of the soul principle "gets enclosed," the *pneuma* "makes a fetation and implants movement in it."[94] Now the Greek association of foam with fertility hearkens back to the mythical scene of Aphrodite's birth from the sea foam, as heard in her very name (*aphros* means foam). According to Hesiod's account, when Kronos castrated his father, Ouranous, he cast his genitals into the sea and around them white foam arose, out of which Aphrodite grew.[95] And it is worth bearing this paternal provenance of the sea foam in mind, because as Aristotle articulates his theory of spontaneous generation, he makes it clear that the spiritized matter that is *pneuma* plays an active role analogous to that of the father, while the material principle is provided by sea water and earth, concocted by the ambient, seasonal heat (just as food provides the material out of which the female residue is formed by her lesser heat in sexual reproduction).[96]

So while active and passive, paternal and maternal elements are produced and act on one another in spontaneous generation in a process analogous with sexual reproduction, there is nonetheless a suggestion once again that matter itself possesses its own kind of motion. It might be argued that *pneuma* is a special case, an exceptional form of soul matter, spiritized substance containing both formal and final cause as part of its constitution. But spontaneous generation, *genesis automatos*, poses certain difficulties for the causal schema of sexual reproduction, indicating that matter as *self-moving* is indeed at work, as disclosed by Aristotle's remarks in Book VII.9 of the *Metaphysics*. Here, strikingly, Aristotle pushes the analysis in a direction that leads him to contradict almost everything he says of matter elsewhere. He starts by asserting that in some instances a thing can be generated both by *automaton* and *technē*, such as health, and says—in a middle-voice formulation—that in these instances (though not others) matter is "such that it can initiate its own motion [*hoia kineisthai huph' autēs*]."[97] And this is a remarkable statement indeed.

What goes unnoticed in his discourse is just how singular and complex the notion of "health" is as a context for these self-initiated motions, even though it appears repeatedly throughout Aristotle's discourses as a paradigmatic telos. For health may be the end product and aim of a *technē*, the medical art, but it is quite unlike a bed or a statue since the "matter" upon which this *technē* operates is a living body, so that health also indicates a body that is *by nature* functioning well, living well, in accordance with its form or actuality, *energeia*. One might say, then, that insofar as the body for the doctor is analogous to the wood for the carpenter, the body is "matter," but insofar as the body itself is already a hylomorph, a composite of form and matter generated *by nature*, it is not mere matter at all but a natural *this*, an organic unity, that an inquirer can theoretically further decompose into material components (flesh and bone, or menstrual blood, depending on whether the analysis proceeds statically or genetically) and form. But Aristotle is not saying this here at all. The statement is, rather, quite explicit: the matter *in itself* (not just qua the object at hand for the doctor) is self-moving. Instead of noting all of this, Aristotle here simply treats health as an example—as if there were many others—of things that are generated both artificially and spontaneously, instead of the remarkable and mysterious confluence of material necessity, bodily practices, and medical art, of *phusis*, *ethos*, and *technē*, that it undoubtedly is. Here, the slippage between subject and substrate, between an essence that is a bearer of accidents and a substrate that receives form, that occurs when the very notion of matter is first introduced in *Physics* I.7 (previously discussed in chapter 1), would seem to return. Health, however, is not an *accident* or attribute of being in the way that Socrates's musicality is accidental, but rather the very sign of living well, a kind of *eudaimonia* at the level of the organism, signifying both its *energeia* and *entelecheia*.

What follows is more confusing. Aristotle tells us that things that have the capacity to move themselves can be divided into two kinds: those that can move themselves in a particular way [presumably animals], and those that cannot—he says, "so as to dance [*orchēsasthai*]."[98] Such dancing, in the middle voice, is a kind of self-motion without form or end. Presumably it is not choreographed or orchestrated, but improvised, mantic, *automatic*. This matter that moves itself in no particular way (*ouk hōdi*), dancing in the middle voice, suggests the Bacchanalian frenzy; the automatism of women dancing in the mountains, far beyond the confines of the *polis*. Strangely, he exemplifies this kind of matter in the following sentence with stones (*lithoi*), and fire. Fire certainly can be said to dance. But stones? Is he thinking of an earthquake? A volcanic eruption? When exactly do stones dance or move themselves in any way at all? In both the *Physics* and the *Poetics*, we also find the falling stone given as an illustration of *automaton*, specifically the stone that uncannily falls on a man. In the *Physics*, Aristotle is illustrating the *auto matēn* (in-itself, to-no-purpose) quality of *automaton*—we say the stone fell by *automaton*, not for the purpose of hitting the man: the chance or coincidental—symptomatic—quality is shown by the fact that we might credibly think that the stone was pushed by someone for the sake of striking him.[99] The uncanny or *unheimlich* aspect of *automaton* here may be described quite literally by Freud's definition as something unfamiliar "which leads back to something long known to us, once very familiar"[100]—the uncaused, unknowable motion revealed as such by its symptomatic coincidence, its "falling together" with an easily assumed explicit, knowable, deathly, intention. The example is further elaborated in the *Poetics*, illustrating a highly effective plot device in which the internal connection between *automaton* and *wonder* is reemphasized. He says, "even among chance events [*tou automatou kai tēs tuchēs*] we find most wondrous [*thaumasiōtata*] those which seem to have happened by design (as when Mitys's statue at Argos killed the murderer of Mitys, by falling on him as he looked at it: such things *seem* not to occur randomly)."[101] The tragedy referred to here is unknown, but the uncanny, symptomatic effect is unmistakable, as the unthinking stone metes out its all-too-human vengeance. The statue of the murdered man falls (*piptō*) coincidentally, but the wondrous effect is of course one created by the skill of the craftsman, in this case the tragedian. We are returned once again to the figure of the *architechtōn*, the puppeteer behind the scenes, knowable, masculine, authoritative, appropriating that wonder to himself that we might otherwise find in the world.

In the brief, elliptical remarks on self-moving matter in the *Metaphysics*, then, Aristotle admits its possibility—matter whose motions issue not from any telos or purpose, but which moves, dances, like the Bacchae, like fire, and like the stones of the earth. At this radical moment, where Aristotle has—most unusually—acknowledged that health is not simply conferred by the physician but may also arise spontaneously, through the self-moving matter of the body, we glimpse a different order of motion: that of aleatory matter.[102] However, in the example of the falling stone we are, if we follow the lead to the *Poetics*, returned once again to the symptomatic conjuncture of *automaton* and *telos*, returned to the mastery of the craftsman or author in whom *automaton* is subsumed. And what is more, the stone that falls, the fire that rises, each is following its own elemental telos, journeying toward its own proper place. So perhaps the usual subsumption of aleatory matter to teleological order is simply inevitable. But if we pursue the passage, we see that this is not exactly the case.

Moving to a discussion of *automaton* and natural becoming, Aristotle writes: "But things by nature which are generated spontaneously [*tautomatou*] are, as in the previous case, those whose matter can be moved also by itself in the way in which it can be moved by the seed; but things without this capability cannot be generated otherwise than by things like themselves."[103] In this passage, Aristotle has indeed discussed how the seed acts just like things produced by *technē*, in the sense that that which issues from the seed comes has the same name (*homōnumon*) as the seed's product. Likewise, the bed is built from the *logos* or idea of the bed within the carpenter—the idea and the product have the same name. He adds that we must not, however, expect to find this homonymy in every case in nature, since we say that a woman—if not a monster (*ean mē pērōma ēi*)—is also produced by a man, and that a mule does not come from a mule.[104] In other words the processes of generation are subject to certain aleatory deviations, may also swerve away from their origin, and dance, like stones or fire. Here, what is produced does not always have the same name as its progenitor—the mating of a horse and a donkey produces something else, called a mule, and a man may likewise produce a woman.

These deviations, then, the articulating deviations of *automaton*, disrupt the *nomos* and *logos* of patrilineal and patronymic succession, the paternal logic of the moving cause. The phenomenon of sexual reproduction is thus explicitly given the same aetiology, the same causal explanation, as that of spontaneous generation, and it is, in short, that "matter has the power to move itself in the same way as the seed."[105] The opaque motion of matter, its automatic spontaneity, is therefore able to intervene in and disrupt the passing down of the patronymic in reproduction, and break the homonymy, force a shift in the *logos*, between one generation and the next. The *automaton* of matter thus articulates both beings and words through time, in a randomly shifting series, in a form of change and temporality characterized by unpredictability, lability, deviation, and opacity. In the phenomenon of *automaton*, where the aleatory motions of matter are exposed, we can glimpse in this unorthodox moment of Aristotle's an astonishing foreshadowing of Darwinism, insofar as this automatism is the unthinking, uncaused, undirected, nonteleological engine for transformations of form over generations.

At *Generation of Animals* II.4 Aristotle further expounds on the powers of feminine matter in reproduction when he argues that if different species copulate and generate offspring, after successive generations the offspring will take after the female as regards their bodily form. Furthermore, when seeds are introduced into a foreign land, the plants will take after the soil (*kata tēn chōran*), which provides both the matter and the body for the seeds.[106] In these cases Aristotle once again grants matter certain powers directly at odds with its construal as passive in the causal account. (The feminine resonances of the *chōra* will be explored at length in chapter 3, while the complex question of the deviations of heredity that take place in and through successive generations will be treated in detail in chapter 5.) Suffice it to say here that in order to explain the passing down of characteristics from mother and maternal ancestors, male and female, to the child, Aristotle must also posit the presence of multiple potencies, *dunameis*, potential forms, and active principles in the menstrual blood which are blatantly at odds with his construal of the feminine contribution to reproduction as purely material and passive.

Material necessity and its opaque, aleatory motions, figured as *automaton*, stands not as something that acts merely in concert with hypothetical necessity, the necessity issuing from ends, but as something which exists in a fundamentally antagonistic relation with it—disruptive, obstructive, unruly, disobedient. It is a necessity that remains exterior to and independent from the teleological regime of nature and human arts, which are ultimately governed by a final cause at once physical, metaphysical and ethical. Material necessity, in its inexorable, unseeing and unpredictable self-motion, always threatens to disrupt the hypothetically necessary order of things issuing from the *telos*. The conflictual nature of this relationship, plus the injunction that hypothetical necessity must prevail over the matter's necessity, is shown by the fact that where hypothetical necessity fails and matter and its motions gain the upper hand, the result is monstrosity.

The female offspring, as I have shown, results *both* from the entelechial imperative to reproduce the species, *and* from a disruption, a fault in the concoction of matter, a glitch in the process by which the form of a man reproduces itself. Aristotle posits that femaleness itself, the "feminine," is in its mechanical provenance less a principle standing opposed to masculinity as it was in the Pythagorean list of opposites, or as possessing its own kind of motion as it is in Plato's *Timaeus*, than a certain deviation *from* masculinity, masculinity deformed, the result of masculinity's failure.[107] The phenomena of *automaton* and material necessity, as well as the facts of heredity, reveal that feminine matter, far from representing a mere passive receptacle, a substrate to be enformed by the masculine, in fact possesses and is capable of producing its own form of motion, aleatory motion, a motion that has effects, identifiable retroactively through observation and thought, but unknowable and invisible to the scientist or philosopher seeking first causes, the why of things. While its movements and principles might not be knowable in a science, the *prōtē hulē* of feminine matter in Aristotelian reproduction also appears to be a receptacle not only of the masculine principle of the sperm, but also of multiple ambiguous figures through which Aristotle attempts to account for its activities and powers: the marvelous automatic puppets, the process of housebuilding, the soil (*chōra*) of foreign lands, the *dunameis* of the multiple parts of the embryo, the female parts of the offspring, the form of the species, as well as the ghostly, insubstantial echoes of the *dunamis* of the mother qua individual and all her ancestors. As will become clear shortly, the feminine resonances of the Platonic receptacle and *chōra* are all too evident here.[108]

In terms of the Aristotelian conception of necessity, female animals might thus be said to occupy a unique position *between* the two conflicting types of necessity here described. The paradoxical and overdetermined position of the feminine between teleological and material necessity, explained by both final causation and by the aleatory *automaton* inherent in matter, places the feminine figure both firmly within and firmly outside the teleological regime of the Aristotelian universe. Like the matter that is her metonym, she is *indeterminately interior and exterior.*

THE FEMININE SYMPTOM

It is finally in this doubling up itself, in this duplicitous positionality, that the female figure appears *symptomatically* in the causal order, in the physics and metaphysics of Aristotle's world. Earlier, the symptom was glossed as something generated by and native to a system, which at the same time threatens to disrupt and unravel the very systematicity of the system. At the same time, behind and anterior to this modern sense of symptom lies the Greek word, *sumptōma*. While occasionally found in a medical context (and not till after Aristotle's time), the more common meanings of *sumptōma* are, according to Liddell and Scott, "anything that befalls one, a chance, mischance, calamity," from *sum*, together, with, *piptō*, to fall, hence "to fall together with." It may also be translated as "coincidence," whose Latin etymology (*co*, together, with + *in* + *cadere*, to fall) is cognate with the Greek. *Sumptōma* can usefully be contrasted with Aristotle's *kata sumbebēkos*, the phrase most frequently translated as "accident" and opposed to essence, from *sumbainō*, to walk together, hence "according to walking alongside." It would seem more random and even less predictable, certainly more chaotic than the polite walking together of the *kata sumbebēkos*. Items that fall together fall where they may, crashing to the ground without a guiding path, even, sometimes, killing a man. Walking, traveling a path, requires on the other hand a certain regulation of movement, maybe intention, volition, certainly directedness, and perhaps even consciousness or freedom. Those who walk together may or may not walk toward a goal, as evidenced by Heidegger's country path conversations.[109] *Sumbainō* is on a path, on the way, and thus at least potentially entelechial. *Sumpiptō* is no longer on any way, it is to be by the wayside. To walk is to be standing upright; to fall or to have fallen is to be supine. Falling is unforeseen, undesirable, unwilled, automatic. It points to a disruption, a break in the normal course of events. More than nonessential, it is unexpected, remarkable, surprising, uncanny, potentially harmful, potentially abyssal or shattering. In Aristotelian terms, perhaps the most important distinction between walking and falling is that one is the result of self-motion of a particular kind, and the other exemplifies *automaton*, as shown by the insistent illustration of the stone. For Aristotle, falling is teleologically explicable because heavier objects such as those of earth fall toward the earth, their proper place, while lighter things, like fire, rise, although downward motion itself carries a devalued and feminine sign for Aristotle, as will be discussed in chapter 5.[110] But the falling *together* of the *sumptōma* has *no explanation*. This "falling with"—the "with," "at the same time"—indicates and presupposes a multiplicity, a plurality which must pertain in the cosmos as the condition of the coincidence. The symptom read as *sumptōma*, then, is itself intimately allied with luck and chance, and, as discussed in my introduction, Aristotle himself occasionally uses *sumptōma* as a synonym for *automaton*, notably in contexts where there is a relation to women and femininity.

Unknowable and exceptional, the feminine symptom at once stands beyond, but also shows the way, gives a sign through which the Aristotelian metaphysical system may be diagnosed and understood. The female figure is also of course *par excellence* knowable in and necessary to the process of reproduction. In this, her role is essential to the entelechy, the teleology of nature. However, as I have shown in my discussion of the *prōtē hulē* of the menstrual blood, this knowability is dependent upon a certain lability, her choric ability to receive, encompass, generate, give rise to, and accept multiple unstable figurations. She is thus a chimerical figure, an *aporia*, a "necessary accident," and as such her existence will never be fully explained or fully accounted for by the extensive lists and categories of which Aristotle is so fond as he seeks to do justice to the complexity of phenomena. Standing simultaneously both inside and outside Aristotle's system, the female figure is herself *aoriston*, she refuses to respect its boundary. She thereby reveals the permeability of that boundary, and gives the lie to its coherence.

CHAPTER THREE

The Errant Feminine
in Plato's *Timaeus*

The previous chapters aimed to establish that the most significant opposition through which to understand sexual difference in Aristotle's physical and metaphysical architecture is not that of form and matter, but rather that between teleology and chance. The masculine *telos*, as prime mover, is explicitly identified as source of all motion in the Aristotelian cosmos. However, the regular and cyclical motions to which it gives rise are subject, in the sublunary realm, to various diversions, disruptions, and disorderings as they encounter the obscure motions of aleatory matter, an errancy I read as both symptomatic and feminine. In later chapters I undertake close readings of Aristotle's accounts of place and motion, tracing the tropes of sexual difference therein, before turning finally to the metaphysical themes of potentiality and actuality, *dunamis* and *energeia*. Place and motion are central notions in Aristotelian physics, and this chapter will take a genealogical detour into the Platonic cosmology delineated in the *Timaeus* to inquire into their gendered resonances. In *In Spite of Plato*, Adriana Cavarero notes that there are still moments in the Platonic corpus where the instituting of patriarchal metaphysics is as yet incomplete, or at least unsutured, and she "steals" feminine figures from Plato's texts to explore their persistence and to carve out a space for women, finding echoes of an archaic, prephilosophical and prepatriarchal cultural moment superseded by Plato in his explicit arguments and discourse.[1] In the *Timaeus* there are no such women, but there is certainly an explicitly gendered "family romance" at work in his account of creation:

demiurge and Forms in the paternal position, receptacle/*chōra* as maternal, and the child which is the world of becoming.[2]

For Aristotle, motion is a fundamental constituent of the cosmos: in the *Physics* he calls it a "kind of life [*hoion zōē*] for everything that is constituted by nature."[3] The kind of motion he thematizes and investigates is that which is knowable and predictable, intelligible in terms of a teleological universe, and which, as we will see, he ultimately defines in terms of potentiality and actuality as the "actuality of the potentially existing qua existing potentially."[4] However, as we have seen, there are also other, opaque, unaccountable, ignoble kinds of motion—those of matter, *bia*, and *automaton*—that carry a feminine mark. The idea that motion—understood as the life of the cosmos—should have two very different manifestations: one orderly, knowable, and masculine, the other random, opaque and feminine, does not appear *sui generis* in Aristotle's philosophy, but rather finds its direct provenance in the cosmological account given by Plato in the *Timaeus*. Plato's account is at once a cosmogony and a cosmology: it is a mythico-philosophical narrative of the beginnings of the cosmos as well as a description of the cosmic order of things. Unlike Plato, Aristotle believes that the universe is eternal, with no end and no beginning to time or motion. The prime mover is not an *archē* in the temporal sense, but in a metaphysical sense. However, given the way that different sources of motion fall along the lines of gender in the Aristotelian text, and Aristotle's own frequent citations of the *Timaeus*, this chapter will explore Plato's dialogue, whose cosmological "likely story" (*eikōs muthos*) contains a rich repository of gendered thematics.[5] Tracing themes of origin, gender, and motion in this dialogue thus provides a philosophical, or more correctly a mythico-philosophical context for Aristotle's gendered metaphysics. Furthermore, a critical feminist analysis of the notion of receptacle/space, the *hupodochē/chōra* in the *Timaeus*, and the fate of this notion in Aristotle's conceptions of place, motion, and matter, will help to situate and more vividly illuminate my account of the Aristotelian teleological cosmos.

THE COSMOGONY OF THE *TIMAEUS*

The cosmogony of the *Timaeus* unfolds in the context of the familiar Platonic distinction between the realm of being on the one hand—knowable by reason, eternal and fixed, and fully real—and the realm of becoming on the other: knowable through the senses and by opinion, characterized by ceaseless change, but itself "never fully real."[6] Timaeus's task in the dialogue is to show how such an eternal realm could initially give rise to the world we see around us: the world of experience, the realm of becoming. In contrast to Arisotle's conception of a cosmos without beginning or end, persisting in perpetuity, the realm of becoming for Plato is not eternal, but must have come into being at some point, precisely because it *is* visible, tangible, and corporeal,[7] and because we know it through the senses and through opinion. However, giving an account of this origin holds an epistemological difficulty for Plato because it tells of a world that can only be known through opinion and belief, and not through reason and truth. Hence even the best cosmogony can only be "likely," and never incontrovertibly true.

Plato identifies the origin of the cosmos as a father or maker (*dēmiourgos*), a god of goodness who sought to create order (*taxis*) from disorder. Having found "all that was visible" in a state of discordant and undisciplined motion (*kinoumenon plēmmelōs kai ataktōs*), rather than at rest, he implanted the highest and best faculty of reason into soul, and soul into body, thus creating a cosmos described as a "living being with soul and intelligence" (*ton kosmon zōon empsuchon ennoun*).[8] The creator, we are told, then made the world from the four elements, using all of the fire, water, air and earth available, a complete unitary and uniform whole, perfectly spherical, smooth, and sufficient unto itself, with no outside and no remainder, "satisfied to be its own acquaintance and friend."[9] The anthropomorphized universe is a living body without any relationship to an outside, without eyes, ears, limbs or organs of ingestion or discharge. Its soul is placed in the center and diffuses through the whole, covering, concealing, or enveloping (*periekalupse*) the body, which moves in perfect circular motion. However, within this unitary body all is not smooth and unitary. God created the soul prior to, and with priority over, the body, and he did so by creating a complicated admixture of the two sorts of existence—indivisible and eternal on the one hand, and divisible and changing on the other, and then the Same on the one hand and the Different on the other (it is not clear if this is a rewording of the first two sorts of existence or is intended to denote slightly different elements): "forcing the Different, which was by nature allergic to mixture, into union with the Same, and mixing both with Existence."[10] Having done this he apportioned and divided this new whole in mathematically determinate ratios, creating cosmic circles of the

Same and Different, the Same being the steady and undivided realm of fixed stars and the Different divided up into the spheres of the sun's ecliptic, the moon, and the different planets.

The created universe could not be eternal like its pattern, an eternal living being, but in order that it could resemble this being as closely as possible, the father made "in that which we call time an eternal image, moving according to number, of the eternity which remains for ever at one."[11] This measurable circular motion, which resembles as far as possible the eternally same and unmoved, gives a form of time that imitates eternity in its regularity and cyclicity (an argument finding clear echoes in Aristotle's cosmos). The heavenly bodies thus "define and preserve the numbers"[12] of time. As in Aristotle, time is dependent upon and produced by bodies in periodic, measurable motion. The motions of the cosmos create the diurnal periods of night and day, the monthly periods of the moon, and the sun's annual cycle, all enumerable and knowable through the faculty of reason.

After this comes the creation of the gods, the earthly creatures, and, as is well known, the two sexes, the better of which, Plato says, is man. A soul residing in a star would be born into a body "by necessity" (*ex anankēs*). If, and here there are allusions to the myth of the *Phaedrus* and the *Republic*'s myth of Er, a soul thus embodied showed mastery of the sensations, desires, and feelings that bodies qua bodies are necessarily subject to, the soul would return to its star. Those who failed to do so would be changed into women or, in the case of more egregious failures, into an animal according to the nature of his wrongdoing. Such a soul "would have no respite from change and suffering until he allowed the motion of the Same and uniform in himself to subdue all that multitude of riotous and irrational feelings which have clung to it since its association with fire, water, air and earth, and with reason thus in control returned once more to his first and best form."[13] Here, as in Aristotle later, we find a hierarchical ranking of men, women, and animals. But for Plato, each is a progressively diluted admixture of the Same (*tauton*) with the Different (*thateron*, a contraction of *to heteron*), that is the multitudinous, unpredictable, elemental riot, whose vicissitudes the embodied being must master (*krateō*) in order to secure eternal happiness.

Like Aristotle after him, Plato also separates causes into "those that operate intelligently and produce results that are good" (*kalos kai agathos*) and those that "operate without reason and produce effects which are casual and random" (*to tuchon atakton*).[14] And as in Aristotle's

Physics, this separation of rational, knowable causes and the type of cause that Plato says operates "through bodies whose motion is derived from others and must be passed on to others " introduces a discussion of necessity. As discussed in chapter 2, for Aristotle the kind of necessity inhering in matter, the disagreeable compulsion that hinders and disrupts *teloi*, indeterminate and unpredictable, chancy and symptomatic, is barely dignified by a place in his typologies, but instead is relegated to the status of the derivative and parasitic. Simple necessity and hypothetical necessity are related to *telos*: the first is that which simply cannot be otherwise because it issues from the prime mover, and the second is that which is related to the realization of specific goals and the existence of entities in the sublunar realm.

This refinement, in which certain kinds of necessity are apportioned to the side of the telic and good, is not present in Plato, who instead understands necessity in atomistic fashion as the random motions of the physical world.[15] He casts intelligence (*nous*) and necessity (*anankē*) simply as dual opposed forces combining in the creation of the world, and the proper relation between them as a subordination of necessity to intelligence, to be achieved by intelligence's reasonable persuasion (*peithous*) of necessity. It is at this point in Timaeus's narrative that he calls for a return to the beginning of the cosmogony, for a new or other original principle (*heteran archēn*), to take into account of what Plato now calls the "errant cause" (*planōmenēs aitias*).[16] This is this same errancy, straying, or wandering (*planōmenon*) that Plato attributes to the womb at the very end of the dialogue, in a passage that (alongside Hippocrates) is a *locus classicus* for the malady of hysteria.[17] Timaeus thus will turn once again to the beginning, another new beginning (and he also reiterates the conjectural or "likely" status of his narrative). Here he will account not only for the establishment of a reasonable world by a reasonable creator, but also for "the nature of fire, water, earth and air before the heavens came to be and what their state [*pathē*] was then,"[18] and the disordering forces of necessity which lead reason astray, and whose subjugation through persuasion is required if order and harmony are to prevail. John Sallis has thematized the proliferation of beginnings in the *Timaeus*, observing that "in the *Timaeus* nothing is more vigorously interrogated than the question of beginning."[19] Sallis's own vigorous interrogations of the *Timaeus*, however, treat only cursorily the way that the question of beginning is also irreducibly interwoven with figures of femininity and sexual difference.[20]

Timaeus's return to a new beginning generates, in addition to the two original forms (*eidei*)—the intelligible and unchanging realm of Forms, and its copy, the visible world of becoming—a third form he calls the receptacle (*hupodochē*), which is also "the nurse [*tithēnē*] of all becoming."[21] This receptacle is apparently very difficult to describe: it is "invisible and formless, all-embracing, possessed in a most puzzling way of intelligibility, yet very hard to grasp."[22] Recognizing such a receptacle in the formation of the cosmos means that, strictly speaking, even the elements must not be thought of as beings or entities, but instead as composed of the unchanging receptacle. In each case the element in question possesses distinctive qualities rather than an essence—"watery" rather than just being water; "fiery" rather than just being fire, and so on. The receptacle itself "must always be called in the same manner [*tauton autēn aei prosrhēteon*]; for from its own proper quality [*dunameōs*] it never departs [*ouk existatai*] at all."[23] It is worth noting a careful distinction here—Plato does not say the receptacle is eternal and unchanging, but that it must always be called in the same manner,[24] not because it is always the same, static, eternally unchanging like the Forms, but because it never departs from (*existatai*) its own *dunamis*, its own potential, power, or possibility. While it is always changing, indeed we might say part of what it gives in creation is movement and change, any specific change remains strictly speaking unaccomplished, unrealizable, unhypostatizable. In Aristotelian terms we might say it will never reach the *telos* of substance or *energeia*, actuality; no matter how much *entelecheia* it might give rise to it will always and forever return to and remain in its own potentiality, its *dunamis* qua *dunamis*. In this way the pluripotent *hupodochē* never takes on any permanent shape or form, but is—and this is merely one of many names that Plato finds for it even in the face of his prohibition on different names—a molding stuff or plastic material (*ekmageion*) for receiving the figures (*eisionta*) that enter and leave it.[25]

THE FEMININE FIGURATIONS OF THE *EKMAGEION*

Ekmageion is a difficult word to adequately translate. It can denote an impress or mold, that is, something that provides a shape and creates an impression in something else. At *Laws* 800b and 801d, Plato uses it in the sense of a model or exemplary case. As in the *Timaeus* and *Theaetetus*, it also means that which receives the impression, that on which an impression is made, as in a wax tablet.[26] Lee gives "neutral plastic material" while Bury and Kalkavage give "molding-stuff" and Jowett merely provides "recipient." Aristotle, describing Platonic doctrine in the *Metaphysics*, uses it as a metaphor for the ability of the dyad of the Great (infinite) and the Small (infinitesimal) to generate numbers,[27] and there Tredennick translates it as "matrix." The primary meaning of *ekmageion*, or at least the first given by Liddell and Scott is, by contrast, that of a napkin or wiping cloth: something that instead of creating marks rather removes them. Later in the *Timaeus*, Plato uses it precisely in this sense when describing the function of the spleen as that which cleans the liver and absorbs its impurities, "as a wiper [*ekmageion*] that is laid beside a mirror always prepared and ready to hand."[28] (It is this organ that, as discussed in chapter 2, Aristotle will say in *Parts of Animals* has no purpose at all but is present merely due to material necessity). The verb from which *ekmageion* is derived, *ekmassō*, means to wipe clean; in the middle voice to wipe away one's tears. It also means to mold or model in wax or plaster, to take an impression of or imprint an image. The verb *massō*, in turn, means to touch or handle, to work with hands or knead, and here its internal connection to figuration more generally may be discerned. To figure, after all, is from the Latin *figura*, from *fingere* (to mold). *Ekmageion* therefore holds together at once the mutually contradictory meanings of mark receiving, mark giving, and mark removing; it offers the possibility that it may even mark itself, perhaps indeterminately generating its own impresses as well as receiving them from others, while continually erasing, renewing and refreshing itself so that the process may begin anew.

All three of these moments—mark receiving, mark giving, and mark removing—are present and thematized separately in the Aristotelian depiction of coming-to-be, which involves privation as well as production at the point of contact between the passive and active elements, matter and form. In the scene of artifact production, continually invoked to explain and illustrate natural reproduction, the potter's active hands work the passive clay: at the place where fingers and clay come together, any prior form, or more strictly speaking the privation of the form to come, is erased and the hands install a new form in the pliant matter. That all three moments or aspects of generation cohabit in Plato's patently feminine *ekmageion* is perhaps indicative of Plato's relative lack of systematicity. But it also points to a reading of the receptacle as potentially a more complex and complexly

generative category of (non)substance, one which might not in fact
have need of either the Forms or a father-creator to effect the work
of becoming, and offering the possibility that it may even mark—and
erase—itself. In the *ekmageion*, then, we perhaps glimpse a rendering of the feminine that has not been "properly prepared" so as to be
"devoid of all the characters which it is to receive."[29] As Plato says: "If
it were like any of the things that enter it, it would badly distort any
impression of a contrary or entirely different nature when it received
it, as its own features would shine through."[30] An *ekmageion* which
indeterminately holds together giving, receiving, and erasing marks
would thus be both endowed with a peculiarly feminine capacity for
generativity and self-motion, as well as the capacity for distortion and
errancy warned of by Plato.

In its capacity to both receive and erase marks, the *ekmageion* as
wax tablet holds together the properties of solidity and fluidity in
its labile passage from solid to liquid form and back again. To further elaborate the gendered stakes of the *ekmageion*, we may turn
to Irigaray's exploration of the embodied topologies of these states
of matter.[31] In *Speculum of the Other Woman*, Irigaray describes
the secret fluidity—"blood, but also milk, sperm, lymph, saliva, spit,
tears, humors, gas, waves, airs, fire . . . light," that "threaten[s] to
deform, propagate, evaporate, consume" the masculine subject.[32]
In order to affirm masculine identity, it is required that the woman/
mother solidifies, that liquid becomes ice, forming a clear reflective
surface or mirror that will protect and preserve the male from "any
possible assimilation into that shapeless flux that dampens, soaks,
floods, channels, electrifies, lights up the apartness in the blaze of its
embrace."[33] Commenting on the *ekmageion* passage in the *Timaeus*,
she writes, "She is always a clean slate ready for the father's impressions, which she forgets as they are made. Unstable, inconsistent,
fickle, unfaithful, she seems ready to receive all beings into herself.
Keeping no trace of them. Without memory. She herself is without
figure or proper form. . . . Needed to define essence, her function
requires that she herself have no definition."[34] While what receives the
imprint, the *hupodochē* or *ekmageion,* must therefore be in an indeterminate state—neither solid nor liquid, or both solid and liquid, but
in any case infinitely malleable—it must also present a smooth reflective surface: "Yet it is certainly the mirror which, memoryless, forget-
ful of all traces and imprints, represents the image of things set before
it. And as far as the intelligible goes, has the mirror any other function

than to define things by withdrawing itself from specific characterization."[35] As noted, in the middle voice, that peculiar reflexive voice
in Greek between active and passive, the definition of *ekmassō*, is a
wiping away of tears. That tears appear here as a hidden figure for
the *ekmageion*'s mark has particular resonance. Tears are after all a
distinctly feminine expression of emotion, of grief, joy or compassion
(one that Plato elsewhere roundly denigrates), a dissolving into fluidity which threatens to deform the smooth surface of the mirror and
render unstable any distinction between self and other, inside and
outside; an act of mourning and remembrance which fails to solidify
into a memorial, a mark made, the distinction between maker and
substrate itself dissolved in the reflexivity of the middle voice, and
simultaneously wiped away, forgotten.[36] This space between active
and passive voices, where the distinction between activity and passivity itself is dissolved, is thus subjected to a dissolution and a fluidity
that carries an irreducibly feminine mark.

Irigaray reads the *ekmageion* as a necessarily entrapping structure
for femininity, a frozen figure providing a smooth reflective surface
ready for masculine imprimatur, but whose capacity for fluidity renders it unable to hold on to itself through time or memory. But these
multiplying resonances of the *ekmageion* also demonstrate and illustrate themselves the generativity and lability of the process of figuration given in and by Plato's rendering of the receptacle/*chōra*. By this I
do not wish to make Plato into a protofeminist, to imply that, *contra*
Irigaray, all is liberatory in this context. However, in the constitutive indeterminacy of this figure there is at the very least an opening
toward refiguration, and therefore a possibility that the receptacle/
chōra might be usefully reread, that as an "impossible yet necessary
site for all further inscriptions," as Butler puts it, it also offers the
possibility for reinscribing, in the vicissitudes of its figural materiality, the very femininity that it represents or figures.[37] What I want
to stress is that among the oppositions held together in the figure
of the *ekmageion*—solidity and fluidity, receptivity and generativity,
inscription and erasure—the activities of molding and writing instan-
tiate a passage between materialization and naming, between the genesis of worldly things, and figuration itself.[38]

How, though, may we locate this figure in relation to Aristotle? The
Platonic distinction figured in the *ekmageion*—between that which
comes into being, that *in which* the being becomes, and the model
which the being resembles—is reminiscent of the later Aristotelian

distinctions between the substance or "this," the matter from which it is made, and the form which enters it. But Plato does not elaborate these distinctions in a formalized metaphysics, and he certainly never uses term "matter" (*hulē*) to describe the substrate or "that in which the being becomes." Plato instead remains in the mythical, figurative register, and asks us to "liken the receptacle to the mother, the model to the father, and what they produce between them to their offspring."[39] In this image of a family unit he quite explicitly places sexual reproduction at the heart of metaphysics. The resonances of this will echo throughout the thought of Aristotle, such that he will write, for example in *Physics* I.9: "Now in things which are generated, one of these [two natures] is an underlying joint cause with a form, being like a mother, so to speak."[40]

BEING, BECOMING, AND PERSUASION

Before Plato moves on to his curious reformulation of *hupodochē* (receptacle) as *chōra* (space), he takes a moment to reiterate the distinction between the first reality of Forms—the unchanging and eternal templates of the physical world—and the secondary world of becoming. He questions the soundness of the distinction, only to more firmly ground it in the epistemological distinction between two modes of knowing: intelligence and true opinion or belief. He says that the rational realm of the Forms is imperceptible to our senses, involves truth, and is known to us and produced in us by teaching (*didachēs*), while the irrational, sensible, physical world is known only by persuasion (*peithous*). One is immovable by persuasion, and the other is alterable by persuasion.[41] The reappearance here of the theme of persuasion is notable since only a few paragraphs previously he has told us that, on the cosmic scale, intelligence (*nous*) must subjugate the realm of necessity (which is then reformulated as the errant cause, the third kind, and the receptacle itself), through persuasion.[42] That necessity itself may be subjugated by persuasion is a testament to the strength of the latter's force. We may come to know the forms through teaching, employing the faculty of intellect, but it is intellect itself that must exert its strong influence on necessity and must master it through persuasion.[43]

Persuasion, Plato now tells us, is also the means by which the physical world, the irrational realm, exerts its influence. This persuasion cannot be understood as either the illegitimate rhetorical strategy of sophists, as in the *Gorgias*, nor the authentic "technique of intelligence" described in the *Phaedrus* and employed by the statesman of *Laws*.[44] On the contrary, the persuasion the physical world exerts can only be understood as a kind of force. Persuasion, then, is equally the means by which the intellect coercively dominates the realm of necessity, and the means by which the sensible, irrational realm in turn coerces us, leads us into errancy and produces opinion in us as opposed to truth. Might we then say that the physical world also seeks to master us, to subordinate us, to lead us away from truth through this coercive, forceful method? Are we then to engage in a conflict of persuasions, bound to meet the persuasion of *doxa* with a counterpersuasion, the *peithous emphronos* of intellect, even though our faculty of intellect cannot be moved by persuasion and ought not to be thereby threatened? There is, once again, an uncanny mirroring at work here, one which, strangely enough, echoes the discussion of Aristotelian necessity in chapter 2, in which the necessity that issues from telos is set against the compulsions of matter that work against it.

One might further ask: if the technique, namely persuasion, by which intellect masters the realm of necessity and the vicissitudes of the physical world is the same as that through which the physical world affects us, does this compromise the clarity of the distinction between the two realms. Does it open us to the possibility, anathema to Plato, that "what we perceive through our physical senses must be taken as the most certain reality"?[45] Presumably, coercive persuasion is the only kind of exertion that the realm of necessity will accept, insensible as it is to teaching and reason. Moreover, it is the privilege of the intellect to be conversant in many modes of transmission, including persuasion as well as the logical rationality of "teaching," but the difficulty is certainly troubling if we are to rely on a distinction between different modes of knowing for our certitude that the realm of the forms is both prior to and more exalted than the physical world. For if the intellect's method of subordinating the physical world is the same as the visible world's method of creating *doxa* in us, then how can a secure distinction between the realms of being and becoming be guaranteed?

It is therefore worth noting that in this textual boundary zone, in the place or space *between* the account of *hupodochē*, receiver of being and that of *chōra*, giver of place to becoming, Plato attempts to set on firmer ground the distinction between being and becoming and "cast his vote."[46] In so doing he raises a problem concerning techniques of power and coercion that are to be employed equally by both realms. On a cosmic scale, it is of course the errant necessity that has its source in *hupodochē/chōra* that must be persuasively subjugated by *nous*. But it is a testament to the incomplete, indeed failed subjugation of errant necessity that that necessity returns in the physical and somatic operations of the visible world, which in turn exerts itself on us through the physical senses. If one is to become one of the "small number of persons" who share in *nous*, along with the gods, this necessity must be strenuously resisted, and indeed countered by *nous*'s own persuasive power. This chiasmatic circuitry of persuasion is thus sustained by its very failure. In this light, it becomes possible to understand the very constitution of intellect and necessity as separate realms as given, at least in part, by their respective resistances to the violent coercion of the force of persuasion issuing in the other. And perhaps this is why Timaeus's discourse can only ever be a likely story, persuasive as can be, and not an unmediated vector of truth.

That the sensible realm, the unruly realm of feminine necessity, is able to resist persuasion, is a condition of possibility of the being/becoming duality. In sustaining itself through such resistance, it holds up an imperfect mirror image to the realm of the intellect, which also cannot be moved by persuasion. At the same time, feminine necessity acts as an "errant cause," posing an unquellable threat to the harmonious order of the cosmos as governed by the intellect. Here, then, we detect a trace of what in Aristotle becomes the feminine symptom, although here it is figured as necessity. For Plato, this necessity not only ensures the systematicity of the system through providing a feminine mirror, a reflective surface for Being's own necessity as *nous*, but also represents an ever-present threat of disruption in the order of things. Necessity ever calls for persuasion to order and subdue it, and this persuasion is ever doomed to failure if the cosmos is to endure, if there is to be anything at all to be ordered by the persuasive force of intellect.

REFIGURING THE RECEPTACLE AS *CHŌRA*

Despite the difficulties Plato encounters in grasping or adequately describing the *hupodochē*, and despite his admonition that it should always be called in the same manner, he produces a surfeit of metaphors through which to characterize it (gold, the nurse, the mother, the *ekmageion*, the substrate for a fragrant ointment), before reformulating it as *chōra* (space). The receptacle or *hupodochē* in itself carries an audible feminine resonance, as evidenced by the structure and various usages of the word: *hupo-*, "under," "underlying"; *dechomai*, "to take," "to accept," "to receive hospitably," "to entertain"; the verbal form *hupodechomai* more strongly indicates the hospitality of entertaining or welcoming under one's roof, and, said of a woman, also means to conceive or become pregnant. Its recasting as *chōra* (space, place, position, territory, but also a land or country, especially the country as opposed to the town), seems at first to evacuate these feminine elements. Surprisingly, this shift has not been thematized by most commentators, including feminists, who tend to note it but have not treated it as a problem.[47] In his essay on these passages of the *Timaeus*, entitled "Chora," Jacques Derrida privileges this particular name, as does Sallis in *Chorology*. Derrida nonetheless insists that the "multiplicity of metaphors (or also of mythemes in general) signifies in these places not only that the proper meaning can only become intelligible via these detours, but that the opposition between the proper and the figurative loses its value."[48] Derrida refuses any identification of *chōra* with a feminine principle or element, on the grounds that as it is neither sensible nor intelligible, it cannot be a thing or determinate existent ("for example an existent of the feminine gender"[49]), and therefore cannot have or own a property such as femininity; it must be not anthropomorphized and reduced to a thing or a subject, whether sensible or intelligible. Instead, he says it is a third *genos*, that is, kind, genus, genre (beyond myth or philosophy), or gender, and as such is a "neutral space of a place without place, a place where everything is marked but which would be 'in itself' unmarked."[50] Derrida, however, also acknowledges that every reading of *chōra* will be anachronistic if not achronous (though the question of the relation of *chōra* to temporality is by no means clear and remains to be elucidated), and indeed my feminist analysis is avowedly anachronistic, yielding explicitly to what he calls "retrospective projections" or "teleological retrospection," in that my very interest in the notion of *chōra* lies in its multivocal feminine resonances.[51]

Conceding that the distinction between the proper and the figurative has perhaps lost its value here, or is bracketed at the very least, close attention should be paid to these properly feminine figures in the *Timaeus*. As noted above, the *hupodochē* connotes welcoming into the home, the *oikos* or domestic sphere, the Greek sphere of women, while *chōra*'s most quotidian usage denotes the countryside, and not

the city, which may also—like the *oikos*—be opposed to the masculine public sphere of the *polis*. Said of a woman, *hupodechomai* is to
become pregnant, to have received the male seed, providing the fertile ground for reproduction, *genesis*. We have already explored the
feminine resonances of the *ekmageion* as a receiver of imprints, but
the most explicitly feminine figures are obviously that of the nurse
and the mother, indeterminately both bearing and nurturing, in the
ur-scene of sexually reproductive cosmic creation. Timaeus's return
to the beginning thus uncovers this more radical scene: a three-term
structure of kinship, a family romance which replaces the prior auto-
genetic picture in which a father-creator causes an unchanging, eternal, intelligible realm to spontaneously give rise to a sensible world of
becoming and change. The feminine figures appear here (as Derrida
notes) almost exactly in the middle of the text, as figures for a nonth-
ing which can only be known through a dreamlike awareness or "bastard reasoning, *logismōi tini nothōi*"[52]—a mode of reasoning where
paternity can no longer be assured and truth no longer authorized
because a space, a chasm, has opened between the Forms and the
world, the intelligible and the sensible, in a classical *mise en abyme*.[53]
Falling into this chasm, we might experience this once again as the
feminine symptom, or *sumptōma*, falling together into the abyss of
maternal materiality even as we are welcomed by the receptacle, held
in its hearth, and suckled by the nurse's breast. Here, then, we might
articulate the shift from *hupodochē* to *chōra* as the protective comfort
of the receptacle giving way to vertiginous open space, to an interval
without orientation, feature, or form; the non-positional condition
of positionality in general. It is not the "void," as Plato makes clear
this cannot exist. But if it is rather something like "place" or "position," or something like magnitude or dimensionality, or something
like "thereness" in general, how is that to be thought? How can place
be generalized or abstracted, apart from specifying locutions such as
"this place," "my place," "your place"?[54]

   Hupodochē, by definition, is that which receives. What then of
chōra—land, country, space, place, room, territory, position, location?
Perhaps the most notable distinction to be drawn between the two
concepts is itself topological: *hupodochē* envelops with a boundary, it
presents a kind of invagination, an opening into interiority, the comfort of welcome, an invitation to filling, inscription, and penetration,
whereas *chōra* does not. *Chōra* denotes rather an exteriority, an opening, giving room, dimension, depth, and magnitude—spacing—but

also, as indicated by the related verb *chōrizō*, separating, dividing, differentiating, and severing. *Chōra* thus provides the possibility of up and down, here and there, and indeed any sort of positioning in a field, a giving of alterity through spatial differentiation. There is also an affinity with the originary Hesiodic *chaos*, or gap, as alluded to by Derrida and explicitly noted by Nader El-Bizri in his essay on *chōra* (I will return to this shortly).[55] To put it another, more anachronistic way, *chōra* gives extension, or from our modern perspective dimensionality in general, perhaps even something like space-time. That *chōra* might temporalize—give time, as well as space, is a possibility Plato does not, or perhaps even cannot consider, though as Derrida's notion of *différance* teaches us, temporal deferral is always at issue in and inseparable from spatializing difference. Shared by the two notions, *hupodochē* and *chōra*, is a sense of creating a position for, giving place to the Forms, and in this giving place there is also a sense of the dependence of place on a boundary for its constitution. Perhaps this sense is more explicit in *hupodochē* than in *chōra*, perhaps, until we remember that what spaces out also divides and differentiates, *chōrizei*.[56] They differ in that *hupodochē* invites in, holds, receives, while *chōra* opens out, provides space, gives.

Derrida notes that *chōra* cannot be thought of as either subject or support for beings, for belonging to neither Being nor Becoming it is not a being at all, and although we cannot help catching or conceiving it "via the anthropomorphic schemas of the verb *to receive* and the verb *to give*," it is "anything but a support or a subject which would *give place* by receiving or by conceiving, or indeed by letting itself be conceived."[57] He then cautions against the ontological effect suggested by this giving of place: "There is *chōra*, one can even ponder over its *physis* and its *dynamis*, or at least ponder these in a preliminary way, but *what is* there is not; and we will come back later to what this *there is* can give us to think, this there is which by the way *gives* nothing in giving place or in giving to think; whereby it will be risky to see in it the equivalent of an *es gibt*."[58] The first question to ask, here, though, is whether the Heideggerian *es gibt*, or "there is," is anything like an "anthropomorphic schema"—and indeed, because we are in ontological territory here, the answer must be no. As a formula for understanding being as *given*, the *es gibt* precisely does not rely upon an anthropomorphic scheme of subject (giver), recipient and object (gift). The second question is whether it will be then possible to conceive of a scene of giving and receiving that is neither anthropomorphic—involving donor, recipient, and the gift that passes between them, nor ontological. Can nothing, a lack of being, give? How could *chōra* help to answer this question? Can what receives also give?

What this choice does not acknowledge is the indeterminate directionality, the simultaneous giving *and* receiving of the receptacle/*chōra*. Perhaps we can imagine the demiurge as the giver of Being, the Forms as the gift, and the *chōra* as recipient. Or the demiurge as giver, Becoming as recipient of Being, and *chōra* as a kind of site enabling the passage between them. Sallis's commentary on the variable ordering of the three kinds is certainly germane here.[59] But it is also possible to imagine that—since the receptacle/*chōra* appears as a third term *between* Being and Becoming—in its relationship to Being it acts as recipient (as penetrable female), and in its relationship to Becoming it gives (as nurturing mother). But despite Plato's designation of it as a mother, it *is* not, is neither a being nor a subject, and cannot be one in this sense. Holding together *hupodochē* and *chōra*, it/she seems to both give and receive, without subjectivity, and outside any ontological schema. What is suggested, and what perhaps can only remain in the realm of suggestion, is an indeterminate, incalculable, ceaseless receiving/giving without arrival, without possession, property, or ownership; a chiasmatic crossing point, constantly changing without alteration, a scene of the condition of possibility of place/boundary through which being is/becomes becoming; a point without extension but giving extension, without concrete or ontological ground but giving the possibility of not only the totality of the sensible world as the Forms enter and pass through it, but also receiving *and* giving the possibility of the very distinction between the sensible and intelligible.

These meditations on *hupodochē* and *chōra* show us that the space where or whereby the intelligible is transformed into the sensible is incontestably marked by maternal and feminine figures. Further, the feminine within sexual difference cannot therefore be confined here to the merely ontic or anthropological, psychological, or biological realms (to use Heidegger's distinction in *Being and Time* §10,[60] the "neutralizing" gesture of which is repeated by Derrida in his remarks on *chōra*), but instead points beyond itself in a restless series of refigurations that complicate endlessly the separation that Plato seeks to enforce between Being and Becoming.

FEMINIST ENGAGEMENTS WITH *CHŌRA*

The reading and analysis of the feminine receptacle/*chōra* as restless, errant, and indeterminate suggests that it may be a potentially useful theoretical locus through which to reread and perhaps displace the metaphysical architecture handed down to us by Plato and Aristotle. However, as Plato offers it, this feminine figure is all too easily absorbed in its entirety into the reproductive function. Although the receptacle/*chōra* may point beyond itself toward endless refiguration, may signify or even be a name or metonym for *différance*, that figuration is nonetheless circumscribed by the receptacle/*chōra*'s decidedly maternal role in the Platonic cosmogony and cosmology. It is more or less axiomatic that any version of the feminine in which it is reduced to the maternal cannot be adequate to a feminist philosophical practice. Before moving to a discussion of the provenance of motion in the *Timaeus*, then, I will turn to some critical engagements with *chōra* in recent feminist literature, in order to see if and how it may be displaced, refigured, or salvaged for feminist ends.

We have seen that trying to think receptacle together with *chōra* (space, gap, interval) means that on the one hand it may be read as that which spaces, which separates and differs qua separation and difference, and on the other as that which provides a place for reception, passively penetrable and calling to be filled—as well as indicating the relation between the two. The resonances of these notions of space and place with the topology of the female body, and in particular the maternal body, have been taken up in a quite divergent context by Kristeva, and have been explored at some length by Irigaray. In turn, Judith Butler has investigated both Kristeva's and Irigaray's engagements with *chōra*, and the consequences of these readings for a thinking of "matter" broadly conceived. While Butler is not concerned with how ideas about or figures of sex and gender inform and are intertwined with ancient accounts of motion and coming-to-be, her reading in *Bodies That Matter* of the status of figures of "woman" or femininity in their relation to the materiality of lived bodies in Kristevan and Irigarayan engagements with Plato and Aristotle are illuminating. In short, Butler draws attention to a crucial difference between Kristeva's understanding of *chōra* and Irigaray's reading: Kristeva accepts and even promotes a certain identity between *chōra* and the maternal body, while Irigaray refuses any such identification.

In Kristeva's psychoanalytic and linguistic project, the body of the mother is quite literally the ordering principle of the semiotic *chōra*, that realm of language in which drives are expressed by means of a mobile, rhythmic, vocal and gestural organization that is for her semiotic and not yet symbolic. Kristeva thus takes literally Plato's figuration of *chōra* as mother or nurse, giving it a definite location and embodiment and role in the development of the infant. Kristeva's *chōra* is somatic and literal: rhythmic, reflecting the mother's heartbeat, breath, and other bodily processes; vocal, reflecting her voice; and gestural, reflecting her movements. Plato's *chōra* is, by contrast, in chaotic unbalanced motion without rhythm or periodicity, and has no vocality or limbs with which to gesture. Strictly speaking, this is not really a reading or analysis of Plato's *chōra*, so much as a deployment of the notion in a quite different register and discursive context, to quite different ends. Kristeva makes no particular effort to systematize or justify her reading either within the logic of Plato's text, or in philosophical terms more generally.

For Irigaray, on the other hand, there can be no such easy identification between *chōra* and its feminine figures, and to this extent, as Butler notes, she accepts Derrida's injunction against anthropomorphism, though for different reasons: "the figures of the nurse, the mother, the womb cannot be fully identified with the receptacle, for those are specular figures which displace the feminine at the moment they purport to represent the feminine."[61] This is not merely the formal observation that what is designated in this field that is *prima facie* a condition for the world of Becoming—and on analysis is revealed as the condition for the very distinction between Being and Becoming—cannot be named or understood as any one of the things for which it is the condition, but rather that any such attempt to locate woman, the feminine, in a definite place, to designate a role for her, is to reduce her immediately and mistakenly to a reproductive function, to perform a violent catachresis which displaces and erases everything about her that is not in the service of maternity or nurturance, everything that resists and exceeds such a reduction.

For Irigaray, a radical indeterminacy persisting between the literal and the figural is a starting point for understanding the condition of women and femininity in general; the female sex is the sex which *is not one*, perhaps not a "sex" at all, and if a sex, then certainly not unitary nor unifiable: "Whence the mystery that woman represents in a culture claiming to count everything, to number everything by

units. . . . *She is neither one nor two.* Rigorously speaking she cannot
be identified either as one person, or as two. She resists all adequate
definition."[62] The figure offered by Irigaray to represent woman's non-
unicity is that of the famous "two lips." The two lips are carnal, and
yet even their carnality is not determinate in that while they are most
obviously the vaginal lips, they are also the lips of the mouth. They
mark yet indeterminately the body's liminality, the boundary between
inside and outside; they are neither (both) shut nor (and) open, neither
(both) one nor (and) two; and they are offered as a polemical intervention into the symbolic regime in the Lacanian sense, whose dominant
metaphor or figure is the rigid and unitary symbol of identity, power,
property, and agency—the phallus.

Where the Lacanian phallus dominates and legislates, and grounds
the possibility of a clear distinction between binary oppositions—
all those in the Pythagorean list of opposites for example, including
the masculine and feminine, as well as the literal and the figural—
the two lips are in continuous contact, incalculably proximate. They
enter into ceaseless exchange and render impossible any guarantee of
fixed identity or of stable distinctions between opposites, including
that of the literal and the figural. In a sense, one could say that Plato's
bastard reasoning is indeed at work here—the father is done away
with as guarantor of reason and legitimacy—and the two lips cannot be properly known or collapsed into any one of their figures any
more than the *chōra* can. In both cases we are faced with a ceaseless
shifting among a range of meanings: recall the etymology of lip (*labi*),
to slip or fall, to slide from meaning to meaning, to be *labile*. Nonetheless, it is true that the feminine mark of *chōra* is always reducible to the reproductive function, whereas the gendered carnality of
the two lips certainly denotes a biological capacity for reproduction,
but it does so alongside a genitality that may be purely pleasurable,
which exceeds the reproductive function, as well as an orality that, as
the site of speech, may also be differently generative, and differently
pleasurable.

Insofar as both receptacle/*chōra* and the figure of the two lips
denote a strictly indeterminable yet undeniably feminine site of incalculable exchange, giving and receiving without reciprocity, restlessly
sliding or falling outside the schemata of traditional metaphysics, the
connection between them is undeniable. To this extent we can detect
an Irigarayan strategy of mimesis at work, in which by "an effect of
playful repetition" what was supposed to remain invisible is rendered

visible.[63] Butler cites this very passage, pointing out that when Irigaray goes on to say that what is rendered visible is the "possible operation of the feminine in language," she opens herself to the oft-levied criticism of essentialism.[64] In another essay in *This Sex*, Irigaray likens the mimetic function to the *chōra* itself in its capacity as receiver or reflector of images: "The mimetic role itself is complex, for it presupposes that one can lend oneself to everything, if not to everyone. That one can *copy* anything at all, anyone at all, can receive all impressions, *without appropriating them to oneself*, and *without adding any*. That is, can be nothing but a possibility that the philosopher may exploit for (self-)reflection. Like the Platonic *chōra*, but also the mirror of the subject."[65] The ever-present risk that mimesis may merely reflect and reproduce the imprints of patriarchal philosophy is vitiated for Irigaray by the fact that woman's sex cannot be exhausted by mere mirroring, "does not postulate oneness or sameness, or reproduction, or even representation. Because it remains somewhere else than in that general repetition where it is taken up only as *the otherness of sameness*." The Irigarayan woman thus "keeps something in reserve with respect to this function."[66] My reading of the multiply figured, pluripotent receptacle/*chōra*, and in particular the figure of the *ekmageion*, shows that far from merely receiving imprints, it/she on closer inspection also marks, erases, gives, receives, even if none of these various functions becomes the "one" which could stand in for all the others, arriving at a stopping place or *telos* of substance or being where meaning is fixed and hypostatized once and for all. The figure of two lips functions similarly—not as a metaphor, which would take the place of the phallus, but rather, as the figure itself suggests, as a metonymic figure of contiguity, of touching, of proximity, or a chiasmatic figure of crossing over and crossing back or mutual penetration, which could neither completely substitute for or take the place of any other figure, nor halt the process of refiguration. The remainder, the something in reserve that is not exhausted in the mimetic function, is therefore not to be found some secret bodily essence of woman, coquettishly withheld as is the way of her sex. Rather it is a part of the very figurality of the two lips which make impossible any arrival or stopping point that would be signaled by the material body *understood under the guise of mute passivity or essence*.

It is beyond our purview to summarize the extensive Anglophone feminist debates that have circulated around the question of Irigaray's essentialism since the translation of her major texts into English in

1985, suffice it to say that this understanding of the two lips as metonym rather than metaphor is a cornerstone of antiessentialist readings of Irigaray developed by thinkers such as Jane Gallop, Diana
Fuss, Margaret Whitford, and Drucilla Cornell.[67] As Fuss puts it, the
two lips are "neither literal nor metaphoric but *metonymic*,"[68] and
further, because the two lips "operate as a metaphor *for* metonymy;
through this collapse of boundaries, Irigaray gestures toward the
deconstruction of the classic metaphor/metonymy binarism."[69] So if
we accept this analysis of the status of the feminine figure as continually pointing to the limitations and conditions of possibility of its own
figurality, we render impossible any direct identification of even this
deconstruction with "the feminine," because it is precisely relations
of contiguity and proximity, not determinations of identity, that are
being described. This feminist analysis, then, deploys the feminine
not as a central feature, or essence, of deconstruction, but as continually drawing attention to the contiguity of what is called feminine
and that which deconstructs, and it is the insistence on this specific
contiguity that we might call deconstructive feminism. In terms of
mimesis, then, we might recast Irigaray's "possible operation of the
feminine in language" as a sort of *via negativa*, in that it continually draws attention to the way that any production of the feminine,
or sexual difference—at least in these exemplary patriarchal texts—
cannot appear as anything but inevitably and necessarily reductive,
systematizing, schematizing, and thereby always at odds with itself.
The feminine thus always points beyond its appearance in any given
order, and this outside is figured by Irigaray not as pure negativity,
nor as a positive essence, but as the excessive, fluid, metonymic, corporeality of the indeterminately feminine/female body.[70]

For Butler, there is no possibility that mimesis—whether deployed
strategically or otherwise—could simply or unproblematically repeat
a phallogocentric order. Mimesis, after all, always errs (and here Butler and Plato make strange bedfellows, for the erring nature of mimesis is precisely his concern in banning the poets from the ideal city in
the *Republic*). While such errancy is neither necessarily radical nor
liberatory, mimetic repetition necessarily and always involves displacement; indeed it is Butler's central contention in *Gender Trouble* that displacement operates as the very condition of repeatability.
Reading receptacle/*chōra* through the two lips in this way, then, discloses a certain displaced repetition, a recontextualization, a rede-
ployment of philosophemes and figures to different ends, and in this

particular case feminist ends. In doing so, the violent constitution of binary oppositions in which the feminine is eternally entrapped by Plato in service to masculine hegemony and order comes to the fore. However, as Butler also points out, when Irigaray insists upon attributing this displacement and its attendant revelations to the operation of the feminine in language, she renders invisible and inarticulable all kinds of other violent exclusions effected by Plato's hegemonic operations. Irigaray halts the polysemy of *chōra*, the two lips, and mimesis itself at the site of the feminine, and at the very minimum we may acknowledge, along with Butler, the slaves, children and animals also excluded and exploited by Plato in his attempts to establish a figure of disembodied masculine reason.[71]

How do these considerations bear upon the present project? In exploring the articulations, both the connections and disjunctions, between Plato's *hupodochē/chōra* and Irigaray's specifically feminist figuration of the two lips, we can more clearly indicate the protofeminist potential of the receptacle/*chōra*. This lies, it seems to me, in its very refusal to respect a stable distinction between the literal and the figurative or between the metaphoric and metonymic, in its incalculably reflexive and self-penetrating giving/receiving, in the irreducible and symptomatic duality of its determinate role in a family romance *within* the creation story, and its constitutively exterior, excessive, bastard, shifting role as the unruly, disruptive, errant cause. But we should be also suitably warned against identifying any of these qualities too closely or permanently with the feminine, because if we do we not only risk resuscitating the traditional binarism (though the Butlerian reading of the Irigarayan strategy of mimesis gives us a model in which this may always be a risk worth taking), but we also effect other kinds of exclusions, installing the "feminine" as a sort of "master figure" which stands in for what is excluded in general. As soon as the feminine is privileged above other kinds of excluded or abjected others—whether racialized others, economically disenfranchised others, differently-abled, differently sexed or gendered others, and so on—the hierarchy of value is merely reestablished on new grounds.

Nonetheless, the figurations of receptacle/*chōra* explicitly involve a tropology of gender. And this inevitably prompts the question of whether in this text of Plato, at the inception of the grand narrative of Western philosophy, there are glimpses of an archaic, originary "feminine" that may be reclaimable for feminism or for women, or an alternate, antihegemonic conception of "woman" that may be stolen from the texts, along the lines undertaken by Cavarero. As Irigaray herself has recently written: "With regard to Greek culture . . . I think we are trying to find the crossroads at which we have taken the wrong path."[72] Earlier tropes of the feminine in the Greek tradition point to an archaic association of woman with the land, the earth. There is Gaia or *Gē*, fecund and ready to be seeded, and the ancient fertility goddesses Demeter and Cybele, and perhaps a lost, archaic matriarchy hearkening back to the Sumerian worship of Inanna whose story of a descent to the underworld echoes loudly in the story of Demeter and Persephone.[73] This, of course, is the thesis of the nineteenth-century anthropologist J. J. Bachofen, whose work on *Mutterrecht* (mother right) and its subsequent supplanting by a patriarchal order proved vastly influential, but which later scholarship has largely disproved.[74] And yet to seek in archaic cultural phenomena an originary, pristine "feminine" unsullied by patriarchy is surely to succumb to a highly charged form of the etymological fallacy. At stake for Irigaray is recovering women's very experience of her own selfhood, her body, her desire, her pleasure, her lived experience, in a way that would not be merely the "other" of the male seen as the seat of all drive, all desire, all symbolic authorship and authority. And indeed, the "errant cause" only arises in the *Timaeus* as a result of a certain inadequacy of the demiurgic model, pointing to a symptomatic failure in the paternal-productive discourse that the feminine, as third term, is brought in to assuage.

Nonetheless, it seems to me that in any era, place, text, sex and gender, reproduction, and sexuality and desire are inevitably the site of contested and contradictory meanings. And what is therefore of value for this feminist analysis of Plato's text is not an imagined glimpse of a not-yet-quite-covered-over elemental feminine, but the particular formation of gender dynamics that it reveals. Plato's formation offers a scene of feminine maternity and nurturance, an order of necessity, the female reduced to function, but a scene that is also, strangely, errant and motile, that does not stand still, is not self-same, that has no "voice" or "substance" of its own, that leaves no permanent mark, but that nonetheless signifies the ever-renewed inevitability of coming-to-be and passing away, of earthly motion, and the ever-present threat of disorder, and the vicissitudes of temporality, remembering, and forgetting.

Such resonances, then, may move us away from the specificities of the body, and into the registers of the geopolitical, of nation, race, and culture. And the very context of the dialogue indeed suggests these associations in its discussion of politics and the ideal city, where the reference seems to be the *Republic*. Indeed *chōra* also appears in *Republic* II, but there it is fully appropriated by the order of the *polis*, fully territorialized as the object of contestation, an arable resource to be fought over in wars between men over land already claimed as property.[75] Nonetheless, the frame also foregrounds the displaced prehistory of cities, and *chōra* here also denotes a realm of *phusis* outside the city where historical markers might be wiped away by environmental forces, suggesting perhaps the inevitable misguidedness of etymological or archaeological projects in general. Here the effect of receptacle/*chōra*'s unquellable errancy may be clearly heard.[76]

Shifting briefly to the register of contemporary feminism, the errancy of receptacle/*chōra* is arguably also at work in the borderlands of Gloria Anzaldúa, where the border—the impossible space in between nations, identities, worlds—is transvalued as a space of creativity and generative, if painful, "psychic unrest."[77] When Anzaldúa writes, "I will have to stand and claim my space, making a new culture—*una cultura mestiza*—with my own lumber, my own bricks and mortar and my own feminist architecture,"[78] might she not also be calling upon the generativity, the irreducible nonself-sameness and self-inscription of the receptacle/*chōra*? Drawing on multiple mythic figures and images—especially feminine figures of pre–Columbian America as well as later syncretic figures, speaking in at least three languages, and in registers of poetry, history, myth, memoir, philosophy, to flesh out, to symbolize, to build a world in which she might dwell— Anzaldúa, like Plato, articulates a choric borderland between philosophy and myth. Noting the commerce and confluence here between an utterly hegemonic text of Western philosophy and a text dedicated to articulating the possibility of living on and through the borders of that hegemony, we are called not to understand one in terms of the other, to subsume one to the other, but rather to pay attention to what is generated in the fertile boundary zone of their proximity, while letting each remain in its specificity.[79] Receptacle/*chōra* does not specify historical, personal, sexual, geographical, cultural, linguistic situatedness; nor does it permit their evacuation into the ideality of abstract Being; *logos* without *muthos*, existence without embodiment, materiality, motion, ground. Elizabeth Grosz's reading of *chōra* as primarily abyss and symptom of masculinist metaphysics concludes in a call for women's return from exile, a restitution in which they may find a proper place in which to forge a feminist architecture, and in which to dwell. Anzaldúa's borderlands may, by contrast, be seen as resonating with the indeterminacy and motile generativity of the receptacle/ *chōra*, as a zone of creativity where dwelling, living, being as becoming, is always already taking place, ongoingly. Receptacle/*chōra* here is less a *condition* of living than its very activity.

Such zones of creativity may perhaps be best illustrated by feminist aesthetic practices, for example by the earth works of Ana Mendieta. Mariana Ortega's suggestive work on existential spatiality in Mendieta's practice reminds us that creativity in the, "space of the exile and in-between-ness" should not be generalized, as, say, a condition of modernity, but must always remain tied to the specificities of history and place, as the materiality of Mendieta's work discloses.[80] Mendieta's *Siluetas* show us spaces that are the remains of her presence, traces of embodiment, a woman's body in the land, of a feminine occupation of territory, country, nature, land as receptacle/*chōra*, nature becoming culture, and returning to nature, a chiasmatic upsurge of culture in nature, and vice versa, where temporary and temporalizing marks are made and erased. The temporality of receptacle/*chōra*—in its evanescence, its dissolving into fluidity, its withdrawal and figuration of loss—does not merely give way to forgetting. Like the *Siluetas*, it may also, by a strange turn, supply a most powerful reminder of the specificity, corporeality, and materiality of time and place, history and politics, figuring loss, but also the unerasable persistence of memory in life.

RECEPTACLE/*CHŌRA* AND MOTION

As my analysis has shown, the receptacle/*chōra* is a restless notion, indeterminately yet ceaselessly giving, receiving, marking, erasing, and eluding our attempts to "determine the truth" since it can only be known via a kind of bastard reasoning, or in a sort of dream state. Plato explicates the difficulty at 52c when he says that the reality after which the image is modeled in the process of becoming does not belong to its copy, and it therefore "exists ever as the fleeting shadow [*pheretai phantasma*] of some other, must be inferred to be in another, somehow cleaving [*antechomenēn*] to existence, or it could not be at all." (I have substituted cleaving for Jowett's "grasping," to reflect the Greek verb *antechomai*, which in the middle voice means both to hold on to something, and to hold out against it). This is, says Plato, clearly at odds with "true and exact reason" which says that "while two things are different, they cannot exist one of them in the other and so be one and also two at the same time."[81] This fugitive image, an elusive phantasm, fleeing and escaping reason's grasp, yet perceptible as in a dream, and itself somehow cleaving to being, reinforces the restlessness and polydirectionality of receptacle/*chōra*, whose indeterminacy may be further characterized by its always being in motion.

It is somewhat surprising that *chōra*'s motion, or indeed the general problem of the beginning of motion in a cosmogony that tells a story of how an eternally unchanging realm gives rise to a realm of continual becoming, has remained largely unthematized by commentators (with the notable exception of Kristeva, who does not, however, draw on the text with an eye to fidelity). And Plato, taking up the cosmogonic narrative once more, indeed goes on to describe an originary elemental chaos prior to the intervention of the demiurge and the coming of order:

> Before the heavens came to be, there were being [*on*], space [*chōra*], and becoming [*genesis*], three things, existing in three ways. The nurse of becoming was watered and fired and received the shapes [*morpha*] of earth and air, and undergoing [*paschousan*] all the other affections [*pathē*] that accompany them, appeared both manifold, and filled throughout with powers [*dunamia*] neither similar nor balanced, with no part of itself in equilibrium, but every part oscillating [*talantoumenēn*] unevenly. She/it was shaken by these, and she/it moreover shook them in turn. These moving things were forever borne this way and that, and dispersed, just like that which is shaken and winnowed by baskets [*plokanōn*] and other instruments [*organōn*] for cleaning corn: the solid and heavy are borne one way, and the loose and light settle in another place. In this way the four [elements] came to be shaken by the receiver [*dexamenēs*], itself moving like an instrument [*organon*] that furnishes shaking; the most unlike were greatly divided [*horizein*] one from the other, the most alike were pushed toward one another, with the result that therefore these kinds were held in different and again different space [*chōra*], even before everything in the universe was ordered and generated out of them. And on the one hand, even before this, all things were in a state without reason and measure, but when on the other hand the whole ordering was taken in hand, mastered, fire first, and water and earth and air, holding some trace [*ichnos*] of themselves, were altogether in truth in a state just as would be expected in the absence of a god; and insofar as this was their nature, he first patterned [*diaschematisato*] them with form [*eidos*] and number. According to his power, god composed them to be most beautiful and best from that which they were not—such an account must always be granted by us above all else.[82]

God has not touched the cosmos yet—but already the elements, or at least a trace of the elements, exist in virtue of a kind of interpenetration of their "shapes" and the receptacle, which is passively "wetted" and "fired" and receives both the shapes and their "affectations" (*pathē*). In subsequent passages, Plato describes how these shapes are the ideal figures, the simplest polyhedra that can convert into one another by virtue of being all composed of the simplest possible plane figure, the triangle. So even prior to the creator's work there is a spontaneous admixture of ideal mathematical form and receptacle. The elements are not yet patterned, ordered, and beautiful but instead shake and are shaken in all directions by the nurse/receptacle and possess yet only a "trace of themselves." However, the shaking, oscillating motion, which Plato likens to women's labor of winnowing grain with a sieve or basket, means that they separate, and come to occupy different regions of space (*chōra*).

The realm of Forms is eternal and unchanging, and therefore we, and Plato, are faced with the question of the source of motion, change, and indeed time if the story of creation of the world of becoming is to be told. We find, then, that it is space, now figured as the "nurse of becoming," that originally furnishes motion in the cosmos, a kind of unbalanced, disorderly motion. This nurse does not tend or nurture, but the motion she provides is rather a shaking, like a bad mother or a maenad in the Dionysian frenzy. The motion is then refigured as the feminine labor of sorting grain with the feminine technology of a woven basket (*plokanōn*) that shakes. The feminine element here, to ventriloquize Irigaray, is not one, but slides from figure to figure: *hupodochē*, *ekmageion*, mother, nurse, winnower, *chōra*. While the motion is not yet strictly that of periodized generation, neither measurable nor regular, it does give rise to boundaries (*horizein*), and different regions of space are thus established.

Chōra, then, effects a sort of self-differentiation out of disequilibration, it separates (*chōrizei*) and blindly and chaotically spaces itself through the powers/potentials (*dunamis*) of its constituents, almost despite itself. Like an instrument (*organon*), it undertakes work (*ergon*), albeit a directionless, feminine labor that nonetheless results in a sort of preordering of the world of becoming, and without which motion, change, and indeed the entire realm of becoming could not come about. While there is not yet proportion, measure or number by which time could be counted, a kind of temporality may nonetheless be discerned in *chōra*'s self-spacing, a duration in which

labor is undertaken and boundaries established, where an unlovely
proto-ordering of the traces of the elements comes to pass—a process
as yet immeasurable, but also necessarily and irreducibly temporal.
The nurse is thus a nurse of becoming in a double sense, in that she
is one kind of reality, *chōra*, nurturing another, *genesis*, but that also
the nurse herself becomes, changes, or develops as the work of self-
differentiation proceeds.

On the distinction between motion and rest, Plato writes that
motion can never take place in conditions of uniformity, while rest is
found in equilibrium.[83] It is thus in the unequal, nonuniform disequilibration just described that the possibility and beginning of motion
can be found. Indeed it is only when the demiurge introduces cosmic order that rest even becomes possible. Plato also explains why
uniformity is never fully achieved, even as the elements separate,
because the compressing (*sphingein*) nature of the spherical universe,
the shapes of the elemental particles, and their abhorrence of a void,
mean that the particles constantly interpenetrate the spaces between
one another even as they constantly seek their proper region. No
space (*chōra*) remains, even though it is the perpetual disorder of the
chōra that gives the grounds for motion and temporality.

It is then this "visible world" that the creator encounters at the
beginning of the dialogue as being in "discordant and disordered
motion" (*kinoumenon plēmmelōs kai ataktōs*). *Plēmmelōs* is a musical term, denoting a making a false note or out-of-tune-ness, and
more generally erring, faulty, harsh or offending. It may be contrasted
with the harmonious periodicity and ordered regularity instituted by
the demiurge and by which time becomes measurable, although it is
hard to see how something may be out of tune unless there is already
a tune, or some harmony, from which it may have erred. I do not
wish to labor the more general paradox that any positing of originary
chaos or errancy in a cosmogony presupposes the later order by contrast with which it receives its definition, so that receptacle/*chōra*'s
appearance in the middle of the dialogue, rather than at the start, may
be understood not simply a narrative quirk, a symptom of *muthos*,
but a logical necessity. Rather, I want to emphasize that these notes
of discordance, these strayings and unassimilable motile differences
of the visible world that appear throughout the *Timaeus*, are irreducibly marked in the dialogue as feminine. This errant feminine will be
carried over into the Aristotelian cosmos, leaving its traces throughout the corpus as symptomatic aleatory matter. One of its names is

automaton, but it also appears as chance (*tuchē*), force, or compulsion (*bia*), and the unassimilable and unruly aspects of plural, indeterminate, matter.

It is a measure of the shift from Plato's mytho-philosophical "likely story" to Aristotle's highly systematized patriarchal architectonic that Aristotle's principal figure for aleatory matter in nature is *automaton*, a name that also signifies a complex technology: "miraculous" automatic puppets that are so clever and sophisticated that they give the illusion or appearance of independent self-motion, when in fact they are the artifactual products of a thoroughly masculine *technē*. By means of this figure, Aristotle reclaims the unruly disruptions of chance and feminine errancy, the opaque spontaneous generations of matter, and recasts them as an elaborate ruse or trick of patriarchal technological expertise and mastery. I will return to the automatic puppets in chapter 6. Here, I simply want to note that while Plato uses figures of human work and technology, it is the distinctively feminine labors of nursing and grain sorting, and the distinctively feminine artifact of the woven basket, that give shape and name, or perhaps more strictly give motion qua "a kind of life," to the strictly unknowable "wandering cause" of the receptacle and *chōra*, and thus to the cosmos itself.

The *Timaeus* has a surfeit of polyvocal and suggestive feminine figures: receptive, containing, nurturing, and abyssal, but always volatile, errant and motile. The chapters that follow will return to Aristotle's writings on place and motion to see how this errant feminine motility is reduced and suppressed, and yet inevitably returns, symptomatically, as the ineffaceable aleatory dimension of matter.

CHAPTER FOUR

The Physics of Sexual Difference in Aristotle and Irigaray

In the *Timaeus*, Plato's feminine receptacle/*chōra* provides the entire worldly fabric and context for the coming-to-be and passing away of the static and ideal forms, giving everything that subtends the world of becoming: extension, location, space, place, potential, materiality, change, time, and motion. Aristotle, in the *Metaphysics* but especially in the *Physics*, will develop his own account of these natural phenomena, and the task of the remaining chapters is to explore their Aristotelian fate, and thus the fate of the feminine portion of the Platonic cosmos, in his systematic natural philosophy. Less a study of the transmutation of a Platonic idea, this chapter rather investigates the Aristotelian concepts in their own right and on their own terms.[1] I will thus examine how Aristotle's notion of place *finds its place* in terms of his own teleological metaphysics, that is, in relation to his philosophy of substance, matter and form, and potentiality and actuality. The task at hand is to examine the strange and unstable exteriority of Aristotelian place in its feminine valence, and to show that place, like matter, also functions as a kind of feminine symptom. Its indeterminacies too undermine the hierarchical teleology, and in particular the gender hierarchy that does so much work to stabilize the Aristotelian cosmos.

Although the incontrovertibly feminine signification of Aristotelian matter is well-established and textually attested, finding the symptomatic traces of the feminine in the phenomenon of place, and—in the subsequent chapters—in motion and potentiality, requires a more explicitly creative kind of reading, a kind of reading that embraces rather than denies the ever-present possibility of misreading, or what Harold Bloom has called *misprision*.[2] While such an approach does not stint on rigorous engagement with the text, it proceeds somewhat elliptically, through metonymic and figurative means, by allusion and suggestion, moving in and out of phase with itself in a slow and uneven accretion. In this chapter I thus take Irigaray's strong mode of feminist psychoanalytic reading as my guide. Page duBois cautions that psychoanalysis, in its appropriation of Greek tragic themes, enacts a colonizing gesture that reduces a rich and multivalent field of representations of women and sexual difference in the ancient world to a crude schematism of presence and absence of the phallus. However, it is evident that such a reduction also operates within the Aristotelian text. As duBois notes: "For both Aristotle and Lacan, the female body is defined in terms of metonymy. The female is the male, but lacking."[3] Clearly, the male subject is paradigmatic for psychoanalysis, and Irigaray is more than aware that psychoanalysis participates in a philosophical genealogy of schematic reductions of sexual difference. But her approach also offers the possibility of immanent critique, in that when deployed critically and to feminist ends psychoanalysis not only foregrounds question of sex and gender in philosophy, but also permits a disclosure of the precise topologies of the reductions at play and the symptoms produced by those reductions. It is in this spirit, and also bearing in mind that Oedipus was a central part of Aristotle's cultural milieu—indeed Sophocles's *Oedipus Tyrranos* seems to function as the paradigmatic tragedy in the *Poetics*—that Aristotle, Freud, and Irigaray may be read with and against one other. In what follows, Irigaray's feminist psychoanalysis will be entwined with a queer critique of ontological sexual difference, engaging the Aristotelian text in a practice that is simultaneously faithful and irreverent, rigorous and deforming, legitimate and bastard—in a word, symptomatic—and also, I hope, illuminating, enabling, and generative.

In its most literal sense *chōra* means space, what later eras will call dimension and extension, giving location, ground, containment and place for Being. In the *Physics* Aristotle recasts this receptive and feminine notion of space as *topos* (place), the gendered resonances of which have been forcefully taken up by Luce Irigaray in her essay "Place, Interval: A reading of Aristotle's *Physics* IV."[4] This chapter follows Irigaray, while noting limitations and enriching the analysis through a psychoanalytically inflected discussion of the topologies of both sublunary and celestial realms in the Aristotelian cosmos.

Irigaray depicts sexual difference in this ancient physics relatively schematically; my analysis elaborates, deepens, and complexifies it by grappling with Aristotle's texts in their resonances and aporias, their tropes and their disavowals, at a finer level of texture, in a register that is simultaneously feminist, queer, psychoanalytic, and phenomenological.[5] We will thus observe how the figuring of place in Aristotle's two realms, the sublunar and the celestial, may be understood in sexed and gendered terms. Furthermore, a topological correspondence may be drawn between these realms and the different kinds of gendered attachment found in successive stages of the Oedipus complex. The hierarchical Aristotelian cosmos therefore may be interpreted as reflecting the developmental and teleological narrative of psychoanalytic subjectification: the relations between lower and higher representing a passage from earlier to later, preoedipal to postoedipal, maternal to paternal, with space and topology reflecting processes that change over time. However, the Aristotelian text also complicates and displaces this narrative in suggestive ways. Looking at Aristotle's theory of motion in its relation to both space and time, we will see that this developmental trajectory is interrupted, that the story might be seen to proceed differently and perhaps even be reversed. In contrast to a developmental and teleological narrative, the relation between celestial and earthly can thus also be read otherwise, as the story of an uneven fall into plural materiality, understood as feminine, supplemental, and symptomatic (in the Greek sense of *sumptōma* as "falling together"). This motile plurality will disrupt Irigarays's reading of Aristotelian place as a static feminine container, such that the feminine here comes to represent not just place, but also *displacement*. This displacement—unpredictable, interruptive, symptomatic—is a kind of nonteleological, subterranean, and aleatory motion that accrues to the side of the feminine, quite illegible according to any of Aristotle's explicit accounts of motion, change, or becoming.

The symptomatic feminine thus opens a space to reconceive not only the ethical relation between the sexes, providing the space and interval called for by Irigaray's critique, but may also disrupt the very developmental trajectories by which sexuation and gendering are guaranteed. Aleatory matter displaces the patriarchal narrative that animates the Aristotelian cosmos—a cosmos in which a clear separation between desire (for maternal place) and identification (with paternal exteriority) is the precondition for the division of the sexes into two. Through a consideration of topologies of Aristotelian place in relation to aleatory matter, then, we will see how a space might be opened up in this physics, and therefore in the ethics of sexual difference, for nonnormative bodies and sexualities, for queer, transgender, and intersex subjectivities, and for a different configuration of sexual difference itself.

PLACE: TOPOLOGIES OF SEXUAL DIFFERENCE

At the start of his discussion of place in Book IV of the *Physics*, Aristotle makes a rather surprising and peremptory identification of the Platonic *chōra* with matter *and* place. He writes: "This is why Plato says in the *Timaeus* that matter [*hulē*] and space [*chōra*] are the same; for the receptacle [*metalēptikon*] and space [*chōra*] are one and the same. Although the manner in which he speaks about the receptacle in the *Timaeus* differs from that in the so-called 'Unpublished Doctrines,' he explicitly states that place [*topon*] and space [*chōra*] are the same."[6] The displacements, reductions and misidentifications here are dense and difficult to track, but it is worth spending some time with them. The first thing to note is that three separate concepts bear an equivalence with *chōra*: *hulē* (matter), *metalēptikon* (participant), and *topos* (place), in that order. And the second thing to note is just how inaccurate this reading of the *Timaeus*, insofar as it is one, really is. Nowhere in the *Timaeus* does Plato make the identification of *chōra* with *hulē*. *Hulē* in the sense of matter is an entirely Aristotelian innovation, and there is of course no conception of matter as such in Plato's universe (where he does use the word *hulē* it is exclusively in the sense of wood or timber, for example, at *Timaeus* 69a). Also, nowhere does Plato call the receptacle (*hupodochē*) a *metalēptikon*—a "participant," from *metalēpsis* (participation, partaking, having a share in). This word in Plato (and perhaps in the "*Unpublished Doctrines*" to which Aristotle refers) usually refers to the notion of the participation of worldly objects in the Forms. Strictly speaking, the *metalēptikon* would be the worldly thing itself, rather than the indeterminate receptacle. Even so, Plato more commonly uses other locutions such as *methexis* to refer to this kind of participation, while—perhaps tellingly—Aristotle himself uses *metalēpsis* in a phrase that has reverberated through the history of Western philosophy, when in his discussion of the prime mover in *Metaphysics* XII he says that, "thought thinks itself [*noēsis noēseōs*] through participation [*metalēpsis*] in the object of thought."[7] This *metalēpsis* thus signifies the divine merging of thinking with the thing thought, the contemplative pinnacle of rational life separated from all worldly things. Metalepsis is also an ancient rhetorical trope that indicates the substitution by metonymy of one already figurative sense for another: a "metonymy of a metonymy" as Harold Bloom calls it.[8] Strangely enough, this sense of an errant figuration that has lost contact with any origin also quite accurately describes Plato's receptacle/*chōra*, according to my analysis in chapter 3. However, Aristotle's insistence on the strict identity of concepts in this passage (despite his own metaleptic chain of substitutions) would seem to foreclose this tropological reading. Nonetheless, it resonates beyond its explicit context and seems to describe Aristotle's distance here from Plato with jarring accuracy.[9]

Lastly, there is Aristotle's identification of *place* and *space*. Plato may of course have proposed such an equivalence in the "*Unpublished Doctrines*," and in the *Timaeus* he does indeed say that objects in a world of becoming come to be and vanish in some place (*topos*),[10] and in describing the "third kind," our dreamlike and bastard reasoning affirms that all that exists must somehow be in a place (*topos*) and occupy a space (*chōra*).[11] However, this hardly amounts to an identification of the two notions. Rather, place (*topos*) is yet another figure along with the litany of others—the material substrate, the nurse, the mother, and so on. None of these quite captures *chōra* with any finality, but are the means by which it might be glimpsed.

In *Chorology*, John Sallis has detailed the many reductions to which *chōra* has been subject in the subsequent philosophical tradition, including Aristotle's. As well as indicating the errors just cited in the *Physics*, Sallis directs us to yet another misreading in *De Generatione et Corruptione*, where Aristotle takes the image or figure of gold in the *Timaeus* as exemplary for what he there calls the "omnirecipient" (*pandeches*), and then rereads it as the substrate or *hupokeimenon*, once again a definition of *hulē* or matter.[12] Having argued that it cannot make sense to call something that has come to be the same as that out of which it has come to be (though it is admissible for alterations), thus exposing the fallacy of understanding *chōra* as gold, Aristotle then asserts the superiority of his own position, which states that "there is matter of which the perceptible bodies consist, but that it is not separable [*ou choristēn*] but always accompanied by contrariety, and it is from this that the so-called elements come into being."[13] The qualities of fleetingness, restlessness, and inassimilability so characteristic of the multiply figured receptacle/ *chōra* are explicitly rejected. Plato's *chōra* is always at distance from itself, self-spacing, but Aristotle's matter is not separable from the contrarieties it embraces as the substrate that persists and is present in the passage from not-A to A. Aristotle's identification—or rather mis-identification of the *chōra* with one of its figures, namely gold—enacts what Sallis calls a "reductive reinscription of the chorology,"[14] and serves to render it easily dismissible and thus easily assimilated into the Aristotelian universe. Of Aristotle's subsequent (mis)identification of *topos* and *chōra*, Sallis says, "It is as if Aristotelian physics remains absorbed in the dream, reducing the *chōra* to *topos*, dreaming of the *chōra* as a place that would have a place within the economy of that physics, that metaphysics."[15]

There should be no question, then, that Aristotle's reading of the Platonic *chōra* is violently reductive. All that is unruly, unstable, rest-lessly motile, and unknowable by legitimate reason is tamed and attenuated through his resignifications, arriving on the stable ground of matter and substrate on the one hand, and at *topos*, place on the other. While it may indeed be possible to trouble Aristotelian phys-ics through this reduction of *chōra*—and Sallis suggests as much in a footnote where he remarks that it "offers a basis for putting in ques-tion the interpretation of Aristotle's thought as belonging to 'the era of completion [*Vollendung*] of Greek philosophy' or at least for reopen-ing the question as to the sense of that completion"[16]—the results of that reduction can also be read through their sexed and gendered the-matics. Indeed one might say that insofar as the receptacle/*chōra* can *only* be misread, the particular misreadings to which it has given rise and the specific configurations of sex and gender that accompany and infuse those misreadings are *a fortiori* worthy of our attention. Sallis points out that such a "distorting identification" was commonplace in the Middle Platonism of both Plutarch and Plotinus, and indeed when Irigaray addresses *chōra* in "Une Mère de Glace" it is to Plotinus and his reductive understanding of *chōra* as matter that she turns rather than to Plato himself.[17] Sallis finds Irigaray's unquestioning accep-tance of Plotinus's reduction "curious." However, Irigaray is precisely interested in such reductions insofar as they illustrate a certain fate of "the feminine" in the history of Western philosophy: reduction as a sort of freezing and congealing in which the feminine is immobilized as the "other of the same."[18] Interpreting such reductions as symp-tomatic, rather than dismissing them as simply mistaken, permits an exposure of the very mechanisms by which the systematic ambitions inherent in the metaphysical project effect their exclusions and establish their hierarchies.

IRIGARAY'S PHYSICS OF SEXUAL DIFFERENCE, AND ARISTOTLE'S

In her reading of Aristotle's *Physics* IV in *An Ethics of Sexual Difference*, Irigaray maps out a sexually marked topology of containment: in this physics woman is the container for the man. Her approach—at once feminist, poststructuralist, psychoanalytic, and phenomenological—treats this ancient physical and metaphysical architecture as a scenography or topography to be read and interpreted in terms of what it can tell us about a dynamic of sexual difference. This dynamic operates in the very structure of the world, but not just in the world; it is for Irigaray a fundamental feature of the psyche—of sexed existence under patriarchy—bequeathed to the West by classical antiquity, with profound ontological consequences for women. She concludes that woman contains and gives place to man, and therefore cannot, strictly speaking, exist in her own right within this philosophical imaginary. Irigaray thus mines the ancient text to disclose a sexual and corporeal imaginary, at once phenomenological and psychoanalytic, in which the very topological and tropological formations of the physical cosmos enact and enshrine a reduction of sexual difference to a relation of containership. Aristotle's writings on place exemplify this erasure, for her, by erecting man as the universal, leaving woman no place to be, no place in which woman, qua woman, might "take her place." She counters that stultifying and suffocating scene with topological figures of her own, using a range of tropes from the discourses of particle physics, fluid dynamics, the body's materiality, and rhetoric itself. Thereby, she seeks to create an alternate imaginary, a landscape for thinking, being, and acting, in which sexuate beings might function as containers or envelopes for one another, and also give space for letting one another be in their alterity. Irigaray is thus less concerned with a faithful reading of Aristotle's remarks than with calling for the possibility of a genuinely heterosexual relationship, that is, for the possibility of a relationship between sexually different beings that would not deny the ontological and ethical significance of such difference. She thus calls for a shift to an "age of difference," an epoch in which each sex might each take its place, as well as for an "ethics of the passions" through which we might give one another place, without eclipsing sex either as a way of being or as a mode of relationship.[19]

In Irigaray's analysis, the concepts of Aristotelian physics correspond to the topologically experienced lived body in its sexual difference; she illuminates these latent dimensions of that physics which is not by any means scientific in our sense, but rather, as Edward Casey has put it, protophenomenological.[20] Woman has been reduced to a topology—she *is* place. As container or envelope—as womb, matrix, vagina, mother, and lover—she gives place to man, granting him existential comfort and consolation, while she is placeless, lost, without any place: "I shall affirm that the masculine is attracted to the maternal-feminine as place. But what place does the masculine offer to attract the feminine?"[21] This placelessness of woman, with its connotation of the abyss, of falling in a void, renders her threatening, terrifying. The analysis here takes us far beyond the Beauvoirean diagnosis of woman as aligned with or representing nature: rather, this territory is primordially existential. This abysmal threat, in turn, provokes in the masculine a need for compensatory containment or fixation, effected by woman's exclusion and entrapment in the role of place giver. Irigaray reveals a gendered asymmetry in both topology and the motility of the contained with regard to the container. Desire, as it is expressed as movement, as locomotion toward, remains the preserve of the masculine. Without her own "proper place," woman moves without direction, wanders or falls, is *mise en abyme*, or, to shift with Irigaray to the language of contemporary physics, she merely revolves about the center like an electron.[22] Having thus diagnosed the situation, Irigaray offers a topological solution: the masculine must offer a kind of place in return, toward or away from which the feminine might then be able to move: "If there is no double desire, the positive and negative poles divide themselves between the two sexes instead of establishing a chiasmus or double loop in which each can go toward the other and come back to itself."[23] Irigaray contends that both sexes should move, and both sexes should find place, containment, shelter with the other, without absorption into or annihilation of the other: "Between the one and the other, there should be mutual enveloping in movement."[24] At the close of her essay, Irigaray introduces the theme of the rotation of the universe in Aristotle's discussion of place, noting that for him the cosmos itself does not change place but moves in a circle. She recalls Aristophanes's speech in Plato's

Symposium, in which men and women were once one conjoint being, locked in embrace and moving in a circle. For Aristotle, by contrast, one sex claims to be the whole, constructing "his world into a closed circle."[25]

To specify Irigaray's critique of Aristotelian place more precisely in psychoanalytic terms, one can note that the main hazard presented by the Aristotelian topology of container and contained is the danger of engulfment faced by the male subject in relation to the maternal feminine. Freud describes such a relation as "anaclitic" or attachment type: the unmediated, pre-Oedipal object-choice characteristic of the little boy's (and it is typically a little boy) love of his mother, and rooted, he says, in the nutritional instinct of attachment to the breast.[26] Irigaray's call for an interval, a spacing between container and contained, is a call for a relation to the sexuate other that would be mediated on and for both sides. However, Irigaray does not acknowledge either the pre-Oedipal nature of this situation of containership and threat of engulfment, nor the traditional conduit by which this untenable situation may be mediated or resolved, namely the familial drama of the Oedipus complex. As is well known, in this classic narrative of male subject development it is the father who appears as the third term and therefore under whose sign resolution is enabled. The father threatens to intervene into the little boy's dyadic bond with the mother, precipitating a struggle unto death, with the threat of castration or feminization of the son as the father's trump card. The little boy fantasizes the elimination or death of the father. The father's law responds thus: "Renounce your claim on the mother, for she is mine. If you do not, you will become like her, lacking, the object to be fought over and not a subject, not a player in this conflict. If you do, you will accede to masculinity." The struggle over the body of the mother is resolved when the little boy indeed renounces her, and accepts the prohibition. His subjectivity and masculinity are guaranteed by the assurance that, not now, but in the future, he may have one "just like her": a woman of his own as a legitimate object of erotic desire.[27]

The danger, or power, represented by the maternal feminine is thus neutralized through the Oedipal drama in which she is reduced to a cipher of phallic power, through whom father and son can enjoy a mediated relationship, now full of interval, allowing them both place and space without threat of obliteration.[28] The spacing afforded by this resolution is also temporal: a deferral is introduced, a relation to futurity that is also a metonymic or analogic difference. In forcing the son to wait, not for his mother but for another *like* her in certain respects (and most assuredly with respect to her femininity, the very quality that makes her capable of possession), and for an intimacy, nourishment and containment that comes later, the father's law also gives temporality, an assuredly masculine temporality.

If, then, we reframe Irigaray's diagnosis of sexual difference in Aristotle's account of place as a pre-Oedipal scene of anaclitic attachment, several questions arise. How might this impossible pre-Oedipal dyad be resolved? Are the logic and dynamics of the Oedipus complex reflected in Aristotelian physics and in the constitution of the Aristotelian cosmos, and what does this reveal about the mechanisms of the erasure of sexual difference in the architecture of Western thought? And might we find hints of a destabilization of that architectonic, a destabilization with potential for enriching Irigaray's feminist philosophy?

In *Metaphysics* XII, where Aristotle finally turns to a discussion of the prime mover as the teleological pinnacle of the text's narrative, we may indeed observe a rather striking illustration of Oedipal resolution. Aristotle's prime mover, the masculine signifier *par excellence* is unmoved and motionless, standing beyond the physical cosmos, outside space and time. And it is in relation to this divine and incorporeal entity that the universe rotates out of love. The divine prime thus creates motion not through any exertion of its own, but passively, through being loved (*kinei de hōs erōmenon*).[29] This love, erotic rather than filial or friendly (*erōs* not *philia*), is not possessive, anaclitic, or sexually differentiated. Rather, it is mediated and identificatory: the moving spheres wish to be as much like the prime mover as possible, moving in perfect circles reflecting its perfection, and not desiring to close up the interval between them by occupying its place or seeking engulfment within it. This love is thus precisely *homoerotic*—an eros of like to like.

There is, in psychoanalytic terms, a clear contrast between the anaclitic container-contained relationship between place and thing in the sublunary realm, and the identificatory, or perhaps narcissistic object choice of the moving spheres in the superlunary realm. This distinction lends itself explicitly to a reading in terms of the Oedipus complex: a pre-Oedipal relationship with an engulfing mother versus a post-Oedipal outcome of identification with the father.[30] What then has transpired in the interval? How is this mediation achieved? Reading Aristotle's cosmos via the developmental narrative of Oedipalization, we may conjecture that the dangers represented by unmediated, sexually differentiated containment in the sublunary world are resolved in the "higher" realm by a suppression or subjugation of the maternal-feminine. The matrilocal scene in which entities move toward place and rest in containment is mediated by the introduction of a third term, that of the father, or the prime mover.

To develop this psychoanalytic reading of the dynamics of the Aristotelian heavens, we can draw on Kaja Silverman's account of the negative Oedipus complex, forged in the context of the development of the superego. According to Freud's *Ego and the Id*, the parent one ends up identifying with becomes the blueprint for the superego, where an image of that parent is set up within the ego and functions as the source of moral imperatives. As Silverman notes, the situation for the male subject is explosive, for if the son tries to become like the father, the superego prevents it "by decreeing: 'You may not be like [your father] . . . you may not do all that he does; some things are his prerogative.' The paternal law thus promotes the very thing that its severity is calculated to prevent, a contradiction which must function as a constant inducement to reconstitute the negative Oedipus complex."[31] In other words, the strength of the prohibitive moral law of the father is such that it threatens to push the son's identification away from the father and onto the mother, while a new relation is established with the father: an erotic one. That paternal identification is haunted in this way by *erōs* is reflected in Aristotle's use of that term, rather than the more chaste *philia*, to describe the affective relation between moving spheres and prime mover. In the Greek context, of course, there is nothing surprising about erotic relations between masculine subjects, especially in the rarified world of the Athenian elite where erotic relations between older and younger citizen, lover and beloved, are hierarchically formalized. The works of Plato constantly dramatize these relationships, especially between the figure of Socrates and his various young interlocutors, although any explicit mention of homoerotic love between men is limited to just a few remarks in the Aristotelian corpus.[32]

In the Aristotelian heavens, however, we can see that the Greek hierarchical ordering of lover and beloved, active and passive parties, is reversed. The heavenly bodies are the active lovers and the prime mover is the *erōmenon*, the beloved.[33] While the divine prime mover does not act upon the world in any direct way, it is the manifestation of the good as such, which is for Aristotle that toward which most things, at least, tend. As the ultimate object of desire it can be understood to exercise a powerful moral and legislative force, a law of the father that paradoxically consists entirely in its unattainable erotic passivity (more usually associated with the boy in a Greek pederastic relationship). The beloved beautiful boy, so inspirational to the philosopher in Platonic philosophical love, thus reaches a kind of apotheosis in Aristotle.

In relation to place, the prime mover, serves as a placeholder *beyond* the cosmos rather than occupying any specific place or space *within* the cosmos. Furthermore, the prime mover, *qua* unattainable paternal love object, points to possibilities beyond the prohibitive either/or of sexual difference decreed by both positive and negative Oedipus complexes, in which one must identify with one parent and desire the other. The Aristotelian heavens are driven by a force that is *both* identificatory and erotically desiring, that queers the Oedipus complex, so to speak, but from which women, the feminine, and sexual difference as such, have all but been eliminated. In contrast to Irigaray, for Aristotle it is not the woman that revolves about the center like an electron, but the masculine heavenly bodies that thus move in perfect circular motion, in a relation of pure, homoerotic identification with an impassive metaphysical father.[34]

In this narrative, then, there is a developmental movement from the local motions of the sublunary realm—rectilinear motions toward goals or places—to the broader, higher, and more perfected circular motions of the celestial realm. In the heavens, the feminine no longer has any place at all, not even as a giver of place. The woman/mother is superseded and the relation between subject and paternal function, now understood as that between heavenly body and divine prime mover, is mediated at her expense, at the price of her disappearance.

In this move from sublunary world to cosmos, what becomes of place? There is interval, to be sure, between the heavenly bodies and their beloved, the divine prime mover, but is there a giving of place? For Irigaray, the desire for place is intimately connected with a quest for the divine. She asks:

> Can the quest to infinity for the mother in women result in a quest
> for infinity in God? Or do the two quests intersect ceaselessly? With
> place indefinitely switching from the one to the other? Modifying
> itself moment by moment. Or even transmuting itself from one
> envelope to the other? I become for God the container, the envelope,
> the vessel, the place for which I quest? Nonetheless the split between
> first and last place still has to be resolved.[35]

Irigaray thus suggests a certain interchangeability between woman and the divine as givers of place, with divine infinity substituting for the abyssal falling of feminine placelessness. This is a complex scene: on the side of infinity she invokes both the abyss of material maternity (mothers of mothers of mothers, and so on) and the superlative transcendence of the divine. And woman and divine also both appear on the side of place, envelope, limit, or container. However, it is not quite clear how Aristotle's rejection of the infinite, and his concomitant positing of the ultimate telos in the figure of the prime mover, may fit into this picture. It is, after all, clear that for Aristotle it is feminine matter that is the place of the indefinite, while the masculine, as form and telos is the definite *par excellence*. At the same time of course it is feminine matter that resolves the paradox of how something may come from nothing, and thereby provides a place of sorts, as the *hupokeimenon* or substrate, for the instantiation of form. The quest, desire itself, is perhaps for both Aristotle and Irigaray a striving for a last place, a future place. But Irigaray wants to emphasize that a certain nostalgia for the mother's womb, the first place, may substitute or stand in for this desire. In her emphasis on the concrete maternal situation as first place, as existential container, Irigaray intervenes into the Aristotelian identification of moving cause with final cause as form, and the ultimately divine telos. Further, for Irigaray, place as containership, as envelopment, as a place to dwell but precisely not of engulfment, is necessary for all of us, both men and women:

> Once there was the enveloping body and the enveloped body, the latter being more mobile through what Aristotle termed *locomotion* (since maternity does not look much like "motion"). The one who offers or allows desire moves and envelops, engulfing the other. It is moreover a danger if no third term exists. Nor only to serve as a limitation. This third term can occur within the one who contains as a relation of the latter to his or her own limit(s): relation to the divine, to death, to the social, to the cosmic. If a third term does not exist within and for the container, he or she becomes *all-powerful*.
>   Therefore, to deprive one pole of sexual difference, women, of a third term also amounts to putting them in the position of omnipotence: this is a danger for men, especially in that it suppresses an interval that is both entrance and space between. A place for both to enter and exit the envelope (and on the same side, so as not to perforate the envelope or assimilate it into the digestive process); for both, a possibility of unhindered movement, of peaceful immobility without the risk of imprisonment.[36]

The divine, here, is one figure (along with death, the social, and the cosmic) for a necessary limit, a third term beyond the two sexes that is required by both if there is to be mutual, open containership between sexually different beings. Are there resources in the Aristotelian text for figuring such a limit? The relationship between the divine prime mover and place needs to be more precisely understood.

It is clear that in its lack of materiality, in its rationality, its full presence and actuality, the Aristotelian prime mover is rigorously masculine and not interchangeable with the woman/matrix in any form. However, as the good, and as the object of desire, it also represents the ultimate telos of all motion and action in the cosmos. Temporally ahead of us, metaphysically separate, always out of reach, the paternal divine stands apart. Free of all matter, as thought thinking itself, it is pure abstraction without incarnation, exemplary of that version of the divine that excludes the feminine. It is not something that could be called with any accuracy a "place." Like the Oedipal father, the prime mover thus gives time and frames futurity without giving place. The Oedipal father guarantees to the son that the place that is woman will, eventually be forthcoming, with all necessary consolation and succor. What, though, is the fate of the woman in the Aristotelian cosmos? Feminine place is to be found below, in the sublunary realm, if the body-subject renounces the heavens and, succumbing to its desire for place, falls to earth.

Aristotle's analysis of place in *Physics* IV rests on four primary axioms: It contains a thing, but is not part of the thing contained; it is neither less nor greater than the thing contained; it can be left behind by the thing contained and is separable (*chōriston*) from it; and all places are characterized by being up or down—"By nature each body travels to or remains in its proper place [*oikeios topos*] and it does so in the direction of up or down."[37] The "proper" of the proper place, *oikeios*, has none of the connotations of legitimacy or rigidity of the English, but rather denotes the ownmost intimacy of the homely hearth, the feminine sphere of the household, the *oikos*, which, like *hupodochē*, Plato's word for the receptacle in the *Timaeus*, denotes a certain hospitality, a welcoming into the home. Objects thus travel by nature toward their homes, toward the sphere of the maternal and the feminine, and arrive in rest and repose. Despite this haunting of *topos* by the Platonic receptacle or *chōra*, place is not the receptacle as such: it does not receive Form nor participate in it, but is always separate and separable from that which it contains. It is essentially topological, enveloping and containing, and both depends on and participates in an essential difference, a boundary and limit, between container and contained. Dismissing both matter and form, as well as the interval between thing and place as suggestive but unacceptable candidates for place, Aristotle tells us that place must rather be "the containing body's boundary which is in contact with what is contained."[38] Finally, he settles on the following definition: place is the "primary motionless boundary of that which contains" (to tou periechontos peras akinēton prōton).[39]

In fleshing out his definition of place as a boundary of that which contains, Aristotle explains that "a place is together with [hama] the thing [contained], for the limit [of that which contains] coincides with [hama] that which is limited."[40] This formulation raises a difficulty about the relationship between place qua a containing boundary and qua that which is exhausted by and fully equivalent with the thing contained. To what extent is the boundary separate from its contents, and to what extent do they coincide? Hama, a small word relied upon to do much work here, may be translated as "at once, at the same time with, together with." Translators have taken pains to point out the difficulty with this passage, because for Aristotle the coinciding of place and thing, between that which limits and that which is limited, is, as Wicksteed and Cornford put it, "the error he is anxious to refute."[41] Casey describes how the limits of Aristotelian place and thing act together: "Not only can one limit not exist without the other, but each actively influences the other, helping to shape a genuinely conjoint space, a space of mutual coexistence between container and contained. This co-constituted, coincidental, compresent double limit is what defines place in its primariness."[42] The confusion over the translation of hama in Aristotle's text may be related to the paradoxical, aporetic, or chiasmatic nature of boundary itself as both separating and joining, and in particular to the difficulty involved in describing the outermost boundary of the universe. Aristotle argues that the cosmos itself is a place, but is not in a place, because "heaven considered as a whole . . . is nowhere and in no particular place, that is if there is no body which contains it; yet with respect to the way in which it is in motion, its parts do have a place, for they are consecutive to each other."[43] The universe does not locomote: beyond it there is no place from which or toward which to move. An entity rotating in a circle, it contains parts that can be said to have place with respect to each other; its plurality, articulation, and motion ground the possibility of place for its parts. However, there is still a perplexity regarding the outer boundary of the universe, which despite its rotating spatial relation to itself is not itself contained by anything.

PLACE AND THE FEMININE SYMPTOM

Aristotle's use of *hama* here, an expression that is ambiguously temporal ("at the same time as") and spatial ("together with") in this context, can be read as symptomatic of this difficulty, hearing here the Greek sense of *sumptōma* as chance occurrence or coincidence (literally a "falling together"). At the edge of the cosmos, *hama* traverses the boundary between the exterior, the nonplace, and interior place, its ambiguity bringing us down toward the feminine and to the possibility of stasis and repose. What is outside the cosmos is, after all, motionless and not in time, whereas time, for Aristotle, is itself dependent upon motion, following on from motion, an affection or *pathos* of motion.[44] The unmoved mover that is the source of circular motion, and thus periodicity and the possibility of measurable time, is located here, beyond the cosmos, but it does not provide the containment of place. The outermost boundary, then, must both distinguish between and articulate the temporal and the eternal, the moving and the motionless, the possibility of place-giving and the nonplace. The masculine prime mover, beyond the cosmos, gives time but not place, while the maternal feminine within the cosmos gives place, but in its stasis and closing up of space between, does not give time. *Hama* provides the place, space, interval, boundary, where one may cross over into the other. As Derrida notes of the appearance of *hama* a little further along in *Physics* IV, it "is neither spatial nor temporal. . . . It says the complicity, the common origin of time and space, appearing together as the condition for all appearing of Being. In a certain way it says the dyad as minimum."[45] So even when the explicit description threatens to founder in incoherence and impossibility, *hama* works to reinscribe a foundational dyad, almost without either ourselves, or Aristotle, noticing it—as Derrida puts it, "He says it without saying it, lets it say itself, or rather it lets him say what he says."[46]

The aporetic founding of space-time, relying on the ambiguity of the insignificant *hama*, separates the divine exteriority from the cosmos and the entities within it. What is more, as both limit *and* spacing, it produces a certain androgyny: the possibility of approach, of the intimacy of the hearth, of containership and repose, as well as the necessary distance to keep engulfment at bay. Is there space, or time, here for a different relation to divinity, one that might give place, or corporeality, and an opening for the feminine? The descending order of the Aristotelian cosmos—prime mover; celestial motion; periodicity and time; the movement and cycles of the sublunar realm; the proper place of the elements and then all the other instances of place—one following on from the other, is disrupted by the symptomatic *hama*, which gives space and time *together*, at the same time. This progressive falling from the highest to the lowest, from a pure masculinity to the material femininity of the earth, literally relies on a *sumptōma*, a falling *together*, a symptom that may itself be read as feminine.[47] The *hama*, then, gives space and time together: it spaces and temporalizes, giving both interval and boundary. As such, it is the indeterminate condition of the possibility of place. In its irreducible duality, between corporeal cosmos and the divine, it corresponds to the Irigarayan sensible transcendental, the possibility of an always open sexuate place.

Aristotle's divinity does not provide a place, but exists beyond an untraversable boundary that permits no locomotion toward, no approach, inspiring instead the eternal circular motion that emulates the circularity of thought thinking itself, in a relation both erotic and identificatory. It provokes or incites desire through its superlative, nonmaterial existence. As an abstract telos that is never arrived at, but always ahead and always ideal, it provides the opening and perpetuity of time. On earth, the proper place, the domestic hearth, the maternal container, is perhaps all too approachable, resulting in the specter of the closing up of interval, a stifling engulfment, a stasis, a stoppage of time. Both the prime mover and sublunar place are motionless (*akinēton*) and nontemporal, and thereby provoke the locomotion of objects—the prime mover by setting them in motion and place by providing a place of arrival and belonging. Aristotle defines rest as a privation of motion, and in the sublunary realm it is feminine place that furnishes the possibility of this privation. While Casey observes that the Aristotelian notion of place thus explains motion and rest and their relationship "economically and effectively,"[48] there are also profound consequences for the topological and temporal figuring of the masculine and the feminine. The material motionless feminine provides intimacy and interiority, yet stops time; the immaterial motionless masculine provides spacing and interval, and also inaugurates time. In a sense, place is the sublunary counterpart of the motionless prime mover of the heavens, providing a passive, containing, immanent, material endpoint toward which things tend—whether the natural motion of the elements toward their *oikeios topos* as the up and down, their bosom, hearth, and home, the movement of animals and men such as Odysseus toward their actual homes as local *teloi*, and the other more random, unpredictable motions that result in things being in places as a matter of accident, the way this ant colony happens to have been established in this particular place and functions as home for these ants, and that water just happens to have ended up in that jug. Feminine place, then, functions as a passive, feminine, material, sublunar counterpart to the masculine, active, immaterial unmoved mover in the superlunary realm. As a local end or telos toward which the elements tend to fall or rise—earth and water downward, air and fire upward—not by desire or love, but simply by nature, the "proper place" itself appears as a supplement, a symptom, a fallen earthly substitute for the masculine divinity of the heavens.

There is a difficulty, however, that needs to be addressed, and this involves the distinction between place *tout court* and the "proper place" toward which elements may rise or fall and in which they come to rest, according to their nature. In *Physics* IV Aristotle is crystal clear that place as such can be neither matter *nor* form, and specifically not form because form is inherent to the thing itself, whereas place is its containing body.[49] But in discussion of elemental motion toward proper place in *De Caelo* he, quite remarkably, equates proper place and proper form: "to be carried toward its proper place [*ton autou topon*] is for each thing to be carried towards its proper form [*to autou eidos*]."[50] In this context *place* seems to be no longer separate from *form*, but is finally and precisely assimilated to it. Movement toward proper place is now cast as a movement from potentiality to actuality, with form as its *telos* (I will return to this development in chapter 5; here I stay with an analysis of place in its psychoanalytic dimension). For as fire moves upward to join fire, and earth moves downward to join earth, that is as like moves toward like, Aristotle says that these places—extremity and center—function as the boundaries (*peras*) of the bodies that move toward them and "in a way become the form of the body they enclose."[51]

In addition to solving a problem about self-moving matter, this is also an elegant solution to the problem of how something like an element—which is after all not a unified thing like an organism with a definite boundary containing parts, but rather continuous, boundariless, and not internally differentiated—might be said to have a form at all. And in the *Physics*, Aristotle notes that when a part of an element joins the whole upon arrival at its proper place, it becomes continuous with it and therefore cannot enter into relations of acting upon and being acted upon with it, and will thus stay there *by nature.*[52] However, in the psychoanalytic dimension, this arrival at *proper place,* in which the part finally merges fully *with its place* and becomes indistinguishable from it, enacts the terrifying threat of maternal engulfment. The unspeakable has come to pass.

We see then the salutary effect of recasting the proper place as form. For instead of a horrifying return, a sinking into and eventual submersion in the abject maternal, this journey's end instead has now been transformed into a kind of apotheosis, a glorious accession from potentiality to actuality, the arrival at and fulfillment of the natural masculine telos. And indeed in *De Caelo* the propriety of the proper place is no longer designated by the homely *oikeios topos* but the *autou topos,* the "place of itself," a self-sameness that signifies the possibility that even the most elemental kind of matter in the sublunary realm may achieve something akin to the divine condition. Conceiving of place as form also, then, serves to consolidate the vertical hierarchy of the cosmos, whereby, "earth is in water, water in air, air in *aithēr, aithēr* is in the heavens, but the heavens are in no other thing."[53] And in *De Caelo* it is plainly put: "that which surrounds is on the side of form, that which is surrounded is on the side of matter."[54] An analogy swiftly follows of the heavy with the diseased, and the light with the healthy.[55] So that as one travels upward from center to perimeter one travels from what is base and earthly, from what is degraded and fallen, to what is noble and divine. Even though the elements are all apparently designated as primary matter, as discussed in chapter 1, according to this hierarchy of place it is earth, what is heavy and drawn to the center, that appears to partake of materiality to the greatest degree, whereas whatever is drawn upward is closest to form.

At the same time, place is still not quite form, because a fundamental feature of place is that things not only strive after it, but they may also leave it. Place is necessarily separable—*chōriston.* And indeed Aristotle tells us that while elements will naturally remain immersed in their proper places, any given part is also divisible and separable from the whole, "as if one were to disturb a part of water or air."[56] The verb here is *kinēsē,* used in the active sense of "to set in motion" (at *Iliad* XVI.264 it is used in the sense of disturbing a wasp's nest), and thus implies the possibility of an external source of motion, another *archē kinēseōs* that would disrupt the tendency of the elements to move toward and remain in their proper places. The implication is that such a disturbance would be of the order of an undesirable or disagreeable compulsion, something that acts *against nature*, dislodging the elements from their repose in proper, natural, teleological belonging.

Of course for Aristotle the sublunary world obeys a certain teleological order: in their teleological striving, the cycles of nature and generation emulate the circular motions of the heavens, in time if not in space, so the cyclical transformation of the elements also align with cosmic teleology. The first several chapters of *Gen. et. Corr.* II are indeed devoted to a detailed account of how the elements are cyclically transformed into one another as the contraries of the hot and the cold, the wet and the dry, come to be and pass away from the material substrate. Further, in sexual reproduction it is heat that carries a masculine sign while cold is a marker of the feminine, so it is hardly surprising that the hotter elements rising toward the outer perimeter of place are designated as more noble. And indeed the approach and the retreat of the sun in its annual cycle provides a physical cycle of heat and cold that lends itself to these cycles of coming-to-be and passing away. So on the one hand, there is a fully teleological account of these "disturbances" or oustings from proper place that is explained by the intervention of heavenly cyclicity, whether this occurs through *mimēsis*—cycles on earth imitating heavenly circularity—or by the sun as a direct motive cause. On the other hand, there is also the simple facticity of aleatory matter in the Aristotelian sublunary: matter that is out of place, matter that may under certain circumstance initiate its own wayward motion, matter that is irreducibly and unaccountably plural and indefinite, that wrests other matter out of its place disagreeably, compulsively, disruptively, like children wont to stir up a wasps' nest.

Certainly, the causal trajectories in which matter is caught up (and which it may also, obscurely, initiate) are plural, indeed innumerable. And here, place itself is also plural and innumerable. There may be proper places, designated by the vertical axis of center and extremity, but there are also endless instances of place as such, for all things that are *anywhere at all* have a primary motionless boundary, and must be in a place. Place, like matter, is inherently plural, and insofar as it designates and portends *displacement* just as much as arrival and containment, it also provides a context, or perhaps a condition of possibility, for all motion, all motility. Aristotle insists that matter and place differ because place is *separable*, a *where* something is, whereas matter is not separable, but a *what* that constitutes a thing.[57] But matter, in its giving of plurality and indeterminacy, as a site of unnatural compulsions and the subterranean movements of *automaton*, and in its fallenness and symptomaticity, is also the *necessary condition of all separation*, all differentiation. In the *chōriston* of place, then, we might hear the remainder of Plato's motile *chōra*, reminding us of the inherent restlessness of matter, its at-odds-ness with respect to itself, its necessary separation from itself. The capricious, forceful, disruptive qualities of matter act upon things to push them out of their places, putting them at odds with their place. Such motions, opaque and unpredictable, immune to reason and knowledge, vitiate the Aristotelian promise of the accession to proper place as the local telos of movement and sublunary counterpart to the divine. Here, elemental matter appears divided against itself insofar as it holds the promise of shedding its heavy, earthly shackles and actualizing its potential, rising to divine masculine nobility, and yet at the same time, by the action of some unaccountable external force, it may yet be transformed back into earth, and fall back down, symptomatically, to the base feminine center.

Now these aleatory motions also ground a different order of motility, and also perhaps portend a different order of gender than that indicated by Irigaray in her designation of the feminine as container, and the masculine as contained. In other words, aleatory matter and the countless pluralities of place, insofar as they give the possibility of disruption and displacement, engender a vision of the feminine not dependent on a structure of stasis and motion toward place as form or telos, but one that utterly bypasses, indeed has no relation to, any kind of teleological desire or inclination. These motions also provide another sort of spacing, another sort of temporalizing, another sort of interval. Once again, in the language of Irigaray, they keep open the threshold between the masculine and feminine, inoculating against engulfment. In their materiality and corporeality, they also give a different periodicity, that of animate matter not moving in cycles in identification with the abstraction of thought directed toward itself, but (and perhaps this is to risk a certain essentialism along with Irigaray and also Kristeva) the ebbs and flows of breath, of blood, of corporeal femininity: what Irigaray calls the sensible transcendental. Such a depiction of feminine, material motions is thoroughly reminiscent of, though not quite equivalent to, Julia Kristeva's heterodox appropriation of Plato's *chōra* as a presymbolic maternal dimension of language, that of "rupture and articulation (rhythm), [which] precedes evidence, verisimilitude, spatiality, and temporality."[58] In force, chance, spontaneity, and coincidence, then, we may discern the nascent possibility of both place and interval, of the possibility of the partially open feminine place, and the new configuration of space-time incorporating the interval that Irigaray proposes as necessary for the flourishing of sexuate beings.

A certain narrative trajectory may thus be traced in the emergence of Aristotelian place from the Platonic receptacle/*chōra*. Aristotle attributes to Plato the position that matter and space are the same, that receptacle and space are the same, and that place and space are the same.[59] Aristotle thus sees in Plato an undifferentiated complex of space-place-receptacle-matter that he will proceed to unpack, primarily by differentiating matter and place. Thus, in the course of *Physics* IV.4 he argues strenuously that place is neither matter, nor form, nor the interval between the thing and its place, but the "primary motionless boundary of that which contains."[60] And finally, as he hints in *Physics* IV.5 and argues explicitly in *De Caelo* IV.3, place as *proper place* is ultimately to be identified with form. This consolidates place as the telos of elemental matter, as the limit and boundary that portends its actualization, its becoming *to autou eidos*, and assures its assimilation into the cosmic teleology. In this way, Aristotle provides an ingenious solution to the problem of elemental motion upward and downward: it is the actualization of a potential. But again, such reduction and assimilation cannot take place without remainder. Just as the conception of matter from the point of view of the potentiality/actuality schema renders it unidirectional, vectoral, appropriate, obedient, and yet is utterly incapable of countenancing the aleatory and disruptive motions of matter, so the designation of proper place as form gives rise to its own symptom. Thus the designation of place itself loses all meaning if it does not also include the possibility of disturbance, disruption, and displacement. The restless, rumbling, complex, figural motility of Plato's *chōra* returns, then, symptomatically, buried both in matter's opaque aleatory propensities that give rise to chance events, and in the plurality of all *improper* places in which things might find provisional rest and repose, but not their final resting places.

So to return to the gendered valence of place and its ontological and ethical consequences in Irigaray's analysis, we can note that the ethical relationship called for by Irigaray does not merely implicate the relations between man and woman, but also woman's relationship to herself, to other women, and indeed to all configurations of sexuate being. Such relationships are indeed conditioned by the metaphysical, theological, philosophical and physical topologies within which we think and live, which in turn give possibilities for experiencing our worlds, our understanding and experience of embodiment, sexual difference and sexuation in general.[61] According to Casey, the Aristotelian place container is necessarily closed, for it to be even partly porous would be "disastrous, since the contents would then flow out and lose their place."[62] However, if we take into account the devalued aleatory motions inherent in matter, we see that, against the grain, the Aristotelian container must be, like the two lips, also partly open. It has, or rather *is* a threshold—mobile, temporal *and* spatial; via this threshold it may transform itself into the contained, find its own place, and, in accord with the topology of the chiasmus, still return to itself. Freeing the dyadic topology of container and contained from the opposition of stasis and mobility indexed to the opposition of woman and man offers the chiasmatic possibility of a restless reconfiguration of relationship of the one to the other, indeed the possibility of a restlessly unpredictable reconfiguration of sexual difference itself.

This interpretation, inspired by Irigaray, of the modes of locomotion in Aristotle's sublunar and celestial realms as representing pre- and post-Oedipal modes of relation, renders the Aristotelian cosmos as a motile, spatial representation of a psychoanalytic developmental narrative of subject formation. The identificatory relation that pertains in the celestial realm between mover and the spheres is not simply mimetic, but also erotic. The post-Oedipal masculine subject of the Aristotelian heavens does not obey the prohibitions of the father's law, or rather the father's law is configured differently to permit eros and mimesis to appear together. Although the subject is rigorously masculine, and the relations here are strictly homoerotic, the compresence of eros and identification means that one need not be forsaken for the other, that contrary to the Freudian account these modes of relation may coexist, albeit in the rarified and noble realm of the male Greek elite. The father does not envelop the son, but remains always apart, at a distance. He may be emulated, desired, loved, but the space between them can never be diminished. He cannot hold, contain, or provide a place to dwell. The paternal divine does not give place.

It is only in the earthly realm, within the material cosmos, that place may be given, and in which the maternal-feminine appears as the giving of place. The heavenly bodies transmit motion downward, to the sublunary realm. And it is only here, where multiple causes and plural forces both with and against nature prevail, where heavy objects fall and light objects rise on a vertical axis, that place can take its place (although perhaps the question of its being as such will still remain in abeyance). And then, here, place is identified with proper place, and proper place with form, so that even the small territory carved out for feminine place is assimilated into the larger teleology in which the feminine is an unbearable position, and is indeed characterized by its—necessarily doomed—desire for the masculine. And this desire is doomed in two ways. First, because if it were to get as close to form as it truly desired, if it were truly to merge with place as form, it would no longer be feminine at all, but would have acceded fully to the desired masculine position and canceled out its sexual specificity. Second, because however close to form, however close to the masculine, however close to the divine it gets, the orectic and obedient feminine is always subject to forces that result from its own differentiation, its nonself-sameness, the multiple aleatory forces outside of it that push it out of its place.

In the developmental narrative I have traced, the feminine-maternal container of place in the sublunary realm is supplanted by an erotic-identificatory relationship to the paternal in the heavens. Reversing this narrative of Oedipal development, we now may see in Aristotelian physics a symptomatic fall from masculine perfection to feminine degradation. Even as place becomes form and desire for the father is reestablished in the sublunar, this scene of heterosexual longing of matter for form is destabilized by the irreducible plurality of matter and places. In this reversal, there is also another scene of space and time, another scene of motion, and perhaps, also, an opening toward another scene of sexual difference. These interstitial, displacing motions of materiality may pose an abyssal threat, the existential threat of a ceaseless exile, a being-not-at-home, and yet we may also glimpse in them something of the nonself-sameness of life inherent in matter, another source of motion far from the perfect circularity of the prime mover, another species of divinity that is corporeal, living, breathing. In foregrounding this narrative of a fall, of the faltering misstep, of interruption, ambiguity, displacement, and symptom, some light is thrown on the processes of Oedipalization and subjectification with which I began. For if the feminine gives both place *and* displacement, how can this be read into the scene of anaclitic attachment, of the nutritional relation to the breast, of the engulfing envelopment of pre-Oedipal attachment to the mother? Certainly, the breast is not always there when the infant wants it—the infant's earliest experience is of privation of the maternal body. In some sense, the maternal place may be just as impassive as that of the father. And this of course is necessary—the story of development is after all in large part a story of the infant's attempts to master the mother's absence (as dramatized by Freud's famous game of *fort-da*) [63] But might the kinds of displacement, openness, ambiguity, and simultaneity found in this analysis of Aristotelian cosmos make it possible to envision different configurations of identification and desire in the specific crisis that is Oedipalization? Could desire persist for both the mother and the father, or if not them, then "ones like them"? Could identification persist with both the mother and the father, *hama*, at the same time, coinciding, in the same place? Could the very multiplicity of places and matter's aleatory movements portend a multiplicity of corporealities, identifications, positions, and perverse trajectories of desire within a complex field of bodies, genders, sexes, and sexual scenarios? Could the very processes of gender identification, of bodily ego formation, indeed also be subject in this complex to many kinds of opaque, unpredictable displacements and reconfigurations?[64]

The fall into sexual difference signaled by Oedipus, with its renunciations and compromises, its nonnegotiable either/or, is inevitably and structurally a tragic narrative. One cannot thwart a tragedy by fiat, by simply replacing it with a comedic delirium of gender profusion or nonidentity. Nonetheless, this analysis has allowed us to catch sight of the fact that the developmental and narrative processes by which we become sexuate beings (biological, psychical, social, historical, and so on) are always already subject, constitutively, to multiple, relentless displacements and deviations, minute and large. These are not inconsequential and thus require close theorization.[65] Here, then, I want to complicate and deepen Irigaray's project, insisting that we cannot restrict an ethics of sexual difference, and a space-time and topology in which such ethics may flourish, to a scene between and among two already constituted sexes, man and woman. In this reading of Aristotelian place the kind of place that Irigaray calls for—for women among themselves, and for women and men in relation to each other—is in turn subtended by instances of taking place, giving place, and unpredictable, aleatory displacement. Such processes may be read into the sexual differentiation and deferral that are the *sine qua non* of sexual subject formation—the formation of subjects as sexuate and sexual beings. They might, further, give myriad possibilities for admixtures of desire and identification, a multiplicity of places in which to be and become, beyond the regime of two.

CHAPTER FIVE

Motion and Gender in the Aristotelian Cosmos

While the ontological status of motion in Aristotle has been a matter of considerable debate, it is clear from even a cursory look at the Aristotelian corpus that the problem of motion takes center stage throughout. In Heidegger's reading of Aristotle, the problem of motion (*kinēsis*) bears a profound ontological significance. Motion is after all the very way beings come to be, and therefore the investigation of motion in nature (*phusis*, from *phuein*, "to grow") is absolutely primary. As Heidegger puts it in his essay on Aristotelian *phusis*, "being-moved is explicitly questioned and understood as the fundamental mode of being."[1] For Plato, as is well known, ontological status is indexed to stasis: the greater the capacity something has for resisting change, the closer to Being it is, and conversely the more subject to change something is, the more it diverges from what is truly real (though it is perhaps telling that the Platonic dialogue most relevant to this study, the *Timaeus*, begins with Socrates's call for a depiction of the ideal city in motion).[2] But Aristotle relentlessly thematizes change and motion in many different contexts: ontological, cosmological, biological, physical and ethical. When we think of motion we tend to think of movement through space, locomotion, but Aristotle uses "motion" to refer to all sorts of change—the ontological change of coming-to-be or passing away,[3] a change in quality or quantity, as well as movement from place to place. Notably, it is first and foremost something that takes place *in matter*.[4] His primary work dealing with motion is obviously the *Physics*, which Heidegger claims is therefore Western philosophy's hidden foundational text; it is also a major theme in *De Caelo*, *De Generatione et Corruptione*, and *De Motu Animalium*, and significant observations on motion may also be found in *De Anima*, the *Nicomachean Ethics*, and the *Metaphysics*.

A comprehensive treatment of Aristotelian motion is obviously beyond the scope of this chapter, and has been treated at length in a substantial literature.[5] Rather, this chapter will focus on certain scenes of motion—of the heavens, of the simple bodies or elements, of animals and of men—and in particular on moments in which a teleological account of motion falters and cannot hold; symptomatic moments, moments of deviation, overdetermination and coincidence that, I will argue, also bear a trace of the feminine. Chapter 4 uncovered an Oedipal narrative of place and telos in the Aristotelian cosmos, from maternal place in the sublunary realm, to the impassive masculine prime mover that is the object of homoerotic love in the heavens. As a counternarrative, we also saw a fall from the outer regions of the cosmos to earth, but one not simply characterized by motion in a downward direction. While downwardness is certainly aligned with the earthbound feminine, and the upward direction with what is divine and masculine, falling to earth is also characterized by the increasing insistence of aleatory matter, the motions of plural and indeterminate matter acting *against* nature and deviating *from* it, threatening disorder and destruction. This chapter thus returns to the theme of the symptomatic feminine fall, the falling together that is the very definition of the *sumptōma*. Here, we will see how it inhabits and haunts the scene of *kinēsis* in its ontological dimension as well as in its various ontic manifestations. Beginning in the heavens, and traveling in a downward direction toward the plural movements on earth, I will first consider the nature of celestial movement, which will lead to an expanded discussion of the significance of the prime mover. Moving toward earth, I trace the transformation of heavenly circular motion into earthly cycles via the slant, the *enklisis* of the sun's ecliptic, and the subsequent movement of the elements in the sublunary realm, before turning to the motions of ensouled beings, especially the involuntary movements characteristic of animals and men. At the close of the chapter the metaphysical register reemerges, in a short discussion of Aristotle's definition of motion in terms of potentiality and actuality; this will be a propaedeutic for a fuller consideration of the resonances of sexual difference in *dunamis* and *energeia* in Chapter 6.

As we examine the world around us, we observe a cosmos relentlessly changing, and relentlessly on the move: the turnings of the heavens, the path of the sun across the sky, the swelling of the tides, the changing of the seasons, the rumbling of earthquakes, the rise of mountain chains, the flash of lightning, the gushing of springs, the falling of rain and rocks, the rotting of wood, the rushing of wind, the proliferations of living things, the purposive, involuntary, and playful movements of animals and people, the rhythms of blood and breath, the flows of electricity and magnetism and the dancing of dust motes. We are enmeshed in and constituted by motive processes. Aristotle is an acute observer of these motions—at least the ones he can perceive—and he follows Plato by considering not just locomotion under the heading of motion, but other changes such as alteration in the quality of a thing, as a leaf turns red in autumn, or growth and shrinkage. As ever, he understands all of this according to a teleological framework. The questions he grapples with have thus to do with what ends motions are directed toward, and by what means motions take place. In what way does one thing move another, and what is in a thing that allows it to be moved? Do things possess a principle of motion in themselves or are they moved only by something else, some alterity such as an exterior force coming from elsewhere, or an aim or goal as an object of desire, or perhaps an interior animating force like a soul? What different kinds of motions are there, and how can motion be defined?

As an object of inquiry in itself, motion is subject to Aristotle's famous classificatory impulse. He divides locomotion primarily into circular and rectilinear motion, and then into movements in which a mover pulls something toward itself, or pushes something away. Motions may be "according to nature," that is, occurring along the lines of natural teleology, or forced, "against nature" (*para phusin*). Motion also may be essential or accidental, continuous or intermittent. There are the perfect circular motions of the heavenly bodies and spheres. There are the self-moving motions of sublunary beings endowed with life and soul: plants, animals, and humans. There is the motion toward "proper place" of the elements. There is the notoriously difficult definition of motion in *Physics* III: "the actuality of the potentially existing qua existing potentially."[6]

Crucially, there are kinds of motion Aristotle acknowledges but does not formally identify under the heading of motion. These opaque, strictly unknowable kinds of motion inhere in matter, but appear only spontaneously and by chance, inexplicable symptoms of a precariously ordered cosmos: the motion of the falling stone that strikes a man out of the blue, the "monstrosities" of nature, and the lowly organisms designated as spontaneously generated, the result of *genesis automatos*. Insofar as these motions do not participate in teleology, they are aligned with motion by force (*bia*), the compulsions that occur *against* nature (*para phusin*) and which serve to disrupt and waylay the unfoldings of natural teleology (it would be a mistake to fully identify the two, however, since, for example, a stone thrown up in the air is a movement against nature by force, *bia*, but is not a case of *automaton*). As discussed in chapter 2, Aristotle's explanation in *Physics* II.6 of such chance forces in nature that act against nature (the earthquake, the drought, the flood that destroys crops) as a species of accidental motive cause is quite inadequate and aporetic, and here a gap opens for speculation. Perhaps we should remember that Aristotle is, despite his originality, also a Greek, and thus an inheritor of a tradition in which such phenomena were attributable to the caprices of the gods, and, more archaically, to chthonic feminine powers. His rational and rigorous inquiry into the knowable leaves these without an essence or a name, but they return, insistently, as symptoms of the cosmos.

Heidegger draws our attention to a locution appearing at the start of *Physics* II, where Aristotle speaks of things that come to be by nature as *sunestōta*, constituted or literally "standing together" (*sun* meaning "together" and *histēmi*, "to stand").[7] Heidegger's account of *phusis*, and thus being as motion, involves understanding arrival at a telos as standing forth in gatheredness, and persisting there in stability. As Walter Brogan puts it, the "being of beings is emerging into presence and standing together; it is also enduring in this presence, preserving itself in its presence."[8] For Heidegger's Aristotle, rest or repose in the telos (*en-tel-echeia*, holding-in-the-telos), is not a beyond of motion, a state when movement is finally dispensed with, but rather a modification of motion and a coming to place *granted by* motion: "Rest is a kind of movement; only that which is able to move can rest."[9] It is worth, then, contrasting such standing together, with the *sumptōma*, the "falling together" that Aristotle renders exterior and threatening to the emergence of beings, and that nonetheless, on closer examination, may be revealed as the very condition that makes "standing together" possible. Coming-to-be, after all, involves a restless equilibration of forces at every moment: false starts, ways through, and endlessly complex interactions with internal and external environments, an out-of-phaseness foregrounded in Gilbert Simondon's twentieth-century critical engagement with

Aristotelian hylomorphism.[10] Indeed, a common Renaissance representation of the Goddess Fortuna (*Tuchē* in Greek) depicts her standing on a ball, an appearance of stasis that is in truth equilibration, a pure result of innumerable unseen fallings and counterbalancings.[11] In relation to natural coming-to-be, one might well also recall the Derridean discourse on autoimmunity, a biological trope he puts to work in many different contexts and that refers to a system's producing the very forces that will destroy it, as seen when the immune system attacks not just "foreign" invaders but turns on healthy cells of the body. Simply put, internal forces of destruction function as a necessary condition of possibility, as a sine qua non, of maintaining an organism's integrity and flourishing.[12] The cell, organ, organism, population and ecosphere surely unfold in presencing, but the stability and continuity of these unfoldings are less grounds than effects of multiple processes and forces, visible and invisible, in constant activity and commerce, both agonic and harmonious. Fortune, *tuchē*, that is, the aleatory more generally, are not only what coming-to-be must resist but, as Darwin showed in the nineteenth century and as modern genetics subsequently confirms, the chance encounter is the very stuff of creation, of the becoming and proliferation of beings. Furthermore, sexual difference itself decisively and unprecedentedly breaks open the field for the aleatory encounter in nature through its capacity to enable the exchange of genetic material and engender variation.[13]

These standings and fallings—teleological desires on the one hand and the downward pull of the earth on the other—reappear symptomatically throughout the Aristotelian cosmos. Following the falling of the *sumptōma*, then, I trace the motions of the teleological Aristotelian cosmos as the story of a fall; a downward fall that is also a descent of and to the feminine.

THE MOTION OF THE HEAVENS

In chapter 4, I proposed that the dynamics at work in Aristotle's celestial realm may be characterized as primarily homoerotic and identificatory. The love of the pure, immaterial divine and the desire to approximate it drives the perfect circular motion observed in the heavens. However, even in these rarified celestial circumstances traces of matter and potentiality nonetheless persist, not only in the divine substance that makes up the stuff of the heavens but also in the very conception of the prime mover.

In *Physics* VIII.9, Aristotle describes how circular motion, unlike rectilinear motion, is eternal. When motion comes to a stop, as is inevitable in rectilinear motion, it is destroyed. Therefore of the kinds of motion, the circular is simpler and more complete (*teleios*), and what is complete is "prior in nature and in *logos* and in time."[14] Motion in a circle has no beginning and no end, is unlimited (*apeiron*), and therefore is perfect, unlike that which is limited, which has an end and a beginning, and which comes into being and passes away. Notable here is the point that the motion of the heavenly spheres, *qua* motion, is *teleios*, complete and fully arrived at its goal even as it undergoes a continual change of place. This movement can thus be sharply distinguished from the ontological motion of *genesis* or coming-to-be, in which the developing being's arrival at the *telos* of *energeia* or *entelecheia* means a transcending of motion, a certain arrival in form as a kind of endpoint.[15] Further evidence for the primacy of circular motion for Aristotle lies in the fact that all other motions are measured by them; the movements of the heavens give the periods by which time is counted and therefore in which its being is grounded.[16] The key question here is whether such motion requires a separate cause.

Aristotle's answer to this question is famously inconsistent. On the one hand, in order for such eternal, continuous, motion to exist, there must also be something continuously at work producing it (recall that the Greeks had no concept of inertia). The movement of the highest heavens must require a mover. On the other hand Aristotle argues in *De Caelo* I that the heavenly spheres move in a circle continuously and eternally simply by virtue of *their own nature*, just as fire moves up and earth moves down. They move in such a way because they are forged of a different kind of physical substance than anything we find on earth, prior to the other elements and divine, namely the *aithēr*.[17] Aristotle gives an illuminating etymology of the term used by the ancients for this self-moving heavenly substance: *aithēr* derives from *aei thein*, meaning "always runs." It is part of the nature of this substance to move in perfect circles, just as it is part of the nature of fire (as element, substance or body) to be inclined upward toward the periphery, and part of the nature of earth to be inclined downward toward the center. The spheres do what they do, travel in circles, simply by virtue of what they are, by virtue of the kind of stuff of which they are made. A cosmos that is inherently in motion by its own nature therefore has circular motion as its perfect completion, and presumably nothing exterior, no mover or motive force, is required.

However in *De Caelo* II.2, and in both the *Physics* and *Metaphysics*, Aristotle argues for the opposite view, and is clear that a separate first mover is required to keep these motions going. The argument as laid out in *Physics* VIII begins by stating that any mover must be either itself immovable or in motion. If it were in motion, the series of movers and things moved would then be unlimited and would result in an infinite regress, so there must be a mover that is itself unmoved. This unmoved mover must continuously and eternally have the power to cause motion, without effort, and without changing itself. Finally the mover must not have a magnitude, for if it did it would be either finite or infinite, and no infinite magnitude can actually exist, but neither can a finite magnitude with unlimited power (*dunamin apeiron*). The prime mover nonetheless causes eternal motion for an unlimited time (*apeiron chronon*).[18]

In this argument, the possibility that a substance might be inherently moving by its own nature is jettisoned. Nothing actually *moves itself*. Even though he clearly states in *De Caelo* II.2 that the heaven is ensouled and holds a principle or source of motion (*empsuchos kai echei kinēseōs archēn*), it is not clear that he thinks a soul is actually the kind of thing that can move itself.[19] In fact he argues in *De Anima* I.3 that soul does *not* strictly speaking move in virtue of itself (*kath' auto*), and this insight can be seen as a consequence of his rigorous insistence that all motions be resolved into *poiein* and *paschein*, a thing that produces motion and a thing that undergoes it—even if both these elements exist within the same being, and even if the agent and patient must share some common nature in order that they may interact.[20] There is always a mover and a thing moved. Aryeh Kosman, indeed, argues that the prime mover *is* the soul that moves the cosmos, such that the ensoulment of the heavens would not be found in the spheres but beyond them.[21] One might respond that the account of the *aithēr* does not require a soul of heavens as such at all, rather the *aithēr* "always runs" in virtue of simply being a certain kind of substance whose nature is to move in just that way. But then recall that, according to the *Metaphysics*, the prime mover causes motion by being *loved*, and that the heavenly spheres must also in some sense be *lovers*, *erastai*, capable of erotic desire.

So is the motion of the heavens immanent to the stuff, the substance, and ultimately perhaps the matter of the cosmos? Or does it require a transcendent unmoved mover as the source of movement, the *archē kinēseōs*, without which nothing would move at all? Many commentators have sought to reconcile this aporia, mostly by suggesting a developmental shift in Aristotle's thinking and concluding that the transcendent source of motion is more authoritative since it appears in more texts.[22] Looking more closely at key passages in *De Caelo*, as Helen Lang has done, shows that these two positions may not be contradictory. Lang directs us to Aristotle's claim that the four sublunar elements move toward their proper place—fire up, earth down, air and water up and down to a lesser degree—in virtue of an *inclination* that constitutes their nature. Inclination (*rhopē*) is understood here as constituting the natural ability to be moved, particular to each element—its very nature due to its weight or lightness, a sort of vectoral tendency in inanimate things to move toward their proper place.[23] Place, as an ordering and determinative boundary, is, in this argument in *De Caelo*, finally understood precisely as *form*, and the dynamic principle here is that which governs ontological coming-to-be, the passage from potentiality to actuality.[24]

In a teleological account, the passive potency to be moved *in a specific direction toward an end* becomes active if there is no hindrance or compulsion preventing it. Moving from the elemental to the metaphysical register, one may recall *Physics* I.9, in which matter desires form and stretches out toward it (*oregesthai*), just as the ugly desires the beautiful and the female desires the male. *Rhopē* or inclination thus appears to be an analogue of *orexis*, desire, and also of *hormē*, impulse: all teleological movements that animate the Aristotelian cosmos in physical, metaphysical, and biological registers.

Matter stretches out toward and desires form. The elements incline toward their proper places. The prime mover affects the cosmos through being loved. Just as the ugly desires the beautiful, and the female desires the male. The passive potentiality for being moved or changed, the *dunamis tou pathein* of *Metaphysics* IX, is *already oriented* toward its end. Lang thus situates the movement of elements, including that of *aithēr*, within the metaphysical scene of potentiality and actuality, an analysis that merges nicely with the Aristotelian definition of motion in these terms.[25] In her analysis the elements move toward their proper places as potentiality becoming actualized, as tending toward place as limit and determinative ordering principle, towards precisely *place as form*. While in chapter 4 I analyzed the motion of the heavens in terms of a different structure of desire, identificatory rather than anaclitic, homoerotic rather than heterosexual, Lang argues that the motion of the divine celestial substance is properly understood along the same lines as the sublunar elements: as driven by impulse, a simple proper motion proper to each kind of element. With divine substance the motion is circular, unique, eternal and without a contrary, as befits the nobler realm. Despite the fact that in the *Physics* Aristotle says that "heaven considered as a whole . . . is nowhere and in no particular place,"[26] in this account place functions as the ordering and determinative principle of the entire cosmos, and becomes in this scene indistinguishable from form and functions as form: as the elements tend toward place, matter tends toward form.

The profound workings of the teleology of potentiality and actuality emerge and become visible in this associative and analogical chain, taking us beyond the traditional discourse that would set in stark opposition a cosmos where the source of motion is either a transcendent active mover or an immanent, middle-voiced substance. What disappears from the account, however, is any possible explanation of what could constitute the hindrance, the force, or the disruption of the sublunar realm. The sublunar elements and the divine *aithēr* are rendered equivalent, moving entirely in service to their own actualization as form, magnetized from the start toward place as a polar north that is both their own *and* outside and beyond them, from which they have apparently fallen away and toward which they reach. The banishment of the aleatory is the achievement of the heavens, mark of the special divinity of the matter that is *aithēr*, neither heavy nor light, fully ordered and eternal, without coming-to-be or passing away, asymptomatic. And yet it is matter's very capacity to be other than *just* a privation or lack, neither a simple contrary or negation of form but rather "near to and substance somehow," that Aristotle insists upon in the argument of *Physics* I.9.[27]

Sublunar matter, like the female, is *symptomatic:* proximal to substance but elsewhere, bearing a capacity for being moved and being changed that involves a capacity for privation and lack but is not simply reducible to that lack, and that is never *merely* an orientation toward form but already capable of innumerable and incalculable orientations as the condition of possibility for any given orientation. Divine matter always runs, never falters, never slips or falls. Nonetheless, in the shiver of undecidability between a movement spurred by a transcendent cause and that resulting from an immanent drive, that is, between motion that is a relation to an absolute, and absolutely specific, alterity (form, the unmoved mover) and an interior capacity for movement that is the being at work of a thing that is simply the kind of thing that is at work, we might also glimpse a kind sympto-maticity. Even with perfect, divine movement that does not and can-not fall, must not fail, the potentiality at work in this locomotion reminds us of matter's continual, restless, nonself-sameness. A similar symptomaticity is also at work in this new identity of place and form, to which I will return in the discussion of simple bodies later in this chapter.

In *Speculum of the Other Woman*, Luce Irigaray investigates Plato's cave allegory at length to explore how feminine place, the maternal womb or container, is pressed into service of a journey teleologically and necessarily oriented toward the truth of Form. By attending to the *scenography* of the womblike cave out of which the prisoner must be reborn into truth, and drawing attention to the hierarchy imposed between the sensible and the intelligible, she rigorously demonstrates the ruse by which our common origins in the body of a woman is eclipsed in the metaphysical discourse. The truth of this origin in the sensible and corporeal is systematically substituted by the realm of the intelligible, the realm of the Forms, the exterior landscape where the dazzling glare of the sun illuminates all; all as One. Irigaray seeks not to simply reverse the terms of this *hystera protera,* as she calls it: for her discovering the contours of the feminine is not a simple reinstall-ing of a regime of a lost, unitary truth.[28] Instead her analysis permits us glimpses, flashes, an *Augenblick* whereby the mechanics, the mate-rial corporeal surroundings, the off-scene mechanisms in the wings and beyond the cyclorama are haltingly revealed. Through a certain attention to the medium, to scene, and to matter, and through an ini-tial strategy of *mimesis*—that bastard, feminine method that copies the masculine discourse yet inevitably leads astray—we open the pos-sibility, if not the guarantee, of chancing upon this as yet unthought difference.[29]

These dimly glimpsed contours of feminine sexual difference—described in Irigaray's early works through the imagery of the two lips, through a topology of proximity and openness rather boundedness, through an attention to corporeal vicissitudes and affects, through a certain maintenance of the *indefinite*—are congealed and frozen over and over again, in slightly different language and contexts, through-out the texts of Western philosophy. As discussed in chapter 4, Iri-garay finds the feminine echoed in Aristotelian *place*. So in this new identification of place and form in *De Caelo*, we find the proper place, first understood as the maternal body as the ordering principle or *archē* for the elements, once again subtending and eclipsed by form, the disembodied intelligible object of pure contemplation. The divine substance, the *aithēr*, in its eternal and perfect circular motion, is no longer encumbered by the unnatural, plural motions of chance—or rather, in Aristotle's terms, *not yet* encumbered by them. And yet even in the heavens there are still the planets (*planētai*), literally the wanderers or drifters (recall the feminine valence of this *planōmenon* in Plato's *Timaeus*: the receptacle/*chōra* is the wandering cause, and the womb suffers from a wandering disorder), as well as aleatory phenomena of comets and meteors. *De Caelo* II.3 lays out the argument for the plurality of diverse revolutions in the heavens that are said to be the cause of planetary motions, while comets, meteors, and the milky way are dealt with in *Meteorologica* I and attributed to transitory sublunar causes— the ignited "exhalations" of air and fire irrupting into the heavens.

Echoing Plato's spheres of the same and the different in the *Timaeus*, Aristotle argues in *De Caelo* II.3 that the eternal, perfect, circular movement produces its own opposite, the central point of rest that is its axis. This center is earth, which in turn requires its own opposite, fire, and the intermediate bodies (air and water). So there is established a vertical axis of up and down, center and periphery. But because the elements are not eternal but transform into one another in an imitation of heavenly circularity, there is coming-to-be (*genesis*). Variations in the heavens in the form of a plurality of revolutions are necessary for this coming-to-be to occur, for if there were just one simple heavenly motion, and setting aside the indeterminacies of aleatory matter, the four sublunar elements would remain unchanged. Here, then, the narrative of the fall at the heart of this argument: Perfect, eternal, circular movement produces, as its *consequence*, a structure of center and periphery. Fire moves toward upward toward the periphery, is more noble, and partakes more in the nature of form, while earth that has more of the nature of matter moves toward the center. Aristotle reminds us that while people think that wind and air have *less* form than earth, "in truth they are more a 'this' [*tode ti*] and a form [*eidos*] than earth."[30] Then there are the unnatural motions, lowly disruptive latecomers, gatecrashers on the scene: "What is *against nature* is subsequent to [*husteron*] what is natural; what is *against nature* is a derangement [*ekstasis*] in the coming-to-be of what is natural."[31]

Haunting the perfect and eternal motion of the divine realm of the heavens, then, are the necessary traces of aleatory matter, displaced and showing up where it does not belong in the case of comets and meteors, of the feminine wanderings of the planets, of the slant of the ecliptic, of the unnatural *ekstases* that plague natural becoming. An inconsistency in the narrative reveals a tremble in the unfolding of potentiality toward actuality, a hint of the operations of the feminine symptom, whereby an alternate shadowy account of immanent sources of motion persists alongside the dominant and explicit account of a separate, masculine, divine entity. Furthermore, alongside the now strangely permeable boundary between the heavens and the sublunary, we can discern, dimly and intermittently, a certain intersubstitutability of feminine place and masculine form; the plural, dispersed, factical maternal corporeality of place gives way to a hierarchy of proper place along a vertical axis, imperceptibly folding into the circular motion of the heavenly bodies, all now caught up in the teleology of the impassive and paternal prime mover.

THE PRIME MOVER

As it is told in the *Metaphysics* as well as in *De Generatione et Corruptione*, the prime mover is a first principle that exists by simple necessity. Perfect, complete, and self-sufficient, its activity is like the best we can have only for a short time, but it exists in this state of pleasurable actuality continuously and eternally. Because thinking (*noei*) is in itself the best thing ("thinking according to itself is of the best [*aristou*] according to itself"), the divine prime mover's existence is that of thought thinking itself.[32] Despite the explicit claim that the prime mover is beyond all of physical nature, fully complete in its end (*en-tel-echeia*, holding in its end), and therefore beyond all splitting into active and passive components that is characteristic of bodies in motion, within "thought thinking itself" there is a complex interweaving of activity/passivity and *dunamis/energeia*. To properly appreciate this we need to look more closely at the argument from the *Metaphysics* wholesale.

Here I follow Christopher Long's translation, which perspicaciously foregrounds the persistence and irreducibility of *dunamis* (capacity, potency, potentiality) and the embodied resonances of sensory and perceptual processes (touching, holding, seeing) in Aristotle's articulation of thought thinking itself:

> But the being-at-work thinking [*noēsis*], the one that thinks
> according to itself, is a thinking of what is best according to itself,

and especially so with what is most of all [thinking]. But thinking
[*nous*] thinks itself by participating in that which is thought [*kata
metalēpsin tou noētou*], for by touching [*thinganōn*] and thinking it
becomes that which is thought with the result that thinking and that
which is thought are the same. For what is receptive of that which
is thought and of the very being [*to gar dektikon tou noētou kai tēs
ousias*] is thinking [*nous*], and it is at work when it has them [*echōn*];
therefore it is the being-at-work more than the receptivity that
thinking has [*echein*] that seems divine, and its theorizing [*hē theōria*]
is pleasantest and best.[33]

Thought thinking itself would seem to require or assume the necessity
of a separation between thinker and thought, a diremption of subject
and object, active and passive, and this is indeed the heart of Hegel's
later understanding of *energeia*. But Aristotle is keen to deflect any
notion that the prime mover is divisible. Ferrarin writes of Hegel's
reading of the Aristotelian prime mover:

> Thus Aristotle's indivisible *noēsos noēseōs* is turned into a
> dialectic activity of thinking that divides itself into an active and a
> passive side and at the same time remains at home with itself, in its
> own element. For Hegel the movement of thought is the perfectly
> self-enclosed and complete (*teleia*, in Aristotelian terminology)
> activity of thinking that, as a subject, relates itself to itself as an
> object. Here subject and object are . . . the opposites within—and
> of—their unity. Hegel knows that divine thinking is indivisible for
> Aristotle; the apparent duality of subject and object introduced
> by Hegel within thinking is his understanding of the identity of
> intellect and intelligible that Aristotle affirms, and that for Hegel
> is a perfect example of *Beisichselbstsein*, thought's being at home
> with itself.[34]

Long, in turn, moves away from the language of subject and object,
describing the participation of the "potency for thinking" in the
"activity of thinking" as an ecological encounter: "Aristotle thematizes this receptive capacity as a kind of active condition, a *hexis*, into
which the soul settles itself as into its very nature."[35] Long creatively
reads this potential or capacity in *noēsis*, in thought itself, as a strange
sort of *dunamis*, one that is not associated with materiality but that
rather persists as an immanent condition of possibility of divine (and
human) thinking as relationality as such, understood as a middle-
voiced encounter of cooperation between the capacity for thinking
and the thing thought. Long's phenomenological reading downplays
Aristotle's insistence that the prime mover be *free of* potentiality or
dunamis and its persistence in eternal completeness and actuality, by

emphasizing *dunamis* as capacity or an ability that is continually at work rather than in abeyance or yet to be actualized.

While the divine is emphatically not in motion of any kind (*akinēton*), Aristotle nonetheless emphasizes repeatedly that the divine is a living being (*einai zōion*) in *energeia*, in a continual and eternal state of being at work: "And life [*zōē*] moreover really belongs [to god]: for the actuality [*energeia*] of thought is life, and god is that actuality [*energeia*]: and the actuality of god according to itself is life best and eternal. We say that god is life best and eternal, for life and continuous existence [*aiōn sunechēs*] and eternity belong to god, for this is god."[36] The actuality or activity (*energeia*) of god is the property of living things: life, but a superlative "best and eternal" (*ariston kai aidion*) life, not a life subject to the vicissitudes of matter and temporality, of coming-to-be or passing away. What are we to make of this word *energeia*, "being in the work," especially when there is no motion or matter on or with which to work? Heidegger parses *energeia* into *en-ergon*, being at work, both in the sense of the activity of working, producing, and in the sense of the end product of work. His understanding of *energeia* in the context of *poiēsis* (production) is often understood as shifting the focus from *energeia* away from the teleological sense of being at an end, being in finality or completion, and toward the sense of a process, that of being in production. Ferrarin, for example, summarizing the views of Strauss, Arendt, and Aubenque as well as his own, says that Heidegger "suppresses any sense of finality from *energeia*."[37] Although Heidegger's remarks in the lectures on Aristotle's *Metaphysics* IX.1–3 may support this view, his comments elsewhere tell a different story. In *The Essence of Human Freedom*, he says "the workhood of work consists in its *being finished*"; and in the *Phusis* essay: "In Greek thought *energeia* means 'standing in the work,' where 'work' means that which stands fully in its 'end.'"[38] Here, finality and completion—the work in its perfectedness and "producedness" are shown to be central to the Heideggerian understanding of *energeia*. If we take *energeia* as signifying being in completion rather than being at work, are we simply assimilating it to *entelecheia* and making it equivalent? What becomes of its lexical specificity? Is there any force in its being in a process that is not primarily and essentially teleological?

To help answer this question, recall Aristotle's affirmation that the intellect is not in a state of potentiality in which it may later be the recipient (*dektikon*) of the object of thought, even if that object is, as it must be, the best thing qua its own best activity, thinking. Rather, the intellect fully possesses (*echei*) thought, and, in that possession, contemplation (*theōria*) is the most pleasurable and the best activity.[39] In his explanation of *energeia* in *Metaphysics* IX.6, as well as in his discussion of the nature of pleasure in the *Nicomachean Ethics* X.4 where *theōria* reigns supreme among pleasurable activities, Aristotle gives *theōria* as an example of that kind of *energeia* which is sufficient in itself. In some activities, those with an end or limit such as building or weaving, *energeia* resides in the completion of the activity: the house built, the garment woven. However in other cases, namely contemplation, seeing (*horasis*), life in the soul, and in happiness, *energeia* resides in itself, is complete and sufficient in itself. At the same time (*hama*), says Aristotle, one both sees and has seen, contemplates and has contemplated.[40] Ferrarin points out that in these cases of *energeia* time, as such, brings nothing new.[41] The distinction between past and present—and therefore also between present and future, indeed time itself—is obliterated. Aristotle achieves this by means of the *hama*, the small word upon which so much hung in my earlier discussion of place, where it functioned chiasmatically to articulate the cosmos and its place, conjoining and separating in both temporal and spatial dimensions. The little *hama* thus explicitly seeks a unity, collapsing the present and perfect tenses, while also marking and giving the possibility of a temporal difference, the possibility of a time other than the present. One can say that the kind of activity that is then not temporal, not in movement, not divisible, but instead a living continuous state of completion and fulfillment and enjoyment, a thinking that is the thinking of thinking: this is the *energeia* of the prime mover. Insofar, however, that in the Aristotelian text this divine activity of thinking receives (*dektikon*), touches (*thigganōn*), holds (*echōn, echein*), sees (*theōria*), is alive (*zōēn*), and is in the metaleptic work of participation, it also in its articulation bears traces of that very materiality, embodiment, and temporality from which it is purportedly free as a superlatively perfect form of life.

In *Metaphysics* XII, then, we apprehend the divine as pure thought, perfect and separate, but this apprehension also *takes place* through an activity and receptivity that is necessarily and irreducibly embodied and perceptual as well as noetic. The transcendence and disembodiment of the divine itself appears as a ruse of language, a function of the superlative taking wing into pure abstraction on the basis of the concrete operation of the comparative. Despite Aristotle's insistence on the motionlessness of divine *energeia*, we can discern a certain movement in the "thinking of thinking thinking," *noēsis noēseōs noēsis*, of *Metaphysics* XII.9, but it is a conceptual or noetic movement, a movement of *logos:* specifically the movement of and from the genitive in relation to the nominative.[42] Long finds here once again a dimension of potency, as the genitive announces the participation of thought in itself, in its own capacity for thought. What are we to make of this movement and potentiality eviscerated of all materiality, haunted by a difference that is immanent within thinking itself, a sign of life without bodies, without matter, and without time? Long's immanentist reading moves quickly over the radicality of this transcending of matter in the figure of the prime mover, instead emphasizing its rootedness in the relationality of perception and thus its continuity with the human experience of thinking as apprehension and encounter with alterity. But the prime mover nonetheless relates only to itself, *in illo tempore,* and it is precisely in its transcendent separation from the material world, and its *impassivity* (as *apathēs*) that it is able to inspire that desire, that *eros,* that sets and maintains the whole universe in eternal motion.

The source, *archē,* of all motion is therefore divine, eternal, living substance, thought thinking itself, the best, most noble entity which has itself no materiality, magnitude, or dimension. It causes motion not by reaching out to the world and acting upon it, but simply by being loved: "it causes motion as being an object of love [*kinei dē hōs erōmenon*], whereas all other things cause motion because they are themselves in motion."[43] Even though it is the object of love, the passive object of *erōmenon,* it remains *impassive* in the face of this love. It does not love back, contemplate outward, respond in any way, but is rather supremely unconcerned with the cosmos or indeed anything outside itself.[44] Nothing issues *from* the prime mover, its existence is only as end. It is separate, though not limited: it has no magnitude, and therefore is neither finite—bounded—nor infinite in space, and is eternal, without a boundary or limit in time. If it is separate but without a boundary, the boundary separating it from us must therefore be our boundary, the boundary of the cosmos. The prime mover exists beyond, outside, in the nonplace and nonspace beyond the outer limits of the cosmos; as such, one might say it is pure exteriority and alterity. As hard or even impossible as it is for us (or at least for us post-Kantians) to think or know such transcendent exteriority, the Aristotelian prime mover is rather the *most* intelligible entity, it is intelligibility and intellection in its highest manifestation. But its separateness also consists in its *energeia* as being-in-completeness, pure self-sufficiency, its self-referentiality, the closed circle of its autocontemplation. Fully absorbed in contemplating itself, the thought and thinker are so intimately intertwined that there is no more room for a distinction, no possibility of diremption. It is in this unconcerned self-sufficiency, in the topology of a figure whose self-referential circularity is so utterly complete and closed up in itself that it has no boundary at all, that it most directly reflects a fantasy of autonomous, impermeable, self-sufficient, autarkical, masculinity.

In the figure of the prime mover, Aristotle therefore provides us with an elegant solution to the beginning of motion. All things in motion, if they are not self-moved, require a prior source of motion to move them. Just as the self-motion of animals is understood through recourse to the ends of desire, the problem of the beginning of motion in the cosmos is solved by recourse to the end of motion. That is, the beginning of motion is the end of motion, and the end of motion is also the beginning. As Aristotle understands the transmission of motion as resolving necessarily into active and passive, then the prime mover, in its capacity as the origin of motion, as the *archē kinēseōs*, is irreducibly passive and decidedly not a motive cause like the sperm or an advisor. It is not passive in the sense that an external mover passes motion to it and transforms it, but it is passive insofar as it is loved, and as such it is the passive object of an action, the action of loving. As such, we might argue that at its heart, *energeia* in its very purest form must possess precisely the capacity for that which it has no part of; it must have a capacity not just in the attenuated sense of embracing thought, but also the capacity to be passive, to undergo, to be affected: *dunamis tou pathein*. At the place where *telos* is *archē*, where end is source, beginning and principle, so the pure activity of *energeia*—thought thinking itself—must also possess another kind of *dunamis* explicitly associated with matter and with the feminine, it must be able to undergo, *paschein*. However, as conceived in chapter 4, the love that comes its way is identificatory and mimetic, a homoerotic love that thrives on the very impassivity of its object, its very resistance to the lover's advances. The prime mover must therefore be the passive object of a love that it assiduously resists, indeterminately passive *and* impassive. And indeed, in *Metaphysics* IX Aristotle follows his description of *dunamis tou pathein* with that of a *dunamis*, that is an "impassive state" (*hexis apatheias*), the power to resist any degradation.[45] It is thus precisely *as* aporetic—as passive/impassive, as singular/multiple, and as active/motionless—that the prime mover exerts and maintains its peculiar and exceptional sovereignty in the Aristotelian cosmos.

FALLING TO EARTH: THE SUN'S *ENKLISIS* AS FEMININE SYMPTOM

As we have repeatedly seen, in the sublunary realm as well as in the heavens, there operates a mimetic teleology of nature which, says Aristotle in *On Generation and Corruption*, "always and in all things strives after the better [*oregesthai tou beltionos*]."[46] Being is better than not being, but some things cannot always have being, because they are too far away from the source, the *archē*. Instead they perpetually *come into being*: "God, therefore, following the course which still remained open, perfected the universe by making coming-to-be a perpetual process; for in this way 'being' would acquire the greatest possible coherence, because the continual coming-to-be of coming-to-be is the nearest approach to eternal being."[47] It is worth noting here the strangeness of this evocation of a demiurgic God, creating and perfecting, since Aristotle elsewhere consistently maintains that the cosmos itself is eternal and never came to be, that there was not a time before it in which such creation or perfection might have occurred. Indeed it should by now be clear that the divine prime mover is supremely impassive and utterly unconcerned with the goings-on of the cosmos. The passage, too, speaks of the approach, the nearness sought by sublunary beings to eternal beings, and of the continuity of generation through time as the proof of that approach.

In emulating the heavenly bodies' circular motion, the simple bodies—the elements of earth, air, fire, and water—transform into one another in a perpetual cycle over time.[48] For their part, living beings also maintain themselves in continuous cycles over time at the level of form, at the level of the species. While this cyclical continuity is mostly attributed to teleological mimesis and identificatory imitation of what is best, there is also a more direct, efficient and material cause of sublunar generations and destructions. Seasonal generation, cyclical generation, is caused not only by the perfect circularity of the heavens, but by an inexplicable obliquity in the heavens, a deviation in that perfection: the double movement back and forth of the sun and the planets along the slant of the ecliptic, the band of sky where the signs of the zodiac are found. The motion of the sun is both perfect and circular, and along an inclined circle (*kata ton loxon kuklon*), giving both continuous circularity and a double rectilinear movement, away from and towards the earth.[49] The inclination (*enklisis*) causes this irregular (*anōmalos*) movement, the approach and withdrawal which is the cause of both the generations and destructions that occur in the annual cycle of the seasons.

Motion in a circle is more perfect than rectilinear motion because it is continuous and uninterrupted, but in the sublunary realm this circular perfection can only be manifested in cyclicity, that is, in a purely temporal, nonspatial kind of circularity. Insofar as sublunar beings are subject both to coming-to-be and passing away (*genesis* and *phthora*), their being is maintained continuously and cyclically at the level of form, *eidos*, and not numerically. From a spatial perspective, and from the perspective of the individual being, sublunary motions are linear, not circular. Nature, then, is able to achieve the excellence of continuous, eternal being neither in the rectilinear motions of simple bodies toward proper place, nor in the short and unidirectional existence of each individual lifespan, but through elemental cycles of transformation, and in the being of the species or form that maintains itself perpetually over time, in cycles, according to the approach and withdrawal of the sun.

Aristotle does not attribute to God the operative imperfection that permits sublunary cyclicity, the slant or incline, the *enklisis*, *kata ton loxon*. The vagaries of sublunary coming-to-be and passing away, subject to the plurality, accident, and chance that are the very marks of our world, thus participate in the whole of nature, in what is best, are able to imitate the perfect cycles of the heavens, due to a tilt, a slant, a swerve away, an *enklisis* or clinamen: something inexplicable which has the character of chance or accident, of something aleatory and symptomatic. The sun's queer obliquity traverses the boundary between the heavens and the earth, providing a material link or *articulation* between sublunar and superlunary realms. The *enklisis* and *ekstasis* of the ecliptic thus provides the material and motive causality for the sublunary phenomena of generation and destruction through the rectilinear motion of approach and withdrawal—as the sun approaches, bringing light and heat, it acts directly upon the natural world causing it to spring to life, to grow and bloom; as it withdraws, it causes withering and decline. In the annual cycle of the seasons, the sun therefore *also* and *coincidentally* acts in concert with cosmological teleology, directly transmitting the perfection of cyclicity by providing a material and efficient cause for the sublunary cycles of coming-to-be, and passing away, which are then seen over time to imitate the circular motions of the heavens.

In his deconstructive analysis of Aristotelian cosmology John Protevi approaches the sun's exceptionality from a somewhat different angle, reading the sun itself as a supplement to a worldly order of perpetual cyclicity: "the thematic paternal immanence of species-generation is broken by the irreducible exteriority of the sun."[50] Protevi reads the sun as posterior and supplementary to the teleology of nature, as representing the "solar disruption of its immanence."[51] But in the downward narrative I am tracing here, Aristotle's sublunar nature is not prior to cosmological causation, but posterior, later, *husteron*. Aristotle's teleological systematicity prioritizes ends, and the prime mover of the heavens is the highest end of all, and thus comes first. As discussed in chapter 2, the kinds of necessity that issue from ends are hierarchized as follows: first comes the simple necessity that is the province of the prime mover and the heavenly bodies (that which could not be otherwise), and then hypothetical necessity—that which issues from the teleological processes of nature and art in the sublunar realm. The third kind of necessity is that of the disagreeable compulsions and obstructions that act *against nature* to prevent ends from being realized. This does not *only* function when the achievement of desired ends is vitiated, but in Aristotle's physics and metaphysics (if not his biology) it is only disclosed as such when it disrupts teleological processes, and is therefore rendered parasitic and supplementary to the different kinds of necessity that issue from *teloi*.

It is in this context of the hierarchy of necessity that one can read the phenomenon of the ecliptic. Insofar as it participates in the circular motion of the heavens out of love for the prime mover, the sun participates in simple necessity: it could not be otherwise. But insofar as the sun is also the direct, motive cause of the comings to be and destructions of the sublunar realm, an active *archē kinēseōs* with concrete material effects, it participates in the sublunar order of physical necessity. That is, the sun gives the very possibility of being and not being, being precisely as subject to generation and destruction. By means of its motion toward and away from the earth, it transmits to the sublunar realm the natural cycles of generation and destruction, creating the very passage between being and not being: "Coming-to-be goes on continuously; for the movement will produce coming-to-be uninterruptedly by bringing near and withdrawing the 'generator' [*to genētikon*]."[52] In a sense the sun is like the instrument of articulation referred to in *De Motu Animalium*, the *organōn* likened to a ball and socket joint, which articulates practical *telos*, desiring soul, and desiring body at the place where beginning and end coincide. Thus the sun participates in and crosses both superlunary and sublunary realms, transgressing the boundary between them. In its simple necessity it cannot be otherwise, but it also provides for the possibility that the sublunary realm might always be otherwise, that the contradictories of coming-to-be and passing away might always pertain.

The uncaused falling together, in the figure of the sun, of profoundly different and separate orders of causation—material and teleological—points once again to the symptomatic character of the *enklisis* of the ecliptic. For cyclicity is not just the result of the periodic approach and withdrawal of the sun, but the realm of changing things also moves cyclically through mimicry or imitation: "Indestructible things are imitated by changing things, such as fire and earth. For these, too, are always in activity; for they move in virtue of themselves and have motion in themselves."[53] The diurnal circular motion and annual cycles of the sun qua indestructible celestial body make it a model to be imitated by self-moving sublunary bodies, as well as an agent of motion through the material contacts of heat and light. The sun plays an overdetermined role in the cosmos, crossing over the boundary set by the moon between heaven and earth, at once model for and agent of the motions of natural teleology.

This causal overdetermination has exactly the same structure as that uncanny, symptomatic confluence of opposed forces which results in the conception of a female in sexual reproduction. In the case of the female offspring, a chance deviation or error in the material conditions of conception is required to create a female, but the existence of females is also teleologically necessary so that the species may reproduce itself in perpetuity. Furthermore, the slant or *enklisis* of the sun's ecliptic bears both a lexical and conceptual relation to the later Epicurean notion of the clinamen, derived as they both are from the verb *klinō*, to slope or slant. The clinamen, in Lucretius's explanation of the Epicurean atomic theory (it does not appear in Epicurus's extant writings), is the imperceptible swerve in the trajectory of an atom that takes place at no determinable time or place, and with no discernible cause. This uncaused and unaccountable swerve guarantees that atoms will not be bound by internal necessity, and that they can strike each other in new ways (according to Lucretius without the *clinamen* atoms would simply fall downward like raindrops and never encounter one another). The swerve also provides an explanation for free will, in that it breaks the chain of cause and effect which would subject all being to an inescapable determinism (though the mechanism by which an uncaused atomic swerve reappears at the level of a willing being's conscious thought is unexplained).[54]

In the twentieth century, the trope of the *clinamen* has been taken up and retheorized by a constellation of thinkers including Gilles Deleuze, Alfred Jarry, Michel Serres, Jacques Lacan, Harold Bloom, Louis Althusser, Jean-Luc Nancy, and Jacques Derrida, who have found within it a repressed and radical element of indeterminate excess, and who have deployed it in various contexts including physics, psychoanalysis, 'pataphysics, poetics, and political philosophy.[55] Derrida, with a particular interest in the resonances of the *clinamen* for the divagations of writing, articulates it with a familiar chain of concepts: necessity, luck, chance, symptom, lapsus, incident, accidentality, cadence, coincidence, and most germane to the present purpose, the many resonances of the notion of the fall—befalling, declining, letting the chips fall where they may: "One can fall well or badly, have a lucky or unlucky break—but always by dint of not having foreseen—of not having seen in advance and ahead of oneself. In such a case, when man or the subject falls, the fall affects his upright stance and vertical position by engraving in him the detour of a *clinamen*, whose effects are inescapable."[56]

The intellectual, literary, political, and especially artistic contexts in which the aleatory has emerged as an explicit theme in the twentieth century have, strangely enough, stringently avoided any acknowledgement of its connection with the feminine. One thinks of Dada and the automatism of the Surrealists, their practices of automatic drawing, automatic writing, and so on, or of the abstract exercises of John Cage and Merce Cunningham's aleatory dance/music collaborations in which consultations with the Chinese divination tool, the *I Ching*, generated both sound and movement. One of the most iconic images of the Surrealist movement is Man Ray's photograph, "Waking Dream Séance," depicting the leading lights of Surrealism crowded ominously around Simone Collinet-Breton, André Breton's wife, the automatic typist (Fig. 1). As Rudolf Kuenzli puts it: "The woman here becomes the medium, the hands, through which the dreams of the

Surrealists are put on paper. She is, so to speak, a recording machine. She of course has no dreams of her own but faithfully encodes men's dreams."[57] The men attend assiduously, almost ravenously, to Breton's automatic productions: as the Surrealists' amanuensis she is indeed an avatar for automatism itself, but there is no suggestion that she is its *source*, the *archē kinēseōs* of the writing thus produced. The links between the automatisms of the female body and psyche that collectively are brought under the term hysteria, and the nineteenth-century history of women as spiritual mediums, as vessels for messages from another realm, to the psychoanalytic and philosophical discourses of woman as not all, and as nontruth, are self-evident and well attested. But while the feminine is in these discourses certainly *symptomatic* of the masculine economy in which they emerge, the feminine has never yet been explicitly associated with the aleatory as such, with the chance swerve of the *clinamen* and its capricious, evental, power, except perhaps unconsciously, as the unremitting silence on the matter on the part of the litany of male artists and intellectuals who engage with the aleatory may attest.

It is worth noting, then, that the swerve or fall (recall the German *Zufall*, "chance") of the *clinamen* is no less necessary for an atomistic universe than it is for Aristotle's teleological cosmos. The Epicureans employ the *clinamen* as a way to escape the determinism of material necessity and thereby account for the apparently undetermined phenomenon of free will. While the *clinamen* itself is a later development, Aristotle himself is profoundly and relentlessly opposed to atomist conceptions of nature: he consistently dismisses Democritean arguments in the doxographies, he judges the material cause to be the least significant of the causes, and he relegates the kind of force (*bia*) or degeneration (*ekstasis*, what no longer stands) that operates "against nature" to a supplementary and nonessential role in his various typologies of necessity. Material necessity as the inevitability of cause and effect in nature barely merits a mention in Aristotle's philosophical accounts of necessity, and only comes to the fore in the biological examples, precisely because, contrary to the later Newtonian account of physics as governed by universal laws, Aristotle finds it neither ordered nor regular. Order is to be found only in teleological processes, governed by formal and final causes, while the intrusive, unpredictable and "uncaused" movements of matter are rather always exceptional: they are the very thing that separates "for the most part" from "always." The *clinamen*, however, represents a

Figure 1.   Man Ray, "Waking Dream Seance: Groupe Surrealiste (Surrealist Group)." © 2014 Man Ray Trust / Artists Rights Society (ARS), NY / ADAGP, Paris.

disruption in both kinds of system. It provides a necessary element of spontaneity or randomness in a physically deterministic universe. In Aristotle, we find its cognate as an uncaused declination by which the circular perfection of the heavenly spheres is transformed into finite, rectilinear, earthly, cyclical rhythms of approach and retreat. The downward pull of earthly matter to which the sun is subject, a feminine fall to earth, to proper place, to embodiment, enclosure and rest (at the limits of the solstices), provides the necessary link between the rarified heavens, realm of the eternal and divine, and the world we inhabit, the world we touch, hear, and see, and in which earthly matter provides the ever-present possibility that things in their perpetual striving for perfection will be thwarted, halted, and thrown off the rails. Indeed, Aristotle remarks that although coming-to-be occurs with the approach of the sun, and passing away when it withdraws, this regularity is also undermined by aleatory matter: "it often happens [*sumbainei*] that things pass away in too short a time owing to the commingling of things with one another, for their matter being irregular [*anomalous*] and not everywhere the same, their comings-to-be must also be irregular, sometimes too quick and sometimes too slow, and through this the coming-to-be of certain things may cause the passing-away of others."[58]

As Althusser stresses, the *clinamen* as the atomic swerve provides just the possibility of the *encounter*, the undetermined conjuncture between disparate entities, both in nature and in history. In Aristotle, for whom both natural and human worlds are equally characterized by a striving toward the telos of what is best, this enclitic encounter—here understood as the encounter between heaven and earth—can only appear under the sign of failure, and yet it symptomatically provides very the condition of possibility for the multidirectional plurality of motion in the sublunar world.

Traced here is a story of a descent, a falling to earth, that is also therefore a fall from masculine perfection to feminine mutability. There is a hierarchy beginning with the prime mover, moving to the outer circle or first heaven of the fixed stars, thence to the spheres of the planets, to the sun, and at last to the sublunary realm. Moving away from the eternal substantiality of *energeia*, the entities we encounter—whether the simple elements, inanimate objects, or living things—have the increasing capacity to be otherwise: to move, to change, to grow, to interrupt and be disrupted, and to cease being, and alongside this narrative of a fall into mortality and alterability, with this proliferation of forms of motion, comes a diminishing capacity for perfection. These sublunar entities are nonetheless to be understood as being in a continual state of striving for the perfection from which they are constitutively disbarred; indeed one might say it is this very disbarment that maintains them in perpetual motion. Aristotle, therefore, gives extended teleological accounts both of the motions both of simple bodies as well as of the living things and artifacts that populate the world around us, and these I treat next.

THE SIMPLE BODIES OR ELEMENTS

The four sublunar elements move by nature toward their proper places—fire moves up, as does air to a lesser extent; earth moves down, as does water to a lesser extent. These simple bodies or elements, indeed, are said to possess their own proper, *oikeios*, motion.[59] Following *De Caelo*, which devotes two entire books to the problem of the sublunary elements and their motion, the question of *how* the elements are moved without an internal source of motion is resolved with a recourse to the notions of potentiality and actuality.[60] Here, place is understood under the rubric of *form* and the natural inclinations as potentials to be moved in a particular direction, toward their proper places, along the vertical axis. But how has place made this quite extraordinary transition to *form*?

Aristotle makes it quite clear in *Physics* IV.4 that though place might have the same *shape* (*morphē*) as the thing inhabiting it, it must be separate and separable from it, because things move in and out of place, as water moves in and out of a jug. But the *proper place* of the elements seems to have a rather different character, because as earth conjoins with earth in the downward direction, according to its heavy nature, and as fire conjoins with fire in the upward direction according to its light nature, each joins with a whole, and it is not clear that this kind of elemental aggregation of selfsame material has *form as such* in the same way that, say, an animal or a bed has a form.[61] Further, as discussed in chapter 4, this move on the part of Aristotle has the effect of managing and overcoming what Irigaray analyzes as the psychical threat of maternal-feminine place and instead installs a kind of accession to the divine at the scene of sublunar elemental motion. Aristotle thus explains that it is the extremity (for the light) and the center (for the heavy) that in a way "constitute the form of the body they enclose" insofar as they provide the boundary for these bodies that move toward their own place (*ton autou topon*).[62] So place is *not quite exactly* form but functions just like it in this context. The more precise claim is that "motion towards its proper place is for each thing motion towards its proper form,"[63] and what is significant here is that "proper" of "proper place" is no longer in this context the "*oikeois*" of *Physics* IV, with its connotations of the feminine hearth and home, but "*autou*," the place in and of itself. It is, oddly enough, *motion itself* now that comes to bear the designation "*oikeios*"—the *oikeios kinēsis* of the simple bodies is thus sharply contrasted with unnatural movements that happen by force, *bia*. And here, in the motion of simple bodies toward their proper places, we catch yet another glimpse of matter initiating its own motion under a feminine sign, in the mode of obedient, natural, orectic motion toward final cause. In an almost imperceptible shift, perhaps in the idea that the boundary of the sublunary world itself gives form, we can once again hear an echo of Plato's *Timaeus* and its analogy of the cosmos with a living being.[64] Aristotle, too, calls the motions that weight and lightness hold within themselves a *zōpuron*—a spark or hot coal, literally a "living fire."[65]

Consolidating this biological, and thus teleological scene, Aristotle then goes on in *De Caelo* IV.3 to forge an extended analogy of such movements with those of a living body that might proceed toward growth, or equally toward health or disease. If a light thing is generated from a heavy, as air from water, he tells us, "it progresses to the upper region. Once arrived, it is light—no longer 'becomes' but 'is.' Clearly then it is arriving from potentiality [*dunamis*] to actuality [*entelecheia*]. . . . For the same reason what already is and exists as earth or fire moves towards its own place unless something prevents it. So too nutriment and the curable, when there is nothing to clog or hinder, enter at once on their motion."[66] This analogy is continued and expanded in the difficult passage that concludes *De Caelo* IV.4, where a hierarchy of value is clearly established along the vertical axis. Aristotle reiterates that that which surrounds (*to periechon*) is on the side of form, where as the surrounded (*periechomenon*) is the matter. And further, that which is above is the determinate (*hōrismenou*) whereas that which is below is the matter (which, as we know from other contexts, is indeterminate). Finally, we are told that matter subtends both weight and lightness, just as it capable of harboring both disease and health, and here the vertical hierarchy of value becomes strikingly clear: weight is on the side of disease, lightness on the side of health.[67]

If this is a satisfactory account of the motions of the simple bodies in an upward or downward direction through the dynamism of potentiality and actuality in an analogy with teleological becoming, something else now stands in need of explanation. That is, the elements continue to be as mixed up together as they ever were and do not seem to show any sign of moving toward a state of separation. As well as the acknowledging the presence of hindrances and forces against nature, Aristotle also, in *On Generation and Corruption* II.10, attributes the continuing heterogeneity of the sublunar realm to a continuous cycle in which the simple bodies change into one another in an effort to emulate the perfect circular motion of the heavens: "For when Air comes-to-be from Water, and Fire from Air, and Water again from Fire, we say that coming-to-be has completed the cycle, because it has come back to its starting-point. Motion in a straight line," he concludes, "is also continuous because it imitates [*mimoumenē*] cyclical motion."[68] Each rectilinear motion upward or downward, when seen from a larger perspective, is thus a temporary move that participates in a greater circularity. And this cyclicity is also that which issues from the simple necessity of the heavens, as noted in the previous section.

In this more sweeping conception then, the end of proper place that represents the actualization of those essential potentials, lightness and heaviness, simply evaporates. Proper place in this perspective becomes a superficial telos, a specious and temporary stopping point, and the rest and repose which things find there—which is after all just the privation of motion—is superseded and overcome. The spatial relation of the container and the contained in rectilinear motions is revealed as a just a pit stop, subsumed in the greater project of a cosmic teleology that extends beyond the sublunar realm. The shift in perspective that allows rectilinear motion to be subsumed in circular motion is precisely a shift from a spatial understanding of motion to a temporal one. It is only over time that the local motions of the sublunary realm reveal themselves as cyclical, as well as rectilinear. The spatial circularity of the motions of the heavens is thus imitated in the sublunar realm in the temporal dimension, through the continuity of cyclicity.

There is a curious reversal here of our modern association of linear modes of temporality with masculinity and cyclical modes with femininity.[69] In the account of place as a surrounding vessel in *Physics IV*, it may be understood along with Irigaray as feminine containment. But in the account of the simple bodies and the movements in an upward and downward direction in *De Caelo*, place is recast as form, now a noble and masculine boundary toward which matter might yearn in the teleological schema of potentiality and actuality. So in the first instance, feminine time in the Aristotelian cosmos is less the cyclical time of bodily rhythms and seasonal cycles, but rather a staccato linearity in which things move toward temporary places of rest, or more specifically, the downward drag of weighty earth, analogized with diseased matter, opposed to the noble upward motion of fire. Linear time in Aristotle is not yet the modern masculine time of historical progress described by Kristeva: "time as project, teleology, linear and prospective unfolding; time as departure, progression and arrival—in other words the time of history."[70] Cyclical time, the time of nature, the time of continuity, of contemplation and of divine metaphysical perfection thus carries for Aristotle a masculine mark.

Linear time—discontinuous and ultimately unsatisfactory—represents the less perfect, fallen time of the feminine, a time whose fate it is to be interrupted by a greater order of things, the order of the divine cosmos.

This association of finitude as such with the feminine appears quite remarkable from our post-Heideggerian perspective, in which finitude is the definitive feature of Dasein's existence. In ancient Greece by contrast, death and birth, the limit markers of corporeal and worldly existence, are distinctively in the domain of the feminine: women are responsible for birth, for death rites and mourning, and are rigorously associated with attachment to the corporeal, both in tragedy and philosophy. The post-Socratic masculine soul by contrast is enjoined to rise up to continuity and eternity, signified *par excellence* by circularity in the Aristotelian discourse. Though it would take us too far from this topic to embark on an extensive engagement with Heidegger, it is interesting to note that in his enthusiasm for a retrieve of the beginnings of thinking in ancient Greece, and particularly in his many engagements with Aristotle that form the backdrop to the thinking of *Being and Time*, he completely overlooks the feminine associations of finitude and *ekstasis*. Finitude, thus appropriated from the side of the feminine, is now the defining condition of Dasein. The primary sense of *ekstasis* in Aristotle, that of a violent derailment from the teleological path, in which any standing at or inclination toward an end is utterly destroyed, is recast instead as Being's standing temporally outside itself in a way that is neither fundamentally nor authentically at odds with the movement of nature's unfolding.

Recall *De Caelo* II.3: "What is *against nature* is subsequent to [*husteron*] what is natural; what is *against nature* is a violent destruction [*ekstasis*] in the coming-to-be of the natural."[71] While the motion of the simple bodies is understood as natural, *oikeios,* motion, the unnatural forces that disrupt them are left unexplained. What has become, in Aristotle's account of the elements' movement toward proper place, of their propensity to sometimes act against nature, to be subject to force, to find themselves far from their proper places or to be restlessly displaced in random and aleatory motions, in phenomena such as earthquakes, raging storms, or winter heatwaves? The threat of engulfment posed by proper place, and the danger of stasis posed by the final separation of the elements, is interrupted by cosmic cyclicity to be sure, but—we must not forget—*also* by the *bia* and *automaton*, the unnatural movements inherent in matter which act to thwart teleological motion. The *lapsus* of the ecliptic gives rise not only to an ordered linearity, but also necessarily gives rise to the forces of disorder, to the agonism of the *para phusin*, nature set against itself. Recasting the scenario once again in the psychoanalytic terms employed in our discussion of place, we can see that Aristotle dignifies the identificatory imitative relation at the level of the cycle, which for him creates the necessary space and breathing room in the sublunar realm. Through cycles of transformation the horror of the anaclitic-type relationship between container and contained and its goal of static engulfment is averted, while aleatory matter once again drop out of the account. The feminine cast as a threat of stasis is overcome by masculine teleology, while the feminine symptoms of errancy, deviation, and chance, the motions against nature, can only appear as illegitimate, violent, and disruptive.

THE MOTION OF ANIMALS

An assumption threaded throughout this study is that the animal, the unified organism consisting of parts and whole, the teleological entity *par excellence*, provides the key to the whole of Aristotle's thinking. Constituting the genus to which man belongs and in which man is distinguished only by his rationality, the animal is a frequent example in accounts of substance, cause, and coming-to-be in the *Physics* and *Metaphysics*. Then there are the many treatises devoted specifically to animals: *History of Animals; Parts of Animals; Generation of Animals*; and—central to my concerns here—*De Motu Animalium*. It is, after all, in animal behavior and in the structure of the organism that a non-rational, natural, self-preserving teleological order of life may be most strikingly observed. Animals of course move randomly, but also quite evidently engage in life-sustaining activities: pursuing shelter, food, and mates and avoiding harm. As a natural and self-evident "good," animal life, *zoē*, in its propensity for preservation, is perhaps the key trope for the Aristotelian telos, at once metaphysical and ethical. Observations about the purposive behavior of animals easily harmonize with Aristotle's teleological cosmos as a whole, and indeed when he tells us at the start of the final book of the *Physics* that motion itself is "a sort of life [*zoē*] belonging to things which are formed by nature,"[72] it is animal life that may most easily occur to us as the model for this claim. And we should also not forget that it is this animal life, *zoē*, that illustrates the activity of the prime mover in *Metaphysics* XII.[73]

Given that the animal is an insistent figure for Aristotle of primary substance, and that Aristotelian motion is not just locomotion but also becoming and change, animal motion also has an ontological dimension, that of development or becoming, raising the question of the relationship of matter to form, and of potentiality to actuality. Here, though, I am primarily interested in animal locomotion in its teleological and aleatory manifestations. Aristotle's account of teleological animal motion notably reveals something of a compromised relation of the organism with the true and the good, especially when it comes to *phantasia,* things that appear that are not actually there. The feminine symptom, I argue, is at work in Aristotle's account of the practical good and *phantasia* in animal movement, as well as in his account of involuntary motions.

Aristotle's notion of *automaton*—chance or spontaneity in nature and a feature of the whole of sublunar nature both animate and inanimate—emerges in the context of animal life. As he explains in *Physics* II.6, animals (as well as children and inanimate objects) are not subject to luck *(tuchē)*, because they do not possess the faculty of choice *(prohairesis)*. Rather, their mode of being subject to randomness is named by *automaton*. Aristotle gives an example of the horse who we say came as a matter of *automaton*, "that is, his coming saved him, he did not come for the sake of being saved," in which *automaton* appears akin to good luck, but in a nonhuman register, one not subject to *logos* or choice: it is a nonteleological motion in nature that nonetheless fulfills the telos of *living,* but coincidentally or symptomatically.[74] Indeed in *Generation of Animals* Aristotle develops the notion of *automaton* most specifically in relation to those lower, ambiguous and liminal creatures: the *ostrakodermata*—literally "animals with earthenware skins"—that are said to generate spontaneously *(kath' automaton)* out of the environmental *pneuma*. In fact it is only in relation to this zoology, this study of what lives, changes, and moves in space, that the very notion of *automaton* as spontaneity in nature becomes intelligible.

Automaton was dealt with thoroughly in chapter 2 as the very site in Aristotle's cosmos where matter itself was finally seen to actually initiate motion, in contrast to almost everything else that is said about matter elsewhere. But even in *De Motu Animalium,* where Aristotle's dominant theory of motion as requiring separate motionless mover and thing moved, an active and passive component, is assiduously followed, there are curious and symptomatic slippages. The account of animal motion as explained principally by desire, *orexis*, in *De Motu*, also renders the animal as the site of a certain inconsistency, insofar as the truth or goodness of what animals desire, that is, what moves them, is far from assured. Insofar as the practical good that they are said to pursue may or may not be an actual good, and is rather a kind of *semblance* and *supplement*, it may be easily read as carrying a feminine sign.

Aristotle's principal discourses on animal motion are found in *De Motu Animalium* and *De Anima*, and both texts agree that this movement is the product of two faculties in the animal—desire (*orexis*) and thought (*nous*), aiming at a *telos* or end; not a speculative end but a practical one: "the first mover is the object of desire [*to orektikon*] and also of thought [*dianoēton*]; not, however, every object of thought but the end in the sphere of things that can be done [*to tōn praktōn telos*]."[75] Since animals are not capable of calculative thought or deliberation, Aristotle posits *phantasia*—what appears, appearance—as a kind of thinking (*hōs noēsis tina*) that most animals at least are capable of, and that is itself able to cause motion.[76] Generally translated as "imagination," *phantasia* is not quite that faculty and must, as Nussbaum argues, be understood not only as a faculty of recalling images, but also in its relation to the verb *phainesthai* (to appear, to shine forth, to be manifest).[77] As described in *De Anima*, *phantasia* is an affection or *pathos* that "does not come to be without perception [*aesthesis*], and without which judgement [*hupolēpsis*, taking up] does not occur."[78] It refers on the one hand to ideations, dream images and so on, but on the other hand to *what appears*, as suggested by its verbal root. As such *phantasia* has a complex and ambiguous relationship to exteriority and a tenuous relationship to the good and the true. *What appears* to the animal is linked to sight, made possible by light— "since sight is the chief sense, the name *phantasia* is derived from *phaos*, because without light it is impossible to see"[79]—and yet may be present to the animal without the operation of either. While *nous* always gives the truth, is always capable of determining the good, *phantasia* and *orexis* are both correct and not correct (*kai orthē kai ouk orthē*).[80] Aristotle goes on to say that the desired object, *to orekton*, (whether real or imagined) excites movement, but this object may be either a real or an apparent good (*to phainomenon agathon*). In this phenomenology of the animal we thus find ourselves in the realm of what Plato called "bastard reasoning," where the laws of non-contradiction do not apply and teleology threatens to go awry. The animal, beset by ideations and perceptions that may be always false, is moved toward what seems good, but may be led astray. The language of *chōra*, too, echoes in these passages: "And we must suppose that the apparent good [*to phainomenon agathon*] holds the place [*chōra*] of the good";[81] and "the practical good is capable of being otherwise" (*prakton dē esti to endechomenon kai allōs echein*).[82] *Chōra* is the indeterminate space in which the good itself may or may not appear, and when it does, it does so restlessly, without ontological guarantee. The latter sentence ought to remind us of the formulation of aleatory matter, what is always capable of being otherwise. But further, it contains at its heart the *endechomenon*, that which receives into itself, the feminine receptacle in the middle-voiced sense, so we might translate: "the practical good is the receptacle that holds otherwise."[83] Receptacle and *chōra*, the ever-present possibility of errancy, and thus the feminine symptom, may be clearly heard in this formulation of the practical good. In *Physics* II.3 in the definition of *telos* (final cause), Aristotle closes the gap between good and apparent good in a time-honored legislative speech act in the imperative: "Let there be no difference [*diapheretō mēden*] here between calling this 'the good' or 'the apparent good.'"[84] Despite this proclamation, the practical good that appears in the *chōra* of the good as its substitute and placeholder nonetheless persists in Aristotle's account of animal motion. It also appears in *akratic* human desire in which mastery has failed, and the forces of *orexis* and *phantasia* override the light of *nous*, as a necessarily degraded and symptomatic form of the good, inseparable from corporeal forces of pleasure and desire, inherently at odds with the unfoldings of natural teleology. In this space or *chōra*, teleological processes *themselves*, what an animal *aims at*, are subject to errancy and potentially send nature off the rails. The practical good thus offers yet another site in the sublunar realm, along with the innumerable nonproper places at which things aim, for a telos *manqué*: fallen, corrupt, oblique: a feminine symptom. The finite linearity of animal teleology aims at sustaining the animal's life, *zōē*, and yet in its corporeal, feminine materiality is haunted by the ever-present possibility of failure, and hence death. Once again we find that, contrary to the modern association of cyclicity with the feminine and linearity with the masculine, that in the Aristotelian text linearity and thus finitude are articulated with the feminine. Desire, *orexis*, he tells us, is tied inherently to the present ("for what is momentarily pleasant seems to be absolutely pleasant"[85]) and cannot look to the future—it is only *nous*, that masculine contemplative faculty, that turns us to the future and thus opens us to the potentially eternal and divine by allowing comparison between contraries, and which permits us to resist deathly desire.

The mechanics of animal motion described by Aristotle are, too, a site of the feminine symptom. Motion results primarily from animals pursuing the pleasurable and avoiding the unpleasurable, although the presence of these things is clearly not required for them to move. As he says in *De Motu*, in *phantasia* the "form that is thought of," *to eidos to nooumenon*, chances to be (*tunchanei*, emphasizing the aleatory relationship) like the actual thing, and indeed we react to it as if it were actually there: "we shudder and are frightened" just thinking of something cold or something terrifying.[86] Through somatic reactions of cooling and heating (often so subtle we do not notice them) in response to both pain and pleasure and the thoughts and *phantasiai* thereof, a small movement of enlargement or contraction takes place. Desire, *orexis*, causes movement through a coinciding and articulation of beginning and end, *archē* and *telos*, that Aristotle likens to a ball and socket joint—they are contiguous but one must remain fixed while the other moves, and then again to a wheel which rotates around a fixed point.[87] We may imagine desire as divided into a "soul part" likened to the trunk of the body, and a "body part" as a limb set in motion—both soul and body, fixed and moving, active and passive, are necessary to the motion. Thus a mechanism is set in motion that once again, strikingly, is likened to the *automata*, the marvelous automatic puppets that he also invoked to explain embryonic development after fertilization in *Generation of Animals*. These *automata*, "which are set moving when a small motion occurs,"[88] are remarkable mechanisms of transmission and magnification. A small motion in one part of the body may thus have far greater consequences elsewhere, and will do so easily and simultaneously due to the actions of contiguous passive and active parts upon one another. This beginning in desire is quickly translated into the transmission and magnification of tiny initial motions throughout the body, a rapid change of scale enabled by the analogy with those technical wonders, the *automata*. The mechanism will thus smoothly articulate active and passive components, unless elements in the process fall short (*apolipēi*) in some way, presumably waylaid by the unexpected privations and obstructions of aleatory matter.[89]

Clarifying the exact mechanism of transmission of motion in more detail, Aristotle says, "It is with good reason that the inner regions and those around the origins of the organic members are fashioned as they are, so as to change from solid to liquid and from liquid to solid, from soft to hard and *vice versa*."[90] Motion is transmitted through the body on the model of *automata*, of the artifacts of *technē*. But the bodily referent exemplary for motions responding to stimuli (including thoughts and *phantasiai*) by hardening and softening is clearly the penis, in its capacity for erection and detumescence, *pace* Nussbaum's commentary which attributes these actions to the joints.[91] Aristotle then proceeds to explain that the *sumphuton pneuma* (*sumphuton* means, literally, "growing together, concrescent"), the element of life or "soul heat" that is the "earthly analogue" of divine *aithēr*, provides the requisite power and strength (*dunamis kai ischus*) to cause movement.[92] The *sumphuton pneuma* resides in the heart (and also in the joints and the genitals). In yet another vividly masculinist analogy, Aristotle says that the *sumphuton pneuma* located here contracts and expands, and governs motion in all parts of the body, just like a "city well-governed by laws."[93] Although using the notion of human law, *nomos*, to describe the somatic unfolding of animal motion may seem almost "natural" to us, it is important to note that despite observations of regularity there is no conception in antiquity of natural processes as "law-governed," and that despite the many instances in which Plato and Aristotle compare the *polis* to an organism, this political sense of biological order must be read as the unusual and specific image it is, prefiguring by two millennia the development of "laws of nature" in the Renaissance and seventeenth century.

What, then, of disruptions in transmission, or indeed of involuntary motions—motions that may be unintended or even undesired, motions that escape the lawful ordering of the well-governed city? Aristotle addresses explicitly the unchosen, unwilled, and irrational movements such as heart palpitations, blushing, and penile erection and ejaculation (distinguishing them from the nonvoluntary motions of sleep, waking, respiration, and growth that are not governed by appetitive desire). He says that often it is observed that these are sometimes moved "when something appears [*phanentos tino*], but without the command of thought,"[94] and sometimes not. The heart and the male sexual organ are, he says, the most conspicuous sources of such movement, each behaving like a "separate living creature [*zōon kechōrismenon*]" containing "vital moisture." One can hear again the *chōra*, the abyssal gap that separates such motions from the reach of the *polis* and its law. He goes on: "In the case of the heart, the reason for this is clear: in it are the origins of the senses. And there is evidence that the generative part, too, is of this kind: for the force [*dunamis*] of the semen comes forth from it like a kind of living creature [*zōion*]."[95] While the identification of *dunamis* with specifically masculine potency will be discussed in chapter 6, we should again be reminded of the *Timaeus*, in which Plato describes man's genitals as "naturally disobedient and self-willed [*phusin apeithes te kai autokrates*], like a creature that will not listen to reason, and will do anything in its mad lust [*epithumias oistrōdeis*] to prevail."[96] After this Plato turns to the female womb, which longs for (*epithumētikon*) children, and if left unfertilized will wander about the body causing "acute distress and disorders of all kinds."[97] Aristotle, however, makes no mention whatsoever of the female genital organs.[98] For him, they do not harbor a life principle of any kind.

By way of explanation for these involuntary and unruly motions characteristic of the male genitals, Aristotle first tells us it is quite reasonable to posit a reverse motive relationship between origin (*archē*) and parts (*morioi*), such that the parts may be the source of motion as well as the center. But this of course will not make for either a "well-governed" or orderly city. There are many examples of such degraded and unsuccessful forms of governance in Aristotle's *Politics*, but the human world is far more susceptible to such vicissitudes than the natural; in politics the people may frequently disrupt and overthrow regimes (indeed both democracy and revolutions are said to result from *sumptōmata*), but in nature such reversals are always exceptional.[99] If the parts initiate motions that reverse the machinery, not only does the chaos of polyarchy or anarchy threaten, but the entire vectoral quality of teleology may break down and with it the integrity of the organism, raising the specter of the *corps morcelé*, Lacan's body in pieces, the fragmented body that lurks beneath the idealization of bodily integrity that is the engine of the mirror stage in his developmental theory.[100] Lacan's theory is instructive here, insofar as bodily integrity *itself* is for him founded on a *phantasia*, an apprehended image of a bounded and totalized body as represented by the image in a mirror. While this does not apply to animal motion, it is clear that Aristotle's references to involuntary motions in this section of the text refer to certain embarrassing human experiences in which the body does not behave as one wishes it to, and in which it exceeds and even overturns the reign of the soul.

The presence of such movements is of course inherently unpredictable—the same thought may give rise to a certain motion at one

time, but not another; the thought of the sexually desirous object may
result in an erection on one day, but not the next. The reason for this,
says Aristotle, is that "sometimes the passive matter [*pathētikē hulē*]
is present in the right quantity and quality, and sometimes not."[101]
Matter thus exerts its ability to interrupt and disrupt teleological
processes through its unpredictable presence or absence, but is once
again designated as "passive" and disbarred from having any motions
of its own, just as the account of genital motions from the *Timaeus* is
apparently redacted in Aristotle's conception, erasing any reference to
feminine motions. The irony here, that the forceful and active motions
of the male sexual organ are attributed to the unpredictable presence or absence of matter, passive and feminine, should not escape us.
In this passage the feminine symptom thus haunts phallic masculinity in the most literal of ways. The tumescence of the penis depends
upon the aleatory vicissitudes of matter: who can tell if such matter
will be "present in the right quantity and quality"? Figuratively, too,
the penis and heart are beyond reach of the governance of the *polis*,
not only producing their own unpredictable motions but also subject
to the separation and errancy of *chōra*, the country beyond the city
walls.

The constant references made by Aristotle to the technical-pro-
ductive power of the craftsman—the by-now-familiar carpenter,
housebuilder, potter, and so on—through which we may comprehend
the active *dunamis* of the sperm that possesses the *archē kinēseōs*,
the paternal source or principle of motion, the "originating ordering" as Heidegger has it,[102] remind us that the source of motion, of
self-motion and indeed all motions in accordance with nature, *kata
phusin*, is marked as masculine.[103] But the active animal may also
move in relation to purposes or places that may or may not be real
or actual goods, and which, in their dissembling capacity, also carry,
irreducibly, a feminine mark. Irigaray reminds us that the finite, discontinuous, rectilinear motions of the sublunary world take place in
an interval bounded by limits, points of arrival and departure both
spatial and temporal, in a scene in which the feminine is locked into
stasis, while the masculine is active and mobile. But at the same time,
the capacity of matter to misbehave, to act in restless and unpredictable ways also forever haunts the scene of motion in the Aristotelian
cosmos; the aleatory capacity of matter constantly undermines the
teleological unfolding of nature, providing friction, force, and disruption; it threatens lack of control and further downfall and chaos.

ARISTOTLE'S DEFINITION OF MOTION IN
TERMS OF *DUNAMIS* AND *ENTELECHEIA*

In *Physics* III Aristotle gives a famously refractory definition of motion in terms of *dunamis* and *entelecheia*: he says motion (*kinēsis*) is the "actuality of the potentially existing qua existing potentially" (*hē tou dunamei ontos entelecheia, hē toiouton, kinēsis estin*).[104] A short discussion of this knotty definition will conclude this examination of Aristotelian motion, and also serves to turn us toward the central concepts of Aristelian metaphysics, namely potentiality and actuality, which will be the subject of chapter 6.

First, the terms of the definition. *En-tel-echeia*, often translated as "actuality" or "actualization" means, literally, "holding-in-the-end." The implication is that whatever *end* or *telos* is being aimed at in any sort of change, motion, or coming-to-be, that end has been attained and is henceforth held within a being, which is therefore at completion or perfection. *Dunamis* is variously translatable as capacity, capability, potency, power, possibility, and potentiality. Of note, then, is that motion is to be defined entirely by terms that already circumscribe a teleology: a potential or capability for X; a completion of X. We have already seen how these terms are used to solve the problem of motion toward proper place of the elements. And as these are the terms to which he turns in *Metaphysics* IX after his long discussion of matter, form, and their relationship in the previous books has finally run aground, we can be certain that we are arriving at the shimmering core of Aristotelian metaphysics. Brague puts it this way: "In the face of Eleatism, Aristotle's project is to reintegrate motion into being and, in order to do so, to show that it can be defined."[105]

As Simplicius explained long ago, and Aquinas and many others have noted since, potency as simply potency cannot be motion, for it implies something lying in wait, yet to occur; and actuality as it exists in actuality can neither be motion, for it implies a process already completed.[106] Motion is characteristic neither of the bricks and wood lying there, qua buildable, nor the house, already built. Neither, as both Aquinas and recent commentators have noted, is it supportable to suppose that Aristotle is in the definition indicating a *passage* or a *process between* potentiality and actuality, for such an insertion begs the question by simply defining motion in terms of another sort of motion: that is, a passage or process still stands in need of an explanation.[107] A little further along in *Physics* III.2 he says, "and although motion is thought to be an actuality [*energeia*] of a sort, yet it is incomplete [*atelēs*]; and the cause of this is the fact that the potential, of which this is the actuality, is incomplete."[108] We thus arrive at the essential difficulty: how can we understanding something to "be in completion" (*en-tel-echeia*) if at the same time it is inherently incomplete (*atelēs*), given that motion always signifies incompletion? This would leave us with a logical violation—a contradiction in terms— what Brague calls an "unbearable oxymoron" that Aristotle would have never permitted.[109] As "incomplete completion," the definition of motion would seem to be an aporetic, or symptomatic, expression of A and not-A at the same time. How, then, to think this through?

Heidegger's approach makes *sterēsis* (privation, or not-being) essential to *genesis*, thus giving rise to what Brogan calls its twofoldness: "an understanding of being as essentially divisive and agonistic" that requires Aristotle to have turned, without quite articulating it, to *time* as ontologically fundamental and central to his understanding of noncontradiction.[110] Protevi seeks to resolve the contradiction via the notion of a "me-ontological interweaving" (using *me-* in the Greek sense of *not*) an interweaving, over time, of potentiality and actuality, of not being and being, but this seems to me overly schematic and insufficiently specific.[111] Introducing time as ontologically fundamental is indeed the radical corollary of understanding being as motion, but it does not quite succeed in helping us understand the meaning of *entelecheia* in Aristotle's definition. As Protevi and Brague note, the definition sought is a *horismos*, it makes de-finite by providing the boundary that is requisite for something to be. This boundary is one that cannot be given by sight alone, but may, according to Brague, only be found within language, in the *logos*. Aristotle himself says motion is "difficult to grasp by sight, but which admits of being [*chalepēn men idein, endechomenēn d'einai*]."[112] It is not through the perception of vision, *idein*, Brague says, that motion is apprehended as such, as *being*, but only through the saying, the *legein*, that is *logos*. *Logos*, he argues, allows us to see beyond what is there before us—the bricks and wood are simply lying there like things—into their possibility. *Logos,* seen in this light, aligns with the conception of *nous* forged in my earlier discussion of animal motion, in that it permits an apprehension of future possibilities, allowing a choice of actions in accordance with the options thus lain before us. It is therefore specifically through the operations of *logos*, and in particular in its inflectedness—its tense- and aspect-granting elements that allow us to distinguish ongoing action (present and imperfect tenses and the gerund, for example) from completed action (e.g., aorist, perfect, and pluperfect tenses)—that motion may be apprehended as a kind of being.

To help flesh out his sparse and abstract definition, "the *entelecheia* of potentially existing as such," Aristotle provides us with a clear and full illustration: "That a motion is what we have stated it to be is clear from the following. When the buildable [*oikodomēton*], insofar as it is said itself to be such, is qua actuality [*entelecheia*], it is then being built [*oikodomeitai*], and this is building [*oikodomēsis*]; and similarly in the case of learning, healing, rolling, leaping, ripening, and aging."[113] There are many things to note about this passage. First, the examples are all potentially teleological processes, phenomena that are moving toward ends whether natural (as in ripening) or artifactual (as in building). But the ends they are moving toward in each case must be sharply distinguished from the end that is at the heart of the *entelecheia* of motion. Brague draws our attention to Aristotle's interpolation, "insofar as it is said itself to be such [*hē toiouton auto legomen einai*]" to emphasize the key role played by *logos* in the definition. And, in favor of this linguistic argument, Aristotle's examples of what can potentially move toward an end (the buildable, *oikodomēton*), in their *entelecheia* qua potential, are found to be gerunds (*oikodomēsis, iatreusis, kulisis, halsis, hadrunsis*, and *gēransis*). Motion as *process* here would seem to be buried in the text's very grammar.

However, and here the analysis departs from Brague, it is not simply through *logos* that we apprehend motion as being. Although the Platonic *idea* may grant a static ideal vision, and the profound link between sight and philosophical contemplation as *theōria* is well attested, vision as a sense grants us apprehension of motion all the time. Our apprehension of the bricks and wood that comprise "the buildable" is not simply a photographic image, frozen in time, for if we linger while the workers arrive and begin their labor we will indeed observe the materials being assembled into a house. Our other senses too, especially hearing, which depends fundamentally on motion for its operation, grant us an unmediated sense of a world on the move. The corporeality of *aisthēsis* gives, and is indeed constituted by, motion without requiring the intervention of *logos*, and indeed in *De Anima* Aristotle states as much: "perception of movement, rest, number, shape and size is shared by several senses. For things of this kind are not proper to any one sense, but are common to all, for instance, some kinds of movement are perceptible both by touch and by sight."[114] But this of course is insufficient to claim for motion Being as such, nor does it grant a definition, falling prey as it does to the unswerving antisensory logic of Eleatism and its Platonic heritage. And when Aristotle says in the *Metaphysics* that motion is something "difficult to grasp by sight, but which admits of being [*chalepēn men idein, endechomenēn d'einai*]," we may again be reminded of *chōra*, the distinctly feminine *receptacle* (*endechomenon*) that accepts or receives being, not knowable according to any Platonic logic of being (*idein*) but only apprehended in a dreamlike way, according to a bastard reasoning.

Looking closely at Aristotle's definition of motion, something strange then begins to emerge that takes us far beyond a claim about linguistic inflection as a way to circumvent the contradiction presented by the *entelecheia atelēs* or incomplete completion. Teleological movements, which Aristotle illustrates by the most emblematic case of building, reach their end in the final product, in this case the built house, in *en-tel-echeia* and completed aspect. The telos here is clear, and achieved, and in its arrival the motion in question, that of building, is destroyed. What Aristotle is indicating in this instance, however, is something else, *another entelecheia* that characterizes *the motion of building itself*, a "potentially this" qua potential, the buildable qua buildable in its end *as such*, holding another telos altogether. In this remarkable moment we may catch sight of an *entelecheia*, a perfection or completion, a being at the end, of a *being*—motion— which is inherently incomplete, an *entelecheia* quite orthogonal to and separate from the familiar Aristotelian teleology as conceived throughout the corpus as arrival at an end. In this definite conception of motion as a complete being with a clear horizon and definition, as a *formula*, we might even, and quite anachronistically, detect a foreshadowing of the infinitesimal calculus to be developed far in the future by Leibniz and Newton, the strange mathematics that captures, formulaically, the rate of change (and perhaps thus "change as such") at a single instant. But this takes us too far from our path. How does Aristotle himself develop this notion?

The examples given in the quotation above: building, healing, learning, rolling, leaping, ripening, and aging; deepen and enrich this understanding of the *entelecheia* of a *dunamis* qua *dunamis*. We find first perhaps the most classic of Aristotelian teleological metaphors, the *technai* of building, healing, and learning. Building builds toward a definite object: the house, a form, and matter composite which stands fully in its work (*en-ergeia*), in which its work and potentiality is fully and completely gathered up and expressed in completeness. Healing is a movement toward health, the proper, integral, and perfect functioning of the organism. Learning moves toward the acquisition of knowledge, and on its basis the divine perfection of philosophical contemplation may ultimately be attained. The next examples, those of rolling and leaping, admit of greater ambiguity. One may, teleologically, roll a log to a desired position for building, and one may leap to safety. But one may also roll and leap in play, in dance, in the Dionysian frenzy; one may in other words roll and leap for their own sake and not for a separate end. Ripening may signify a move toward perfection, the fruit reaches a point at which it is perfect to eat, but aging, the final example, indicates instead a movement toward passing away, *phthora*, destruction and death, signifying our mortal ends rather than an attainment of any sort of completed perfection to which a becoming might teleologically aspire. While Aryeh Kosman insists that Aristotelian motion does not contain its own end, but is always directed elsewhere and therefore must always expire when the end is reached (as in the case of building), here, by contrast, we find illustrated the possibility that motion may indeed be its own end. Oddly, Kosman adds strolling to the classic examples of nonkinetic *energeia* in *Metaphysics* IX.6, namely seeing and thinking—*energeiai* that have left motion behind and are to be rigorously distinguished from it.[115] Strolling, like seeing and thinking, and like playing or improvisational dance, is an end in itself. But surely no one would argue that these are not also instances of motion.

Such a conception of motion, and especially corporeal motion, as an end in itself and not directed elsewhere finds contemporary philosophical resonance in the feminist phenomenology of Iris Young, who asks us to consider a scene from a Tillie Olsen story in which a farm woman "cans her tomatoes while mindful of the colicky baby she holds between her arm and her hip. The movement is plural and engaged, to and fro, here and yonder, rather than unified and singly directed."[116] Young asks what a phenomenology of action would look like which started from the premise that women often do many things at the same time, but here I want to emphasize the aleatory and dancing quality of such forms of motion as well as their simultaneity; to and fro, hither and thither, chaotic, perhaps rhythmic,

indeterminately both rectilinear and circular, and also distinctly feminine. The plurality of ends typical of women's labor, the places where
means and ends become indistinguishable, and where motion for corporeal, material beings becomes an end in itself, haunt the nonkinetic
purity of *energeia*, the protodivine activity in seeing and thinking.
Even if, as is strenuously argued in *Physics* VIII.8, circular motion
is the most divine because continuous and complete in itself, we may
discern anterior to this in the definition the endless aleatory restlessness of dustmotes, the ever-living fire of Heraclitus, the unpredictable
and indeterminate motions that characterize matter in the sublunary
realm.

Here, then, at the heart of the Aristotelian definition of motion is a
kind of being that is an *entelecheia* of potential qua potential that *may*
describe teleologically oriented motions, but may *also* peel away from
them and take us in another direction entirely. This other direction
is not vectoral, telic, at all but, as Aristotle's examples of rolling and
leaping disclose, may be playful, multidirectional, plural, aleatory.
Young notes that the kinds of motion that are the typical concern of
the phenomenological tradition, are the intentional, paradigmatically
masculine, activities of "sports, labor, and travel,"[117] and it is easy to
see how these are rooted in the paradigmatically masculine and teleological Aristotelian figure of the craftsman. This other *entelecheia*,
by contrast, draws us toward another kind of motion, symptomatic
and in the tradition inaugurated by Aristotle marked with a feminine
sign: the unforeseen, the unpredictable, the chance vagaries of matter
in motion that do not participate in teleological processes, and that
indeed, as we have seen, often serve to derail them.

CHAPTER SIX

Sexual Difference in Potentiality and Actuality

At the start of *Metaphysics* VI.2 Aristotle gives an instructive summary of the "many ways" in which being is spoken (*legetai pollachos*). First, there is being according to accident, second, being according to the true (and not-being in the sense of the false), third, being according to the schemata of the categories (the "what," the "how much," the "where" and so on), and finally, besides all these, being according to *dunamis* and *energeia*.[1] There is something of a teleological movement at work in this ordering, in which each account is surpassed by the next, and this is reflected in the movement of the *Metaphysics* over the next several books. The remainder of Book VI dispenses with being as accident, and being as truth, because, briefly put, "the cause of one is indeterminate [*aoriston*] and the other is an affection of thought."[2] Books VII and VIII offer a detailed investigation into categorial being in the primary sense of the "what"; here the operative question is: what constitutes the "what it is to be" (*to ti ēn einai*) or "essence" of primary substance which could ground the unity of a being conceived deictically as a "this"—the bronze sphere, or the living organism? Matter and form are each considered in turn as likely candidates, but the inquiry finally runs aground, and the matter-form schema is abandoned since neither can give the matter-form composite or "hylomorph"—the "this" that is Aristotle's concern—the requisite ground for its unity. In Book IX he turns finally to the last of the four modalities of being listed in VI.2: being according to potentiality and actuality, or *dunamis* and *energeia*. (As in previous chapters I leave these terms mostly untranslated, since *dunamis* may be translated by English words as diverse as power, potency, potential, ability, capacity, force, appropriateness, and possibility, while *energeia*—with *ergon*, "work," at its heart—may be variously rendered as actuality, activity, actualization, being at work, being in the work, and so on. *Energeia*'s sometime alternate *entelecheia*—with *telos*, "end," at its heart—signifies holding at the end, being in completeness, perfection, and so on.[3])

To follow Heidegger's lead, thinking about being in these terms takes us to the heart of Aristotle's most radical contributions to philosophy, offering an understanding of metaphysics at its most profound as an account of *how* being is, its "ways of being" as Charlotte Witt puts it, rather than analyzing it as a *what*.[4] In Heidegger's reading of Aristotle, this understanding of being as a "how" or a "way" discloses being as essentially noncategorial and in movedness, and therefore "in time," and fundamentally temporal. While temporality is fundamental for Heideggerian being, for Aristotle it is motion, rather than time, that is the fundamental category of philosophical inquiry and it is therefore *motion* in its ontological dimension, that is my primary concern both in the previous chapter and in this one.[5] Thinking being through *dunamis* and *energeia* in such a way that motion becomes central to the way that beings appear requires a subtle understanding that proves both revelatory and fruitful for a feminist analysis, and in which corporeality and aleatory matter play a crucial role.

I am not seeking here to clarify the relation between the *dunamis/energeia* analysis in Book IX and the earlier books of the *Metaphysics*, nor to establish clear and definitive distinctions among the thorny concepts of *dunamis, energeia,* and *entelecheia*.[6] My concern, rather, is to continue tracing the thematics of sex and gender in the Aristotelian cosmos. The analysis will therefore focus in particular on Heidegger's engagement with Aristotle and some feminist appropriations of this Heideggerian uptake of Aristotelian philosophy, showing more clearly how sex and gender function in, and a feminine symptomaticity emerges from, Aristotle's thought in this new context.[7] Once again, the account of sexual reproduction in *Generation of Animals*, and its deployments of *dunamis* and *energeia* will take center stage, in concert with the discourses of *Metaphysics* IX. If Aristotle indeed displaces or even supersedes the matter/form distinction through his notions of *dunamis* and *energeia*, we may inquire after the fate of the female/male distinction in this new territory. How are *dunamis* and *energeia* themselves enmeshed with tropes and figures of sex and gender in Aristotle's texts? What becomes of aleatory matter and the feminine symptom in this thinking of being according to *dunamis* and *energeia*? Read with sexual difference as a guiding question, and particularly in conjunction with the sexuate discourse of *dunamis* and *adunamia* in *Generation of Animals*, *Metaphysics* IX proves itself to be bristling with aporias that may be best clarified through the logic of the feminine symptom.

Up until this point the alignment of the feminine with matter and the masculine with form has been basic to this study, and so before embarking on a discussion of *Generation of Animals*, the immediate question is whether sexual difference can be similarly mapped onto the opposition between *dunamis* and *energeia*. The resonance is unmistakable, insofar as *energeia*, and especially *entelecheia*, signifies perfection and completion, and *dunamis* as what is potential signifies the *incompletion* of what is yet to come. Within Lacanian psychoanalysis and its associated feminist tradition it is indeed a commonplace that woman is the "not all" or "not whole" (*pas-tout*); she signifies *lack*, while the phallus symbolizes an (albeit impossible) wholeness and perfection.[8] Closely examining the Aristotelian text we are able to uncover how this association is established within the very framework of Western metaphysics, rather than being simply rooted in a prephilosophical mythical unconscious, as the aetiology of the "Oedipus complex" in myth and tragedy would imply. For Aristotle, the relationships among female and male, matter and form, and *dunamis* and *energeia* are far from simple or even analogical. Matter and form, after all, are different aspects of a static being, a being understood at a single moment in time, while the *dunamis-energeia/ entelecheia* couplet can only be understood of a being in time, of a being that is becoming, and whose way of becoming is irrevocably teleological. *Dunamis*, as possibility and potential for being, is in this schema necessarily preoriented toward a determinate future, on a journey that in a teleological universe is always governed by being's movement toward completeness, and in which *completion* is, by definition, *better* than incompletion.

However, while completeness and perfection may be easily marked as masculine, and incompletion and lack as feminine, *dunamis* is not the simple obverse or privation of completion. Rather, as possibility, potential, capacity, and power, *dunamis also* falls on the side of the masculine. In *Generation of Animals* we find that the male possesses great power or potency (*megalēn dunamin*),[9] while the female is frequently characterized by her *lack* of *dunamis*: *adunamia*.[10] Thus the female not only lacks the completeness of *entelecheia*, she also represents a lack of power, potency, and capability, and thus also falls short in relation to *dunamis*.

In what follows, I will discuss the relationship between *dunamis* and matter, where I show how shifting to the language of *dunamis* more effectively embeds matter within a teleological vector, but also fails to erase matter's polyvocality or pluripotency. Then I move to Aristotle's remarkable definition of *dunamis* in *Metaphysics* IX, examining the causal assumptions embedded within it specifically in relation to natural coming-to-be, *phusis* and *genesis*, including sexual reproduction and spontaneous generation, development and growth. By tracing the textual links in the *Generation of Animals* and *Metaphysics* between *dunamis* and masculine potency on the one hand, and *adunamia* and feminine lack on the other, one can see how Aristotle consolidates his hierarchical teleology on the basis of the technical paradigm, that is, on the model of the craftsman's activity. Following the lead of feminist readers of Heidegger, I will consider how "passive *dunamis*" (*dunamis tou pathein*) provides an alternative site for thinking being's twofoldness and sexual difference beyond the logic of presence and absence, A and not-A, but then follow Book IX as it unfolds toward its teleological conclusions, tracing the subterranean operation of the feminine symptom as both consolidating and undermining the teleological hierarchy.

DUNAMIS AND MATTER

So far, matter has been understood as the site of the appearance of the feminine, insofar as it is simultaneously what is passively acted upon by form, what desires form, *and* the site of disruption, of aleatory and subterreanean movements that give the possibility of being otherwise. Matter has, *prima facie*, a ready-made affinity with *dunamis*, as Aristotle understands matter precisely as a *potential for* form. This parallelism is demonstrated nicely toward the end of *Metaphysics* VIII: "the proximate matter [*hulē*] and the form [*morphē*] are one and the same; the one exists potentially, the other as actuality [<*to men*> *dunamei*, *to de energeia*]. Therefore to ask the cause of the unity is like asking the cause of unity in general; for each individual thing is one, and the potential and the actual are in a sense one."[11] The importance of this sentence for Aristotelian metaphysics cannot be underestimated. But it is important to interpret it correctly, because he is not claiming here that matter and form are somehow identical. Rather, the unity of the individual thing understood as primary substance—the goal unsuccessfully sought throughout the central books of the *Metaphysics*—is finally established by asking us to look at substance in a different way. Instead of being comprised of two irreducibly opposed substances, matter and form, each of which in any case is inadequate in itself and cannot appear without the other, and whose confluence is in itself inexplicable, the individual thing is now disclosed *as a unity* that may be understood in *two ways*: in one way according to potentiality (correlated with matter), and in the other according to actuality (correlated with form).

This connection between matter and *dunamis* is affirmed elsewhere, for example, in *De Anima* where Aristotle says, "Substance is used in three senses, form, matter, and a compound of the two. Of these matter is *dunamis*, and form *entelecheia*; and since the compound is ensouled, the body cannot be the *entelecheia* of a soul but the soul is the *entelecheia* of the body."[12] Matter, form, and the composite are affirmed as the three senses of substance. Matter is body to form's soul, and what is more, it is a body of a particularly appropriate kind:

> [Soul] is not a body, it is associated with a body, and therefore resides in a body, and in a body of particular kind; not at all as our predecessors supposed, who fitted it to any body, without adding any limitations as to what body or what kind of body, although it is unknown for any chance thing to admit any other chance thing. But our view explains the facts quite reasonably; for the actuality [*entelecheia*] of each thing is by nature engendered [*enginesthai*] in the *dunamis* that belongs to it, and in its proper [*oikeiai*] matter. From all this it is clear that the soul is a kind of actuality [*entelecheia*] and *logos* of that which has the *dunamis* of having a soul.[13]

Here, *dunamis* and the proper (*oikeios*) kind of matter (in one way the menstrual blood, in another flesh, bones, and so on in the case of vertebrates) engenders the form in question (soul). What is more, there is something in the matter that lends itself to its telos in advance, that makes it is suitable, able, and appropriate for receiving a form and therefore, *qua dunamis*, it is found to be already incipiently oriented toward form, and thus a full participant in teleology. Hypothetical necessity, or necessity thought teleologically, tells us that knife-blades after all *must* be made of substances of a certain hardness, such as steel or obsidian, and vertebrate bodies *must* be made of flesh and bone and skin.[14] *Energeia* as logically and metaphysically prior to *dunamis* is thus determinative of the properness, we might say the appropriateness or propriety, of the matter and its *dunamis*.

Turning this scenario on its head and seeing it from the point of view of matter, we may recall the passage at the end of *Physics* I.9 in which matter appears as a kind of obscure subject of desire, yearning for and stretching out toward (*ephiesthai kai oregesthai*) the divine and the good on account of its inherent lack. Matter here literally *desires* form, "like the female which desires the male and the ugly which desires the beautiful."[15] Here matter's otherwise untheorized capacity for motion is made manifest, as substance that *desires*, but once again matter appears in the mode of *propriety*: its proper and homely (*oikeios*) motion directed obediently toward a telos, toward a specified and determinate completion. This propriety is also indeed characteristic of the household (*oikos*) for Aristotle: in the *Politics* the household exists as the internal part and natural support of the *polis* that is the whole and the end.[16] Matter, considered on its own terms, may elsewhere be the site of compulsion, *automaton*, aleatory activity that goes against nature, but this kind of movement is never dignified as desire, *orexis*. We might say, indeed, that there is no non-teleological, nonheterosexual, nonmetaphysical desire for Aristotle, even though, as discussed in chapter 5, animals, because of the phenomena of *phantasia* and the practical good, may often be mistaken about their objects of desire. But matter understood as *dunamis* is already taken up into the teleological project, properly directed toward *energeia* and "appropriate for . . ." as Heidegger puts it in his essay on *phusis*.[17]

What is at issue at the beginning of the *Physics* is nothing less than determining the nature of becoming, since it is absurd to claim that something comes from nothing. In a certain sense, Aristotle argues, something does come from nothing, since form arises where there was none previously. When a lump of clay becomes a pot, the "lump," insofar as it represents the absence of the pot, is destroyed. Aristotle argues that in coming-to-be it is not the matter but instead the *privation* (*sterēsis*) of a determinate form that the opposite of form, and it is *this* that is therefore destroyed in the process, while the matter persists throughout. The matter, then, is the substrate: the site and object of change, while the contraries as "qualities" (pot, privation) do not in themselves change. Matter is thus what permits all change.[18] Insofar as matter exists *kata tēn dunamin*, according to potential, it is necessarily, he says, ungenerable and indestructible.[19] This *dunamis*—potentiality or capability—thus allows us to conceive matter as an eternal underlying substrate (*hupokeimenon*, "that which lies under"). Matter's uncanny capacity to *admit privation* and thereby undergo change makes coming-to-be possible, though for all that it still must not be understood as primary substance and cannot exist separately from some form. What is important here is that matter is not the *opposite of form*; rather it is the *privation* which matter encompasses, the absence which it is somehow able to incorporate, that stands in that place. In the argument of *Physics* I.9 (whose primary interlocutor is Plato in the *Timaeus*), the nonbeing, absence, falling short, or privation that thus haunts and enables all coming-to-be is quite explicitly figured as feminine ("as the female desires the male"), and the feminine is hereby characterized by privation. In its rigorously patriarchal and heterosexual expression as *dunamis*, this feminine is inherently oriented toward masculinity as site of the good, as form and being.[20]

Matter understood as *dunamis* is always already on the way to form, swept up in teleology in advance, in its deepest nature determined by and oriented toward the being to which it is destined. Heidegger's translation of *dunamis* as "appropriateness for . . ." reflects this sense of preparedness for form and orientation toward an end.[21] Even if we normally understand *telos* as something external and separable (on the model of technics), it would seem that, in nature, *telos* is also encrypted in the very heart of matter insofar as its ownmost possibility, its *dunamis*, is always a possibility *for* some determinate form. This permeation of matter by telos is signified as a hole or space yearning to be filled, a hole that is only defined by the peg that will come to fill it, *as the female desires the male*. However, as soon as matter is understood as thus *invaginated*, as incorporating a penetrable privation at its heart, this determination by telos in advance is displaced, and an indeterminate field of becoming is thus necessarily opened.

Understanding matter as *dunamis* shackles it necessarily to *energeia* as the realization or actualization of a potential for a specific form, but it is as a site of privation that matter provides the possibility of *becoming anything at all*, not merely *becoming some determinate thing*, teleologically predetermined. In its most radical dimension, then, *dunamis*

as potential or capacity or possibility, as the condition for possibility
for becoming in general, must give way to an open field of possibilities.
This is a delimited field to be sure, for an elephant does not give birth
to a mouse, but within those limits—whatever they may be—the possibilities are theoretically infinite because fractionally and infinitesimally
different from one another. In this light, then, matter's *appropriateness
for* a given form is just *one* orientation among myriad possibilities, and
a given form just *one* possible outcome.

  Aristotle falls just short of acknowledging these plural possibilities
inherent in matter, but it is worth noting that *dunamis* also appears
in his "other" definition of matter as "what is able [*dunaton*] to both
be and not be" or as the potentiality (*dunamis*) "for each of them to
be, and also not to be."[22] Rather than its usual appearance as the passive recipient of form, or as necessarily oriented toward some form,
matter in this conception appears rather as the very site of indeterminacy and the aleatory, the site where A and not-A may both tran-
spire, even if the potentially infinite field of possibility that matter
represents is reduced to a simple opposition, the primary contrary of
being or not-being. Yet, as evidenced by all the ways that nature does
not go according to plan, through chance, plural *archai*, and the indeterminacy of matter, a restless rumbling of plural possibilities may
be discerned beyond and behind this congealed logical formula of
noncontradiction.

  The female offspring, after all, is not simply a not-A, but a deviation or deformation that appears as an opposite or contrary in nature
bearing the mark of privation. The female, in her capacity to be filled
by form, thus appears as matter's avatar and teleology's symptom: she
is both contrary *to* form and a falling short *of* form. The female being
discloses that matter's capacity for not being is apparently capacious
enough to encompass what is nearly A, almost A, not quite A, quasi
A, more than A, other than A (that is, B, C, Q) and so on, as well as
the simple absence of being thought according to the logic of negation.
And in Aristotle's biology the female is the primary and privileged sign
of this lack, now understood as excess. *Dunamis*, thought therefore
in accordance with the feminine symptom, names not just a capacity
for being, the alternative to which is simply not-being in a zero-sum
binary, but also, I want to argue, names precisely that way of matter's
being through which it is not simply appropriate *for* a given form, but
also *in*appropriate. Matter as *dunamis* may be oriented toward and
set along a *proper* path, but may also, teratologically, reorient itself

and in turn (in quite un-Aristotelian fashion) even send form itself in a new direction, toward other as yet untold shapes and configurations.

While Aristotle's linkage of matter and *dunamis* binds matter to its teleological destiny, a more careful consideration reveals that matter's possibilities always exceed this unitary outcome. In this way matter's privation must be understood not merely as contrariety or negation, the "not" of an A that is already posited in advance, nor as a modality of being that runs contrary to that of becoming, signifying destruction or passing away rather than coming-to-be. Nor may it be easily identified with the movement of withdrawal that for Heidegger always accompanies presencing (of which more presently). Rather, thinking *dunamis* according to the feminine symptom opens here a radically non-Aristotelian field of contingent pluralities, encompassing infinite possibilities of infinitesimal difference that may unfold, or fail to unfold. In fact, the possibility that *dunamis* may fail to unfold functions appropriately as a condition of the possibility of its very unfolding, and signifies the always present possibility of other unforeseen kinds of becoming.

SEXUAL DIFFERENCE AND THE DEFINITION OF *DUNAMIS*

Aristotle's primary definition of *dunamis* (the "guiding definition" as Heidegger calls it) at the beginning of *Metaphysics* IX is intended to unify a phenomenon that is, like being itself, "spoken of in many ways" (*legetai pollachōs*). Aristotle refers to the many senses in which *dunamis* and the related verb *dunasthai* (to be able, to be capable of, to have the power to do something) may be used, and points us to his enumeration of these different senses in *Metaphysics* V, his "philosophical dictionary." In formulating a definition that would unify this multiplicity, he tells us that apart from meanings that are equivocal or analogical, *dunameis* "that are related to the same form or appearance [*pros to auto eidos*] are all sources out of which something comes [*pasai archai tines eisi*]," and can therefore "be spoken of in one primary way [*pros prōtēn mian legontai*]."[23] He then encapsulates *dunamis* as "a source or principle of change in another thing or in the thing itself qua other [*archē metabolēs en allō ē hēi allo*]."[24]

The definition contains both a reference to *dunamis* as a source or principle of change, and an insistence upon the alterity of this source. This motive power or capacity is not apparently something a being can simply have in itself, in a selfsame unproblematic way. Rather, the origin of a change is located in some otherness, either exterior, or found within. Further, the paradigmatic instance of *dunamis* is found when it is "the source out of which something comes," so we should be clear that we are dealing specifically with *coming-to-be* rather than something like a change of quality or size. The external/internal distinction maps neatly onto the *technē/phusis* distinction, insofar as nature is famously defined by Aristotle as that which has an internal source of change (as opposed to *technē* in which the source of change is always exterior—it is the potter who alters the pot).[25] The insistence, then, on the *alterity* of the *archē* of change would seem to reinforce the dominance of the paradigm of *technē*, the craftman creating a product, in coming-to-be. In natural things, with their source of motion *within*, this craftsman would appear to be enfolded into the changing thing, encrypted within it as an internal alterity, and this is confirmed by the fact that in nature the three nonmaterial causes converge, such that final and formal causes are also identical, at least generically, with the cause of motion. For Heidegger, then, the Aristotelian notion of *phusis* is particularly suggestive for a critique of instrumental reason since the relation of *appropriation* found in *technē* is displaced by that of *appropriateness* in *phusis*.[26] However in sexual reproduction this source of internal change is reexteriorized and literalized as the father, thus reestablishing an appropriative technical relation at the heart of *phusis*, insofar as the male is defined in *Generation of Animals* as that which generates in another, while the female generates within herself, providing only the site and the material substrate for the offspring. Sexual reproduction is thus paradigmatic of all change: according to its template the source of change and motion is in the male; the thing changed is given by the female. For a thing to have its own source of motion, then, it must be self-divided, not selfsame—and sexual difference appears as the primary example of that division in nature. The scene of sexual reproduction cements the definition of *dunamis* as "a source of change in another," taking place *in* the female with the exterior source of motion as male. Yet an important questions remains. What, exactly, is the nature of the source of motion in the definition that is found internally—in the same thing *qua* other?

While in sexual reproduction the *arche kinēseōs* is clearly the father, and specifically the sperm, how might we understand the *dunamis* as a source of motion that is an alterity within a natural being? As discussed in chapter 5, the soul—understood as separate from the body but nonetheless within the organism—is the motive force within an animal or plant. In the case of the simple elements it is less clear where this internal distinction may be found, since they appear to possess an *inclination toward proper place* that is expressed as an undivided *dunamis*.[27] Living things have a soul—this is the form and "first *entelecheia*" of the organism.[28] To complicate things further, this "first *entelecheia*" also functions as a capacity or *dunamis,* a potential for many kinds of activity. In the simple case of locomotion, this soul moves the animal that desires, in turn stretching out toward something else external, and here both the soul and the externally desired object may be understood as the source of the change or movement. The soul is the internal alterity, divided from the body, and the object of desire is the external alterity, and in a teleological gesture in which these two *teloi* somehow act in concert or perhaps even coincide, so the being moves. And in the situation of ontological change, in for example the developing embryo, the situation is even more complex, to the extent that it becomes quite indiscernible (recall Aristotle's recourse to the automatic puppets as an explanation for embryological development, discussed in chapter 2). Despite Aristotle's intentions that *dunamis* and *energeia* should preserve the unity of the composite, this scenario—in which there is a fundamental difference between the source of change and thing changed—implies that a natural entity must be necessarily divided against itself, folded back or turned on itself in some respect or another, always split into active and passive components if change or movement is to take place. *Entelecheia* in this way seems to turn back upon the ensouled being and act upon it, actualizing its potential, enacting its own sort of *metabolē*, a *metabolē* that may be found the heart of the guiding meaning of *dunamis*, the *archē metabolēs en allō ē hēi allo.*

Looking more closely at the Greek, we find the noun commonly translated as change (*metabolē*) is formed from the verb *metaballō* (to turn about, to reverse, to turn oneself), from *meta-* and *ballō* (to throw, strike, push or let fall). While Aristotle in his focus on coming-to-be foregrounds a unidirectional change from privation to presence, the word itself signifies a backward-turning: throwing, turning, twisting, pushing, falling—a forceful, perhaps violent motion as well as an allowing, the letting fall when what is thrown completes its arc or *parabola*. Indeed the noun *bolē* indicates a throw, a stroke, or the wound of a missile—a blow or coup. Heidegger suggests that *metabolē* should be understood in an "active" sense, "to transpose or to shift, for example, to shift the sail, to transpose goods,"[29] yet this cannot account for the movements of *metabolē* as backward turning, torquing, overturning, or falling, which are made invisible in Aristotelian coming-to-be, with its smooth passage from privation to substance. *Metabolē* thus works against Aristotle's insistent teleology, hinting that beings may also be folded back upon themselves, making it difficult to distinguish passive and active elements in change or a clear direction toward a higher or better form. Indeed, *metabolē* thus understood recalls Heidegger's 1940 reading of Aristotle's *Physics* II.1 (and Brogan's subsequent analysis of this reading) in which nature, and thus being, appears as *twofold*. Heidegger discerns this twofoldness in Aristotelian being insofar as the privation (*sterēsis*) that characterizes matter and potentiality is understood not as a *negation* or even as an *absence* of being, but instead as a kind of *presencing*, "namely, that kind in which the *absencing* (but not the absent thing) is present."[30]

This insight is rooted in a remark made by Aristotle at the very end of *Physics* II.1: "For privation [*sterēsis*] is in a way [*pōs*] a form [*eidos*]."[31] What Heidegger elsewhere calls withdrawal or concealment is always simultaneously at work in appearing or presencing; *eidos* here is to be understood not as "form," but in the phenomenological sense of that which appears.[32] Privation, as withdrawal, appears alongside becoming, part and parcel of becoming. Rather than understanding this dialectically, with privation as the negation of a given positivity, being is rather to be understood as primordially and fundamentally twofold. As he puts it later on in the essay: "With its very coming-to-life every living thing already begins to die, and conversely, dying is but a kind of living, because only a living being has the ability to die."[33] This may be confirmed by the discussion in *On Generation and Corruption* I.3 in which Aristotle affirms that, "the passing-away of one thing is the coming-to-be of another thing, and the coming-to-be of one thing the passing-away of another thing."[34] Yet despite finding grounds for this twofoldness in Aristotle, there is also something profoundly at odds here with Aristotelian teleology. Aristotle is, after all, quite explicit that death is primarily a kind of accident and not merely a necessary counterpart or counterbalancing of birth. And as a kind of "end" it is certainly not a modification of or modality of telos. As a pungent passage in *Metaphysics* VIII explains, "There is also a difficulty as to why wine is not the matter of vinegar, nor potentially vinegar (though vinegar comes from it), and why the living man is not potentially dead. In point of fact they are not; their degeneration [*phthora*] is accidental [*kata sumbebēkos*]."[35] The idea that privation itself might have a way of presencing, a way of appearing, appears here only in the terrain of the symptom: accidental, chancy, aleatory. The female herself, in Aristotle, might, after all, be accurately characterized as *the* paradigmatic way of appearing of privation: as a *de-formation*. In this way the symptomatic feminine, matter's avatar, may in fact stand in for all of life's vicissitudes, whether natal or mortal, and still remain strictly unaccountable within the teleological system taken as a whole.

If the *archē* of change, in the sense of both beginning and principle, is the *end* or *telos* of that change, how can a transitive action of this *archē-telos* upon *what is moved* be explained? How does one thing act upon another in teleological causation? Since Aristotle studiously avoids the billiard ball conception of causation found in atomism, this is not an easy question to answer. His treatise *Acting and Being Acted Upon* (mentioned in *Generation of Animals*) is lost, but in *On Generation and Corruption* he makes a valiant, convoluted, attempt. Aristotle first specifies that agent and patient must come into some sort of contact (*haphē*),[36] and they must be contraries that share a genus (e.g., color affects color, and "whiteness could not affect *grammē*").[37] Second, telos has an assimilative and appropriative effect on what is being changed: "what is active assimilates that which is passive to itself [*to poiētikon homoioun heautō to paschon*]; for the agent and patient are contrary to one another, and coming-to-be is a process into the contrary, so that the patient must change into the agent [*hōst' anankē to paschon eis to poioun metaballein*], since only thus will coming-to-be be a process into the contrary."[38] Aristotle says here both that the contrary is changed into its opposite (e.g., that illness becomes health), and that the subject undergoing change now has an opposite quality (the man who was sick has regained his health). Despite the many possible agencies at work in this scenario—which might include the doctor, the medical art, the doctor's drugs or scalpel, and the living body itself—the *poioun* or agent is here specified as the end, the *telos* of the process. According to this conception Aristotle designates health itself as the real agent of change rather than, say, the doctor, who is merely the proximate agent or motive cause. The sick man, after all, does not change into the doctor, nor into the art of medicine. Surely, however, health is not an "agent" in the sense that we normally understand it? So despite the remarkable claim that change occurs through a process of assimilation ("the agent makes the patient like unto itself") this strange scene in which the doctor's agency is displaced by the greater end of health (which has no agency) must be resolved. Aristotle indeed concedes that health can only be understood as an agent in a *metaphorical* sense, because states (*hexeis*) such as health do not "act upon" as such, but rather occupy that ground of the self-same impassive *energeia* or *entelecheia* we saw in the case of the prime mover. But he seems to balk at identifying a real agent, such as the doctor, and chooses instead to highlight matter's passivity: "The active agency [*poiētikon*] is a cause, as being the source from which the origin of the movement [*archē tēs kinēseōs*] comes, but the end in view is not 'active' (hence health is not active, except metaphorically [*kata metaphoran*]); for, when the agent is present the patient becomes something, but when 'states' [*hexeis*, e.g., 'health'] are present the patient no longer 'becomes' but already 'is,' and the 'forms,' that is the 'ends,' are a kind of 'state' [*hexis*], but the matter, qua matter, is passive."[39] An active agency as a source of motion is mentioned yet not specified, but by means of a rhetorical flourish that reestablishes matter's intrinsic passivity, Aristotle manages to pass this over, leaving the question of the agent open. And this is all the more striking since in the case of becoming healthy the matter at hand is clearly not "mere" matter, the dead wood designated by *hulē*, but living matter with all kinds of unruly potential to comply or not comply with the doctor's ministrations. Seen in this light, the "patient" *as such* appears as something like a phantasmatic construction of the medical art, just that *upon which* it works. Furthermore, in the shift to the language of form and matter, the passage abruptly moves from a scene of technical change, the administering of the medical art, to an ontological register. Form takes the place of the state of health, and the patient's body appears as passive matter as such, whose only role is to be *acted upon*. Here, in a kind of question-begging sleight of hand, the many metaphorical and literal nonmaterial sources of change (health, the doctor, the medical art, the scalpel) seem to consolidate and converge. And unfortunately Aristotle sheds no further light on the problem (next, there is an obscure comment about matter, fire, and heat, followed by a long doxographical section, and then another attempt to describe action and passion which is corrupted and extremely difficult to parse).

Through the thoroughly ambiguous example of medicine and the opaque processes of healing, Aristotle effects a strange transgression of *technē* and *phusis* wherein the medical art, health, and the doctor's actions—form, telos, and motive cause—mysteriously unite in a grand teleological agency acting on passive matter. And he conveniently erases the fact that the "matter" in this scene is actually a living body that may also participate actively (or not, according to its aleatory propensities) in the healing process. While the problem of teleological change has not been satisfactorily resolved, we have seen how Aristotle tries, and fails, to grapple with the problem, and in so doing consolidates his technical conception of causation in which the three active causes converge and act together upon passive matter. Health, a state of the body, is in this way apportioned to the doctor and the medical art, rather than to any bodily or material agency. The body, matter, and the realm of the feminine are passive and mute. *Dunamis*, then, understood as the "source of change in another or in the same thing qua other" has undergone a remarkable transformation. Rather than falling on the side of matter, potentiality, seen as the transitive action of a source of motion or *archē kineseōs* upon something else, is now definitively aligned with form, with telos, with being at the end: *energeia/entelecheia*. What, then, has become of the matter's relation to *dunamis*?

PASSIVE *DUNAMIS* AND THE FEMININE SYMPTOM

In Aristotle's definitive account of *dunamis* in *Metaphysics* XI.1, he first gives the "guiding definition" of *dunamis*,[40] but then turns immediately to a different kind of *dunamis* that would seem to speak to the issue of feminine passive matter, namely *dunamis tou pathein:* the capability of or capacity for being *acted upon*, or *passive dunamis*. He writes: "For one kind is a *dunamis* of being acted upon, a source of passive change in the acted-upon-thing itself by another or by itself qua other. [*Hē men gar tou pathein esti dunamis, hē en autōi tōi paschonti archē metabolēs pathētikēs hup' allou ē hē allo.*]"[41] The difficulty here is not so much in the language but in the thought of an *archē*, a beginning or source of passive change as something with originating force. How indeed can something that is passively changed *have* an internal source of change? The immediate and most obvious way to interpret this notion of a "passive *dunamis*" is to think of it as that which in the substance allows change (originating elsewhere) to happen—a kind of malleability or receptivity, a distinctively feminine mode of being. Indeed Heidegger's formulation, in his translation and close reading of this passage, echoes this reading: "that which itself is in the tolerant as the origin of tolerable change, tolerable from another, or else from itself, to the extent that it is another."[42] He explains, "The lump of clay tolerates something; it allows the formation, that is it is malleable as a way of force."[43] However, the strangeness of the *archē metabolēs pathētikēs*, the "source of passive change" ought to strike us. Why, here, would we not hear *archē* as an initiating force encrypted within the matter, acting in some sort of confluence or concert with that which acts upon it from outside?[44] Heidegger's use of "tolerating" (*Erleiden*) for what is translated as "passive" has its own peculiarity—he means it in the sense of "allowing" or "permitting." This evocation of consent, of some capacity that would perhaps rather not "allow" an intervention and yet yields, reinforces the unmistakable feminine resonances of *dunamis tou pathein*. Indeed, a certain refusal to surrender to this external, penetrating "change from another" is immediately taken up by a couple of lines later when Aristotle speaks of an "impassive state" (*hexis apatheias*), describing it as a tendency to resist deterioration or destruction (but never, one should note, is it a resistance to the seductions of form or *telos*). Such a persistive tendency is reminiscent of Spinoza's *conatus*, specified as the desire or tendency of existing things to persist in their being, such as when living things act to save (*sozei*) themselves, and this is of course fully in line with a larger teleology. However, the duality and juxtaposition here of the passive and impassive *dunameis*, one allowing and the other resisting change, also speaks to the possibility of matter's closure to change or becoming as such, a certain refusal of form, as well as to its surrender to and desire for being taken up into and assimilated to form in telic becoming.

Even at this early stage of the discourse on *dunamis* we find a schema of active and passive powers and capacities, delicately and mysteriously intertwined, and carrying unequivocally gendered resonances. The twofoldness of being that Heidegger unearths in Aristotelian *phusis* is a touchstone for the development of this later thinking. Heidegger draws attention to *absencing* in Aristotelian *phusis* as precisely an *eidos*, an appearing and presencing. And indeed, certain feminist readers of Heidegger—such as Jean Graybeal, Carol Bigwood and Patricia Huntington—have found gendered significance in this interplay of powers as expressed in the late Heidegger's thinking of the movements of unconcealment and concealment, appropriation and receptivity, involved in the presencing of being. Bigwood, in particular, has sought in the movements of concealment, withdrawal and reclining that Heidegger discerns in *phusis* echoes of a suppressed femininity worthy of feminist revaluation.[45] Bigwood interprets Heidegger's emphasis on concealment as having the potential to bring to light a feminine dimension of being that has been typically covered over in metaphysics, "encompassing what the history of Western thought has associated with chaos, mystery, darkness, silence, movements back, the earth, and the primitive."[46] She argues that reclaiming such values would lead to a nondominative and ecologically sensitive consciousness: "fostering and understanding of the positive qualities of dependency and need, receptivity, passivity and responsiveness might help release ourselves from the binding power of the age while at the same time working toward a reconceptualizing of power."[47] Huntington, by contrast, brings a welcome Irigarayan critique to bear on Bigwood's observations, noting that associating movements of withdrawal and darkness with the feminine simply reenacts a metaphysical opposition in which the "feminine" is inevitably only permitted to appear as the other of the same, a specular mirror secured merely to support the life and functioning of a masculine regime.[48] Indeed the twin poles of Aristotelian *dunamis*—the potential to *act* and the potential to *be acted upon*—exemplify a profoundly entrenched metaphysics of sex and gender in which agency is located entirely on the side of the masculine, and any attempt to revalue or transvalue this opposition is bound to run aground on the shores of sexual *in*difference, as Huntington succinctly shows. By shifting our attention, then, to a different dimension of matter, to its indeterminate, aleatory, nonself-same, and strangely self-moving properties, to the ways that it is not oriented toward or appropriate for form, perhaps this deeply entrenched opposition between a dark and passive feminine withdrawal, with all its associated abyssal terrors, and a blithely proactive masculine potency, has some hope of being undone.

The Aristotelian scene itself with regard to *dunamis* is, however, not exactly simple, and pursuing its manifestations further complicates these gendered dynamics. We have already seen that the "impassive habit" of *dunamis* gives a certain power to resist change, to "say no" or deny penetration from without. Such impassiveness at the heart of matter has its metaphysical echo or counterpart in only one other location in the Aristotelian corpus—in the figure of the prime mover itself, the ultimate object of the cosmos's desire, whose very impassiveness arguably produces and maintains desire, and through which motion is thereby enabled, in perpetuity. Such resistance, then, as *dunamis tou pathein*, is precisely the uncanny capacity of matter to sustain itself in separation, to remain in a certain abeyance. As such yet another instance of feminine sympomaticity reveals itself: the matter or potential whose task it is to merely receive form also has a subterranean role as preserver, and thus a certain suppressed middle-voiced role in ontological coming-to-be. This glimmer of impassivity in *Metaphysics* IX is the first sign of a more complex scene of gender at work in the notion of *dunamis*. But *dunamis* also has another sort of gendered life, and this is found in Aristotle's biology of sexual reproduction.

DUNAMIS AND SEXUAL REPRODUCTION: THE PROBLEM OF HEREDITY

As should be familiar by now, Aristotle in *Generation of Animals* defines male and female respectively as that which generates in another, and that which generates in itself. The male possesses the principle of movement and generation, and the female possesses that of matter.[49] But he also elaborates as follows: "There must be that which generates, and that out of which it generates; and even if these two be united in one, at any rate they must differ in form (*eidos*), and in that the *logos* of each of them is distinct. In those animals in which these two *dunameis* are separate, the bodies (*somata*) and nature (*phusis*) must be different."[50] Even if the distinction is ultimately characterized as that between a motive and generating principle and matter, as it is in the sentence that follows this quote, Aristotle also articulates the distinction in terms of a separation of *logos*, of form, of body, of nature, and of *dunameis* (powers).

In its simplest and most schematic form, sexual reproduction requires the passive matter of the menstrual blood, and its passive potential to receive form, to be transformed by the active male principle of motion and *logos* in the sperm into an actuality (*energeia*) without remainder. The conception of *dunamis* as a source of motion in another finds here its paradigmatic illustration. But, as *Generation of Animals* and its exemplary attentiveness to the phenomena quickly reveals, things are not so simple. The powers and potentials attributed to male and female in their contributions to the offspring are in fact quite hard to pin down, so the next task is to try to make some sense of them by looking closely at how he describes and interprets the details of sexual reproduction. While Aristotle is keen to portray the female contribution as merely passive matter and even prime matter, it also teems with strange powers and figures. In addition to a distinctive power or *dunamis*, her own form (*eidos*), nature (*phusis*), and *logos*, the parts of the offspring, including those specific to the female, are also said to exist potentially (*dunamei*), in the female residue.[51] Further, embryonic development is likened to the action of automatic puppets, in which great complexity is as it were coiled up in advance within the fetation, in *potential,* and to which the male sperm contributes the initiating motion.[52] And then, in addition to all this, Aristotle must grapple with the problems posed by the phenomena of heredity, in which sons may look like mothers or grandmothers, and daughters like fathers or grandmothers.

So first, how might one understand the separation of these powers or *dunameis* that Aristotle attributes to male and female? Following from the discussion in *Metaphysics* IX, one might easily assume that he attributes an active power to the male sperm, a *dunamis tou poiein*, and the passive ability to be acted upon to the female menstrual blood, a *dunamis tou pathein*. And indeed, throughout *Generation of Animals* the male is said to possess *dunamis*, in fact the semen is said to "possesses great potency" (*megalēn dunamin*).[53] However, while— as in the above passage—a certain *dunamis* is sometimes ascribed to the female, she is also more regularly characterized by her *inability* (*adunamia*), as lacking a certain power or capacity:

> But the male and the female are distinguished by a certain ability
> [*dunamis*] and inability [*adunamia*]. Male is that which is able to
> concoct, to cause to take shape, and to discharge, semen, possessing
> the principle [*archē*] of the form [*eidos*], and by principle I do
> not mean that sort of principle out of which, as out of matter, an
> offspring is formed belonging to the same kind as its parent, but I
> mean the *proximate motive principle* [*tēn kinousan prōtēn*], whether
> it is able to act thus in itself or in something else. Female is that
> which receives the semen, but is unable [*adunatoun*] to cause semen
> to take shape or discharge it. And all concoction works by means
> of heat. Assuming the truth of these two statements, it follows of
> necessity that male animals are hotter than female ones, since it is on
> account of coldness and inability [*adunamia*] that the female is more
> abundant in blood in certain regions of the body.[54]

The ability and inability, *dunamis* and *adunamia*, described here are, respectively, the ability of the male to form a potent residue in the form of the sperm, capable of acting as a primary motive force in another,

and the inability of the female to produce a residue with a comparable active power. Masculine potency is then precisely an active moving
force, a *dunamis kata kinēsin*, able to transitively affect and produce
effects in another. Instead of a passive *dunamis*, the female rather possesses a lack or privation of *dunamis*, a powerlessness or weakness:
adunamia. The presence of *dunamis* in reproduction is characterized
by the presence of heat, enabling concoction (*pepsis*) of the fetus, while
its lack (*adunamia*) is evidenced by the female's relative coldness. Sexual reproduction thus requires the extraordinary transmutation of a
scalar phenomenon, that of temperature, into a field of contraries:
heat and cold, ability and weakness, presence and absence (signified
by the alpha privative of *a-dunamia*), A and not-A, male and female.[55]
These contraries in turn are the very stuff of Aristotelian becoming
and Aristotelian teleology, not to mention the famous Aristotelian logic
of noncontradiction: indeed they are operative even in his theory of
the elements, which are constituted by the primary contrarieties of hot
and cold, wet and dry: "there is matter of which the perceptible bodies
consist, but it is not separable but always accompanied by contrariety,
and it is from this that the so-called elements come into being."[56] Even
more broadly, contraries are always involved in change from one state
to another, from not cultured to cultured, not white to white, from not
being to being, and in the most general terms from potentiality to actuality.[57] Before exploring in more detail, then, the considerable reverberations of this designation of the female as a *privation* of *dunamis*, as
adunamia, it necessary to examine the operation of this reproductive
dunamis, and how, precisely, Aristotle articulates and apportions it.

Aristotle elaborates semen's "great potency" as follows: "Thus, the
semen of the hand or of the face or of the whole animal really *is* hand
or face or a whole animal though in an undifferentiated [*adioristōs*]
way; in other words, what each of those is *in actuality* [*energeia*],
such the semen is *potentially* [*dunamei*] . . . since neither a hand nor
any other part of the body whatsoever is a hand or any other part of
the body if it lacks soul [*psuchē*] or some other *dunamis*; it has the
same name, but that is all."[58] Here, there are several things to note.
First, body parts *in potential* are attributed to the sperm. Second,
the difference between sperm and the body it has come from and
is destined to become is precisely that between an undifferentiated
and a differentiated entity. The undifferentiated semen *is* the whole
animal potentially (*kata dunamis*), while the differentiated organism
exists in actuality (*energeia*). As the Greek suggests, differentiation or

distinction (*diorismos*) requires the introduction of an internal boundary (*horismos*): a separation or division, and really, this is the core of
the problem of embryology in general. To try to think it through in
Aristotle's own terms, recall the earlier discussion of the definition of
dunamis as "a principle of change in another or in the thing itself qua
other." One might ask, how does the distinction between an internal
and external source of change apply in this scenario? How is such
a boundary introduced? Is the capacity for differentiation inherent
within the sperm, in other words is *dunamis* here precisely a capacity
or potency for differentiation itself? Or does it presume or imply a call
for the sexually other, the female matter, to provide the alterity necessary for differentiation? At *Metaphysics* IX.7 Aristotle qualifies the
notion of spermatic *dunamis* with the comment, "the seed is not yet
potentially a man; for it must be placed in something and change. And
when it is already such that it can be moved by its own principle, it is
then potentially a man; but prior to this it has need of another principle [*archē*]."[59] The great power of the semen, then, is not the power
to become a man in itself, but is rather the potential for this power, a
dunamis for a *dunamis*, and thus requires another principle, *archē*, in
order to act. The menstrual blood thus appears here in the guise of an
unspecified feminine *archē*, necessary if the sperm is to be "such that
it can be moved by its own principle." Simply put, active sperm acts
on passive menstrual blood, and conditions of *dunamis* are fulfilled,
enabling the fetus thus to arrive in its potential to be man.

A slightly more complex account of the powers of the menstrual
blood is given in the following passage from *Generation of Animals*
II.3:

> As semen is a residue, and as it is endowed with the same movement
> as that in virtue of which the body grows through the distribution of
> the ultimate nourishment, when the semen has entered the uterus it
> "sets" [*sunistēsi*] the residue produced by the female and imparts to
> it the same movement with which it is itself endowed. The female's
> contribution, of course, is a residue too, just as the male's is, and
> contains all the parts of the body *potentially* [*dunamei*], though
> none *in actuality* [*energeia*]; and "all" includes those parts which
> distinguish the two sexes. Just as it sometimes happens that deformed
> offspring are produced by deformed parents, and sometimes not, so
> the offspring produced by a female are sometimes female, sometimes
> not, but male. The reason is that the female is as it were a deformed
> male; and the menstrual discharge is semen, though in an impure [*ou
> katharon*] condition, for it lacks one constituent only, the principle of
> soul [*tēn tēs psuchēs archēn*].[60]

As the semen meets the female residue, it "sets" it (on the analogy of rennet with milk), though *sunistemi* also means "to place or set together, to combine, unite, to associate, also to organize, compose, create, or frame," as well as "to make firm or solid."[61] As the semen imparts a movement of solidification, it also seems to have a compositing or assembling action. However, the female residue, understood hitherto as prime matter, *prōte hulē*, passive and devoid of all form as far as possible, now appears to *already* contains all the parts of the animal (including all sexual parts of both sexes) *potentially*, indeterminately, perhaps jostling for expression, though not in actuality. The female residue is thus "*potentially* the same in character as the body whose secretion it is."[62] We are thus presented with a mechanical picture in which the essential principle that is imparted by the semen is a motion that assembles, and in which fetal development is understood through the analogy with the *automata*, the automatic puppets.[63] A motion occurs that impels a process whose unfolding is preordained, there from the start *in potentia,* and the strength of the initial movement determines the "successful" outcome of the process. As ever, there is a normative injunction for males to take after the father, for the male principle to "gain the mastery," though females are said to take after their mother. And further, "Some take after none of their kindred, although they take after some human being at any rate; others do not take after a human being at all but have gone so far that they resemble a monstrosity, and, for the matter of that, anyone who does not take after his parents is really in a way a monstrosity, since in these cases nature has in a way strayed [*parekbebēke*] from the genus."[64] In this story of a progressive degeneration we can, despite Aristotle's scientific language, hear loud echoes of Hesiod's archaic narrative of a fall from a state in which men live according to justice, and in which "women bear children that are like their fathers."[65] By contrast, in the morally degenerate stage of the race of iron, "a father will not be like his children, nor will they be like him."[66] The specter here, in both Hesiod and Aristotle is surely not just that of a failure of heat, but also the possibility that women themselves might wander, stray and commit adultery, disrupting the always phantasmatic certainty of the paternal trajectory in the well-ordered household.

Aristotle, nonetheless, provides clear mechanisms for how the outcome may not be "successful," and how the offspring may "depart from type" or "degenerate" (*existasthai*). As he explains in *Generation of Animals* IV.3: "That which is acted upon [*to paschon*] degenerates [*existatai*] and is not mastered [*ou krateitai*] through a) deficient potency [*elleipsin dunameōs*] in that which is concocting and moving or b) the bulk [*plēthos*] and coldness of what is being concocted and differentiated."[67] These processes may give rise to a "polymorphous assemblage," something that also might occur if an athlete eats too much and his body parts "turn out ill-assorted," and similarly in the "disease known as satyriasis."[68] So according to the soul heat theory, the masculine potency may somehow itself be deficient in itself, due to something like youth or old age or a fluidity or femininity of body, as he points out in the aetiology of the female offspring in *Generation of Animals* IV.2, but also there may simply be too much *katamēnia*, resulting in a derangement of embryonic parts. Any of these things, along with external factors like winds in the south or a waning moon, might create the breakdown in mastery, giving rise in small measure to a female, and to monstrosity if the deficiencies or overloads are more extreme. Still, though, the feminine contribution is represented not as a parallel or opposing power, but simply as something capable of diluting and undermining a thoroughly masculine enformation. So if the potential for the offspring's form is in the sperm, how might the offspring ever come to resemble his or her mother? And by contrast, if the body parts are nascent in the menstrual blood, how might an offspring look like his or her father?

Aristotle often refers to the sperm as containing the *logos* of the creature, the *ratio*, reason, account, formula, just as the carpenter has the *logos* through which the bed will come to be. The following is a typical passage:

> As for hardness, softness, toughness, brittleness and the rest of such qualities which belong to the parts that have soul in them—heat and cold may very well produce these, but they certainly do not produce the *logos* in direct consequence of which [*hōi*] one thing is flesh and another bone; this is done by the movement which derives from the generating parent who is *in actuality* [*tou entelecheia*] that from which the offspring is formed *potentially* [*dunamei*].[69]

Montgomery Furth interprets this *logos* associated with the sperm's movement as a kind of informational power, giving a "pre-determined sequence of physical and chemical formative activities."[70] On this reading, which perhaps owes more than a passing debt to contemporary scientific knowledge, there is no form as such in the sperm, but rather a *dunamis* understood as an informatic *logos*. That it is always given by Aristotle as the *logos* of a *movement* (*kinēsis*) shows us that perhaps it is in the sperm that we ought to locate the genius that lies behind the mysterious working of the automatic puppets. Even though the *dunamis* of the parts, the material substrate appropriate for fetal development, may lie in the menstrual fluid, the movement which animates the puppets, sets them in motion at the start by providing the *archē kinēseōs*, may also provide the introduction of internal boundaries in virtue of which one thing is flesh and another bone. The sperm not only sets the puppets in motion, it also provides a determining *logos* that provides for the nature of their parts, and in particular for their differentiation and articulation, their development over time. This is further illustrated by a technical analogy in the passage that directly follows the one cited above:

> Heat and cold soften and harden the iron, but they do not produce the sword; this is done by the movement of the instruments [*kinēsis tōn organōn*] employed, which contains the *logos* of the art [*technē*]; since the art is both the principle and form [*archē kai eidos*] of the thing which is produced, but it is located elsewhere than in that thing, whereas nature's movement is located in the thing itself which is produced, and it is derived from another natural organism which possesses the form *in actuality* [*energeia*].[71]

Just as in the productive activities of *technē*, the sperm is the producing agent, which is likened to the productive, directed, movement of the instruments, the anvil and hammer, transmitting the craftsman's *logos* in the creation of a sword. The form resides in the blacksmith's art, and as *energeia* in the begetter, the father, but the sperm and the instruments are the vehicles of the *logos*, and thus the *dunamis* of the *energeia*, the form to come. The dual role of *archē* as both source and principle is evident here, consonant with the Heideggerian rendering of *archē* as an "originating ordering" which both begins *and* continues to exert dominance over the process, while *hulē* (matter) remains utterly passive in its role of "appropriate orderable."[72]

This solution to the provenance of the offspring's form in the sperm thus reasserts the Aristotelian order of the primacy, priority, and activity of masculine *dunamis*, now understood as *logos*, on the model of *technē*. Despite the passages that indicate that the female residue contains all the parts of the organism potentially, the aetiology of sexual difference reappears once again as the direct result of the mastery or failure of a thoroughly masculine *dunamis*, and girl children bear the unmistakable mark of that failure, indeed of the inevitability of that failure.

The question of how the mother's characteristics may be passed down to the offspring still remains to be addressed. However, Aristotle offers a detailed and ingenious theory of heredity, in which the kinds of *dunameis* in maternal and paternal contributions may be further specified. Is it possible to identify, here, a specifically female *dunamis*? Aristotle's discussion of heredity throws light on his distinction between species and individual, as well as the way that *dunamis* functions in sexual reproduction. It is clear that male and female are said to differ by *logos* and by *dunamis*, but sex is not the only thing that is passed down. In reproduction, as in Aristotle's metaphysics of substance, it is always the peculiar and individual (*to idion kai to kath' hekaston*) that exerts the stronger influence.[73] He says, "*Dunamis*, in each case, I use in the following sense: The generator [*to gennōn*] is not merely male, but also a particular male such as Coriscus or Socrates, and it is not merely Coriscus, but in addition a human being."[74] The species and genus to which a thing belongs specify it, but its individual being as a this [*tode ti*] is what constitutes its substance and its being, and its greatest *dunamis*. In reproduction and heredity, this hierarchy of substance also makes itself felt:

> Now everything, when it departs from type [*existasthai*], passes not into any chance thing [*to tuchon*] but into its own opposite [*antikeimenon*]; thus, applying this to the process of generation, that which does not get mastered must of necessity depart from type and become the opposite in respect of that *dunamis* wherein the generative and motive agent has failed to gain the mastery. Hence if this is the *dunamis* in virtue of which the agent is male, then the offspring formed is female; if it that in virtue of which the agent is Coriscus or Socrates, then the offspring formed does not take after its father but after its mother, since, just as "mother" is the opposite of "father" as a general term, so also the individual mother is the opposite of the individual father. The same applied to the *dunameis* that stand next in order, since the offspring always tends to shift over [*metabainei*] to that one of its ancestors which stands next, both on the father's side and the mother's.[75]

We now see that there are multiple *dunameis* at work in the agonic scene of fetation: those that give rise to the characteristics of a father and mother, those that give rise to sex, and those of the other ancestors. We now see how a male offspring may resemble his mother, and a female offspring her father. But rather than countering the male power with a female power, a male's resemblance to his mother is made possible by the departure from type or degeneration (*existasthai*), of the father's *dunamis*, not now *qua* male but *qua* individual. The mother's characteristics appear in the son not as a result of the *presence* of any specific *dunamis* on her part, but merely as a result of an absencing, a privation, of the individual *dunamis* of the father. Aristotle further distinguishes this presence and absence in terms of *energeia* and *dunamis*—some movements are present as *energeiai*, as actualities, these are those of the male parent, and of generic things such as being human and being an animal; some only *dunamei*, potentially, such as those of the female and the ancestors.[76] There are apparently specifically female movements, lying in wait, in potential, but the actually existing movement that may activate them is on the side of the male. What is more, the possibility of multiple paths for development, the potential characteristics of a multitude of ancestors, also obscurely appears on the side of feminine *dunamis*.

Aristotle then distinguishes two decisive mechanisms—*existasthai*, which signifies a degeneration and transformation (*metaballein*), into the opposite, that is, into the opposite sex; and *luesthai*, a lapsing, loosening, or slackening in which case the characteristics of grandparents (of the same sex) and former ancestors will come to the fore: thus if the father's *dunamis*, qua individual, lapses, the son will resemble the grandfather. *Existasthai* occurs when the male principle fails to achieve mastery. In *luesthai*, the agent (*poioun*) in turn gets acted upon by that upon which it acts, and thus a heating agent may end up being cooled, or vice versa.[77] In Aristotle's *Poetics lusis* also signifies the denouement of a tragedy, a kind of undoing,[78] and it is also most notably part of the epithet for *erōs* that appears in the first lines of Hesiod's *Theogony* and in many other epic and lyric contexts: "limb-loosening" (*lusimelēs*). So there is certainly a sense of giving way here—of contraries melting into one another—that resonates with the receptivity of *dunamis tou pathein*: indeed here that which is *acted upon* more or less takes center stage, and acts back upon that which would act on it. He illustrates thus: "a thing which heats may get cooled, or one which cools may get heated, either without having acted at all, or by having acted less than it has been acted upon."[79] And while one might read this perhaps as a kind of salutary deliquescence, or even as an emergence of buried, feminine, "passive" agency in heredity, it strictly speaking operates for Aristotle only within and not between the sexes. *Luesthai* represents a dilution of the *dunamis* that makes things individual and separate, ultimately leading once again to a kind of corruption and degeneration.

The vagaries of aleatory matter in sexual reproduction, hitherto understood as *automaton*, are thus now refigured in terms of the specific mechanisms of *existasthai* and *luesthai*. Loosening (*luesthai*) is a rather passive failure of the generative principle, and results merely in a walking over (*meta-bainei*) to the next same-sex ancestor in line. *Existasthai* marks a misdirection or deviation in matter that results in radical transformation into a contrary: a *meta-ballei* or throwing over into sexual alterity. The forceful *ek-stasis* of *existasthai* is a departure from standing, a pushing out of place of the self-standing uprightness of masculinity, easily interpreted as a violent unmanning that results in a symptomatic fall into femininity. In Aristotle's usage, *existasthai* signifies the destruction of a thing's very nature, which in this case means the seed's *logos,* form, or soul principal is transformed into its opposite, the female.[80] The mastery of masculinity, whose principle signifier is the erect, upright phallus, is thus subject to a destructive deviation at the hands of restless and obstructive matter, a ruinous *clinamen* overthrows the active masculine power of production, *dunamis tou poiein*, into its *antikeimenon*, its supine and passive opposite, the female.

Aristotle's quite brilliant solution to the problem of inherited characteristics nevertheless results in a profound incoherence in relation to his theory of sexual reproduction, because it requires a balance of powers (*dunameis*) between the sexes that cannot be effectively translated into the matter-form distinction. It remains obscure how any "information" for the mother's form, the mother's *logos*, can be present in the menses, even if the menses has the potential, that is, is the *right kind of matter*, to be formed into all the female parts as well as the male parts. If the father's *dunamis* qua individual (rather than qua male) fails to master the matter, we see how it degenerates, but Aristotle still offers no account of how the mother's specific characteristics may emerge in its stead. Without positing a formal principle, a *logos* present in the female residue, this is an impossible situation. Aristotle requires us to assume or imagine the presence of the *dunamis* or *logos* of the mother's form, qua individual, as well as those of her parents and other ancestors, in the cold, inert, passive matter of the menstrual blood.

Aristotle's discussion of heredity thus articulates a profound metaphysics of presence rooted in sexual difference, in which masculine *dunamis* confronts feminine *adunamia*, and either masters it or fails to do so.[81] Failure results in a violent transformation into the opposite, the female sex, which functions as a sign of privation and failure. In more extreme cases such failure results in a deviation even from the species form into monstrosity. However, in order to explain the handing down of characteristics from parents to child, Aristotle must posit a burgeoning multiplicity of powers on both male and female sides, *qua* individuals, *qua* species and genus, and qua ancestors. Sperm— as source of motion, vehicle of soul principle, *pneuma*, *logos*, and potential form—is well-equipped to harbor such powers, while menstrual blood, as prime matter, is *appropriate for* enformation by the sperm, but cannot intelligibly transmit specific characteristics. Again we encounter the symptomatic structure: matter must both be pure passive receptivity *and* a kind of receptacle or *chōra*, a site for multiple and unpredictable figurations that may or may not come to presence in the offspring.

DUNAMIS AND *ADUNAMIA*: THE SPECTER OF CASTRATION

Since the search for a specifically female *dunamis* seems to have run aground, what of the powerlessness or incapacity, the *adunamia*, that is ascribed to the female? At the end of the treatise on *dunamis* in *Metaphysics* IX.1, Aristotle defines *adunamia* and the *adunaton*, incapacity and the incapable, as the privation (*sterēsis*) of *dunamis*. Recall that in the formulation of coming-to-be according to the matter/form schema in *Physics* I.9, privation is a necessary element. To reiterate, matter provides the locus of privation, and thus gives the possibility that things in the sublunary realm may be and not be. It fundamentally subtends the possibility of the generation and destruction of all substance, *ousia*: "Now all things which are generated, whether by nature or by art, have matter; for there is a *dunamis* for each of them to be, and also not be, and this *dunamis* is the matter in each."[82] Neither form nor matter in themselves are generated or destroyed, but the capacity of the matter to admit of privation is what makes change possible. If the female, as I have claimed, is indeed matter's avatar, we might want to propose that she is *also* a *dunamis* for being and not being. And this, indeed, would be in line with a more archaic conception of the feminine. For the *dunamis* that enables becoming and not becoming might appear in the human world as something like a power over life and death. More powerfully yet, as in Cavarero's reading of the Demeter-Kore myth, it might signify the power over birth and not birthing, over fertility and thus the very possibility of life itself.[83] But no—the privation that characterizes the female in Aristotle is in fact far more profound than this. It is a privation of ability *as such*: the absence of power to accomplish anything at all.

In defining *adunamia* Aristotle gives several senses of privation. The first distinction is between the case of a thing simply not having a particular attribute, and a thing not having something when it should by nature possess it. The latter case is further qualified: "In some cases, we say that things are deprived [*esterēsthai*], if by nature they would have something but by force [*bia*] they do not have it."[84] What can he mean here? With Aristotle's abstract classifications, he often has some exemplary figure in mind, and identifying this figure can help to clarify what is at stake. Turning to the philosophical definition of *adunamia* in *Metaphysics* V we find the following: "For we would not use the expression 'incapable of begetting' similarly for a child, a man, and a eunuch."[85] That is, a child is incapable of begetting by nature; a man is incapable of begetting as a result of a failure in nature—impotence or "erectile dysfunction" as it is now known; and the eunuch has been deprived of his natural potency *against* nature, through the use of force. The primary referent of Aristotelian *adunamia* is, like that of the English "impotence," a lack of generative power, or sexual *dunamis*, on the part of the male.

Throughout *Generation of Animals*, females are indeed characterized by inability, *adunamia*. The implicit association of the feminine with privation, *sterēsis*, is further cemented when we remember that in Greek the womb, *hustera*, is at least homonymically, and arguably also etymologically related to *husterēsis*, a coming short, a want or need, and *husteron*, the latter, the inferior, the weaker, what comes later.[86] A man, on the other hand, is the *proteron*, the foremost, and only against his nature does he suffer a privation of *dunamis*, impotence (while the eunuch suffers this privation by force). This specter of castration in the definition of *adunumia* can therefore be read as a figure for the possibility that feminine matter, as the possibility of not being, can always waylay, disrupt, or in some way violently prevent the unfolding of becoming. This finds further confirmation in Aristotle's definition of privation (*sterēsis*) in *Metaphysics* V, where the example given is that classical analogue of castration, namely blindness. The types of privation follow the same scheme as those in the definition of *adunamia*: not having a thing by nature, for example, the plant is said to be deprived of eyes; not having something by genus, like the blindness of a mole; not having something which by nature it ought to have, like a blind man. The fourth kind of privation is given as "the taking away of something by force."[87] Aristotle does not give an illustration in this case, but the absent figure of a man blinded by force, that of Oedipus himself, is easily supplied, and the Freudian resonances here are inescapable. The power of seeing is linked fundamentally for the Greeks to the power of speculative knowing as *theorein*, and is extolled by Aristotle as the best aid to knowledge in the famous opening lines of the *Metaphysics*: "All men naturally desire knowledge. An indication of this is our esteem for the senses; for apart from their use we esteem them for their own sake, and most of all the sense of sight. Not only with a view to action, but even when no action is contemplated we prefer sight, generally speaking, to all the other senses. The reason of this is that of all the senses sight best helps us to know things, and reveals many distinctions."[88] Seeing, furthermore, is closely associated with thinking in all the examples given of *energeia* that has surpassed motion (where there is no other *ergon* than the *energeia* itself).[89] The removal of sight would lead directly to the impossibility of philosophy itself.

That *adunamia* has an intimate connection with castration should come as no surprise to the reader of *Generation of Animals*, where Aristotle describes the female as both *anapērian* (deformed, castrated) and as possessing *adunamia*. The female is the lacking male, and with these designations Aristotle renders her utterly powerless. Also, according to the logic of the feminine symptom, she is not simply on the side of powerlessness but represents a threat in her very being, a threat that in turn stands in need of neutralization. Indeed, the power of aleatory matter exceeds any attribution of *adunamia*, returning in the face of this designation as a subterranean material agency that might unman a man, and that indeed unmans the potency of his sperm in the battle for mastery that results in the female offspring.

By contrast, Heidegger's reading of the twofoldness of being erases without a trace these sexuate dimensions of privation. In the *Phusis* essay he reads privation (*sterēsis*) as absencing that is *in* presencing. He says that the lack, the "goneness" of a thing (as when, for example, one's bicycle is stolen) *irritates* us and is therefore present to us constituted as a positive manner of being.[90] In *phusis*, "while the blossom 'buds forth' [*phuei*], the leaves that prepared for the blossom now fall off. The fruit comes to light, while the blossom disappears."[91] In this vegetal example of natural growth sexual difference is totally obscured. He pays no attention to the fact that it is the *dunamis* of matter, precisely as the capacity for being and not being, as the harboring the capacity for privation and for being otherwise, that allows for these successive stages of presencing, nor that this privation is relentlessly constituted in relation to the normative force of sexual difference. In fact, Heidegger's own translation of the passage on *adunamia* in *Metaphysics* IX entirely erases the differences noted above between a natural lack and violent removal or castration. His rendering simply asks, "for are we not inclined to call the boy, the man, and the eunuch powerless to procreate in the same sense?"[92] And instead of noting the implicit anxiety of a masculinity under threat in Aristotle's categorizations, his translation of *dunamis* as *Kraft* (force) leads him to understand the relation of impotence to procreation as revealing only a positive and naturalized connection between an implicitly masculine potency and life: "This points to a special bond between 'force' and 'life' (as a definite mode of *einai*, of *being*), a bond with which we are acquainted from daily experience and common knowledge, without scrutinizing its inner essence and good."[93] The dynamics of sexual reproduction and the necessary contribution of the symptomatic female contribution (as the complex *adunamia*/aleatory materiality) are thereby thoroughly obfuscated in Heidegger's reading.

The mood of masculine castration anxiety in Aristotle's definitions of *adunamia* and *sterēsis* may in turn serve to illuminate the distinction between *dunamis alogon* and *dunamis meta logou* in *Metaphysics* IX. In the second chapter, Aristotle introduces a distinction between *dunamis alogon*, that is, the *dunamis* of things without *logos*, and the *dunamis* that pertains to *logos*, *dunamis meta logou*. He explains that some *dunameis* are present in inanimate things, while others are in living beings and in the soul. *Dunamis meta logou* is the power of the soul that has reason, *logos*. Hence all the arts (*technai*), and what he calls the productive sciences, are *dunameis meta logou*, powers that arise from the faculty of *logos*. He then states: "Every *dunamis meta logou* is capable of causing both contraries, but every *dunamis alogon* can cause only one; for example, heat can cause only heating, but the medical art can cause sickness as well as health."[94] As he develops this position, which is once again about how things are able to act on other things, he explains that the sciences (*epistēmas*) have the capacity for contraries, and the scientific man (*epistēmōn*) can produce both contraries, one essential, one accidental (like health and sickness). He concludes that "things which are capable with respect to reason [that is, things that have *dunamis meta logou*,] produce contraries in things without reason, for the contraries are held together in a single principle, in *logos*."[95] *Logos*, then, encompasses and reveals contrariness, opposition, and the power of *logos* is the power of producing both contraries. That which is *alogon*, without reason, on the other hand, has the power to produce one outcome only.

This formulation is certainly both surprising and puzzling in light of the Aristotelian definition of matter as the possibility of being and not being. Matter, the *alogon* par excellence, bears the potential for the most fundamental of contraries, the ontological contrary of being and not being. As such, it is the condition of possibility of the unexpected, unintended, or chance outcome, and bears no guarantee. Further, to continue with Aristotle's example of heat, it is certainly true on one level that something with the power of heating, say fire, produces only heat and cannot produce its opposite, cold, whereas the *logos* enables a person to either heat or cool something at will. If Aristotle's point is about the power of choice, certainly he is right, but he does not frame it this way. Rather, the distinction he gives is that between a unitary outcome of a power, and a power from which either of two contraries may result. In the context of sexual reproduction, we have seen how, when the sperm implants its masculine *logos*, an imperceptible shift in the correct amount of heat due to a south-facing copulation can give rise precisely to a major transformation into the opposite sex, producing a female instead of a male. This is certainly an instance of *dunamis alogon,* and it is determinative of sexual difference. This conception of the univocal inevitability of outcomes issuing from natural things is also surprising in another way: Aristotle, as a teleological thinker, consistently polemicizes against such physical necessity elsewhere. In the *Physics*, for example, he argues that any regularity we see in nature, what happens "always and for the most part," issues precisely *not* from any sort of necessity inhering in the material nature of things but indeed from final causes, for the sake of some good, such as keeping the cycles of nature going. Thinkers such as Anaxagoras and Empedocles who believe in physically necessitated causation, who argue that, "since the hot and the cold and each of such things are by nature of such-and-such a kind, certain other things must exist or come to be,"[96] are relentlessly discredited. This is because all those phenomena that might be attributed to physical necessity alone, beyond the reach of final cause, are those which fall *outside* the expected—such as frequent rains in summer or heatwaves in winter. These are the result of the aleatory phenomena of *automaton* or *sumptōma* for which matter is the vehicle. Because of their material nature, things which don't have *logos* always harbor possibility of different futures: due to the unpredictability of material vicissitudes a contrary may indeed come to pass, in defiance of our expectations.

Aristotle's example of the medical art once again sharply discloses what is at stake. He claims that "the healthy produces only health," but that the doctor—the scientist or *epistēmōn*—may produce both health and illness.[97] Equipped with his *logos*, his knowledge, and his tools the doctor may indeed lead the body toward health *or* toward sickness. However, this scenario utterly obscures the patient's own opaque and unpredictable responses to treatment. The body, as *alogon*, of course *may or may not* comply with the doctor's ministrations, and may also harbor *within itself* the capacity for both health and illness in spite of the doctor's artful *logos*. As soon as we leave the very simplest of contexts, the vagaries of matter begin to intervene and give contrariness—no *logos* is required.

But Aristotle, here, seems to be interested in specifying and establishing the role of the craftsman, especially the scientist or doctor, as definitively determining between contraries. The rational soul is distinctive in that it can make decisions. It can desire and choose one thing and discard others, and is not driven by any sort of necessity whether physical or teleological (although *that it desires* discloses it as a fundamentally teleological being, oriented toward that which it desires as the best). Indeed later in *Metaphysics* IX he clarifies his point: "[In the case of *dunamis meta logou*] there must be something else which decides, and by this I mean desire or choice. For whichever of two things an animal desires by decision [*kuriōs*], this it will bring about when it has the *dunamis* to do so and approaches that which can be acted upon. Therefore every thing that is capable *kata logon* must act on that which it desires, whenever it desires that of which it has the capability and in the manner in which it has that capability."[98] Desire, choice, decision, and mastery are therefore key to the understanding of *dunamis meta logou*. Note the strangeness here of illustrating a point about *logos* with an animal, which seems to reinforce for Aristotle the *necessity* of acting when desire, capability, and decision come together. The whereabouts of *akrasia* and *hamartia*, indeed of any kind of hesitation or error in this scenario is unclear—they seem, oddly, to have dropped out of the account. But they, too, would seem to be part and parcel of what *logos* enables.

In Heidegger's analysis (which also does not consider *akrasia* or *hamartia*), in *dunamis meta logou* both contraries are *evidently maintained* even after a path has been decided upon. He puts it this way: "Thus *logos* . . . is constantly what excludes, but this means that it is what includes the contrary with it. What this says is that the contrary is 'there' and manifest in a peculiar way in the very fact of avoiding it and getting out of its way."⁹⁹ The Heideggerian theme of a present and manifest absence, a twofoldness in being that exceeds mere positing and negation, will be by now familiar. But can a meaningful distinction be maintained here between *manifest* contraries in *logos*, and a cluster of opaque or hidden possibilities in nature? However, such a split is not satisfactory, for, as we learn from psychoanalysis, in desire and decision there are also surely a cluster of opaque and hidden unconscious possibilities, not necessarily available to the all-seeing eye of the hyperconscious master of discernment. And in the scene of choice that *logos* enables, we might also ask about what has become of the failings and errancies of *akrasia* and of *hamartia*. In Heidegger's own discourse, after all, it is not just in *logos*, as the laying that gathers, that twofoldness unfolds, but also in *phusis* itself.

In the work of *logos*, in *technē*, and in *epistēmē*, then, there is a decision, *kurion*, an act of mastery. In making a work, the craftsman decides, and thereby creates a boundary. Heidegger draws our attention to the fact that in production the *eidos* (form) of the work (*ergon*), is already seen in advance:

> It is seen precisely in what it comes to in the end, if it is to be fully ended and finished. In the *eidos* of the *ergon*, its being-at-an-end— the ends which it encloses—is in advance already anticipated. The *eidos* of the *ergon* is *telos*. The end which finishes, however, is in its essence, boundary, *peras*. To produce something is in itself to forge something into its boundaries, so much so that this being-enclosed is already in view in advance along with all that it *includes and excludes.*¹⁰⁰

Poiēsis, human making, then, is understood here as the installation of a boundary, a decision that cuts off other paths. This boundary excludes that which will not be, and this has a spatial and temporal aspect: the potter determines the shape of the pot, and also determines the being-at-an-end of the productive process and decides when it is has arrived in its final form. In this de-scission, this cutting away, the mastery and decisiveness of the craftsman is paramount as the *ergon*, the product, takes shape and becomes concrete. Each contrary possibility that is annihilated is deemed—as *epistēmē* and *logos*—to be fully manifest, fully known to the craftsman, and is actively discarded. The craftsman, the builder, the doctor, has absolute mastery over the work and his own body: he holds in his hands the responsibility for establishing boundaries, creating limits on space and time, producing works and health from the capacities given by an omniscience-granting *logos*.

Following this Heideggerian reading, it now appears unsurprising that Aristotle establishes the power of the craftsman over contraries with *dunamis meta logou*, and in particular over the primary contrary of possession and privation,[101] at the beginning of IX.2, directly after the discussion of privation and impotence, with their immediate resonances with castration, at the close of IX.1. In the fantasy of mastery presented by *dunamis meta logou*, the specter of castration is itself mastered and held at bay in the image of the good doctor, the good father, who nurses his patients and sons back to health and does not wield the knife as a mutilating force upon them. The contraries of being and not being are thoroughly accounted for in the *logos*, and the very tools for decision and determination of an impermeable boundary between inside and outside, as the form of the work, are placed in the master's hands.

The problems caused in natural coming-to-be by the chance vicissitudes, coincidences and compulsions of material necessity are thus set aside in this opposition between *dunamis meta logou* and *alogon*. Instead, Aristotle offers an image of necessity in nature that is not haunted by such contrariness: "when the agent [*poiētikon*] and the patient [*pathētikon*] approach each other, the former must act and the latter must be acted upon, each in the manner in which it is capable."[102] Every coming-to-be in nature is, therefore, on this view, exactly what it will have been; there are no other options. At this moment in Aristotle's text the distinction between *alogon dunamis* and *dunamis meta logou* is observed from the point of view of the thing already at completion, in *entelecheia* or in *energeia*, in the future anterior of *what it will have been*. Time has stopped. Becoming has come to an end and rests in being. Change and chance, the possibility of not being, are cast aside. The phenomena of nature reappear as absolutely inevitable. On the other hand, the power of *logos* means that the results of

human making can always be different, due to the enduring copresence of the contraries. Heidegger, for whom the *logos* signifies "the
laying that gathers," emphasizes not the decision-making power of
the craftsman as a result of his possessing *logos*, but the ontological givenness inherent in *logos* itself: "No judgments and forms of
judgment are meant here, but the inner movement and lawfulness
which lies in the openness of the world and which presents itself
for the Greeks primarily and essentially in *logos* and as *logos*."[103]
In the invocation of an "inner movement and lawfulness," Heidegger's account brings *logos* into intimacy with *phusis*, finding the
inner movement of *phusis* present also in *logos*. But in my reading,
one that attends to the resonances of sexual difference, Aristotle's
dunamis meta logou rather masters nature's vicissitudes, and functions instead to provide a vision of full and unchanging presence,
in which no loss or privation may be countenanced. In the figure
through whom *logos* is manifested, and the product of his labor at
the moment of completion—the *ergon* standing fully upright in its
being at its end, the healed body or indeed, the mutilated eunuch—
we find the most iconic representation of twentieth-century feminism's analyses: the phallic, architectonic, power of the craftsman,
the master and his tools, the father's law.

The point of view expressed at this stage in the definition of *dunamis* thus remains as an *aporia* in Aristotle's text and thought, in
that it apparently abolishes in one gesture the possibility inherent in
materiality that something might not come to be, a being at work or
energeia without remainder. Through the fantasy of total disclosure
offered by *dunamis meta logou*, the symptomatic threats of materiality and privation (*sterēsis*)—including the coming short (*husterēsis*) of
the feminine matrix (*hustera*); the deformity (*anapēria* or castration)
of the female; and the errant, obstructive, deviating, and mutilating
possibilities of feminine matter—are thereby quelled and suppressed.

ENERGEIA/ENTELECHEIA: BEING AT INCOMPLETION

Aristotle's account of *energeia*, that state of being in the work that is
also a being in completion, *entelecheia*, is less an example of the decisive mastery that *logos* may offer than a scene of multiple analogical
figures that do not rest together in any easy way.[104] As *Metaphysics*
IX proceeds toward its teleological culmination in *energeia*, *dunamis*
itself is redefined in its terms. *Energeia*, however, is approached at

first not with a definition, but via a series of analogies: "As that which builds is to that which is capable of building, so is that which is awake to that which is asleep, or that which is seeing to that which has its eyes shut but has the power to see, or that which is separated from matter to matter itself, or the finished project to the raw material. Let the term *energeia* signify the first part of each of these differences and *dunamis* signify the second part."[105] From this analogical series, it is not hard to see how the usual Latinate translations of *energeia* as "in act," "actuality," and "activity" have persisted. In the first case what is signified is an activity, that of actually building contrasted with what *can* build; the second case, a state of being active: being awake contrasted with what *can* be either awake or asleep; the third, the activity of seeing contrasted with what *is capable of* seeing. For the fourth, "that which is separated from matter to matter itself," various examples of *technē*, *eidos*, and *logos* can be provided: the art of the builder, the form of the house that is in the craftsman's soul, the soul of a creature, or the *logos* for which the sperm is vehicle in reproduction. For the final example, the finished product, one may supply the finished house or the developed offspring, as compared with the bricks and stones, or the menstrual fluid. In the vexed relationship between *energeia* as movement (*kinēsis*) and *entelecheia* as arrival at an end, Aristotle ultimately forges a separation between *kinēsis* and a transcendent and motionless *energeia*, exemplified by the act of thinking and instantiated *par excellence* in the figure of the prime mover, finally freed from the vicissitudes and the finitude of materiality. At the start of the *Nicomachean Ethics*, furthermore, Aristotle argues that the ends of various arts and science are varied, but in the case of an art where there is a final product, that product, the *ergon*, that which is separate, completed, and thus *finally at rest*, is superior to any activity requiring movement.[106]

Aristotle tells us that *energeia* is prior to *dunamis* in several senses: in *logos*, in substance, and also in at least one sense of time. In becoming, the *energeia* will come at the end of the time it takes for generation to occur, so that generation is completed, and the entity can merely exist, qua entity, in the fullness of its being, and in this sense *energeia* is temporally posterior, the *husteron* to *dunamis*'s *proteron*. However, he also writes that, "the actually existent [*to energeia on*] is always generated from the potentially existent [*tou dunamei ontos*] by something which is actually existent [*to energeia ontos*]; for example, a man by a man and the musical by the musical, as there is always a first mover, and this mover already exists in actuality [*energeia*]."[107] On questions of temporal originality, then, Aristotle clearly sides here with the chicken over the egg. All *energeiai*, actually existing beings, are in both nature and the human world, temporally prior to their potentiality or possibility. What this formulation also reveals, however, is a certain *husteron proteron*, for if *energeiai* are temporally prior how may the gaps, the lacks, the disruptions and the vicissitudes of materiality required by *dunamis* appear? The material cause and its privations appear, from this perspective, as sort of fallen bastard offspring, necessary for the cycles of nature to perpetuate themselves in time, but nonetheless always getting in the way—the feminine symptom in action.

The restlessness figurality of *energeia*, sliding from figure to figure, evoking kinds of work and activity as well as form, *logos*, and finished product, is made explicit by Aristotle when he states his hope that induction, *epagōgē*, will make his meaning clear, and a plea for his analogies to be "seen together" (*sunoran*), because we should not seek a definition or boundary (*horos*) for everything.[108] The instability of such a definition that is really not a definition at all once again evokes Plato's description of the receptacle/*chōra* in the *Timaeus*, knowable only through its multiple figures via the operations of "bastard reasoning."[109] Aristotle's *energeia* includes activities that are clearly motile and material (the act of building), activities that are not so clearly material (seeing, contemplation) but which still from the point of view of nature require the metabolic processes of the living body as their substrate, and then those things that are separate from and transcend materiality: *logos* and *eidos*, instantiated in the prime mover. Seeing these different elements of *energeia* together has typically required of the reader a kind of illegitimate idealization that works to conceal its motility, its polyvocality, and its precarity. But I want to insist on their unerasable, symptomatic compresence in Aristotle's discourse.

Aristotle's reformulation of the question of being or substance in terms of *dunamis* and *energeia* in *Metaphysics* IX has the undeniable effect of entrenching his natural teleology more profoundly. Reformulating matter as *dunamis*, as *appropriateness for*, renders it vectoral, introduces into it a *telos* from the start, and erases its aleatory dimension, its plurality, its capacity for unbecoming as well as for becoming. Nonetheless, close examination of the textual vagaries of *dunamis*, *adunamia*, and the various kinds of *dunamis*, especially in relation to the articulation of sexuate powers in *Generation of Animals*, reveals profound difficulties that once again may be read and understood clearly in light of the notion of the feminine symptom developed in the course of this work. In the mysterious and unpredictable phenomena of *automaton* such as mutation and spontaneous generation, in the restless motions and multiple *dunameis* of matter such as the nascent organs and ancestral forms within the *protē hulē* of the menstrual blood, in the capacity of the body to exceed or refuse medical ministrations, in rains in summer and heat waves in winter, we find manifestations of "the indeterminateness [*aoristian*] of matter and the existence of a plurality of principles which impede the natural processes of generation and destruction, and so are often the causes of things coinciding [*sumpiptontōn*] contrary to Nature."[110] These feminine *sumptōmata* wrench open the stable presencing of *energeia* in nature, revealing it is as continually under threat of destabilization, continually subject to the risk of nonbeing, and thus never fully present or secure.

In his essay on potentiality, Giorgio Agamben reminds us, without noticing the pertinence of sexual difference, that for Aristotle *dunamis* also contains at its heart *adunamia*: "Every human power is *adynamia*, impotentiality; every human potentiality is in relation to its own privation."[111] In this call to embrace privation or concealment in human power, we might also hear an echo of Heidegger's Heraclitean call in the *Phusis* essay to return to nature its own propensity to hide: "the task is the much more difficult one of allowing to *phusis*, in all the purity of the essence, the *kruptesthai* that belongs to it."[112] Agamben asserts that, in the human realm, freedom itself consists in being "*capable of one's own impotentiality*, to be in relation to one's own privation."[113] This call for acceding to one's own impotentiality and one's own privation, as well as for a "potentiality that conserves itself and saves itself in actuality,"[114] is a call to understand freedom as radical passivity or receptivity that may be productively reread in relation to a topology of sexual difference. Indeed, Patricia Huntington's feminist appropriation of Heidegger makes much the same argument. Feminist psychoanalytic insight adds to this a call for a nonanxious relation to castration which would require neither the shield of a *logos* that defines itself in opposition to materiality nor the dream of an *energeia* of full presence to protect itself from threats of feminine materiality and privation. Despite Aristotle's explicit statements to the contrary, feminine materiality cannot remain a supine, passive, receptive substrate gladly accepting the imprints of masculine form. Nor is it just a sign for privation or lack. In addition to these, it is also a restless, aleatory lability. Such restlessness gives an alternate kind of motion, opaque and incalculable, and thus also suggests another register of becoming: a becoming according to a feminine temporality of interruption, not tied to and indeed exceeding the unfolding of *entelecheia* and *energeia* as presencing. The motile, aleatory characteristic of matter may also reappear on the side of *logos*, not as its capacity for negation and the encompassing of negation, but rather as the restless, endless push to multiple figurations that inhabits *logos* as its necessary condition, and which makes thinking, and therefore philosophy, possible.

Coda: Matters Arising

From the Aleatory Feminine to Aleatory Feminism

They call you lady luck
But there is room for doubt
At times you have a very un-lady-like way
Of running out

FRANK HENRY LOESSER

Matter, and thus the feminine, appears in the Aristotelian cosmos in three main guises. First, and paradigmatically, matter is the substrate of a change that necessarily comes from elsewhere. It is passive, what is acted upon, it is weighty and falls to earth, it is potential insofar as it lies patiently in wait for form, and is appropriate to and for that form. Second, there is the characterization in *Physics* I.9 of matter as *desiring*, as *stretching out toward* form: here it appears as a strange kind of subject of desire, even harboring its own obscure sort of movement. One might also connect this to the inclination (*rhopē*) that impels the elements toward their proper places in the latter books of *De Caelo*. Here, matter is already folded in advance into the potentiality-actuality schema, into the teleology. Its incipient, vectoral orientation toward form is evident in its very being, at its very heart, and its appropriateness here appears akin to obedience. Insofar as such matter is "like the female desiring the male" she is a "good girl."[1] However there is a third aspect of matter pursued throughout this book: matter as disruptive, as disobedient, as compulsive, as aleatory, as harboring manifold movements *against nature*.[2] This disagreeable aleatory matter gives rise as such to the female offspring, a being that is nonetheless *teleologically required*, and this inexplicable confluence of errancy and teleology I have characterized as "the feminine symptom."

What possibilities, then, might this reading offer for the contemporary philosophical scene, in particular for thinking about feminist philosophy or political theorizing more generally? Throughout these

chapters, Luce Irigaray's recommendations for feminist philosophical practice in "The Power of Discourse and the Subordination of
the Feminine" have been assiduously activated: seeking and exposing
the scenography and conditions of philosophical systematicity, proceeding psychoanalytically to uncover unconscious gendered commit-
ments, mimetically inhabiting and "reopening" the texts of Western
philosophy, and especially and specifically seeking what she calls the
"elsewhere of 'matter.'"[3] But what is the political and philosophical meaning for sexual difference of this identification established
between chance and the feminine in Aristotle's texts? Certainly, the
claim is *not* that the feminine and the aleatory are to be in any sense
essentially connected or identified, or that the aleatory is a long-bur-
ied site of essential feminine sexual difference, finally uncovered and
resurrected at last. Rather, this connection arises in and through Aristotle's establishment of a long-reigning and vastly influential teleological metaphysics, and it is a connection that has survived, quite
unscathed, the supersession of this teleological metaphysics in the
epistemic, philosophical, and political revolutions of modernity—
indeed its echoes may be found in cultural figures from Boethius,
Machiavelli, and Goethe to Frank Sinatra and his Lady Luck.

At the same time the aleatory itself has also recently emerged as a
fecund site for political theorizing, perhaps most centrally in Althusser's late work on aleatory materialism, but also as a key element of
various contemporary "new materialisms" influenced by the works
of thinkers such as Bergson, Whitehead, Merleau-Ponty, Simondon,
Deleuze, and Guattari as well as the American Pragmatist tradition,
and taken up into feminism notably by Elizabeth Grosz, Rosi Braidotti, and Clare Colebrook, among others. The central insight of these
thinkers—that matter is essentially moving, processual, self-organiz-
ing, and riven with the capacity to unfold in unexpected directions
(whether to destructive or productive ends)—is thoroughly of a piece
with what I have excavated as intrinsic to Aristotle's texts. A short
coda is not the place to engage substantively with these bodies of
thought, nor to work out theoretical specifics in relation to a contemporary philosophical scene. However, I would like to at least gesture
toward some of the ways the analysis of Aristotle undertaken here
might bear on some current issues and debates.

Certain crucial questions immediately present themselves: How
can theorizing about matter in metaphysical, physical, and biological
registers reflect upon or help us think through phenomena of human

history and politics, if at all? Analogical associations between the physical body and the social order are of course rampant in both antiquity and modernity, but what is the force of such analogies, and is this relationship indeed simply analogical? What is the value, if any, of remaining *within* the ancient texts of Western metaphysics while undoing them, as opposed to claiming an alternative and external philosophical genealogy that might include Democritus, Epicurus, and Lucretius as well as Spinoza and Nietzsche, what Althusser has called a "materialist underground"?[4] And what might an aleatory feminism, understood as a tactical alliance that seeks the overcoming of patriarchy even as it is generated by a thoroughly patriarchal architectonic, even look like?

Aristotle himself, of course, wrote an entire treatise on politics and it is therefore to him that we should first turn for some clues about how a teleological metaphysician understands the vagaries of political life. However, since the political scene of antiquity as he countenances it embraces only the rational deliberations of elite men, there is no space for a positive valuation of the aleatory, of the random, of the voice and force of the subaltern who would challenge, divert, or recast the very ground of the *polis*. The *polis* is rather understood, in its ideal form, as the privileged and *sui generis* site of beautiful dialogue among equals, sharing rule by turns, and bound by affective ties of friendship.[5] Furthermore, while Aristotle explicitly states that the *polis* in its irreducible multiplicity must not be understood as a unity or as an individual, and ought not therefore to be understood on the model of the organism, he has frequent recourse to this analogy.[6] Throughout the *Politics*, in fact, he is liberal with bodily analogies, and the norms of health—not to mention the pathologies of corporeal disproportion—are central metaphors in his discourses concerning degenerate regimes.[7] The aleatory, for Aristotle, can in other words only play a destructive role in matters of human relations, just as it does in nature. Indeed he designates the *sumptōma*—the chance occurrence—as the source of both democracy and of revolutions: disruptive upsurgings of the people of which he does not approve in the least.[8] This connection between the natural and human worlds is evident in a passage that appears toward the end of *Metaphysics* XII, the chapter on the prime mover, where the referent is not the *polis* but the household:

> For in an army goodness exists both in the order and in the general, and rather in the general; for it is not because of the order that he

exists, but the order exists because of him. All things, both fishes
and birds and plants, are ordered together in some way, but not in
the same way; and the system is not such that there is no relation
between one thing and another; there is a definite connection. For
all things are ordered together to one end, just as in a household, in
which the freemen have the least liberty to act at random [*etuchē*]
but all or most things are ordered, while slaves and wild animals
contribute little to the common good but these for the most part act
at random [*etuchen*].[9]

Here the unsuitability (and, I submit, untranslatability) of Aristotle's
political discourse for the contemporary globe is laid bare. Not only
does freedom, that value of Western modernity *par excellence*, function quite differently here, but the actions of slaves and wild animals
(and, implicitly, women) are relegated not simply to nature but appear
on the side of the aleatory, which acts *against nature* to disrupt and
waylay its proper unfolding. Freemen are bound necessarily to the
good (in a formulation that can only appear stingingly ironic to the
modern eye), and in the ideal *polis* are bound to the good and well-
being of all. These are the only true political actors in this encounter
between order and chaos. There is no room for Machiavelli's prince,
understood by Althusser on the model of Lucretius's *clinamen*, as
the one who arises from no specified place or time, and who enables
a properly historical and political *encounter*. There is no space for
understanding and analyzing the complex dynamics of colonialism
or capitalism, since Aristotle simply decrees that *poleis* should not
expand, and that the accumulation of wealth for its own sake should
be outlawed. Neither is it possible to consider the rise of social movements that rearticulate the entire space and meaning of the political, such as feminism, queer struggles, disability rights, animal rights,
and environmental movements, in which matters of the household
and kinship, of the body, of love and sex, of healthcare, of nature,
biology, and ultimately of philosophy itself, are disclosed as harboring profoundly political and ideological dimensions.

   Where Aristotle does, strangely, coincide with at least some contemporary materialist theorizing, is in the scope of his thinking. The
dynamics of teleology, the priority of the end as *energeia*, as a unified
living activity signified *par excellence* by the activity of the organism
with language that is man (the famous *zōon echon logon*), governs the
entire field of his thought, whether biological, physical, metaphysical,
cosmological, logical, political, ethical, rhetorical, or poetic. So that
while the model for a teleological cosmos may derive from biology,

and especially the biology of man, there is a distinctly antihumanist character inherent in the teleological approach. In each area of inquiry, then, Aristotle observes and documents the phenomena with an acute and attuned eye, listens to and incorporates the things said by predecessors, and finds certain principles continually at work: things act for the sake of the good and what is best, and what is essential, whole, unified, healthy, and harmonious is what is best. Central to this harmony is an equilibration of the ubiquitous dynamics of activity and passivity—ruling and being ruled—and this is as true in the political sphere as in the biological and metaphysical. Contemporary phenomenological scholars of Aristotle such as Claudia Baracchi and Christopher Long have resisted hegemonic readings of Aristotle in radical ways, and emphasized the political and ethical value of such an approach for thinking through critical issues of our times.[10] However, holding sex and gender as central guiding questions in an analysis of the texts, as I have done, reveals a structural commitment to gender hierarchy throughout the Aristotelian corpus that cannot, it seems to me, reasonably be evaded.

Reaching into antiquity and encountering its strange complexities does nonetheless permit a sidestepping and sidelining of certain modern legacies. The world-founding Cartesian subject, the Kantian transcendental subject, the Hegelian dialectic of subject and object, Newtonian laws of nature governing a mechanistic universe, the overweening value of individual freedom, the triumphs and dangers of technoscience, political formations such as the nation-state, modern colonial empires and postcolonial struggles, and the entanglements of identity politics are just some of the notions simply unthinkable from the standpoint of classical Greek thought. Nonetheless, the two opposing strains in Aristotle's thought, toward both system and phenomena, give grounds for a certain, possibly productive, ambivalence for thinking in a contemporary frame. For Aristotle may on the one hand be easily read as a totalizer, his thought dominated by what Reiner Schürmann has called Greek antiquity's hegemonic fantasm of "the One": an ontotheological unity underlying nature's multifarious phenomena that can be traced to the earliest thinkers of Presocratic Greece.[11] In this light, one might interpret his philosophical project as driven by a fantasy that the world's secrets can be finally yielded up by a grand unified theory—what Donna Haraway has called the "god trick."[12] On the other hand, his piecemeal yet of-a-piece approach to his various areas of inquiry, and his fidelity and attunement to articulating both the phenomena he encounters and the ways things are spoken of (what Christopher Long has called his "legomenology") may also have something in common with Haraway's liberatory vision of overlapping, partial perspectives.[13] While similar teleological dynamics may be observed over and over again in each field of study—whether metaphysics, physics, biology, poetics, politics—the specificities and singularities of each field are unique and untranslatable. The fantasies of ultimate mastery over and possession of nature represented by Haraway's "god trick"—not to mention the imaging technologies that permit a smooth and uninterrupted phantasmatic "zoom" from the subatomic, through the molecular, the cellular, the human sized, and the cosmic—are thus arguably specific excrescences of modernity and have not yet congealed in Aristotle's philosophy.

Seen in this way, then, a curious confluence emerges between Aristotle's thinking and the insights yielded by recent developments in chaos theory. According to the latter, phenomena both natural and human, as diverse as hurricanes, political movements, intracellular processes, economic cycles, fetal development, chemical reactions, internet sensations, geological formations, phase transitions, plant growth, the spread of disease and so on, are describable by the same nonlinear mathematical equations and broadly topological concepts such as attractors, bifurcations, vortices, and solitons.[14] Notable here is that both positions, ancient and contemporary, displace the sovereignty of the human subject characteristic of modernity, and each finds movement and life inherently at work in both organic and inorganic phenomena. At the same time, the differences are profound. The Aristotelian cosmos is, after all, driven by teleological desire in a scene at once metaphysical, ethical, and paternal-theological, while the world presented by chaos theory and its uptake into philosophy and political theory is one of spontaneous, immanent, aleatory, self-assemblage, knowable only dimly through stochastic and higher-mathematical means. This distinction, and its political stakes may be investigated more closely by returning once again to a consideration of the long, vexed relationship between matter and teleology inaugurated by Aristotle, epitomized in the central figure of the organism.

If one starts one's inquiry into the nature of reality by the phenomenological observation of natural beings, with the animal organism as the paradigm, as I believe Aristotle does, the intuition that teleological processes are at the heart of life springs forth quite naturally.[15] Certainly, the becoming of the organism involves development toward a

fully realized, reproductively mature, adult form. And certainly living
beings act (for the most part) to preserve the life and integrity of their
being (whether on an individual or transindividual species level). Flies
act to evade the swatter, vines stretch toward the light, animals and
plants display all sorts of adaptive features—camouflage, dentition,
sensory apparatuses, behavior patterns, sexual displays—that allow
them survival and flexibility in their specific environments. Physiological processes aim toward homeostasis and maintaining a stable
internal environment for the organism, ensuring smooth interactions
between various physiological systems (circulatory, nervous, diges-
tive, lymphatic, excretory, and so on). The perspective and experience
of the knower as an embodied being also contributes to such a phenomenology: after all the highly unpleasant disequilibrations and rav-
ages of disease are incontrovertible signs of breakdown and errancy
in relation to the desirable harmony that is health. Understood on this
basis, it is easy to see how Aristotelian phenomenology is thus transformed into an ontoethical metaphysics in which all things (natural
and human) clearly act "always and for the most part" toward what
is *best, to beltion.*

It would be a mistake, however, to imagine that such a style of
analysis is archaic, simply evaporating in modern scientific accounts
of the natural world. Indeed, Darwin himself was in favor of teleological explanation of natural phenomena, and throughout *The Origin of Species* subscribed to the view that natural selection "acts *for
the good of each being,* and that its products are present *for* various
functions, purposes and ends."[16] Even if there is no design, no ultimate purpose, no grand unifying reason, no emulating or striving
toward the divine in natural world; even if every gene mutation and
symbiosis is the result of a chance occurrence, teleological explanations still persist. And this is because biology has traditionally dealt
at the level of totalities—cells, organs, and organisms—that are seen
as unified individuals. The Aristotelian approach that understands
the existence of substances *in relation to one, pros hen,* results in the
primacy of functional and teleological explanations that continue to
abound sensefully and, I think, with a certain precarious legitimacy,
into the present day.

However, more recent biological thinking has also shifted focus
decisively away from the hegemony of the functional totality whose
paradigm is the organism, or has rethought the organism's becoming
in such a way that shatters its hegemonic unity. The mid-twentieth

century work of Gilbert Simondon, for exampled, incorporates the social collective and sensory environment, as well as the pluripotentiality of the developing being and its inherent out-of-phaseness with itself, into a new conception of "metastability" that fundamentally displaces the substantial finality of the adult individual.[17] Disciplines such as immunology, cellular and molecular biology, ecology and medical ecology emphasize the permeability and precarity of boundaries, as well as web-like, constitutive interrelationships between the organism and its surroundings, at both macro and microscopic levels, and introduce concepts such as the microbiome in place of the traditional organism.[18] Here, health appears less as a feature of a well-oiled and functional machine, clearly bounded, pure, and well-defended against outside attack, than as a question of a diverse and flourishing ecosystem in which humans and a range of external and internal stimuli and microorganisms all play their part in fostering an environment of immune functioning. As the discourses of the later Derrida have forcefully shown, rigid boundaries and defenses that refuse to acknowledge this kind of constitutive alterity—both within *and* outside (and Derrida writes especially in the political register but in a way that might be extended to all beings)—result typically in disorders of autoimmunity in which the very mechanisms whose function it is to protect the organism end up destroying it as well.[19] In evolutionary terms, too, the rise of that most unitary of creatures, the eukaryotic single-celled organism, is now widely understood to be the result not simply of accumulated genetic mutations but of certain chimerical, symbiotic incorporations, such that intracellular organelles like mitochondria or plasmids are thought to have once been prokaryotic bacteria in their own right, ingested but not digested by a host bacterium.[20] This leads to a very different view of the organism, and of health and disease, displacing the view that even a disease as life threatening as cancer should be thought of as an external enemy to be vanquished. Dorion Sagan puts it this way: "[Organelles that were once bacteria] are now generally well behaved, although cancer is noteworthy for the rampant multiplication of the occasionally vampiric mitochondria."[21] The phenomena of life thus appear irreducibly plural and relational, and the "norms" of "normal" and "healthy" versus "pathological" or "diseased" are, as Georges Canguilhem presciently argued from the 1940s onward, no longer easily opposable or extricable.[22]

There is, of course, also an antiteleological strain in natural philosophy whose roots reach back to earliest antiquity. Aristotle himself attributes the view that parts of animals may randomly aggregate into whole creatures to Empedocles in *Physics* II.8, where he asks whether suitable dentition and other teleologically explicable parts of animals could indeed appear by coincidence, *sumptōma*. "If so," he writes, "then whenever all the parts came together as if generated for the sake of something, the wholes which by chance (*automaton*) were fitfully composed survived but those which came together not in this manner, like the man-faced offspring of oxen mentioned by Empedocles, perished and still do so."[23] He refutes this possibility by recourse to the regularity of natural phenomena—things happening by chance and "against nature" are *infrequent*, while those that are properly natural occur *always or for the most part*. However Theophrastus, Aristotle's student, strenuously disavowed his teacher's foundational claim about the frequency of the good and the orderly in nature. In his *On First Principles* (known as his *Metaphysics*) he asserts instead that, if one observes nature closely, things *rarely* if ever act for the best but by coincidence (*sumptōmatikōs*) and by necessity, and that "there is much that neither obeys nor receives the good—or rather, it is much more by far."[24] More famously, the ancient atomists, Leucippus, Democritus, and Epicurus, admitted only atoms and void into their ontologies, and believed that natural bodies were formed through chance and necessity, as aggregates resulting from either from the movement of a primal cosmic vortex, or simply from random collisions and interlockings of differently shaped atoms.[25] For Lucretius, whose first-century BCE *On the Nature of Things* is the fullest account we have of the Epicurean philosophy, the earth in an originally fecund state gave rise to "grasses and saplings first, and then created animals—many species variously produced in many ways."[26] According to this Epicurean view, an infinitely large number of atoms existing in infinite space over an infinite time period must necessarily give rise to innumerable sorts of aggregation, in particular the earth with its peculiarly maternal fecundity, none with any ontological or essential supremacy over any other. "Monstrous" forms were created on an equal par with the regular forms we know, but like Empedocles's man-faced oxen, died out on account of failure to survive and reproduce:

> At that time the earth experimented with the creation of many prodigious things, which were born with bodies of grotesque appearance. There were androgynes—beings halfway between the two sexes, belonging to neither, differing from both; there were some creatures devoid of feet or deprived of hands; there were others dumb

for want of a mouth, or blind for want of eyes. . . . Other equally
monstrous prodigious beings were produced by the earth. But they
were created in vain, since nature denied them growth and they were
unable to attain the coveted bloom of maturity or find food or be
united in the acts of Venus.[27]

The theme of a Venusian maternal-feminine fecundity infuses the
entirety of Lucretius's poem; indeed it begins with an extended invocation of Venus's many wondrous qualities and delights. Matter, in its
new philosophical manifestation in the Latin language now appearing as *materia* rather than *hulē*, is of course directly related to *mater*
(mother). The centrality of this feminine principle in Lucretius's work
cannot be overestimated: "In expounding our philosophy I often call
these elements 'matter' [*materiem*] or 'generative particles of things'
[*genitalia corpora rebus*] or 'seeds of things' [*semina rerum*]; and
since they are the ultimate constituents of all things, another term
I often use is 'ultimate particles' [*corpora prima*]."[28] In assimilating the male seed (*semina*) thusly to the maternally signifying matter
(*materia*), in his refusal to accept the tragic patriarchal sacrifice of
Iphigenia by Agamemnon that he finds so emblematic of obfuscatory
and oppressive religious discourse, in elevating maternal and earthly
fecundity and establishing an unequivocally feminine principle at the
root of all existing things, and in foregrounding the originary role of
chance in the form of the *clinamen*, the uncaused swerve that ensures
the collision of atoms, Lucretius is thus the mirror image of Aristotle.[29] The aleatory feminine appears in this remarkable text no longer
as a symptom of a patriarchal metaphysics, but as the plural and generative origin of the entire cosmos.

In his genealogy of the "underground current" of what he calls the
"materialism of the encounter" in the Western tradition, Althusser
includes a whole alternate genealogy that includes Democritus, Epicurus, Machiavelli, Spinoza, Montesquieu, Hobbes, Rousseau, Marx,
and Heidegger. Outside of Lucretius's Epicureanism, none of these
thinkers, with the notable exception of Machiavelli, draw attention to
the feminine valence of matter and chance. Absent here is Giordano
Bruno, who, particularly in *De La Causa*, satirizes the Peripatetic
position on passive, feminized matter, and takes up the Epicurean
mantle, offering *mater-materia* instead as fundamental substance, an
unfolding potential out of which form transiently emerges and passes
away.[30] Machiavelli of course famously aligns women and luck—the
last part of *The Prince* is devoted to a program for managing fortune

and her feminine wiles, and the virile Renaissance man of *virtù* is just the character to whip her into shape.[31] Speaking of women and whips, it is worth noting that Friedrich Nietzsche undertakes a profound transvaluation of the aleatory in the form of the Dionysian force of disruption, generativity, and ecstasy, but he almost without exception eviscerates it of its bacchic, feminine qualities, aligning it instead with the hypermasculinized figure of the satyr.[32] This assimilation and appropriation is all the more remarkable since Nietzsche's main source for the Dionysian-Apollinian distinction, indeed its originator, was J. J. Bachofen, theorist of archaic *Mutterrecht*, who, in the tradition of Euripides's *Bacchae*, identifies the Dionysian unequivocally with the unboundaried feminine qualities of the fecund earth.[33]

A manifestation of the aleatory feminine may be found also in Goethe's botanical writings of the early nineteenth century, in which he writes of the "spiral tendency" of plants as contrasted with their tendency for vertical growth. The spiral system which causes plant growth to turn in on itself governs development, nourishment, and reproduction, but is prone to excess and as such is also the source of "the extremely diverse misgrowths that appear as deviations from the law of definite forms."[34] The spiral tendency is thus also *symptomatic* in the sense I have developed here, in that it both "fosters completion" but "also occurs erratically, prematurely, and destructively."[35] As a deviation from the straight path, the spiral tendency might well be compared with the Lucretian *clinamen*, an errancy that is both productive and destructive, without a natural or ethical compass. Goethe himself explicitly identifies the vertical and spiral tendencies with masculinity and femininity, each equally necessary in his view: "Let us recall the figure of speech we ventured to use with the convulvulus and the staff. Let us go a step further and visualize a vine entwining itself about the elm. Here we see, drawn to our attention by Nature herself, the male and the female, the giver and the receiver together, growing in a vertical and spiral direction." Goethe consummates the romance thus: "In the course of the transformation of growth the two systems are separated, in obvious contrast to one another, and take opposing courses, to be reunited at a higher level."[36]

The difficulty with elevating a philosophy of matter, of the aleatory, and of the feminine, to the level of a foundational cosmic principle is that with matter's generativity and life-giving qualities inevitably come decay, destruction, mortality, death. The Epicurean philosophy is thus explicitly dedicated to accommodating oneself to this factical

situation through a cultivation of *ataraxia*, a kind of equanimity, as
well as joy and pleasure in friendship that "dances around the world,"
and an ethic that delights in movement rather than stasis.[37] However,
as Simone de Beauvoir explained so vividly in *The Second Sex*, and
is well-traveled terrain in psychoanalysis, "woman" as she appears
in the Western tradition has been mostly reduced to a repository
for such anxieties about our mortal being, as well as uplifted as an
always available source of comfort and delight capable of assuaging
such anxieties, at least momentarily.[38] Irigaray's *Speculum* describes
at length how philosophers have thus, consciously or not, transformed woman into a mirror or screen upon which both the pro-
foundest fears and the most exhilarating and comforting consolations
may be projected, thereby managing existential anxieties by locating
both threat and (an inevitably short-lived and failure-bound) succor
outside and beyond their own all-too-human bodies.[39] Taking up the
disruptive and motile possibilities signified by the aleatory feminine,
a feminine that is evental, that "comes from nowhere" and *cannot
stand still*, and *mobilizing deliberately* such fears and hopes in order
to reveal the contingency of their association with women, is one possible tactic, therefore, for a politics of resistance to this entrenched
patriarchy. Echoing an Irigarayan trope, in the wake of the twentieth-century demise of the possibility of metaphysics, the dehiscence
of this construct of "woman" as existential solace and endless disap-
pointment, as container and abyss, is perhaps *the* philosophical and
political challenge of our own time.[40]

But before going further with this thought of aleatory feminism
as an aleatory materialism, a further consideration of teleology and
materialism is in order. Not this time in the biological or natural
register, the sense in which teleology signifies a relation to a larger
unity thought primarily according to a spatial logic, but rather in its
explicitly political-temporal-historical expression. This is not to say
that we should not speak of organic or organicist conceptions of the
social body as teleological, strictly speaking.[41] But teleology's much
more renowned role in modern philosophy of history stems from
Kant, is articulated in Hegel's dialectic, and finds its feet, as it were,
in Marx's materialism. It is this element to which Althusser's aleatory
materialism of the historical encounter is most strenuously opposed.
Althusser states, perhaps crudely, that the materialism (or "surmate-
rialism," on the model of "surrealism") he is attempting to develop
is "opposed totally" to the materialisms on record, including that of

Marx, Engels, and Lenin. This, he says, "like every other materialism in the rationalist tradition is a materialism of necessity and teleology, that is to say, a transformed, disguised form of idealism."[42] In
his recent essay, "Non-dialectical Materialism," Pheng Cheah echoes
this sentiment when he speaks of Marx's theory of labor in teleological terms "as a process of actualization whereby the given reality or
matter 'is negated' through the imposition of purposive form," and
says that in both Marxism and Hegelianism "negation is a source of
actualization."[43] We may put aside here the large-scale historical stag-
ism and "dialectical materialism" of Engels, in which opposing economic forces within a given mode of production come inevitably to
a revolutionary head, giving rise to subsequent modes of production
with the final form of a fully functional, state-free, and self-governing
communism. Not because such a future is impossible, although the
notion that spirit, history, or relations of production tend toward a
state in which contradictions are finally overcome supposes an intol-
erance for contradiction that appears to be highly uncharacteristic of
contemporary economic and social orders in a global frame. Indeed
to set aside a dialectical-teleological conception of history in favor of
aleatory materialism is not at all to imagine that history (qua modes
of production) has already reached its end.

Cheah goes on to explore Derridean and Deleuzian modes of non-
dialectical materialism which, along with Althusser's conception,
may be read under the sign of the aleatory. According to Cheah's incisive reading of Derrida on matter from the 1972 *Positions* to *Specters
of Marx* in 1993, matter for Derrida appears first as a radical alterity,
one that always risks being fully inscribed in and by the traditional
oppositions of Western metaphysics. This conception is developed in
his later work as an inappropriated and inappropriable other that is
a site of the event, of the gift of time, that signifies the arrival of the
future (*avenir*), as the "to-come" (*à-venir*) and that has a weak messianic or eschatological dimension that renders us passive in its operation but also has the capacity to activate us, to arouse a response,
both ethically and politically. As Étienne Balibar makes clear in his
important essay on the "suspended dialogue" between Derrida and
Althusser, it is precisely this eschatological or messianic dimension
that separates these two nondialectical thinkers.[44] Derrida on the one
hand carefully separates teleology as a metaphysical notion from an
eschatological or messianic dimension in ethico-political life. In the
place of the "good as such" (whether thought as Aristotelian telos or

Kantian ideal), he mobilizes conceptions such as the gift, forgiveness, justice, event, and hospitality, and draws attention to their irreducible operation in the discourses under his inquiry. In an extended footnote in *Specters of Marx*, he famously speaks of Walter Benjamin's "weak messianic power" as *messianic without messianism*.[45] Such messianicity is for Derrida *incalculable*, appearing only as *différance*, nonself-identical and continually deferred: not arrived, nonpresent, always to come. There is clear risk here of falling back into an ontotheology— but the risk is mitigated vastly, it seems to me, by reading this, as Cheah does, as a dimension inherent in and immanent to materiality itself. Althusser on the other hand dispenses with any and all conceptions of futurity, defending a radically disenchanted Hegelianism that goes beyond teleology as "a process without subject or end."[46]

Althusser's aleatory materialism utterly evacuates from politics and philosophy any notion of origin and telos: no cause, no morality, no theology, no metaphysics. There is for him simply the facticity of the random encounter, which, like Machiavelli's prince and Lucretius's *clinamen*, comes from no specified place or time, the effects of which may or may not take hold:

> Since every encounter is provisional even when it lasts, there is
> no eternity in the "laws" of any world or any state. History here
> is nothing but the permanent revocation of the accomplished fact
> by another undecipherable fact to be accomplished, without our
> knowing in advance whether, or when, or how the event that revokes
> it will come about. Simply, one day new hands will have to be dealt
> out, and the dice thrown again on to the empty table.[47]

The historical or political encounter may appear to involve the "exceptional individual" on the model of Machiavelli's Prince: Napoleon, Rosa Parks, Mohamed Atta, or Nelson Mandela might stand as examples although it would surely be a mistake to imagine that these familiar names arose in vacuums on the strength of some inner *virtù*, rather than as a product of the highly organized circumstances for which they metonymically stand (perhaps lone assassins such as Lee Harvey Oswald stand as exceptions). More credible as historical actors here are collective social movements and blocs: the forces giving rise to May 1968, the Arab Spring, or Occupy. Nothing specific gives birth to them, nothing sustains them, there are no guarantees of their effectiveness, merely the chance coming together of circumstances that may or may not effect lasting change. However, Althusser's aleatory encounter is not simply between historical actors, but

also between the prince and the goddess of fortune herself. Glossing
Machiavelli, he writes: "Encountering *Fortuna*, the Prince must have
the *virtù* to treat her as he would treat a woman, to welcome her in
order to seduce or do violence to her; in short, to use her to realize his
destiny."[48] Chance, then, is itself, or herself, to be managed, mastered,
seduced, manipulated, violated, and instrumentalized, and the ability
to accomplish this is the very mark of the man of *virtù*. A consequence
of this politics of aleatory materialism is, then, the promotion of a
certain skill, of a hypertechnics capable of managing *chance itself*,
produced by ideologies of gender and manifesting in a certain masculine style. Chance, of course, as Althusser would insist, refers to the
field of the constitutively unpredictable and unmasterable, and any
claim to a technics of the aleatory must necessarily be phantasmatic.
Phantasms notwithstanding, recent work in areas such as economics,
ecology, and chaos theory nonetheless articulates a limited technics
that might be used to map or manage complex systems. As described
by Manuel DeLanda, such frameworks suggest ways that complex
systems might be manipulated in certain directions, though this is
a far cry from the decisive manliness of *virtù*. Policy decisions may,
for example, nudge economic systems away from inefficient attractors, or certain environmental management strategies might encour-
age ecosystems toward an optimal region of instability "on the edge
of chaos" that encourages resilience and flexibility, even though a
small risk of catastrophe may also be present.[49] There is certainly
some scope here for a limited, risk-aware agency in an aleatory world,
though it must draw back considerably from the fantasies of technical mastery governing modernity since Renaissance man first bravely
broke through the layered hierarchies of heaven and earth determined
by a sedimented Aristotelianism.

    While Althusser's materialism of the encounter thus decisively dis-
penses with a paternalist metaphysics, it does not quite do away with
a masculinist humanism in which man stands over the world as over
a cacophonous orchestra, still hopeful of conducting something rec-
ognizable as music even in the absence of guarantees. The Derridean
approach, by contrast, requires a constant enmeshment in the world,
in which I am understood to be always ethically and politically at stake
in my dealings with the world, subject to unconscious drives in choice
and decision, as much subject to the world as it is subject to me, as
passive as I am active. Cheah puts is this way: "We would have to
thus rethink the philosophemes of decision, of that foundational couple

activity and passivity, as well as potentiality and actuality."[50] He continues: "the force of materiality is nothing other than the constitutive
exposure of [the subject of] power to the other," and this carries the
messianic thought of "an absolute or incalculable hospitality."[51] In light
of my analysis of Aristotle's *dunamis tou pathein* or capacity for *being-
acted-upon* as carrying a distinctively feminine valence (not to mention
Derrida's own reliance in his work on hospitality upon ancient scenes
in which the bodies of women typically play a central and sacrificial
role), such recommendations for laying oneself bare to the world need
to be approached with considerable caution.[52] Women throughout history have certainly not been well served by subscribing to sacrificial
logics. Nonetheless, the call for responsibility and responsiveness, to a
realization of and accession to one's own implication in alterity, for a
stepping back from a desire for mastery in politics and ethics, or indeed
in what we might call the politics of knowledge or in philosophy writ
large, is undeniably urgent.

As well as in Derrida, this strand may be found in the late Heidegger's notion of *Gelassenheit*, in the Levinasian ethics of the face
of the other, and in Jean-Luc Nancy's thought of Being Singular Plural, as well as in numerous feminist and queer thinkers.[53] We might
simply mention here Heideggerian feminists such as Patricia Huntington, the deconstructive feminisms of Gayatri Chakravorty Spivak,
Drucilla Cornell, and Gloria Anzaldùa, and feminist philosopher of
technoscience Donna Haraway. What is distinctive in these thinkers
is their articulation of an engagement with the world that takes primary responsibility for the stakes of that engagement, in other words
an awareness that in claims to knowing and speaking there is also
silencing and concealment, but also (and here is the materialist or
deconstructionist departure from Heidegger) always an indeterminate
array of possibilities for transformation in the space of the encounter.
Any attempt to responsibly grasp reality recognizes that such "grasping" is never a grasp at all, but rather a reaching toward or stretching out without guarantee. It carries with it evasions, blind spots,
and the ever-present and yet unpredictable possibility of change. Haraway's recommendations for feminist science, for instance, suggest
that it should not encounter its fields of investigation as an agent con-
fronting passive objects of knowledge, nor should it treat the world as
a chthonic, fecund, "mother earth," but rather it should engage the
world as a kind of "witty agent," a trickster with whom we might
converse without assurances or guarantees (a formulation in which

the Presocratic echo of Heraclitus's "nature loves to hide" may be loudly heard).[54] Such encounters and dialogues, a "political ecology" among human and nonhuman (and partially human) entities: animals, plants, artifacts, natural phenomena, social and economic phenomena, hybrids and cyborgs, understood as agents rather than patients, has been promulgated in a trove of recent thought, much of it inspired by the immanentism of Deleuze and Guattari. Perhaps the most explicitly political formula is given by Bruno Latour, who has proposed a radical "parliament of things" in which all such beings would be granted a voice and a vote.[55] Of course, the ethical questions raised by who might claim to speak for or represent whom or what in such a parliament are legion. Sensitive to these problems, thinkers such as Jane Bennett and William Connolly have articulated new, complex, conceptions of political ecology that push it in promising directions, while Karen Barad's work provides an elaborate and impressive philosophical underpinning for this new multiagentic world.[56] New philosophical movements have emerged, such as object-oriented ontology, that grant new liveliness and significance not just to natural things and complex systems but also to artifacts.

In the wake of these brave new materialisms, a feminist critique is still urgent and necessary. A stark illustration of how just how persistent and pervasive the reduction of women to passivity and objecthood continues to be may be found, oddly enough, in news reports of the death of Osama bin Laden in May 2011. The very first press release, by John Brennan, the White House's counterterrorism chief, announced that bin Laden had used his wife as a "shield," and that she, as a consequence, had been killed—a story eagerly embraced by a public intent on envisioning the last moments of a misogynist Islamic monster. The next day, White House spokesperson Jay Carney revealed that bin Laden's wife had instead *rushed the invading commandos* and was shot in the leg, but was still alive. It is worth considering how the almost unimaginably courageous action of Amal Ahmed Abdulfattah, this then unnamed woman, screaming and swerving in as if from nowhere like Lucretius's *clinamen, rushing the commandos*, became so quickly reformulated as mute passivity, how she was so quickly reduced to an object, tool, and obstacle—a shield—in a scene of action that can and must take place between men alone.

Aristotle's metaphysical construal of matter as passive, as malleable and capable of being *worked upon*, so decisive for the fate of the female in both Christian and Islamic worlds, entails that it is also a site of privation. And this lack has not just a logical aspect but also a gendered valence. Chapter 6 shows how Aristotle consolidates a conception of the feminine as *lack* and *inability* on this basis, a conception that remains alive and well in the Western imaginary up to and including Lacanian psychoanalysis. This lack on the side of the feminine opens up a *mise en abyme*, what Irigaray has called, "the horror of the abyss, attributed to woman."[57] Under this rubric, any thorough consideration of one's origin in the body of a woman and the maternal line that precedes that, announces the threat of an endless, boundaryless descent into materiality, the terror of the replicative automatisms of biology, and ultimately the deadly stases of inorganic matter. In the face of this abyss, the saving force of the spermatic, transcendent father can only provide welcome relief, profound existential consolation. Hence Irigaray's call for a relation among women that subscribes neither to abyssal boundarylessness, nor to bounded subjectivity secured on the basis of objectal exchange or projection of lack onto a sexual other ("forgive me, mother, I prefer a woman").[58] Irigaray's feminine to come thus follows the logic of a half-open, self-touching, nonappropriative corporeal discursivity characterized by nearness and proximity, the *"nonsuture of her lips,"* rather than the fully substantial unified individuality of the phallus.[59] We can see, then, how Irigaray makes clear the sexual stakes of Heidegger's reading of Aristotelian becoming as twofold, in which absencing becomes a mode of being, or presencing, rather than a mere negation. But, as shown in chapter 6, in the discussion of Bigwood's feminist Heideggerianism, even with the elevation of privation to the status of a mode of being, this hermeneutic of gender leaves us with ineluctably feminine supineness, a passivity or receptivity that reinscribes the metaphysics of gender.[60] And it is this metaphysics that aleatory feminism challenges.

Aristotelian matter appears in its dominant guise as passive, receptive, malleable, moldable, *appropriate for* the form to come, and even stretching out toward it. But, according to the reading developed in this book, it also, necessarily, harbors a quite different subterranean character. It is the source of everything that is unexpected, forceful, and surprising—happy coincidences and monstrous, devastating disruptions. This conception of matter as inappropriable and excessive—not merely a placeholder for negation or privation but as the very possibility of otherwiseness, as harboring a field of potentials any one of which might be realized, dependent on an indeterminate confluence of factors, has found distinctive resonance in twentieth- and twenty-first century materialisms—both biological and political. But I also want to insist upon the political force of the symptom as *feminine*—the conjunction of this aleatory field of the event with antipatriarchal feminist politics. In the space of the aleatory, the hierarchies of ruler and ruled, of passive and active, and of stable configurations of masculine and feminine have, strictly speaking, no purchase or meaning. Nonetheless the Aristotelian feminine symptom, traversing the interior of teleology as mute passivity or complicity and the exterior as interruptive event, may also be harnessed as a site of feminist power.

It is important to be clear. Asserting such intimacy between the feminine and the aleatory is not an essentialist or eternalizing claim about the nonself-sameness of woman as such, nor an Irigarayan claim about the nature of an as-yet-unthought feminine. Rather, the call here is for a feminist politics to *tarry with the aleatory*, to see what sorts of working through (of metaphysics and of patriarchy) might be accomplished via this uncanny and all too metaphysical confluence. In Nietzschean style, the aleatory feminine must undergo *transvaluation*. No longer a threat to be feared or kept at bay, it is a capacity for difference, change, even for ecstasy. A feminist conception of aleatory politics is aligned with what Rosi Braidotti has called the teratological, and what Donna Haraway has called the cyborg. It embraces monsters, hybrids, the mutant generativity of automatons, and the disfigurement and mortality of corporeal beings. Its mode of proceeding can be defined as *interruptivity*.[61]

Neither active nor passive, interruptivity signifies a capacity both *to be interrupted* and *to interrupt* existing orders. Women's corporeal and social experience has been typified by relentless interruptions, but interruptivity signifies *also* that which disrupts, simply because that is part of what it means to be on intimate terms with the aleatory encounter, and this interruptivity thus signifies and lays bare the precarity of any existing (heteropatriarchal, white-supremacist, capitalist) order.[62] Aleatory feminism thrives in lively collectivities, and takes to the streets in the fashion of the many women involved in the Arab Spring and Occupy movements, and in the Guerilla Girls and Riot Grrl aesthetic movements.[64] The slogan of Belgrade Women in Black: "Always disobedient to patriarchy, war, nationalism and militarism" indeed exemplifies this aleatory spirit. Aleatory feminism plays anti-state and antireligion punk music in orthodox churches in the style of

Russian feminist band Pussy Riot, rising up *seemingly from nowhere
at no specified time* and celebrating with an eye to neither origin nor
telos, but with humor, guile, and an incisive critical understanding
of authority's ruses.[64] Unlike Machiavelli's prince, aleatory feminism
does not act in the name of national constitution but undercuts it:
Djamila Bouhired, a key player in Algeria's mid–twentieth-century
independence struggle, continues to fight for women's legal, political,
and social justice in a struggle that necessarily exceeds any national-
ist agenda. Aleatory feminism urges us not simply to treat the *world*
on Harawayan terms as a witty agent, but also to *embody* the active
passivity and passive activity of Dionysus and the trickster. Reveling
in corporeality, sensation, play, and sexuality, it indicates a sensuous
activity that is also always responsive—motor *and* sensory. In all its
openness and motility, the radically counternormative force of aleatory interruptivity cannot ultimately sustain or retain its articulation
with what is specifically feminine. Aleatory feminism countenances
all possibilities, all reconfigurations of past and present circumstances, including queer and transgender reconfigurations of gender
and sex. As much transgender and intersex as it is feminine; what
is aleatory welcomes alterity—all differences in embodiment and
circumstance—race, class, ability, ethnicity—among and between
women and queers, or indeed anyone, male or female, intersex or
trans bodied, committed to challenging unified, fortified, essential-
ized, and teleologically egoic modes of subjectivity and sociality.

Arising as it does from foundational texts of Western thought, as
a political reconfiguration of the feminine symptom, aleatory feminism cannot be easily or cleanly separated from that tradition. Unlike
Deleuzian-inspired political thinking, it necessarily involves inhabiting, reckoning with and engaging with the patriarchal, metaphysical
legacies to which it is opposed, both from the inside *and* the outside.
It portends less a brave new world than the unpredictable possibility of an impious taking up, a becoming conscious, and a working
through: an immanent yet unpredictable possibility that goes back
through its roots while arriving from nowhere, in order to branch out
into as yet unthought social, political, economic, erotic, and embodied configurations.

NOTES

INTRODUCTION

1. *Historia Animalium* X contains much similar material, however, it is widely accepted that Aristotle was not its author, and it is not considered closely here. See Allan Gotthelf's introduction to Aristotle, *Historia Animalium*, vol. 1, bks. I–X, trans. D. M. Balme (Cambridge: Cambridge University Press, 2002), 2.

2. Martin Heidegger, "On the Essence and Concept of Φύσις in Aristotle's *Physics* B, 1," trans. Thomas Sheehan, *Pathmarks* (Cambridge and New York: Cambridge University Press, 1998), 185, hereafter "*Phusis.*"

3. E.g., at *GA* I.2 716a6–7; I.22 730b9–23; II.1 734b31–36; II.3 737a17–30, and II.4 738b20–27.

4. *GA* I.22 730b14–20.

5. *GA* IV.2 765b28–76a1; 766a9–12.

6. See *GA* IV.3 767b3–15.

7. This formulation is elaborated in Gayatri Chakravorty Spivak, "Feminism and Deconstruction, Again: Negotiations," in *Outside in the Teaching Machine* (New York: Routledge, 1993).

8. Eve Kosofsky Sedgwick, "Paranoid Reading and Reparative Reading, Or You're So Paranoid, You Probably Think This Essay Is About You," in *Touching Feeling*, 123–51 (Durham, NC: Duke University Press, 2003).

9. I thank Damon Young, in conversation, for the formulation of this idea specifically in terms of the transference.

10. Jacques Derrida, "Autoimmunity: Real and Symbolic Suicides: A Dialogue with Jacques Derrida," in Giovanna Borradori, *Philosophy in a Time of Terror: Dialogues with Jurgen Habermas and Jacques Derrida*, trans. Pascale-Anne Brault and Michael Naas, 85–136 (Chicago: University of Chicago Press, 2004).

11. Louis Althusser, *Reading Capital*, trans. Ben Brewster (London and New York: Verso, 1979), 86.

12. Judith Butler, *Bodies That Matter* (New York: Routledge, 1993), 39.

13. "It is not during the winter that frequent rain is thought to occur by chance [*tuchē*] or by coincidence [*sumptōmatos*], but during the summer, nor frequent heat during the summer, but during the winter. So if these

be thought to occur either by coincidence [*sumptōmatos*] or for the sake of
something and if they cannot occur by coincidence [*sumptōmatos*] or spontaneity [*automaton*], then they occur for the sake of something. . . . There is,
then final cause in things which come to be or exist by nature." *Physics* II.8
199a1–7. Translation modified.

    14. A passage in *De Anima* appears to give an account of the relation
between nature and *sumptōma* that is somewhat less oppositional than in the
Physics: "An animal must have sensation, if nature does nothing in vain. For
all things that exist by nature are for the sake of something, or are things that
coincide [*sumptōmata*] with being for the sake of something." III.12 434a32–
4. This contrast illustrates quite neatly the traversing of teleology's interior
and exterior characteristic of the feminine symptom. Other occurrences of
sumptōma or the related verb *sumpiptō* in the corpus can be found at *Meteorologica* I.5 343b and I.7 344b (production of comets is due to a coincidence of meteorological forces); repeatedly in *On Prophecy in Sleep*, e.g.,
I.463b1–11 (referring to the coincidental nature of most dreams); in *On Respiration* V.472b26 (the theory that breath is contingent [*sumptōmatos*] to life
and death is debunked); in *Historia Animalium* I.16 495a15 and III.2 511b15
it describes certain biological phenomena (ducts leading from eye to brain
do or do not coincide; blood happens to flow out of vessels when animals
die making it impossible to observe the vessels clearly); at *Metaphysics* VI.2
1026b13 (the fact that accident is only a name coincides with [*sumpiptei*]
what is said well) and XIV.6 1093b17 (number sometimes coincides with
other beautiful attributes, as in the list of opposites, but this is analogical);
Nicomachean Ethics IX.10 1171a8 (having too many friends is undesirable
since it is a likely coincidence that one would have to share in pleasure with
one and sadness with another at the same time); *Prior Analytics*, I.9 30b4 (if
a particular premiss is apodeictic, the conclusion will not be, since no impossibility occurs [*adunaton sumpiptei*]); *Posterior Analytics* I.5 74a14; I.12
77b32 (parallel lines do not coincide); *Topics*, IV.5 126b34–127a1 (immor-
tality isn't a kind of life, an everlasting kind in a species-genus relation, but
rather a coincidental property [*sumptōma*] or affection [*pathos*] added to
life), also V.2 130a35 and V.5 134b28; *Poetics* XIV.1453b14 (what sort of
incidents [*sumptōmatōn*] in a narrative strike one as pitiable or terrible?)

    15. Jacques Lacan, *Écrits: A Selection*, trans. Alan Sheridan (New York
and London: W. W. Norton, 1977), 154.

    16. *Soph. El.* XIV.174a7–9.

    17. *Soph. El.* XIV.174a5.

    18. Lucretius, *De Rerum Natura*, trans. W. H. D. Rouse (Cambridge,
MA: Harvard University Press, 1975), II.292.

    19. *Rhet.* I.9 1367b25.

    20. The relevant passage may be found in Thucydides, *The Peleponnesian
War*, trans. Richard Crawley (London: J. M. Dent, 1910), LIX.3.

    21. *Rhet.* I.9 1367a17–18.

    22. *Pol.* V.4, 1303b39–1304a4.

    23. *Pol.* II.12 1273b42–1274a20; the occurrence of *sumptōma* is at
1274a13.

24. *Pol.* V.6 1306b6.

25. See Louis Althusser, *Philosophy of the Encounter: Later Writings, 1978–1987*, trans. G. M. Goshgarian (London: Verso, 2006).

26. The Aristotelian answer to Sherry Ortner's famous question, "Is female to male as nature is to culture?" is thus a resounding "no." See Sherry B. Ortner, "Is Female to Male as Nature is to Culture?" in *Woman, Culture, and Society,* ed. Michelle Zimbalist Rosaldo and Louise Lamphere. 67–87 (Stanford, CA: Stanford University Press, 1974).

27. *Timaeus.* 47e.

28. See *Met.* V.5 1015a29.

29. Luce Irigaray, *This Sex Which Is Not One,* trans. Catherine Porter (Ithaca, NY: Cornell University Press, 1985), esp. 28–31.

30. See Elena Tzelepis and Athena Athanasiou, eds., *Rewriting Difference: Irigaray and "The Greeks"* (Albany: State University of New York Press, 2010); Luce Irigaray, *The Marine Lover of Friedrich Nietzsche,* trans. Gillian C. Gill (New York: Columbia University Press, 1991) and *The Forgetting of Air in Martin Heidegger,* trans. Mary Beth Mader (Austin: University of Texas Press, 1999).

31. See John Sallis, *Chorology: On Beginning in Plato's "Timaeus"* (Bloomington: Indiana University Press, 1999).

32. *Tim.,* 52b.

33. See especially Aquinas's commentaries on the *Metaphysics* and *Physics,* as well as those of Simplicius.

34. Classic feminist readings include Lynda Lange, "Woman is Not a Rational Animal: On Aristotle's Biology of Reproduction," in *Discovering Reality: Feminist Perspectives on Epistemology, Metaphysics, Methodology, and Philosophy of Science,* ed. Sandra Harding and Merrill B. Hintikka (Dordrecht, Holland: D. Reidel Publishing Company, 1983); Genevieve Lloyd, *The Man of Reason: "Male" and "Female" in Western Philosophy* (Minneapolis: University of Minnesota Press, 1984); Luce Irigaray, "How to Conceive (of) a Girl," in *Speculum of the Other Woman,* trans. Gillian C. Gill (Ithaca, NY: Cornell University Press, 1985); Judith Butler, *Bodies That Matter*; Cynthia A. Freeland (ed.), *Feminist Interpretations of Aristotle* (University Park: Pennsylvania State University Press, 1998). For a comprehensive review of the legacy of Aristotle's theory of reproduction in the West, see Nancy Tuana, "The Weaker Seed" *Hypatia* 3, no. 1 (1988): 35–59.

35. Christopher P. Long, *Aristotle On the Nature of Truth* (New York: Cambridge University Press, 2011), 7. The tradition of phenomenological readings truly begins with Heidegger's own writings, especially the early lecture series published as Martin Heidegger, *Phenomenological Interpretations of Aristotle,* trans. Richard Rojcewicz (Bloomington: Indiana University Press, 2001), the lecture series on *Metaphysics IX*: Martin Heidegger, *Aristotle's "Metaphysics" θ 1–3: On the Essence and Actuality of Force,* trans. Walter Brogan and Peter Warnek (Bloomington: Indiana University Press, 1995), and the *"Phusis"* essay. Walter Brogan, *Heidegger and Aristotle: The Twofoldness of Being* (Albany: State University of New York Press, 2005) has been an invaluable resource, while John Sallis's interpretations of

Plato in *Being and Logos* (Bloomington: Indiana University Press, 1996) and especially his work on the *Timaeus* in *Chorology* have been singularly helpful. Other works in this tradition include, significantly, Christopher P. Long, *The Ethics of Ontology: Rethinking an Aristotelian Legacy* (Albany: State University of New York Press, 2004), and Claudia Baracchi, *Aristotle's Ethics as First Philosophy* (New York: Cambridge University Press, 2008).

36. Brooke Holmes, *The Symptom and the Subject* (Princeton, NJ: Princeton University Press, 2010), 2.

37. Martin Heidegger, *Being and Time*, trans. Joan Stambaugh (Albany: State University of New York Press, 1996), 25–6.

38. Margaret Whitford, *Luce Irigaray: Philosophy in the Feminine* (London: Routledge, 1991), 114. See generally ch. 5, "The same, the semblance, and the other."

39. *Phys.* I.9 192a24. In fairness to Aristotle he does qualify this by noting that femaleness and ugliness are "accidents" of subjects rather than subjects in themselves, but this does not obviate the force of the analogy.

40. See, for example, "The proximate matter [*hulē*] and the form are one and the same; the one existing potentially [*dunamei*], the other as actuality." *Met.* VIII.6 1045b18–20, translation modified.

41. *Met.* VII.7 1032a20–23; *Gen. et Corr.* II.9 335a34.

42. Page duBois, *Sowing the Body: Psychoanalysis and Ancient Representations of Women* (Chicago: University of Chicago Press, 1988), 16. In addition to Irigaray, authors who have put psychoanalytic theory to the work of illuminating ancient and classical texts include Jean-Pierre Vernant and Nicole Loraux, though these latter authors attempt to describe broader formations across multiple genres and disciplines, including literature, anthropology, and history as well as philosophy, that would characterize and diagnose something like "the Greek mind." This work makes no such claims about an entire culture, but limits itself merely to the philosophical and scientific writings of Plato and Aristotle.

43. If part of the impetus for this project is approaching problems traditionally thought to be universal through an analysis that seeks to do justice to the particularity of lived bodies, we might then legitimately ask, why sex and gender and not other ways in which bodies are particularized, marked, and rendered subaltern within a system in which those in power—whose assumptions masquerade as universal—are still overwhelmingly white, straight, moneyed, able-bodied, older men? In foregrounding one kind of particularization, this approach necessarily elides the intersecting tissue of modes whereby bodies are produced, marked, and particularized: race, sexual orientation, class, bodily ability, and so on. It is undoubtedly the case that in foregrounding sexual difference, I do not sufficiently address other ways that bodies and persons are differentiated and hierarchies established in Aristotle's writings. Racialized figures (though one must be careful of anachronism) certainly appear throughout the corpus, as evidenced, for instance, by Aristotle's frequent use of the example of the "white man" alongside the "cultured man" to illustrate the distinction between essence and accident. His remarks on monstrosity rely on and entrench norms of bodily ability. The

absence of commentary on homosexuality or pederasty in the corpus is notable in itself. And his notorious designation of natural slaves in the *Politics*
renders them, like women, lacking in a part of the soul (*Politics* I.5 1260a12–
14), and yet they are deemed necessary to both *polis* and *oikos*. While this
book's focus is on sexual difference, the notion of the symptom may also be
applicable to the many axes of hierarchy thrown up by Aristotelian teleology,
and the politics of aleatory feminism developed in the Coda makes clear that
it is part of the swerving nature of aleatory uprisings that they may occur in,
among, and in the name of every kind of subaltern being.

44. See Homer, *Iliad*, trans. A.T. Murray, rev. William F. Wyatt (Cambridge, MA: Harvard University Press, 1999), XIV.187, where Hera is the
one so bedecked highly effectively for the seduction of Zeus, and Hesiod,
Works and Days, trans. Glenn W. Most, in Hesiod, *Theogony, Works and
Days, Testimonia* (Cambridge, MA: Harvard University Press, 2006), 76,
where during the fashioning of Pandora by Hephaestus she is given adornments by Athena, along with Persuasion and the Hours (not to mention
deceitfulness by Hermes).

45. John Sallis reminds us of a further connection in Plato: the luxurious
city in the *Republic* 372c–e, the city that necessitates war and thus guardian-
ship, includes "those having to do with women's adornment (*peri ton gunai-
keion kosmon*)." *Chorology*, 142.

46. To my mind one of the most powerful descriptions of the ambiguity
represented by women's adornment is still to be found in Simone de Beauvoir,
The Second Sex, vol. 1, part 3 "Myths," ch. 1., trans. Constance Borde and
Sheila Malovany-Chevallier (New York: Alfred A. Knopf, 2009).

47. *Phys.* IV.2 209b13–17.

1. ARISTOTELIAN CAUSATION, REPRODUCTION,
AND ACCIDENT AND CHANCE

1. *GA* IV.6 775a15–16.

2. E.g., at *HA* X.631b31.

3. An obvious example of such a scheme is that of Boethius in his *Consolation of Philosophy*, trans. V. E. Watts (London: Penguin Books, 1969).

4. Montgomery Furth, *Substance, Form and Psyche: an Aristotelian
Metaphysics* (Cambridge: Cambridge University Press, 1988); Robert Mayhew, *The Female in Aristotle's Biology* (Chicago: University of Chicago
Press, 2004); Devin M. Henry, "How Sexist Is Aristotle's Developmental
Biology?" *Phronesis* 52, no. 3 (2007): 251–69 are largely representative
of this trend, although Henry is sympathetic to at least some versions of
a feminist critique. Karen M. Nielsen, "Private Parts of Animals: Aristotle on the Teleology of Sexual Difference" *Phronesis* 53, nos. 4–5 (2008):
373–405, to my mind addresses these positions more than adequately, and
my analysis proceeds along lines sympathetic, if methodologically divergent,
to hers. Aryeh Kosman, in "Male and Female in Aristotle's *Generation of
Animals*" (unpublished paper on file with the author) and Daryl McGowan
Tress in "The Metaphysical Science of Aristotle's *Generation of Animals*

and its Feminist Critics" *Review of Metaphysics* 46 (1992): 307–41 represent male and female as complementary and different rather than hierarchically ordered. Tress takes much of the textual evidence I produce here
not to show fundamental and untenable inconsistencies with an overarch-
ingly masculinist metaphysics, but she instead argues that Aristotle places
unusual and notable metaphysical weight on the material, passive, feminine
principle which then acts in concert with the formal, active, masculine principle. Tress thus applauds Aristotle for upholding a regime in which women,
though "valued," are nonetheless necessarily and fundamentally secondary,
a position which should be summarily rejected on standard humanist, and
not even radical feminist grounds.

   5. See Introduction, n. 29.
   6. *GA* I.2 716a6–7.
   7. *Phys.* II.7 198a25.
   8. "The relation of male to female is by nature a relation of superior to
inferior and ruler to ruled." *Pol.* I.5 1254b13–15. For a development of a
notion of these groupings as "principle bundles" which operate similarly
across many of Aristotle's texts see Judith M. Green, "Aristotle on Necessary Verticality, Body Heat and Gendered Proper Places in the Polis: A Feminist Critique," *Hypatia* 7, no. 1 (1992): 70–96.
   9. *GA* I.2 716a15.
   10. This conception is neither Deleuzian nor Badiouian, to make a germane distinction on thinking the event in contemporary philosophy, but is
rather native to Aristotle's system and must remain within its conceptual
and textual terms. Perhaps, though, contextualizing "the event" in terms of
an Aristotelian legacy may help to clarify the ontological stakes or commit-
ments inherent in thinking through the possibilities of a postmetaphysical
event, by working to disclose its indebtedness to a lingering metaphysical
ancestry.
   11. "All causes are beginnings." *Met.* V.1 1013a17.
   12. *Met.* I.3 983a25–27.
   13. The argument is made in *Met.* II.2.
   14. *Met.* II.2 12–13.
   15. *Met.* II.2 994b14–17.
   16. *Met.* V.1 1013a17–24.
   17. This account of modern causation is obviously schematic, and has
been subjected to a great deal of contestation. It does, however, have its provenance in the work of Renaissance scientists such as Bacon, Kepler, Gali-
leo, and Newton. Cartesian dualism gives it a certain metaphysical credence,
though the account undergoes rigorous examination in Locke's empiricism
and is famously subjected to a searingly skeptical debunking by Hume. The
spirit of these critiques, however, is that of skepticism with regard to any
ontological claim at all that may be made for cause, rather than the provi-
sion of a superseding model. It may also be noted that teleological causal
explanations in science have persisted throughout modernity, especially in
philosophy of biology; see, for example, Ernest Nagel, *Teleology Revisited
and Other Essays in the Philosophy and History of Science* (New York:

Columbia University Press, 1979). In recent physics, too, a simple billiard-ball theory of causation has been brought into question with notions such as observer-dependence at the quantum level. Chaos theory also brings a whole new dimension to thinking about predictability and its limits, which a billiard-ball causal theory treats unproblematically, with its assumption that given the total information about any system at time *t*, one can accurately predict the configuration of the system at any given future time.

18. In her essay, "Accidental Causes and Real Explanations," in *Aristotle's Physics: A Collection of Essays*, ed. Lindsay Judson (Oxford: Clarendon Press, 1991), Cynthia A. Freeland cites a virtual unanimity among contemporary Aristotle scholars that, "the theory of the four causes is really a theory of explanation" (49). Among the authors to whom she attributes this position are Julius Moravcsik, Julia Annas, Jonathan Barnes, William Charlton, Martha Nussbaum, Richard Sorabji and Bas van Fraassen. By contrast, I reject the suggestion that Aristotle himself makes any senseful distinction between "cause" and "explanation," and I therefore want to resist the modern temptation to reduce one to the other. For something to count as an *aitia*, "that which is responsible," it must satisfy for Aristotle both ontological and epistemological criteria, which he does not separate in any meaningful or rigorous way.

19. This is the substance of Apostle's *Physics* commentary, 209n4. Aristotle himself writes, "the bronze is a cause of the statue, and the silver, of the cup, and the genera of these [are also causes]." *Phys.* II.3 194b25.

20. *Phys.* 195a15–17; *Met.* 1013b18–21.

21. By, for example, Bertrand Russell in his *History of Western Philosophy* (New York: Simon and Schuster, 1945), 169.

22. As Aristotle points out in *Gen. et Corr.* I.7 324a30, we speak both of the doctor, and of the wine, as healing. He goes on, however, to identify the doctor's art as the motive cause, because it moves without being moved, rather than the wine, which, although it is the proximate mover and comes into contact with the (literal) patient, is also itself moved. Here not the doctor but his art counts as the cause; it is this specific capacity of the doctor (and not, for example, his musical skill), the doctor *qua* doctor, which sets in motion the chain of events and substances which contact each other and end up acting upon the patient. It is thus logically separable and fully identifiable in this capacity.

23. *Phys.* II.3 195a24–25; *Met.* V.2 1013b26–27.

24. See *Met.* XII.

25. The account here is quick and does not take into account issues raised by apparent goods that are not good at all, by *phantasia*, by the phenomenon of *akrasia*, and so on. For a striking recent interpretation of these issues see Jessica Moss, *Aristotle on the Apparent Good: Perception, Thought, and Desire* (Oxford: Oxford University Press, 2012).

26. *Phys.* II.3 194b26–29.

27. *Met.* I.3 983a28–30.

28. The question of the relationship between the many metaphysical concepts cited in these definitions, including the large and difficult question of

the relation of form to primary substance in Aristotle that is inevitably raised by the distinction between genera and particulars, is unfortunately beyond the scope of the present study.

29. Apostle, *Aristotle's Physics*, 209n6.

30. Martin Heidegger, "Logos (Heraclitus Fragment B 50)," in *Early Greek Thinking*, trans. David Farrell Krell and Frank A. Capuzzi (San Francisco: Harper & Row, 1984), 63.

31. The Heideggerian formulation of the *logos* as "a making something accessible in a gathered and unified way" through recounting and speaking, through discourse (Heidegger, *Aristotle's "Metaphysics"* θ *1–3*, 3), also conveys well the simultaneously disclosive and productive effect for which I am arguing.

32. Christopher Long, in *Aristotle and the Nature of Truth*, understands Aristotle's method as a "legomenology," and under this rubric he develops this notion of *logos* as essentially dialogic. According to Long's suggestive analysis the "saying of things" in dialogue is inseparable from what they are.

33. I deliberately echo Judith Butler's position from *Gender Trouble* (New York: Routledge, 1990) here, in which she argues that the materiality of natural sex is a product of irreducibly discursive practices of cultural gender. Indeed, the argument in this book is premised on the idea that the very concept of matter itself is a direct product, indeed a symptom, of the Aristotelian (and Platonic) discourse as such, albeit one that cannot remain stable within the terms explicitly apportioned to it.

34. *GA* I.2 716a14–15.

35. *GA* I.20 729a24–28.

36. *GA* I.20 729a33.

37. *Met.* VII.10 1035a9, 1036a9, see also *Gen. et Corr.* II.1 329a9–13.

38. *Met.* IX.7 1049b2; *GA* IV.10 778a7. The menstrual blood is also said to contain all the parts of the animal *in potential* (*GA* II.3 737a22–25), and must also be the site of the maternal resemblance discussed in *GA* IV.3.

39. *Met.* V.4 1015a7–11. Likewise, at *Met.* VIII.4 1044a21, he says that mucus is constituted by the viscous, which is in turn constituted by the sweet—things can be thus analyzed (*analuesthai*) into their *protē hulē*. And at *Met.* IX.7 a suggestive argument is made for the adjectival, and thus affective and indeterminate nature of prime matter: "If there is some primary stuff, which is not further called the material of some other thing, this is the prime matter, so that if earth is airy, and air is not fire but fiery, then fire is prime matter, but if this last is a *this*, then it is a substance." 1049a25–28.

40. See, for example, Peck's footnotes in *GA*, 109–10; Balme in Aristotle, *De Partibus Animalium I and De Generatione Animalium I (with passages from II. 1–3)*, trans. D. M. Balme (Oxford: Clarendon Press, 1992), 152; Mayhew, *The Female in Aristotle's Biology*, 42.

41. *Met.* VIII.4 1044a34–b3, translation modified.

42. *GA* I.20 729a21–31, translation modified.

43. *GA* I.20 729a31–32, translation modified.

44. *GA* II.2 736a1.

45. Irigaray, *Speculum*, 167.

46. *GA* IV.3 767b3–15.

47. *GA* IV.2 765b28–76a1; 766a9–12.

48. *GA* IV.2 766a12–14, translation modified.

49. Put thus in statistical fashion, this is what Karen M. Nielsen identifies as "the puzzle" in "Private Parts," 385f.

50. *GA* IV.4, 770b15–17.

51. *Phys.* II.3 195a4–5, my translation.

52. Heidegger, *Aristotle's "Metaphysics"* θ 1–3, 10. The passage referred to is at *Met.* VI.2 1026a33–b2: "But since the simple term 'being' is said in many ways, of which we saw that one was accidental, and another true (not-being being used in the sense of 'false'); and since beside these there are the categories . . . and further besides all these the potential and actual."

53. For an extended account of Aristotle's preservation of appearances, see Martha C. Nussbaum, *The Fragility of Goodness: Luck and Ethics in Greek Tragedy and Philosophy* (Cambridge: Cambridge University Press, 1986), especially ch. 8.

54. Cf. Heidegger, *Aristotle's "Metaphysics"* θ 1–3, 18–27.

55. In the context of an argument for the "reality" of Aristotelian cause, Freeland, ("Accidental Causes"), characterizes the *kath' hauto* relation in terms of "natural" or "objective entailment" inhering in "powers and natures" of things in the world (59). While I reject the premises upon which her argument rests—which presume an unproblematic disjunction between "real cause" and "explanation"—I do accept an understanding of the character of causation *kath' hauto* as internal in Aristotle. However, as I will show, accidental causes may *also* be internal, lurking as they do in the indeterminate vicissitudes of the material cause. My purpose here, however, is to examine the distinction between *kath' hauto* and *kata sumbebēkos* as it is produced textually and rhetorically by Aristotle; it is therefore somewhat beyond my purview to investigate the nature of the *kath' hauto*'s grounding in reality. For further illuminating discussion of this point see Cynthia A. Freeland, "Aristotle on Possibilities and Capacities," *Ancient Philosophy* 6 (1986): 69–89.

56. A bold and suggestive attempt at a unified theory of Aristotle's various statements on accident is undertaken by Alban Urbanas in *La notion d'accident chez Aristote* (Paris: Les Belles Lettres, 1988). It is worth mentioning here that in Book V of the *Metaphysics*, the philosophical dictionary, Aristotle identifies the *kath' hauto* locution ("According to," or "That in virtue of which") with cause (*aitia*) itself: "In general 'that in virtue of which' will exist in the same number of senses as 'cause.' For we say indifferently 'in virtue of what has he come?' or 'for what reason (*hou heneka*) has he come?' and 'in virtue of what has he inferred or inferred falsely?' or 'what is the cause of his inference or false inference?'" (*Met.* V.18 1022a19–23). Aristotle goes on to explain that the *kath' hauto* (in virtue of itself) thus has several meanings: the essence (*to ti ēn einai*) of each particular; everything contained in the definition (genus or universal) of a thing; any attribute which a thing has received directly in itself (such as man's receiving life from his soul), and that which is not caused by something else. The text gives a

further definition of *kath' hauto* concerning the things which belong to a thing alone qua alone, and hence separate. This seems to be an extension of the previous point, although there is some corruption in the manuscripts that makes it impossible to determine the exact sense. However, it is notable that he introduces the notion of separateness here, which is one of his criteria, along with independence, for identifying primary substance. That "the that in virtue of itself" and "primary substance" are intimately related for Aristotle is unquestionable; the extent to which they may be identified with one another is, again, a question for another time. Suffice it to note here that the chain of concepts *aitia–kath' hauto–ousia* invoked here provides further support for treating questions of causation as fundamental to an understanding of Aristotelian metaphysics.

57. *Met.* V.30 1025a14–16. The discussion follows the remainder of V.30.

58. *Phys.* I.7 190b1–5.

59. *Met.* V.30, 1025a26–30.

60. *Met.* V.30, 1025a30–35.

61. *Met.* VI.2 1026b3–6.

62. *Met.* VI.2 1026b14–22.

63. *Met.* VI.2 1026b28–33.

64. In "On the Alleged Impossibility of a Science of Accidents in Aristotle" *Graduate Faculty Philosophy Journal* 13, no. 2 (1990): 55–78, Alban Urbanas argues that certain kinds of accident, objective attributes of individual things—black, white, sweet, etc.—are caused by necessary and formal causes and are therefore metaphysically grounded and knowable in a science. Necessary accidents are therefore substantial and metaphysical. However, Urbanas's project involves finding within an Aristotelian framework a causal and metaphysical ground for accidents that does *not* reduce them to the material, potential, or the indeterminate. My concern is rather to show how the material, the potential, and the indeterminate, especially as disclosed by the Aristotelian account of sexual difference, are pervasive and both exterior and interior to the metaphysical system, and therefore function as the simultaneous condition of possibility and condition of impossibility of that system.

65. As I complete this book, a new comprehensive study of chance in Aristotle: John Dudley, *Aristotle's Concept of Chance: Accidents, Cause, Necessity, and Determinism* (Albany: State University of New York Press, 2012), has just been published, and I regret being unable to incorporate its insights.

66. *Phys.* II.4 195b32, translation modified.

67. *Phys.* II.4, 195b36–196a5. Both Apostle and Wicksteed and Cornford attribute this position to Democritus and Leucippus, thinkers that attribute all things to necessity, however the goal-oriented example Aristotle gives as an illustration is far from atomist in spirit, but rather thoroughly Aristotelian.

68. *Phys.* II.4, 196a15–17, translation modified.

69. *Poet.* IX.1452a3–10.

70. *Phys.* II.5 197a9–22.

71. *Phys.* II.6 197a36–197b5.

72. *Phys.* II.6 197b22–33.

73. *Phys.* II.6 197b30–33. One wonders at the awkwardness of this passage, especially in its resonance with the example of *automaton* from the *Poetics* IX.1452a5–9, in which the stone falls and strikes the man, and in so doing does not vitiate final cause (qua the man's life) but rather very much fulfills the telos of the plot. It seems that Aristotle is keen to emphasize the nonhuman spontaneity of the falling stone as an instance of *automaton*, but finds it difficult to leave behind a teleological context.

74. *Phys.* II.6 197b.

75. *Phys.* II.6 198a2–5, my translation.

76. *Phys.* II.6 198a13.

77. *Poet.* XIII 1453a9–16.

78. *Phys.* II.8 199a33–199b5.

79. *Phys.* II.7 198a27.

80. *Phys.* II.7 198a37.

81. *Gen. et Corr.* II.9 335b24–31.

82. *Met.* VI.2 1027a14–15.

83. *GA* IV.10 778a5–9.

84. *Phys.* II.8 198b11.

85. *Phys.* II.8 198b19–21.

86. *Phys.* II.8 198b24–26.

87. *Phys.* II.8 198b29–32.

88. *Phys.* II.8 199a1–2.

89. *Phys.* II.8 199a31–32.

90. *Phys.* II.9 199b33–35.

2. NECESSITY AND *AUTOMATON*: ALEATORY MATTER AND THE FEMININE SYMPTOM

1. On the goddess *Anankē*, and especially her role in Plato's *Republic*, see Jane Caputi, "On the Lap of Necessity: A Mythic Reading of Teresa Brennan's Energetics Philosophy" *Hypatia* 16, no. 2 (2001): 1–26.

2. *Phys.* II.9 199b33-35.

3. *Phys.* II.8 198b17–19.

4. *GA*, Peck's introduction, xlii. The discussion begins on xli.

5. *Met.* XII.7 1072b11–13.

6. *Met.* V.5 1015a29.

7. *Met.* V.5 1015a30–32. The quotation is from Sophocles, *Electra* 256 and he makes a slight error in transcription, if not in meaning, itself a nice example of *hamartia* (he writes, "*all' hē bia me taut' anankazei poiein*," whereas Sophocles says not "*poiein*" but "*me dran*").

8. Aeschylus, *Eumenides*, 658–61.

9. *Met.* V.5 1015a32–34.

10. This is a translation by David Farrell Krell of Nietzsche's rendition of the fragment in *Philosophy in the Tragic Age of the Greeks*, as cited by Heidegger in "The Anaximander Fragment," in *Early Greek Thinking*, 13.

11. Indeed Aristotle mounts an argument against the Anaximanderian idea that entities arise out of and return to an infinite material substrate

at *Met.* I.3 983b8–11 and *Phys.* III.5 204b30–35, and he mentions Anaximander specifically in polemics against previous thinkers who suggested that
all things arise out of a material mixture (*to migma*), at *Met.* XII.2 1069b22,
and *Phys.* I, 4 187a21.

12. *Met.* V.5 1015a34. The same formula is given at *Met.* XII.7 1072b13.
13. *Met.* V.5 1015a35–1015b6.
14. "Necessity" is reformulated as the "errant cause" at *Tim.* 48a.
15. *Met.* XII.7 1072b13.
16. *Met.* V.5 1015b12.
17. *Met.* V.5 1015b15–16, translation modified.
18. *Gen. et Corr.* II.11 338a4–5.
19. *Gen. et Corr.* II.11 338a14–17, translation modified.
20. See *Gen. et Corr.* II.10.
21. *Met.* V.5 1015b.
22. At *An. Post.* II.11 95a1–3 he puts it this way: "Now necessity is of two
kinds: one acts in accordance with nature and impulse (*hormē*), the other is
a force (*bia*) acting against impulse, just as a stone is borne downward and
upward, but not through the same sort of necessity."
23. In an extended commentary note to his translation of *Parts of Animals*, David Balme takes this position, arguing that the proposition that
material necessity is absolute or simple gives rise to an untenable dualism
that renders teleology toothless. He says that if material necessity is posited
as a factor in generations, there is no meaning left for the final cause, the
"for the sake of which": "Horns are formed out of material which is 'flowing upwards of necessity' (*PA* III.2 663b34): are we to suppose that the necessary movement stops at a point and some other force takes over, and if so
what force?" (79). However, his position means he is also unable to appropriately grapple with the problem posed by the insistent appearance of this
sort of necessity in the text. Rather, it seems that in the biological texts this
kind of necessity is seen as operating all the time, but only gains significance
and appears *as such* in relation to natural teleology, that is, insofar as it is
either taken up and utilized by nature, or, especially, if it goes against nature.
Also, see John M. Cooper, "Hypothetical Necessity and Natural Teleology"
in *Philosophical Issues in Aristotle's Biology*, ed. Allan Gotthelf and James
Lennox (Cambridge: Cambridge University Press, 1987), who defends the
position that hypothetical necessity is different from material necessity, but
appears alongside it, the latter being subsumed to but not reduced to the
former. Cooper argues that material necessity is a proximate cause but not
an ultimate cause (267), and while this sounds right, he does not explore
the consequences for this in relation to the broader theory of causation that
identifies the proximate moving cause with form and telos. In a footnote he
argues that the "simple necessity" of the *Metaphysics* must include Democritean or material necessity (260n20), but I see no textual grounds for this.
24. *PA* I.1 639b21–23.
25. *PA* I.1 640b5–17. The question of the natural motions of the elements
is examined at length in chapter 5.
26. *Phys.* I.1 200a1–3.

27. *Phys.* II.9 200a31–2, translation modified. In his introduction to *GA*, Peck quotes this line in support of his mistaken notion that Aristotle's simple necessity inheres in matter (xlii–xliii).

28. *Phys.* II.9 200a29.

29. *Phys.* II.9 200a32–34.

30. *PA* I.1 639b12–13. He goes on to say that the first is primary and the second, secondary.

31. *PA* I.1 642a2–9, translation modified, emphasis added.

32. D.M. Balme, in "Teleology and Necessity," in Gotthelf and Lennox, *Philosophical Issues,* 285n32. Peck basically agrees, and in an editorial footnote suggests that the two must be "simple" and "coercive."

33. *An. Post.* II.11 94b32–95a3.

34. *PA* I.1 642a31–b4, translation modified, emphasis added.

35. *PA* III.7 670a30; III.7 670b23–24.

36. *GA* IV.3 767b8–12, translation modified.

37. *GA* IV.1 766a18–22. At 766b15–16 he says, "If [the male semen] gains the mastery, it brings [the material] over to itself; but if it gets mastered, it changes over either into its opposite or else into extinction." That the continuous scale of temperature should manifest itself "necessarily" in the opposites, as manifested by male and female is difficult to understand. The necessity operating here becomes clearer if we recall Aristotle's insistence that all coming-to-be involves a diremption into active and passive components and thus into male and female in sexual reproduction.

38. One might supply an argument about freezing or condensation, but Aristotle does not do so.

39. *GA* II.4 738a34–b2. On the topic of biological "residues" in general, he says in the *PA*, "I agree that occasionally nature turns even residues to use and advantage, but that is no reason for trying to discover a purpose in all of them. Some are present for a definite purpose, and then many others happen to be (*sumbainei*) of necessity (*ex anankēs*) in consequence of these" (*PA* IV.2 677a16, translation modified).

40. *GA* IV.8 776a15–35. At IV.8 776b32–34 he also says: "the place around the breasts is just such an empty space, and it is so for both of the two possible causes: for the sake of the best and by necessity" (translation modified). And at *HA* IX 582a6–13 an account is given for the size of breasts: if menses are due and have not yet come, the excess residue fluid will travel upward "of necessity" and create larger breasts.

41. *GA* II.4 739b28–31. A fuller description of the various membranes (*humenes*) in the development of a bird's egg is given at *HA* VI.3 561b16–562a5. The formation of the membrane in its "necessarily accidental" (*ex anankēs sumbainei*) aspect is also given in *PA*'s discussion of the omentum, *PA* IV.3 677b22–33. A similar confluence is proposed regarding the formation of the viscera or internal organs: "they have been formed of necessity at the inner ends of the blood-vessels, because moisture . . . must of necessity make its way out there, and as it sets and solidifies, form the substance of the viscera" (*PA* III.10 673a33–673b2). Each of them obviously has its own purpose, which has been described in turn by Aristotle in *PA* III.6–10.

42. *GA* III.4 755a22–23.

43. See Jacques Derrida, "The Double Session," in *Dissemination*, trans. Barbara Johnson (Chicago: University of Chicago Press, 1981), 212ff. It should be noted that there is no ancient attestation of *humēn* that attributes to it our modern sense of hymen as the membrane of the vagina that signifies virginity.

44. The formation of blood is described at *PA* II.4 651a17–19, the ink of cephalopods at IV.5 679a25–30.

45. Irigaray, "The 'Mechanics' of Fluids," in *This Sex*, 106–18.

46. *PA* III.2 663b32–35.

47. *PA* III.2 663b12–14.

48. *PA* III.10 672b8–24.

49. *GA* II.6 743a21–23.

50. *GA* 743a23–26.

51. *GA* 743a35–b2, translation modified, emphasis added.

52. *GA* 743b20–24.

53. The metaphors of nature as craftsman are noted by Cynthia A. Freeland, "Nourishing Speculation: A Feminist Reading of Aristotelian Science," in *Engendering Origins: Critical Feminist Readings in Plato and Aristotle*, ed. Bat-Ami Bar On (Albany: State University of New York Press, 1994), 155–56, although she does not see in them grounds for a specifically feminist critique of Aristotle.

54. *GA* I.21 729b15–18.

55. *GA* V.8 789b7–13. The passage begins at 789b3.

56. *GA* V.8 789b13–15, translation modified.

57. *De Cael.* I.2 269a18 and *passim*; *Phys.* IV.1 208b20.

58. *GA* IV.10 778a5–9.

59. Balme, defending Aristotle's teleology, says that it is only teleological explanation that provides the limits that make scientific explanation possible, the alternative being chaos: "The elements act in their own natural ways, but the actions are unlimited. This is the sense of the 'indeterminacy' (*aoristia*) that Aristotle attributes to proximate matter. It does not mean uncertain quality of action, nor an inscrutable intractability as some have suggested, but simply that the matter has not yet been formally determined into a precise state" ("Teleology and Necessity," 283). Balme makes Aristotle's very move in *Physics* I.9 here, understanding matter as *destined* to form, as yearning vectorally for enformation, which it has "not yet" achieved. That is, he sees matter through the rubric of potentiality and actuality, rather than in its aleatory or compulsive dimension. Again, what I understand as the primarily conflictual nature of the relationship between material necessity and teleology is not addressed.

60. *Met.* VII.7 1032a20–23.

61. The argument is made at *GA* III.11 762a8–763b16.

62. *GA* III.11. See especially 762a9.

63. *GA* II.3 737a22–25. The apparent contradiction here between menstrual blood as "prime matter" *and* as containing the parts *potentially* will be explored in chapter 6.

Notes

64. *GA* II.5 741b8, translation mine.
65. Plato's *Rep.* 514b. The puppets are also mentioned in *Laws* at 644d, 645d, and 658b. In each case Plato uses *thaumata* to describe them, and not *automata*. For later ancient sources describing the puppets see Galen, *On the Usefulness of the Parts of the Body (De Usu Partium)*, trans. Margaret Tallmadge May (Ithaca, NY: Cornell University Press, 1968), 91, 202, and Heron of Alexandria, *Automatopoietica*, translated in Susan Murphy, "Heron of Alexandria's 'On Automaton-making,'" *History of Technology*, 17 (1995), 1–44. Galen's references echo Aristotle's own, regarding the movement of the joints, at *De Motu* VII 701b1, to be discussed in chapter 5.
66. *Met.* I.2 982b12–13.
67. *Met.* I.2 983a12.
68. I am indebted to a conversation with Aryeh Kosman for prompting this investigation.
69. These include Eric Partridge, *Origins: An Etymological Dictionary of Modern English* (New York: Routledge, 2009), Calvert Watkins, *The American Heritage Dictionary of Indo-European Roots* (Boston, MA: Houghton Mifflin Harcourt, 2000), Hjalmar Frisk, *Griechisches etymologisches Wörterbuch* (Heidelberg: Carl Winter Universitätsverlag, 1970), Émile Boisacq, *Dictionnaire étymologique de la langue grecque* (Heidelberg: Carl Winter's Universitätsbuchhandlung, 1923).
70. Hesiod, *Works and Days*, 103.
71. Ibid., 120.
72. Homer, *Iliad*, II.408; V.748; XVIII.376.
73. *Iliad*, XVIII.377.
74. Michel Bréal, "Étymologies grecques," *Memoires de la Societé de linguistique de Paris* 10 (1898): 402–7.
75. R. Grandsaignes d'Hauterive, *Dictionnaire des racines des langues européenes* (Paris: Librairie Larousse, 1949), translation mine.
76. Julius Pokorny, *Indogermanisches etymologisches Wörterbuch* (Bern: Francke Verlag, 1959), 727; Pierre Chantraine, *Dictionnaire étymologique de la langue grecque* (Paris: Éditions Klincksieck, 1968).
77. F. E. J. Valpy, *Etymology of the Words of the Greek Language* (London: Longman, Green, Longman and Roberts, 1860); Pokorny, 693; J. B. Hofmann, *Etymologisches Wörterbuch des Griechischen* (München: Verlag Von R. Oldenbourg, 1949).
78. Hesiod, *Works and Days*, 101–4.
79. René Descartes, "Meditations on First Philosophy," in *Discourse on Method and Meditations*, trans. E. S. Haldane and G. R. T. Ross (Mineola, NY: Dover Publications, 2003), 77.
80. Hal Foster, *Compulsive Beauty* (Cambridge, MA: MIT Press, 1993), 129.
81. *Phys.* II.6 197b32, my translation.
82. Aquinas, Albertus Magnus, Apostle, and Richard Hope say *automaton* is internal; Sachs's translation retains Aristotle's ambiguity on the matter. Charlton, Hardie and Gaye, Barthélémy Saint-Hilaire, and Ross follow Simplicius and Philoponus (*On Aristotle's Physics 2*, trans. A. R. Lacey

[London: Duckworth, 1993], 292.20–29, in associating *tuchē* with what is internal and *automaton* with the external, presumably because the beginning of the passage specifies *automaton* as an external cause (II.6 197b20).

83. Simplicius, *On Aristotle's Physics* 2, trans. Barrie Fleet (London: Duckworth, 1997), 352.34–35.

84. Apostle, *Aristotle's Physics*, 215n11.

85. *GA* II.1 734b13. As addressed at some length in chapter 5, Aristotle also uses the analogy of the automatic puppets in *De Motu Animalium*, in which they are used to account for the instantaneous transmission and magnification of small motions deriving from the soul's seat in the center of the body throughout the body in the explanation of motion. See *De Motu* VII 701b1–15.

86. For an extended discussion of the analogy of the automatic puppets with spontaneous generation, see James Lennox, "Teleology, Chance and Aristotle's Theory of Spontaneous Generation," *Journal of the History of Philosophy* 20, no. 3 (1982): 219–33. While Lennox discusses the substantially the same material as I do here, and I agree with much of his analysis, he does not find the technical analogy of the puppets particularly significant in itself, and certainly does not thematize gender in his analysis.

87. *GA* II.1 734b13–18.

88. D. M. Balme, in "The Place of Biology in Aristotle's Philosophy" in Gotthelf and Lennox, *Philosophical Issues*, argues that the analogy with the automata reveals that this "complex of movements can control and direct itself" (18). The analogy with the house and house building, however, reveals the source and ground of this control and direction as the form and the final cause.

89. The feminine valence of this class of creatures is made manifest by Simone de Beauvoir, when she writes in *The Second Sex*, "Feminine heat is the flaccid palpitation of a shellfish" (398). The analogy with the situation of spontaneous generation as described by Aristotle is further confirmed when De Beauvoir writes of the feminine sex organ that it is "hidden, . . . mucous, and humid . . . it has a secret and dangerous life" (397), and that feminine sexuality is like "a carnivorous plant [that] waits for and watches the swamp. . . . She is sucking, suction, sniffer, she is pitch and glue, immobile appeal, insinuating and viscous" (398). De Beauvoir's horrifying description of the feminine sexual condition can be read as a diagnosis of a sexual imaginary which has its roots in the very architecture of sexual difference as constructed by Aristotle. This also may remind us that the Greek middle voice, neither passive nor active, so often the site of postmetaphysical philosophical aspirations, may also occasion a certain disgust and abjection.

90. *GA* I.1, 731a25–29.

91. *GA* II.3 737a18; II.3 737a28–30. Jessica Gelber, "Form and Inheritance in Aristotle's Embryology," *Oxford Studies in Ancient Philosophy* 39 (2010): 183–212, has argued that since the mother provides nutritive soul (the kind of soul that plants share), as evidenced by Aristotle's account of wind eggs and also in particular a passage about nutritive soul's actions at *GA* II.4 740b25–34, there must be movements in the menstrual blood that

contribute to the offspring's form, which are therefore not simply the aleatory movements of heat and cold. But she also argues that these movements are used as tools, which seems to confuse a formal principle with a tool or material. There are, undoubtedly, as I am arguing, aleatory movements in matter, but in animals the sensitive soul principle is required for generation, and this must come from the male as he argues at 741a9–13. At *GA* II.1 734b31–36 he writes, "As for hardness, softness, toughness, brittleness and the rest of such qualities which belong to the parts that have soul in them—heat and cold may very well produce these, but they certainly do not produce the *logos* in direct consequence of which one thing is flesh and another bone; this is done by the movement which derives from the generating parent (*gennēsantos*) who is in actuality (*entelecheia*) what the material out of which the offspring is formed is *potentially.*" Since the *archē kinēseōs* is always the male parent in sexual reproduction it is unequivocally the father that is referred to here. Also, in the discussion of *mulēs* or uterine fibroids, these growths are attributed not to any independent movement or growth in the womb but to a lack of heat in the fetation (*GA* IV.7 775b25–776a9).

92. *GA* II.3 736b33–737a5. For a description of *aithēr* as the element of the heavens see *De Cael.* I.2 269a31, I.3 269b30–270b25.

93. *GA* III.11 762a22–24.

94. *GA* III.11 762b16–18.

95. Hesiod, *Theogony*, trans. Glenn W. Most, in Hesiod, *Theogony, Works and Days, Testimonia* (Cambridge, MA: Harvard University Press, 2006), 176–206.

96. The process is described in *GA* III.11 762a36–762b18.

97. *Met.* VII.9 1034a13.

98. *Met.* VII.9 1034a16.

99. *Phys.* II.6, 197b29–33.

100. Sigmund Freud, "The Uncanny," trans. Joan Riviere, *Collected Papers*, vol. 4 (London: The Hogarth Press and the Institute of Psycho-Analysis, 1953), 369–70.

101. *Poet.* IX.1452a5–9.

102. This is confirmed by the passage on dual causes in *Posterior Analytics*, in which he admits that, unlike things done by rational design which are never due to *automaton* or necessity, health and preservation (natural *teloi*) may be due to chance (*tuchē*) as well as to purpose. *An. Post.* II.11 95a5–6.

103. *Met.* VII.9 1034b5–7, translation modified.

104. *Met.* VII.9 1034a35–1034b4.

105. *Met.* VII.9 1034b5–7.

106. *GA* II.4 738b28–36.

107. *Tim.* 91c. This account of Aristotle's position is in alignment with Thomas Laqueur's one-sex model in *Making Sex: Body and Gender from the Greeks to Freud* (Cambridge, MA: Harvard University Press, 1990).

108. Lesley Dean-Jones, in "Aristotle's Understanding of Plato's Receptacle and Its Significance for Aristotle's Theory of Familial Resemblance," in *Reason and Necessity: Essays on Plato's "Timaeus,"* ed. M. R. Wright (London: Duckworth, 2000), argues that understanding Aristotle's theory of

reproduction in terms of the Timaean reproductive scene of demiurge, receptacle, and their offspring—the world of becoming, solves various difficulties Aristotle encounters in terms of accounting for transmission of maternal
qualities in the offspring. I do not believe she succeeds in providing a solution for these difficulties since the receptacle is not a being, has no qualities,
predicates of its "own" that could be transmitted on to the offspring. However, as will be developed in the following chapters, there are good grounds
for understanding the errant feminine motions of the Platonic receptacle and
chōra as persisting and returning symptomatically throughout Aristotle's
account of generation.

109. See Martin Heidegger, *Country Path Conversations*, trans. Bret W.
Davis (Bloomington: Indiana University Press, 2010).

110. The association of the feminine "principle bundle" with downward
motion is well developed by Judith M. Green in "Aristotle on Necessary
Verticality."

3. THE ERRANT FEMININE IN PLATO'S *TIMAEUS*

1. Adriana Cavarero, *In Spite of Plato: A Feminist Rewriting of Ancient
Philosophy*, trans. Serena Anderlini-D'Onofrio and Áine O'Healy (New
York: Routledge, 1995).

2. This portrayal is faithful, but somewhat reductive: the ordering and
ambiguities of this schema is discussed in detail by John Sallis, *Chorology*,
125f.

3. *Phys.* VIII.1 250b11–15, trans. Wicksteed and Cornford.

4. *Phys.* III.1 201a11.

5. *Tim.* 29d, 59c.

6. *Tim.* 28a.

7. *Tim.* 28b, *horatos gar haptos te esti kai sōma echōn*.

8. *Tim.* 30a–b.

9. *Tim.* 34b.

10. *Tim.* 35a.

11. *Tim.* 37d, translation modified.

12. *Tim.* 38c, *diorismon kai phulakēn arithmōn chronou*.

13. *Tim.* 42d.

14. *Tim.* 46e.

15. "[On the nature of necessity], Democritus means by it the resistance
and movement and blows of matter." Aetius I.26, 2, cited in G. S. Kirk, J. E.
Raven, and M. Schofield, *The Presocratic Philosophers*, 2nd ed. (Cambridge:
Cambridge University Press, 1983), 419n.

16. *Tim.* 48a.

17. *Tim.* 91c. This errancy or wandering (*planē*) is a leitmotif throughout the dialogue. It appears first as an attribute of the sophists, who wander
from city to city unlike philosophers and statesmen (19e), and at 38c and 40b
refers to the wandering heavenly bodies, the planets (*planēta*), whose wandering, we are told at 39d, forms the basis of time itself. At 43b and 47b errancy
describes the movements of earthly bodies created by the gods, while at 86e

it relates to the bilious humors that wander the body, and penetrate and attack the soul. Strikingly, at 88e, we are told that the particles and affections that wander in the body (*planōmena*) may be resisted, and health thus maintained, if one imitates the "nurturer and nurse of the universe" (i.e., the errant cause) by keeping oneself in motion (i.e., exercising) rather than remaining at rest. In this way, errancy aligns with errancy and "friend is set beside friend."

18. *Tim.* 48b, translation modified.

19. Sallis, *Chorology*, 5. See also John Sallis, "Reception," in *Interrogating the Tradition: Hermeneutics and the History of Philosophy*, ed. Charles E. Scott and John Sallis (Albany: State University of New York Press, 2000), 91.

20. Sallis's observations on sexual difference in the dialogue find it significant in so far as it indicates an order of *phusis* and *erōs*, that is of procreation, that stands in a certain tension with the order of *technē*—a natural order of threefold reproduction supplanting a technical order of production that requires only two terms, a maker and his product (or if not quite a supplanting, "a hovering between"), *Chorology*, 110. Given Plato's insistence in the *Symposium* upon the subordinate nature of the reproductive *erōs* between men and women vis à vis the philosophical *erōs* that takes place only between men, it is somewhat surprising that Sallis should characterized the reproductive realm so insistently as *erotic* in this discourse (e.g., at 58, 137). The textual precedent for Sallis's identification is a passage in the *Republic* in which Glaucon refers to procreation as an "erotic necessity," in the comedic passage about men and women exercising together in the gymnasium (*Rep.* 458d, cited in *Chorology*, 27). It seems to me that in this formulation it is in the *necessity* rather than the *erōs* strictly speaking that continuity with the *Timaeus* might be found.

21. *Tim.* 49a. *Tithēnē*, from the verb *tithēneō* (to take care of, tend, nurse, cherish, foster). The directly feminine root of this word is *titthē* (the teat or nipple of the breast).

22. *Tim.* 51a–b. *anoraton eidos ti kai amorphon, pandeches, metalambanon, de aporōtata pēi tou noētou kai dusalōtotaton auto legontes ou pseusometha.*

23. *Tim.* 50b. The translation here is Bury's. Bury uses "quality," Lee, "characteristics," Zeyl, "character," and Jowett and Kalkavage, "nature" to render *dunamis*.

24. This point of translation is noted by Jacques Derrida in his essay "Chora," trans. Ian McCloud, in *Chora L Works: Jacques Derrida and Peter Eisenman*, ed. Jeffrey Kipnis and Thomas Leeser (New York: The Monacelli Press, 1997), 18.

25. *Tim.* 50c. Regarding the constantly violated prohibition on naming the feminine receptacle, Judith Butler, in *Bodies That Matter*, writes the following: "In a sense, this authoritative naming of the receptacle as the unnameable constitutes a primary or founding inscription that secures this place as an inscriptional space. This naming of what cannot be named is itself a penetration into this receptacle which is at once a violent erasure, one

which establishes it as an impossible yet necessary site for all further inscriptions. In this sense, the very *telling* of the story about the phallomorphic genesis of objects *enacts* that phallomorphosis and becomes an allegory of its own procedure" (44).

26. Plato, *Theaetetus,* 191c, 196a.

27. *Met.* I.6 988a1.

28. *Tim.,*72c.

29. *Tim.* 50d.

30. *Tim.* 50e.

31. Here in Irigaray's psychoanalytic territory of the topology of gendered bodies and the unconscious processes that subtend the psychical operations by which sexual difference is itself produced, we find a distinct resonance with Freud's "A Note upon the Mystic Writing Pad," trans. James Strachey, in Sigmund Freud, *Collected Papers,* vol. 5 (London: The Hogarth Press and the Institute of Psycho-Analysis, 1953)—the wax tablet which both retains and erases marks and as such provides an extended analogy for memories that are laid down, inscribed, and periodically erased while leaving their traces hidden beneath the surface, and which is discussed at length by Derrida in his "Freud and the Scene of Writing" in *Writing and Difference,* trans. Alan Bass (London: Routledge & Kegan Paul, 1978). The *locus classicus* for the wax tablet as figure for memory is Plato's *Theaetetus,* later elaborated by Aristotle in *On Memory and Recollection,* I. 450a30f. It perhaps also should not go unmentioned that the figure of wax, its changeability and lability, is the theme at the heart of Descartes's Second Meditation (in Descartes, *Discourse on Method*), the fêted site of the turn to a philosophy of subjectivity in the modern era.

32. Irigaray, *Speculum,* 237.

33. Ibid., 238.

34. Ibid., 307.

35. Ibid., 308

36. Cf. Katrin Pahl's work on the moments of emotionality, especially dissolving into tears, in Hegel: *Tropes of Transport: Hegel and Emotion* (Evanston, IL: Northwestern University Press, 2012). In an uncorroborated lexical/etymological link, *ek-mageion* also has a mystical resonance, the verb *mageuō* denoting being a magician or magus, enchanting or bewitching. We might read this as illustrative of the indeterminate status of the *Timaeus*'s narrative, especially in its resonances with the *pharmakeus,* the sorcerer (related to *pharmakon*—indeterminately a healing drug or poison), famously drawn out by Jacques Derrida in "Plato's Pharmacy," in *Dissemination.*

37. Butler, *Bodies That Matter,* 44.

38. Drawing a connection between genesis and naming cannot but remind us of the Judaeo-Christian creation story, the many resonances of which I am unfortunately unable to pursue here.

39. *Tim.* 50d.

40. *Phys.* I.9 192a14.

41. *Tim.* 51d.

42. *Tim.* 48a.

43. In attempting to show that the rational intentionality of a demiurge is not incompatible with the existence of a disorderly realm of necessity for Plato's teleological cosmology in the *Timaeus*, Glenn R. Morrow in "Necessity and Persuasion in Plato's *Timaeus*" *Philosophical Review* 59 (1950): 147–63, argues that such persuasion is not at odds with necessity, but rather brings together into order suitable powers and forces of this realm in the service of rational, purposeful ends. First noting that the rhetorical art of persuasion is heavily criticized by Plato in the *Gorgias* as the province of sophists and politicians, he goes on to examine Plato's distinction in the *Phaedrus* between genuine persuasion—presumably to be identified with the *Timaeus*'s *peithous emphronos* (48a)—and the more degraded rhetorical art. Such genuine persuasion is a "psychagogy"—the art of leading souls, and it requires knowledge of both the good and the end to be accomplished, as well as a thoroughgoing understanding of souls, the different types, and the types of argument each will respond to. "Persuasion," writes Morrow, "in its broadest sense, is the technique of intelligence. It is the proper means for accomplishing what we will with others—whether inanimate materials or thinking men—by understanding them so thoroughly that we can use the forces inherent in them to bring about the end we desire" (156). Morrow's vision, that persuasion elicits order "easily and naturally" (155), and that "the divine craftsman therefore sets the example and provides the setting for the activity of the intelligent statesman, by bringing into being a cosmos built upon the friendly co-operation of its varied parts" (162), requires of the realm of necessity a transparency and knowability that is rendered unavailable by even the most cursory account of the receptacle/*chōra*. That necessity may in fact be somewhat less than cooperative to demiurgic persuasion, if not downright agonistic, is indicated explicitly by Plato at 56c when he write that "God . . . brought [the elements] in every way to the exactest perfection, insofar as the nature of necessity submits willingly or by persuasion." The disjunction here opposes persuasion to willing submission, and clearly reveals persuasion of feminine *chōra* by the masculine demiurge as violent and coercive.

44. Morrow, "Necessity and Persuasion," 156, 162.

45. *Tim.* 51d–e.

46. *Tim.* 51d.

47. The feminist literature on the *Timaeus* is not insubstantial, and includes Judith Butler's *Bodies that Matter*, Judith Genova "Feminist Dialectics: Plato and Dualism" in *Engendering Origins*, ed. Bar On, as well as Irigaray's *Speculum*. Julia Kristeva, *Revolution in Poetic Language*, trans. Margaret Waller (New York: Columbia University Press, 1984) famously uses the concept of *chōra* as a key element of her theoretical work of semiotics at the border of linguistics and psychoanalysis, in which it represents an unregulated, temporary ordering and articulation of drives in a mobile, gestural, vocal, "nonexpressive totality" (25, 40). While this is not the occasion for a critical engagement with Kristeva's semiotics, it should be remarked that she is perhaps the only reader of *chōra* who foregrounds its motile and movement-giving character.

48. Derrida, "Chora," 31.

49. Ibid., 18.

50. Ibid., 23.

51. Ibid., 16.

52. *Tim.* 52b.

53. Derrida, "Chora," 20–21.

54. For an extended analysis of the notion of place in the history of West-ern philosophy, see Edward S. Casey, *The Fate of Place: A Philosophical His-tory* (Berkeley: University of California Press, 1997).

55. Derrida, "Chora," 21; Nader El-Bizri, "*'Qui Etes-vous Chōra?'* Receiving Plato's *Timaeus,*" *Existentia* 11 (2001): 473–90, 475.

56. Sallis's analysis in *Chorology* emphasizes that Socrates's call at the begin-ning of the dialogue for a speech describing the ideal city in glorious motion, namely the city at war, refers us back to the *Republic*'s description of the luxuri-ous city, whose many demands necessitate military expansion. Sallis quotes the *Republic* 373d: "'And the land [*chōra*] of course . . . will now be [too] small,' so that we must 'cut off a piece of our neighbor's land [*chōra*]'" (24). Here, the *chōra* is not certainly space as an ontological opening out, but space as already instrumentalized, territorialized, contained within the logic of ownership and possession, over which glorious wars might be fought between armies of men.

57. Derrida, "Chora," 17.

58. Ibid., 18.

59. Sallis, *Chorology,* 125–56.

60. Heidegger is notably unforthcoming on the subject of femininity or sexual difference, although as Derrida relates in his essay "*Geschlecht*: Sex-ual Difference, Ontological Difference," *Research in Phenomenology* 13 (1983): 65–83, Heidegger, in a course given at the University of Marburg/Lahn in 1928, elaborates *Dasein*'s nonanthropological "neutrality," specify-ing that, "*Dasein* is neither of the two sexes [*keines von beiden Geschlecth-ern ist*]."

61. Butler, *Bodies That Matter,* 41.

62. Irigaray, *This Sex,* 26.

63. Ibid., 76.

64. Butler, *Bodies that Matter,* 47.

65. Irigaray, *This Sex,* 151, emphasis in original.

66. Ibid., 152, emphasis in original.

67. See, for example, Jane Gallop, *Thinking Through the Body* (New York: Columbia University Press, 1988); Diana Fuss, *Essentially Speaking: Feminism, Nature and Difference* (New York: Routledge, 1989); Margaret Whitford, *Luce Irigaray: Philosophy in the Feminine*; and Drucilla Cornell, *Beyond Accommodation: Ethical Feminism, Deconstruction, and the Law* (New York: Routledge, 1991).

68. Diana J. Fuss, "'Essentially Speaking': Luce Irigaray's Language of Essence," *Hypatia* 3, no. 3 (1989): 62–80, 68–69.

69. Fuss, "Essentially Speaking," 72.

70. Here, reading *chōra* as restless and moving, one may find a conflu-ence with the materialist Irigarayan feminism of Elizabeth Grosz and her

groundbreaking theorization of bodies as *volatile* rather than static; see *Volatile Bodies* (Bloomington: Indiana University Press, 1994). However Grosz's own writing on *chōra* takes place in the context of a discussion of the gendering of lived space, and emphasizes simply its maternity and spatiality rather than its motility. See "Women, *Chora*, Dwelling" in *Space, Time, and Perversion: Essays on the Politics of Bodies* (New York: Routledge, 1995).

71. Butler, *Bodies That Matter*, 48.

72. Luce Irigaray, "The Return," in *Rewriting Difference*, ed. Tzelepis and Athanasiou, 262.

73. See Hesiod, *Theogony*; the *Homeric Hymn to Demeter* in *Homeric Hymns, Homeric Apocrypha, Lives of Homer*, trans. Martin L. West (Cambridge, MA: Harvard University Press, 2003); and Dianne Wolkstein, *Innana: Queen of Heaven and Earth* (New York: Harper & Row, 1983).

74. See Lynn E. Roller, *In Search of God the Mother: The Cult of Anatolian Cybele* (Berkeley: University of California Press, 1999) for an incisive assessment of this scholarly tradition.

75. See note 54.

76. The references to *chōra* occur at 19a, 22e, and 23b. Sallis, *Chorology*, ch. 1, "Remembrance of the City" provides a fine overview of these issues.

77. Gloria Anzaldúa, *Borderlands/La frontera: The new mestiza*, 2nd ed. (San Francisco: Aunt Lute Books, 1999), 95.

78. Ibid., 44.

79. Recognizing that in life we simultaneously negotiate multiple, layered, crossing, shifting identities, sexual, racial, and so on, Butler also articulates the need for "an economy of difference . . . in which the matrices, the crossroads at which various identifications are formed and displaced, force a reworking of that logic of non-contradiction by which one identification is always and only purchased at the expense of another" (*Bodies That Matter*, 118). Receptacle/*chōra* as errant matrix, apprehensible through "bastard reasoning," supplies a rich figure for imagining that economy.

80. Mariana Ortega, "Exiled space, in-between space: existential spatiality in Ana Mendieta's *Siluetas* Series," *Philosophy and Geography* 7, no. 1 (2004): 25–41, 37.

81. *Tim.* 52c, Jowett's translation, modified.

82. *Tim.* 52d–53b, translation mine.

83. *Tim.* 58a.

4. THE PHYSICS OF SEXUAL DIFFERENCE
IN ARISTOTLE AND IRIGARAY

1. There is a long established critical tradition exploring Aristotle's interpretation of the *Timaeus*, ranging from from Harold F. Cherniss, *Aristotle's Criticism of Plato and the Academy* (Baltimore, MD: Johns Hopkins University Press, 1994), Friedrich Solmsen, *Aristotle's System of the Physical World: A Comparison with his Predecessors* (Ithaca, NY: Cornell University Press, 1960) and David Keyt, "Aristotle on Plato's Receptacle," *American Journal of Philology* 82 (1961): 291–300, to Richard Sorabji, *Matter, Space*

and Motion: Theories in Antiquity and Their Sequel (Ithaca, NY: Cornell University Press, 1988).

2. Harold Bloom, *A Map of Misreading* (Oxford: Oxford University Press, 2003).

3. duBois, *Sowing the Body*, 30.

4. Luce Irigaray, "Place, Interval: A Reading of Aristotle, *Physics* IV," in *An Ethics of Sexual Difference*, trans. Carolyn Burke and Gillian C. Gill (Ithaca, NY: Cornell University Press, 1993), 34–55. The piece is structured like a traditional commentary, with sequential passages from *Physics* IV quoted at length, followed by "commentaries" that are anything but traditional, but rather meditations on sexual in/difference inspired by the Aristotelian text. Tina Chanter, in *Ethics of Eros: Irigaray's Rewriting of the Philosophers* (New York: Routledge, 1995), 151–59, gives an illuminating exposition of this essay. Rebecca Hill, in *The Interval: Relation and Becoming in Irigaray, Aristotle, and Bergson* (New York: Fordham University Press, 2012) provides a highly sympathetic analysis and meditation in relation to the thought of Henri Bergson. For an incisive critical engagement, see Gayle Salamon, "Sameness, Alterity, Flesh: Luce Irigaray and the Place of Sexual Undecidability," in *Rewriting Difference*, ed. Tzelepis and Athanasiou, 191–201.

5. The thinking here also responds to Elizabeth Grosz's call for feminist theory to "explore non-Euclidean and non-Kantian notions of space. . . . [and] different 'pre-oedipal' or infantile non-perspectival spaces [that] may provide the basis for alternatives to those developed in dominant representations of corporeality." Elizabeth Grosz, "Notes Towards a Corporeal Feminism," *Australian Feminist Studies* 5 (1987): 1–16, 11.

6. *Phys.* IV.2 209b13–17. More traditional analyses of this passage can be found in Solmsen, *Aristotle's System*, 124ff. and Henry Mendell, "Topoi on Topos: The Development of Aristotle's Concept of Place," *Phronesis* 32, no. 2 (1987): 206–31, 213ff., both of whom also review the available interpretive history quite adequately. Heinz Happ's monumental study *Hyle: Studien zum aristotelischen Materie-Begriff* (Berlin: Walter de Gruyter, 1971) stresses the continuity of Aristotelian matter with the Platonic notion of the Indefinite Dyad from the "Unwritten Doctrines," reconstructed in the Tübingen tradition from the writings of other academicians such as Speusippus. While the idea of Aristotelian matter as a principle with mathematical roots in Platonic Pythagoreanism presents a fascinating line of inquiry, I must restrict the present study to Plato's extant text.

7. *Met.* XII.7 1072b20.

8. Bloom, *Map of Misreading*, 102.

9. Apostle, in his translation of the *Physics*, does nothing to disabuse us of Aristotle's own error when he translates *metalēptikon* as receptacle, and then writes in his commentary on this passage that "Plato seems to use 'receptacle,' 'space,' and 'matter' synonymously" (240n5). El-Bizri, perhaps taking his cue from Apostle, compounds the error by citing the Aristotelian passage as follows: "According to Aristotle, Plato believed that 'the receptacle (*hupodokh*'), *khōra* and *matter* (*hulē*) are all one and the same'" ("*Qui Etes-vous,*"

482). See also Alfredo Ferrarin, *Hegel and Aristotle* (Cambridge: Cambridge University Press, 2001), 122n19, for an argument that Hegel's translation of *metalēpsis* as *Aufnahme* (reception) is correct. As to the reappearance of *metalēpsis* in Aristotle's description of thought thinking itself (*noēsis noēseōs*), it is perhaps worth speculating on the fact that at the moment of this most radical statement of the kind of being and *energeia* possessed by the ultimate being— "the chief moment in Aristotle's philosophy," according to Hegel, G. W. F. Hegel, *Lectures on the History of Philosophy: Plato and the Platonists*, vol. 2, trans. E. S. Haldane and Frances H. Simson (Lincoln: University of Nebraska Press, 1995), 148—a term that Aristotle also uses to denote the Platonic receptacle/*chōra* appears. The haunting of the prime mover by the irreducibly feminine *chōra*, and that the taking of itself as an object of thought may require separation, *chōrismos*, into thinker and participant/receptacle as a prerequisite for thinking, are themes to which I will return in chapter 5.

10. *Tim.* 52a.

11. *Tim.* 52b.

12. *Gen. et Corr.* II.1 329a.

13. *Gen. et Corr.* II.1 329a24–27.

14. Sallis, *Chorology*, 153.

15. Ibid., 153–54.

16. Ibid., 154n12. Sallis quotes Martin Heidegger, "Vom Wesen und Begriff der Φύσις: Aristoteles, Physik B, I," in *Wegmarken*, vol. 9 of *Gesamtausgabe* (Frankfurt a. M.: Vittorio Klostermann, 1976), 241f.

17. Sallis, *Chorology*, 151n9. Irigaray's essay appears in *Speculum of the Other Woman*, 168–79.

18. Judith Butler also finds Irigaray's embrace of Plotinus's reduction of *chōra* to Aristotelian matter significant, remarking that it involves "a twist that the history of philosophy has perhaps rarely undergone" (*Bodies That Matter*, 43).

19. Irigaray, *An Ethics*, 12.

20. Casey, *Fate of Place*, 53. He also says here, "A complete consideration of place will have to take both matters into account: how place is "in itself" and how it is relative to other things."

21. Irigaray, *An Ethics*, 39.

22. Ibid., 9.

23. Ibid. Irigaray's invocation of the chiasmus refers to Merleau-Ponty's treatment of that figure in his essay "The Intertwining—The Chiasm" in Maurice Merleau-Ponty, *The Visible and the Invisible*, ed. Claude Lefort, trans. Alphonso Lingis (Evanston, IL: Northwestern University Press, 1973). Irigaray's essay in *An Ethics of Sexual Difference* entitled "The Invisible of the Flesh" also subjects Merleau-Ponty's privileging of vision over the tactile to a thoroughgoing critique.

24. Irigaray, *An Ethics*, 54.

25. Ibid. According to Aristophanes's speech in Plato's *Symposium* it is love between men that is judged the highest and best, because it is driven by "boldness, manliness, and masculinity, feeling affection for what is like to themselves" (192a).

26. Sigmund Freud, *Introductory Lectures on Psychoanalysis*, trans. and ed. James Strachey (New York: W. W. Norton, 1977), 329, 426; also Sigmund Freud, *The Ego and the Id*, trans. Joan Riviere, ed. James Strachey (New York: W. W. Norton, 1960), 21.

27. I owe my understanding of these passages in Freud to Kaja Silverman's seminars at UC Berkeley. Further, the language of "struggle unto death" is not idle here. Gayle Rubin, "The Traffic in Women: Notes on the 'Political Economy' of Sex," in *Toward an Anthropology of Women*, ed. Rayna Reiter (New York: Monthly Review Press, 1975), brilliantly demonstrated the socio-political dimensions of the Oedipus complex in its relationship to structures of kinship and sexual difference. Furthermore, it is perhaps one of Freud's most significant interventions into the history of Western philosophy that he makes possible a rendering of the Hegelian struggle unto death for pure prestige, and hence for subjectivity itself, in terms that disclose a hidden drama of sexual difference—the lord and bondsman are refigured as father and son, and the mother/woman appear as mediating objects of exchange. This drama of sexual differentiation is thus not that of Hegel's *Antigone*, in which the feminine survives only as irony in the life of the community and the masculine law of the polis supersedes all in ethical life (G. W. F. Hegel, *The Phenomenology of Spirit*, trans. A. V. Miller [Oxford: Oxford University Press, 1977], 266–89), but that of *Oedipus Tyrranos*, in which sexual difference itself is disclosed as fundamental to the reproduction of relations between men, which are sustained by and made possible by the mediation of the intergenerational exchange of women as objects.

28. Kaja Silverman, in *Male Subjectivity at the Margins* (New York: Routledge, 1992), 192–94, emphasizes that according to Freud's account in *The Ego and the Id*, for both boys and girls the Oedipus complex can be both "positive" and "negative"—little boys can identify with the mother and take the father for an object, and little girls can also "go both ways." Freud attributes this to the fundamental bisexuality of all individuals, and this certainly has value insofar as it gives a psychoanalytic account of the possibility of non-normative gender and sexuality; but the process—involving a primary splitting of desire and identification along sexed lines—nonetheless results in a quelling of bisexuality in the name of a fixed homo- or heterosexuality, and in early twentieth-century fashion directly indexes sexual orientation to gender identification. This account would also seem to imply that men are subject to exchange equally with women, which certainly flies in the face of the facts of the matter under patriarchy.

29. *Met.* XII.7 1072b4.

30. Freud, *Ego and the Id*, 22.

31. Silverman, *Male Subjectivity*, 194.

32. For example, at *Prior Analytics* II.22 68a40–b7 where he uses it as an example to illustrate a hierarchy of preferences. It is unclear whether his reference at *Eth. Nic.* III.10 1118b6 to the refined pleasures of friction (*tripsis*) and warm baths in the gymnasium refers to sex between men, or simply massage. For an overview, concluding that Aristotle's remarks about sexual behavior are mostly neutral with regard to the gender of the partners, see

Juha Sihvola, "Aristotle on Sex and Love," in *The Sleep of Reason: Erotic Experience and Sexual Ethics in Ancient Greece and Rome*, ed. Martha C. Nussbaum and Juha Sihvola (Chicago: University of Chicago Press, 2002), 200–21. Given that many of Aristotle's erotic examples involve the description of behaviors and attitudes that may pertain equally to one partner or the other, and refer to inequalities or equalities arising therefrom, it seems he is mostly not thinking of erotic relationships between men and women (which are necessarily unequal for Aristotle and could not involve this kind of transitivity).

33. This role-reversal whereby the most elevated being becomes the object of desire finds a certain prefigurement in Plato's erotic dialogues *Phaedrus* and *Symposium*, in which Socrates finds himself in the place of the beloved rather than the lover vis-à-vis a younger man. Toward the end of the *Symposium*, Alcibiades describes his fruitless attempts to seduce Socrates. Socrates remains resistant and impassive in the face of Alcibiades's advances, and this resistance combined with Socrates's inner beauty so frustrates Alcibiades that he claims, "While deceiving [young men] into thinking of him as the lover, [Socrates] brings it about that he is the beloved rather than the lover" (222b).

34. It is important to note that while the Aristotelian prime mover is a patriarchal divinity, it is not a demiurge or creator. "Father" in this sense functions phantasmatically rather than literally.

35. Irigaray, *An Ethics*, 35.

36. Ibid., 12.

37. *Phys.* IV.4 211a1–6.

38. *Phys.* IV.4 212a6–7.

39. *Phys.* IV.4 212a20–21.

40. *Phys.* IV.4 212a30.

41. In the 1957 Loeb edition this appears on 315nb. Apostle's commentary simply glosses over the problem, stating, "The inner boundary of a containing body coincides with the shape of the contained body, if the latter is contained primarily, as in the case of a can full of water" (248n48).

42. Casey, *Fate of Place*, 58. Casey further develops the notion of a double limit in the Aristotelian understanding of place, and argues for a distinction between a boundary, *horos*, which he says belongs to the place or container, and limit, *peras* belonging to the contained (63). The stability of this distinction is somewhat vitiated by Aristotle's use of *peras* to describe the boundary of place in his definition.

43. *Phys.* IV.4 212b9–11.

44. *Phys.* IV.4 212a19, also VIII.1 251b28–29.

45. Jacques Derrida, "*Ousia* and *Grammē*: Note on a Note from *Being and Time*" in *Margins of Philosophy*, trans. Alan Bass (Chicago: University of Chicago Press, 1982), 56. The passage discussed by Derrida is at *Physics* IV.10 218a, on the aporias presented by the concept of time.

46. Ibid., 56.

47. Green, "Necessary Verticality," demonstrates the association of the feminine with downward motion across many different texts, including the

distinction between ruler and ruled in the *Politics*. Aristotle in the *Physics* also explicitly disavows the identification of downward motion with chance: "The up-direction is not any chance direction but where fire or a light object travels, and likewise the down-direction is not any chance direction but where heavy or earth bodies are carried" (IV.1 208b20). In *De Generatione et Corruptione* and *De Caelo*, however, it is clear that up and down do not bear a simply equal-and-opposite valence, but that up is more noble than down. In a discussion of the nature of the simple bodies or elements he says, for example, that "fire alone—and to a greater extent than the rest—is of the nature of 'form' (*tou eidous*), because it naturally tends to be borne towards the limit" (II.8 335a18–20). There is a hierarchy of value here along the vertical axis, and downwardness is clearly inferior.

48. Casey, *Fate of Place*, 68.

49. *Phys.* IV.4 211b14.

50. *De Cael.* IV.3 310a34–b1, translation modified.

51. *De Cael.* IV.3 310b10.

52. *Phys.* IV.5 212b32–34.

53. *Phys.* IV.5 212b21–22, translation modified.

54. *De Cael.* IV.4 312a12–13.

55. *De Cael.* IV.4 312a19–22.

56. *Phys.* IV.5 212b35–213a1.

57. *Phys.* IV.4 211b35–212a1.

58. Kristeva, *Revolution*, 26.

59. *Phys.* IV.2 209b12–16.

60. *Phys.* IV.4 212a20–1.

61. See for example Iris Marion Young, *On Female Body Experience: "Throwing Like a Girl" and Other Essays* (Oxford: Oxford University Press, 2005), for phenomenological analyses that think through sexual difference and embodiment along these lines.

62. Casey, *Fate of Place*, 325.

63. See Freud, Sigmund. *Beyond The Pleasure Principle*, trans. James Strachey, in vol. 18, *The Standard Edition of the Complete Psychological Works of Sigmund Freud*, 1–64 (London: Hogarth Press and the Institute of Psycho-Analysis, 1955), 14–16.

64. As Gayle Salamon, "The Bodily Ego and the Contested Domain of the Material," *differences: A Journal of Feminist Cultural Studies* 15, no. 3 (2004): 95–122, suggests in the context of a psychoanalytic and phenomenological account of transgender: "arguably psychoanalytic theory's most important insight about the relation of the subject to his or her body . . . is that bodily assumption, and hence subject formation itself, is a constant and complex oscillation between narcissistic investment in one's own flesh and the 'necessary self-division and self-estrangement' (to borrow a phrase from Butler) that is the very means by which our bodies are articulated" (119).

65. Butler's—particularly in *Gender Trouble, Bodies That Matter*, and *Undoing Gender* (New York: Routledge, 2004)—and Grosz's (in *Volatile Bodies*) stress on the proliferative capacities of both sex and gender is particularly relevant here (Butler emphasizing the performative dimensions of such

proliferation and Grosz the corporeal). In a more directly biological register, Anne Fausto-Sterling, *Sexing the Body* (New York: Basic Books, 2000) presents extensive documentation of the many vagaries of becoming sexed, also taking into account the psychical, social, and political phenomena involved in this complex and dynamic process, and arguing for the acknowledgment of an entire spectrum of possible and livable positions beyond the duality of "man" and "woman."

5. MOTION AND GENDER IN THE ARISTOTELIAN COSMOS

1. Heidegger, *"Phusis,"* 187.
2. *Tim.* 19b–c.
3. *Phys.* V.1 225a35–b2: "Since . . . changes with respect to generation and destruction are not motions but are changes with respect to contradiction, only a change from a subject to a subject must be a motion."
4. *Phys.* V.1 224b5.
5. A comprehensive and still definitive analysis can be found in Solmsen, *Aristotle's System*, while the most comprehensive and incisive work in recent years is undoubtedly Helen S. Lang's *The Order of Nature in Aristotle's Physics* (Cambridge: Cambridge University Press, 1998). Other notable contributions in English include Sorabji, *Matter, Space, Motion*; the essays by David Furley, Mary Louise Gill, Cynthia A. Freeland, Susan Sauvé Meyer, Michael Wedin, Christopher Shields, Aryeh Kosman and Lindsay Judson collected in *Self-Motion: From Aristotle to Newton*, eds. Mary Louise Gill and James G. Lennox (Princeton, NJ: Princeton University Press, 1994), and works by Sarah Waterlow including *Nature, Change, and Agency in Aristotle's "Physics"* (Oxford: Clarendon Press, 1982) and *Passage and Possibility* (Oxford: Clarendon Press, 1982).
6. *Phys.* III.1 201a11.
7. *Phys.* II.1 192b13. The parsing of the word is performed by Brogan in *Heidegger and Aristotle*, 33.
8. Brogan, *Heidegger and Aristotle*, 35.
9. Heidegger, *"Phusis,"* 189.
10. See, for example, Gilbert Simondon, "The Genesis of the Individual," trans. Mark Cohen and Sanford Kwinter, in *Incorporations*, ed. Jonathan Crary and Sanford Kwinter (New York: Zone, 1992), 297–319.
11. As Michael Witmore puts it in a meditation on this image in "We Have Never Not Been Inhuman," *postmedieval: a journal of medieval cultural studies* 1 (Spring/Summer 2010): 208–14: "Dynamism creates conditions in which a body's capacity for movement is not fully visible: for any apparent state of balance, there may be hundreds of forces acting on the system of ball, figure, and ground which are reconciled in the shiver of balance" (211).
12. Derrida uses this concept in many of his later works, developing it most fully in *Rogues: Two Essays on Reason*, trans. Pascale-Anne Brault and Michael Naas (Stanford, CA: Stanford University Press, 2005), esp. at 109ff.
13. In both *Time Travels* (Durham, NC: Duke University Press, 2005) and *The Nick of Time* (Durham, NC: Duke University Press, 2004), Elizabeth

Grosz elaborates a Darwinian account of sexual difference as kind of "difference engine"—an amazingly effective method for combining DNA and an impetus for phenotypical efflorescence through the mechanism of sexual selection. Darwin, she says, "makes sexual difference one of the ontological characteristics of life itself, not merely a detail, a feature that will pass. Although sexual difference—the requirement of genetic material from two sexes—emerges for Darwin contingently or randomly, an ingenious "invention" of primitive life that maximizes individual variation by ensuring each generation varies from the previous one, it is now so well adapted to the generation of variation that it would be hard to imagine an invention that life might generate to compete with and supersede it. Sexual difference is an ineliminable characteristic of life because of its peculiar economy of combination, exchange, and variation, and because of its pervasive historical force and effectivity" (*Time Travels*, 31). In the wake of this, the question of the ontological status of sexual difference in nature has been hotly contested by Deleuzian feminists such as Luciana Parisi and Jami Weinstein who argue rather for "matter's unpredictable, inhuman, unbounded, irreducibly heterogeneous and multiple, preaccelerated, relational forms of sex that are infinitely open to future variation and self-overcoming." Jami Weinstein, "A Requiem to Sexual Difference: A Response to Luciana Parisi's 'Event and Evolution,'" *Southern Journal of Philosophy* 48, Spindel Supplement (2010): 165–87, 177, and Parisi's "Event and Evolution" in the same volume, 147–64. While it is true that bacteria frequently exchange genetic material non-sexually, any approach that would diminish the importance and relevance of sexual reproduction in natural becoming would, it seems to me, no longer be able to lay claim to being a phenomenology of any kind.

14. *Phys.* VIII.9 265a23–24.

15. While *energeia* has often been translated as *activity*, thus denoting a sort of being in motion, Aristotle carefully distinguishes it from motion in *Met.* IX.6.

16. Aristotle's definition of time is "a number of motion with respect to the prior and posterior and that it is also continuous (for it is of something [i.e., circular motion] which is continuous)" (*Phys.* IV.11 220a25–27). Unfortunately, a discussion of this is beyond the scope of this book.

17. *De Cael.* I.2 269a19ff.

18. *Phys.* VIII.10 267b18–28.

19. *De Cael.* II.2 285a29–30.

20. *De An.* I.3 407b 17–19. Cf. *Met.* IX.1. The essays in *Self-Motion*, ed. Gill and Lennox, treat these questions in considerably greater detail and subtlety than I am able to offer here.

21. Kosman, Aryeh, "Aristotle's Prime Mover," in *Self-Motion: From Aristotle to Newton*, ed. Mary Louise Gill and James G. Lennox (Princeton, NJ: Princeton University Press, 1994), 135–54.

22. Solmsen thinks the *aithēr* is a later development. However A. P. Bos, in *On the Elements: Aristotle's Early Cosmology* (Assen: Van Gorcum, 1972) goes so far as to argue that the central chapters of *De Caelo* (I.4 to the end of Book II) are a later interpolation, written once Aristotle had broken

away from an earlier and more rigorously immanentist anti-Platonism represented in an earlier part of Book I and Books III and IV. Lang summarizes the various positions at 177ff.

23. Relevant instances of *rhopē*, often translated as impetus or impulse, occur at *De Cael.* II.1 297a28, b7f, at III.2 310a22f, at II.2 305a25, and at IV.1 307b33.

24. "We may say, then, that the cause of motion upwards and downwards is equivalent to that which makes heavy or light, and that what is moved (*kinētikon*—the "movable") is the potentially heavy or light, and to be carried toward its proper place is for each thing to be carried towards its proper form." *De Cael.* IV.3 310a32–b1 (translation modified).

25. "As moved *all* the elements are construed according to the same causal model: Aristotle's definition of motion as the actualization of the potential insofar as it is such." Lang, *Order of Nature*, 170, emphasis in original.

26. *Phys.* IV.4 212b9.

27. *Phys.* I.9 192a6.

28. Irigaray, *Speculum*, 244.

29. Irigaray, "Plato's Hystera," in *Speculum*, 243–364. The procedure of *Speculum* is illuminated by Irigaray's own discussion of her methodology in "The Power of Discourse and the Subordination of the Feminine," in *This Sex Which is Not One*. The relationship between place and form in Irigaray is explored in very different ways by Claire Colebrook, "Dynamic Potentiality: The Body that Stands Alone," and Gayle Salamon, "Sameness, Alterity, Flesh: Luce Irigaray and the Place of Sexual Undecidability," both of which appear in *Rewriting Difference*, ed. Tzelepis and Athanasiou.

30. *Gen. et. Corr.* I.3 318b32.

31. *De Cael.* II.3 386a19–20, translation mine, emphasis added.

32. *Met.* XII.7 1072b18f, Apostle's translation.

33. *Met.* XII.7 1072b18–25, translated in Long, *Aristotle on the Nature of Truth*, 232, 235.

34. Ferrarin, *Hegel and Aristotle*, 122.

35. Long, *Aristotle on the Nature of Truth*, 235.

36. *Met.* XII.7 1072b27–30, translation mine.

37. Ferrarin, *Hegel and Aristotle*, 20.

38. Heidegger, *Aristotle's "Metaphysics"* θ 1–3, 41; *The Essence of Human Freedom*, trans. Ted Sadler (London: Continuum, 2002), 48; "*Phusis*," 217.

39. See *Eth. Nic.* X for Aristotle's argument that contemplation is the highest and best pleasure. I return to a more critical discussion of *energeia* in chapter 6.

40. *Met.* IX.6 1048b23–24.

41. Ferrarin, *Hegel and Aristotle*, 24.

42. *Met.* XII.9 1074b35.

43. *Met.* XII.7 1072b4, *kinei de hōs erōmenon, kinoumena de talla kinei.*

44. Ferrarin puts it this way—in a formulation he attributes to Aubenque—"the relation of God to the world is not a communication from a principle to a consequence" (*Hegel and Aristotle*, 375–76).

45. *Met.* IX.1 1046a14.
46. *Gen. et Corr.* II.10 336b28.
47. *Gen. et Corr.* II.10 336b32–337a1.
48. *Gen. et Corr.* II.10 337a4–7.
49. *Gen. et Corr.* II.10 336a33ff.
50. John Protevi, *Time and Exteriority: Aristotle, Heidegger and Derrida* (London: Associated University Presses, 1994), 42.
51. Protevi, *Time and Exteriority*, 43.
52. *Gen. et Corr.* II.10 336a17–19. See also *Met.* XII.5 1071a14–17: "The cause of a man is his elements: fire and earth as matter, and the particular form, some external formal cause, viz. his father; and besides these the sun and the ecliptic, which are neither matter nor form nor privation nor identical in form with him, but cause motion."
53. *Met.* IX.8 1050b29–31.
54. Lucretius, *De Rerum Natura*, trans. W. H. D. Rouse (Cambridge, MA: Harvard University Press, 1975), II.216–93.
55. See Gilles Deleuze, *The Logic of Sense*, trans. Mark Lester with Charles Stivale (New York: Columbia University Press, 1990); Alfred Jarry, *Exploits and Opinions of Doctor Faustroll, Pataphysician*, trans. Simon Watson Taylor (Boston, MA: Exact Change, 1996); Michel Serres, *The Birth of Physics* (Manchester: Clinamen Press, 2000); Jacques Lacan, *The Four Fundamental Concepts of Psycho-Analysis*, trans. Alan Sheridan (London and New York: W. W. Norton, 1981); Harold Bloom, *The Anxiety of Influence* (New York: Oxford University Press, 1973); Althusser, *Philosophy of the Encounter*; Jean-Luc Nancy, *Being Singular Plural*, trans. Robert D. Richardson and Anne E. O'Byrne (Stanford, CA: Stanford University Press, 2000); Jacques Derrida, "My Chances/*Mès Chances*: A Rendezvous with Some Epicurean Stereophonies" in *Taking Chances: Derrida, Psychoanalysis, Literature*, ed. Joseph H. Smith and William Kerry (Baltimore, MD: Johns Hopkins University Press, 1984).
56. Derrida, "My Chances/*Mès Chances*," 5.
57. Rudolf E. Kuenzli, "Surrealism and Misogyny," in *Surrealism and Women*, ed. Mary Ann Caws, Rudolf Kuenzli, and Gwen Raaberg (Cambridge, MA: MIT Press, 1991), 19.
58. *Gen. et Corr.* II.10 336b20–24.
59. *De Cael.* III.2 300a23, 3 302b6, and 4 303b5.
60. See Lang, *Order of Nature*, for a comprehensive and convincing account of this argument.
61. See *De Cael.* IV.3 310b5–12.
62. *De Cael.* IV.3 310b10–11.
63. *De Cael.* IV.3 310a34–b1.
64. *Tim.* 30b.
65. *De Cael.* IV.1 308a2.
66. *De Cael.* IV.3 311a3–10.
67. *De Cael.* IV.4 312a13–21. The Greek here is more suggestive than clear. He says "*hē men toiouton dunamei, bareos hulē, hē de tououton, kouphou*" (312a17–19). One might speculate that it is not, as most translations have

it, that matter is either potentially heavy or light in equal measure, but that it is perhaps rather heavy *qua potential*, but light *qua actuality*. Supplying the missing *energeia* may be an over-read, but it would certainly be consistent with the foregoing claim that what is above is determinate and closer to form, while what is below is indeterminate and closer to matter.

68. *Gen. et Corr.* II.10 337a4–8.

69. For example by Simone de Beauvoir, *The Second Sex*, and by Julia Kristeva,"Women's Time," trans. Alice Jardine and Harry Blake, in *The Kristeva Reader*, ed. Toril Moi (Oxford: Blackwell, 1991).

70. Kristeva, "Women's Time," 192.

71. *De Cael.* II.3 386a19–20.

72. *Phys.* VIII.1 250b15.

73. *Met.* XII.7 1072b26–30.

74. *Phys.* II.6 197b15–16. See chapter 1 for a more detailed analysis of this passage.

75. *De Motu* VI 700b23–25.

76. *De An.* III.10 433a11. I leave *phantasia* untranslated, firstly because any given English translation (imagination, presentative power, making visible) specifies it inappropriately, and secondly in order to preserve its relation to the verb *phainesthai*. There is considerable variation in translation choices for the main concepts in these texts. Confusingly, Nussbaum chooses "desire" for *orexis* and "appetite" for *epithumia*, whereas Hett opts for the exact opposite usage in his translation of *De Anima*.

77. See Nussbaum's Interpretive Essay 5, "The Role of *Phantasia* in Aristotle's Explanation of Action" in *De Motu*, 221–69.

78. *De An.* III.3 427b16, my translation.

79. *De An.* III.3 429a2–5.

80. *De An.* III.10 433a28.

81. *De Motu* VI 700b26–29.

82. *De An.* III.10 433a30.

83. I thank Christopher Long for an illuminating exchange about this sentence.

84. *Phys.* II.3 195a24–26.

85. *De An.* III.10 433b7–10.

86. *De Motu* VII 701b20–22.

87. *De An.* III.10 433b19–27.

88. *De Motu* VII 701b1.

89. *De Motu* VIII 702a14.

90. *De Motu* VIII 702a7–10.

91. See Nussbaum's "Commentary" in *De Motu*, 357.

92. *De Motu* X 703a9–10.

93. *De Motu* X 703a30.

94. *De Motu* XI 703b7–8.

95. *De Motu* XI 703b21–26

96. *Tim.* 91b. I substitute "to prevail" for Lee's "for possession." *Kratein* signifies ruling, conquering and mastery, rather than mere possession. Nussbaum's commentary (*De Motu*, 384) also refers to this passage.

97. *Tim.* 91c.

98. It should be noted that, to Aristotle's credit, he does in *GA* acknowledge and describe the phenomenon of female ejaculation in some detail, and even offers the beginnings of an explanation despite its irrelevance to reproduction: "There are some who think that the female contributes semen during coition because women sometimes derive pleasure from it comparable to that of the male and also produce a fluid secretion. This fluid, however, is not seminal; it is peculiar to the part from which it comes in each several individual; there is a discharge from the uterus, which though it happens in some women does not in others. Speaking generally this happens in fair-skinned women who are typically feminine, and not in dark women of a masculine appearance. Where it occurs, this discharge is sometimes on quite a different scale from the semen discharged by the male, and greatly exceeds it in bulk. Furthermore, differences of food cause a great difference in the amount of this discharge which is produced: e.g., some pungent foods cause a noticeable increase in the amount" (*GA* I.20 727b30–728a9). It is entirely unclear whence Aristotle derives his bizarre typology and science of ejaculation in women, but also quite extraordinary to find in his writings an account of a phenomenon which is entirely unacknowledged in later and even in most contemporary biological accounts. Indeed, it is only due to the efforts of feminists working at the fringes of contemporary medical, therapeutic, artistic, and academic establishments that female ejaculation, and the organs and processes that lead to it, have been afforded any attention or ontological status today. Peck adds a footnote to his 1942 translation stating that Aristotle is mistaken and must be describing a disease: "This apparently refers to the so-called vaginal discharge, which is a natural secretion, but the latter part of the paragraph seems to describe leucorrhoea, which is pathological. The two have apparently been confused" (101nc). The history of the suppression of the biology of women's sexuality aside, Aristotle nonetheless does here attribute a kind of ejaculatory force to women which might be seen as parallel to the *dunamis* of the "separate living creature" to which the male organ is analogized. In light of this, his failure to acknowledge any active or separate *dunamis* on the part of the female in *De Motu* is all the more striking.

99. *Pol.* II.12 1274a13; V.6 1306b6.

100. Lacan's presentation of this idea in the mirror stage essay is all the more apt given that the idealization of the totalized body in the imaginary is articulated precisely through the language of "phantasy," and its breakdown as the hysterical symptom: "The fragmented body . . . usually manifests itself in dreams when the movement of the analysis encounters a certain level of aggressive disintegration in the individual. It then appears in the form of disjointed limbs, or of those organs represented in exoscopy growing wings and taking up arms for intestinal persecutions—the very same that the visionary Hieronymus Bosch has fixed, for all time, in painting, in their ascent from the fifteenth century to the imaginary zenith of modern man. But this form is even tangibly revealed at the organic level, in the lines of 'fragilization' that define the anatomy of phantasy, as exhibited in the schizoid and spasmodic symptoms of hysteria" (*Écrits*, 4–5).

101. *De Motu* XI 703b36–704a1.

102. Heidegger, *"Phusis,"* 189. In a passage that strikingly emphasizes the dominative, paternal hue of *archē* he writes that, "On the one hand *archē* means that from which something has its origin and beginning; on the other hand it means that which, *as* this origin and beginning, likewise keeps rein *over*, i.e., restrains and therefore dominates, something else that emerges from it. *Archē* means, at one and the same time, beginning and control" (ibid.).

103. Specific analogies between craftsmen and the sperm's actions occur at *GA* I.21 729b17 and I.22 730b6–8, but these and other *dēmiourgoi* are endemic throughout the *GA*, *Physics*, and *Metaphysics* as figures illustrative of natural coming-to-be.

104. *Phys.* III.2 201a10f.

105. Rémi Brague, "Aristotle's Definition of Motion and its Ontological Implications," *Graduate Faculty Philosophy Journal* 13, no. 2 (1990): 1–22, 3.

106. Simplicius, *On Aristotle's "Physics 3"*, trans. J. O. Urmson, notes by Peter Lautner (Ithaca, NY: Cornell University Press, 2002), 414.1–7; Thomas Aquinas, *Commentary on Aristotle's Physics*, trans. Richard J. Blackwell, Richard J. Spath, and W. Edmund Thirlkel (New Haven, CT: Yale University Press, 1963), §285.

107. L. A. Kosman's key essay, "Aristotle's Definition of Motion," *Phronesis* 14 (1969): 40–62, makes this point extremely clearly and argues for the "actuality as product" view, distinguishing between deprivative and constitutive kinds of actuality and suggesting that the former is what Aristotle really means in the motion definition. While Kosman's "actuality as product" view has been highly influential, it has had its detractors, including James Kostman, "Aristotle's Definition of Change," *History of Philosophy Quarterly* 4, no. 1 (1987): 3–16, and D. W. Graham, "Aristotle's Definition of Motion," *Ancient Philosophy* 8 (1988): 209–15.

108. *Phys.* III.2 201b31f. It is possible (as Simplicius attributes to Porphyry and Alexander) that *energeia* and *entelecheia* are functioning differently here, but Aristotle states this paradox using both terms at different places, viz. at *Phys.* VIII.5 257b9 he uses *entelecheia atelēs* whereas at *Met.* IX.6 1048b29 and *Met.* IX.9 1066a20f it is *energeia atelēs*. *Energeia* does have work, *ergon*, at its heart, which one might associate with motion, *activity* rather than rest, although Aristotle's statements at *Met.* IX.6 that *energeia* is not a sort of motion are crystal clear.

109. Brague, "Aristotle's Definition," 20n12.

110. Brogan, *Heidegger and Aristotle*, 108–9. The argument starts at 102.

111. Protevi, *Time and Exteriority*, 51. A straightforward deconstructive account would emphasize that it is precisely in something like a definition of motion that *différance* must operate as both temporal deferral and difference as spatial or logical distinction.

112. *Phys.* III.2 202a2f, Brague's translation, "Aristotle's Definition," 13.

113. *Phys.* III.1 201a15–19, translation modified.

114. *De An.* II.6 418a17–20.

115. Kosman, "Aristotle's Definition of Motion," 58. Seeing is of course corporeal and thus kinetic, but to grant Aristotle his argument one may see moving things while in a state of stillness, even as the breathing, living body subtends the activity of seeing.

116. Iris Young, "'Throwing Like a Girl': Twenty Years Later," in *Body and Flesh: A Philosophical Reader*, ed. Donn Welton (Malden, MA: Blackwell, 1998), 289.

117. Young, "Twenty Years Later," 288.

6. SEXUAL DIFFERENCE IN POTENTIALITY AND ACTUALITY

1. *Met.* VI.2 1026a33f.

2. *Met.* VI.4 1028a1f.

3. The occurrence of each term and relationship between *energeia* and *entelecheia* is quantified, mapped out and analyzed extensively in George A. Blair, "The Meaning of 'Energeia' and 'Entelecheia' in Aristotle," *International Philosophical Quarterly* 7 (1967): 101–17.

4. Charlotte Witt, *Ways of Being: Potentiality and Actuality in Aristotle's Metaphysics* (Ithaca, NY: Cornell University Press, 2003).

5. For a profound and far-reaching analysis of Heidegger's Aristotle that has greatly contributed to my understanding, and which affirms the ontological primacy of motion in Aristotle, see Brogan, *Heidegger and Aristotle.*

6. Witt, *Ways of Being*, and Stephen Menn, "The Origins of Aristotle's Concept of Ἐνέργεια: Ἐνέργεια and Δύναμις," *Ancient Philosophy* 14, no. 1 (1994): 73–114, respectively, address these questions broadly and incisively.

7. Witt, in *Ways of Being*, ultimately argues that Aristotle's gendered hierarchy is extrinsic to the normative and teleological account of Being in *Metaphysics* IX. My contention throughout this book is rather that Aristotelian metaphysics is thoroughly permeated by and inseparable from a patriarchal hierarchy of sex and gender, upon which it relies to establish its very coherence and through which a certain symptomaticity in the text is disclosed.

8. See Jacques Lacan, *On Feminine Sexuality: The Limits of Love and Knowledge*, trans. Bruce Fink (New York and London: W. W. Norton, 1998), where, for example, he writes that, "when any speaking being whatsoever situates itself under the banner 'women,' it is on the basis of the following—that it grounds itself as being not-whole in situating itself in the phallic function. . . . There's no such thing as Woman because, in her essence—I've already risked using that term, so why should I think twice about using it again—she is not whole" (72–73). Lacan here reveals himself as Aristotle's loyal heir.

9. *GA* I.19 726b12.

10. See esp. *GA* IV.1 765b9–19.

11. *Met.* VIII.6 1045b18–22, translation modified.

12. *De An.* II.2 414a14f.

13. *De An.* II.2 414a14–29, translation modified.

14. See *Phys.* II.9 and the discussion of Aristotelian necessity in chapter 2.

15. *Phys.* I.9 192a24. In fairness to Aristotle he does qualify this by noting that femaleness and ugliness are "accidents" of subjects rather than subjects in themselves, but this does not obviate the force of the analogy.

16. See for example *Pol.* I.2 1253a19–24.

17. Heidegger, *"Phusis,"* 214.

18. See *Met.* XII.1–2 1069b2–15.

19. *Phys.* I.9 192a13–29.

20. It is worth recalling here that the feminine is not the only politically charged "opposite" characterized by privation in Aristotle's text. The contemporary eye is struck by the introduction to Book XII of the *Metaphysics*: "[Quality and quantity] hardly exist at all in the full sense, but are merely qualifications and affections of Being. Otherwise 'not-white' and 'not-straight' would also exist; at any rate we say too that they 'are,' e.g., 'it is not white'" (XII.1 1069a22–24). The "not-straight" and the "not-white" qualify as privations of an otherwise positive quality, despite the fact that the verb "to be" is used here, but possibly in a fashion that is merely analogical with a proper predicative usage. While "not-straight" (*ouk euthu*) is lifted directly from the Pythagorean table of opposites given in Book I of the *Metaphysics* (986a25) and reflects a hierarchy of value inherited from this tradition, the valuation of "whiteness" over the "non-white" is echoed throughout the text in Aristotle's many examples of "the white" as a quality in itself and as an "accident" of man (see, for example, the discussion at *Met.* IV.4 in which whiteness and culturedness are parallel positive accidents of a man, in this case Socrates). While race and sexuality as determinate axes of human difference only develop in modernity, and these categories have no specific purchase or any meaningful correlates in antiquity, it is still worth noting that an ontological hierarchy in which whiteness and straightness are explicitly valued over their opposites are live and operative in the classical Greek philosophical imaginary.

21. Heidegger, *"Phusis,"* 214.

22. *Gen. et Corr.* II.9 335a34, *Met.* VII.7 1032a22–23.

23. *Met.* IX.1 1046a9–11, translation mine.

24. Ibid. In *Met.* V, the philosophical dictionary, Aristotle offers a definition of *dunamis* that is similar to, though not exactly the same as that in Book IX. The Greek runs as follows: *hē men oun holōs archē metabolēs ē kinēseōs legetai dunamis en heterōi ē hēi heteron, hē d' huph' heterou ē hēi heteron.* "Thus *dunamis* means the source in general of change or motion in another thing, or in the same thing *qua* other; or the source of a thing's being moved or changed by another thing, or by itself *qua* other" (*Met.* V.12 1019a19–21, Apostle's translation). Here, in addition to the source of change being found *in* another, it is also *by* another. In this formulation an extra dose of agency and transitive power is seemingly added to the source of change, and the thing changed thereby appears more definitively in a passive mode.

25. "All things existing by nature appear to have in themselves a principle of motion" (*Phys.* II.1 192b14).

26. For a thorough account of this contrast see Trish Glazebrook, *Heidegger's Philosophy of Science* (New York: Fordham University Press, 2000), esp. 180, 190–1, 201.

27. In accordance with Lang's reading in *The Order of Nature*.

28. *De. An.* II.1 412a28.

29. Heidegger, *Aristotle's "Metaphysics" θ 1–3*, 72.

30. Heidegger, "*Phusis*," 227.

31. *Phys.* II.1 193b 20.

32. For example, "Because the sheltering that clears belongs to it, Beyng appears originarily in the light of concealing withdrawal." Martin Heidegger, "On the Essence of Truth," trans. John Sallis, in *Pathmarks* (Cambridge and New York: Cambridge University Press), 154.

33. Heidegger, "*Phusis*," 227.

34. *Gen. et Corr.* I.3 318a24–25. At *GA* II.V 741b21–24, by way of explaining that in death the heart fails last, just as it is formed first, Aristotle also compares nature with a runner, "covering a double course there and back, and retracing her steps towards the starting-point whence she set out. The process of generation starts from not-being and advances till it reaches being, that of destruction starts from being and goes back again till it reaches not-being." One might say, though, that while this describes the mechanism of death, it does not define its status vis-à-vis the teleology.

35. *Met.* VIII.5 1044b34–1045a1.

36. *Gen. et Corr.* I.6 323a10–11 and *passim*.

37. *Gen. et Corr.* I.7, 323b26, translation modified.

38. *Gen. et Corr.* I.7 324a11–14.

39. *Gen. et Corr.* I.7 324b14–19.

40. Heidegger, *Aristotle's "Metaphysics" θ 1–3*, 57.

41. *Met.* IX.1 1046a14–16, translation mine.

42. Heidegger, *Aristotle's "Metaphysics" θ 1–3*, 73.

43. Ibid., 74.

44. Indeed Tredennick's translation, "the principle in the patient itself which initiates a passive change in it" (*Met.* IX.1 1046a12–13), positively encourages this reading through the idea of initiation.

45. Carol Bigwood, *Earth Muse: Feminism, Nature, and Art* (Philadelphia: Temple University Press, 1993); Patricia J. Huntington, *Ecstatic Subjects, Utopia, and Recognition: Kristeva, Heidegger, Irigaray* (Albany: State University of New York Press, 1998); Jean Graybeal, *Language and "the Feminine" in Nietzsche and Heidegger* (Bloomington: Indiana University Press, 1990). See also generally Nancy J. Holland and Patricia Huntington, eds., *Feminist Interpretations of Martin Heidegger* (University Park: Pennsylvania State University Press, 2001).

46. Bigwood, *Earth Muse*, 99.

47. Ibid., 97.

48. Huntington, in *Ecstatic Subjects*, resists any such easy set of oppositions, finding in Bigwood's gesture of revaluation a problematic romanticization of the "feminine abyss" that is necessarily bound to terror in the patriarchal imagination. However, she does find in the late Heidegger's notion of *Gelassenheit* a particular vision in which receptivity and a nonappropriative relation to others and the world provides a new ethical mode profoundly conducive to feminist and other liberatory projects.

49. *GA* I.2 716a5–15.

50. *GA* I.20 729a24–27, translation modified.

51. *GA* II.3 737a22–24.

52. For an analysis of the mechanical *dunamis* Aristotle draws on in his recourse to the automatic puppets see Jean de Groot, "*Dunamis* and the Science of Mechanics: Aristotle on Animal Motion," *Journal of the History of Philosophy* 46, no. 1 (2008): 43–68.

53. *GA* I.19 726b12.

54. *GA* IV.1 765b9–19.

55. This is of course not an Aristotelian innovation—the oppositions of hot and cold, wet and dry are endemic in Presocratic natural philosophy; their alignment with hot and cold with male and female is well attested in Empedocles—see the Testimonia, mainly of Aristotle and Aëtius, grouped as A81 in *The Poem of Empedocles*, ed. Brad Inwood (Toronto: University of Toronto Press, 2001)—but the mechanism by which the scale of temperature is transformed into a logical opposition is Aristotle's contribution.

56. *Gen. et Corr.* II.1 329a25–26.

57. See *Phys.* I.6 and I.7.

58. *GA* I.19 726b15–24, translation modified.

59. *Met.* IX.7 1049a15–18, Apostle's translation.

60. *GA* II.3 737a18–30, translation modified.

61. Henry George Liddell and Robert Scott, *A Greek-English Lexicon*, rev. and aug. throughout by Sir Henry Stuart Jones with the assistance of Roderick McKenzie (Oxford: Clarendon Press, 1940), Perseus Digital Library, accessed June 18, 2012, http://tinyurl.com/greek-engl-lexicon.

62. *GA* II.4 738b4.

63. *GA* II.5 741b8.

64. *GA* IV.3 767b4–8.

65. Hesiod, *Works and Days*, 235, my translation.

66. Ibid., 182, my translation.

67. *GA* IV.3 768b26–28. Peck's marginal paragraph label rather beautifully calls this "Uneven development."

68. *GA* IV.3 768b30–35.

69. *GA* II.1 734b31–36, emphasis in original. Other references to the sperm's movement as possessing *logos* occur at 735a2, 740b33, and 767b20.

70. Furth, *Substance, Form and Psyche*, 117.

71. *GA* II.1 734b37–735a5 translation modified, original emphasis.

72. Heidegger, "*Phusis*," 214. Heidegger argues at length against a reading of natural processes in Aristotle on the model of *technē*, saying instead that *phusis* is rather a "going back into itself and emerging out of itself" (221). Of the role of *archē* in *phusis* he writes: "Hence the *archē* is not like the starting point of a push, which pushes the thing away and leaves it to itself. Rather, something determined by *phusis* not only stays with itself in its movedness but precisely goes back into itself even as it unfolds in accordance with the movedness (the change)" (195). However, in this conception is a fundamental refusal to bring into view the phenomena of sexual reproduction. Instead, *phusis* is illustrated by means of the growing plant: "While

the 'plant' sprouts, emerges, and expands into the open, it simultaneously
goes back into its roots, insofar as it plants them firmly in the closed ground
and thus takes its stand. . . . But it must not be thought of as a kind of built-
in 'motor' that drives something, nor as an organizer on hand somewhere,
directing the thing." And in the same paragraph against the technical analogy he writes, "No doubt a good deal of time has yet to pass before we
learn to see that the idea of 'organism' and of the 'organic' is purely modern, mechanistic-technological concept, according to which 'growing things'
are interpreted as artifacts that make themselves" (195). While I agree that
understanding nature as self-replicating artifacts is undesirable, it is nonetheless the Aristotelian text that leads us not so much to an understanding of
the *product* of *genesis* as an artifact, but of the *producer* in sexual reproduction as possessing a kind of masculine mastery modeled precisely on that of
the craftsman.

73. *GA* IV.3 767b31.
74. *GA* IV.3 767b23–25, translation modified.
75. *GA* IV.3 768a3–12, translation modified.
76. *GA* IV.3 768a12–15.
77. *GA* IV.3 768b14ff.
78. See *Poet.* XVIII 1455b24ff.
79. *GA* IV.3 768b21–24.
80. The force of *existasthai* as that which simultaneously diverts and
destroys may be demonstrated by Aristotle's usage in some other passages:
in *Nichomachean Ethics* III.12 he writes,"Pain may drive a man distracted
and destroy his nature [*lupē existēsi kai phtheirei tēn phusin*]" (1119a23);
in making the argument in *Gen. et Corr.* I.7 that agent and patient must
be alike in genus but not in species: "For whiteness could not be affected in
any degree by line, or line by whiteness, except perhaps incidentally . . . for
unless the two things are contraries or made up of contraries, one cannot displace the other from its natural condition [*ouk existēsi gar allēla tēs
phuseōs*]" (323b28); and in describing different kinds of change in *Physics*
VII.7: "A thing in motion departs least from its substance if it is in locomotion rather than in any other [kind of] motion [*dioti hēkista tēs ousias
existatai to kinoumenon tōn kinēseōn en tōi pheresthai*]" (261a20). In a discussion of how the spermatic residue is formed in *GA* I.18 he says, "whereas
everything that undergoes colliquescence (melting together) gets destroyed
and departs from its proper nature" (*suntēkonmenon de phtheiretai pan kai
existatai tēs phuseōs*) (725a29).

It is also impossible to ignore in this context Heidegger's designation in
Being and Time of the "*ekstatikon* pure and simple" as temporality (377).
That which stands outside, outside of itself, gives for Heidegger the primordial character of temporality, whether in past, present, or future, and primarily shows itself in the existential projecting into the future. As the translator's
note points out, "The root-meaning of the word 'ecstasis' (Greek *ekstasis;*
German, 'Ekstase') is 'standing outside'. Used generally in Greek for the
'removal' or 'displacement' of something, it came to be applied to states-of-
mind which we would now call 'ecstatic.' Heidegger usually keeps the basic

root-meaning in mind, but he also is keenly aware of its close connection with the root-meaning of the word 'existence'" (377n2). In this Aristotelian context, *existēmi* seems not to carry the meaning so much of standing outside itself, as being ousted from standing. That which *existatai* does not stand outside itself, manfully project itself into the future, but its character as standing is destroyed *as such* as it is pushed from its rightful place and feminized. A suggestive connection thus emerges between feminization, "becoming woman" to give it a Guattarian formulation, and the temporal dimension of *ekstasis*, which unfortunately cannot be explored here.

81. That the metaphysics of presence and gendered apportionment of activity and passivity still haunts and informs the biology of sexual difference in contemporary scientific theory and practice is explored in Emily Martin, "The Egg and the Sperm: How Science Has Constructed a Romance Based on Stereotypical Male-Female Roles," *Signs* 16, no. 3 (Spring, 1991); 485–501, and in Cynthia Kraus's analysis of genetics research into sex difference using the fruit-fly *drosophila*: "Naked Sex in Exile: On the Paradox of the 'Sex Question' in Feminism and Science" in *The Science and Politics of the Search for Sex Differences: A Special Issue of the National Women's Studies Association Journal* 12, no. 3 (2000); 151–77.

82. *Met.* VII.7 1032a20–22, Apostle's translation, modified.

83. See "Demeter" in Cavarero, *In Spite*, for a rendering of this myth in which a feminine power over not just birth and death, but birth and the possibility of no more birth is foregrounded: "It is not the nothingness of male philosophers who identify it with death which provides the measure the world, and its destiny; it is rather the *nothingness* of birth, a mute petrification of *phyein*: the desolate land where even death dies of unmourned immobility" (61).

84. *Met.* IX.1 1046a33–36, Apostle's translation.

85. *Met.* V.12 1019b18–19, Apostle's translation.

86. The homonymic connection between *hustera* and *husteron* is remarked upon orthogonally by Irigaray when she thematizes Plato's cave as the womb, in which men are prevented from turning around toward the *proteron*: "Head and genitals are kept turned to the front of the representational project and process of the *hystera*. To the *hystera protera* that is apparently resorbed, blended into the movement of *hysteron proteron*. For *hysteron*, defined as what is behind, is also the last, the hereafter, the ultimate. *Proteron*, defined as what is in front, is also the earlier, the previous" (*Speculum*, 244). The etymological issue is more difficult and yet suggestive: David Farrell Krell makes a convincing argument for a connection between the two in "Female Parts in *Timaeus*," *Arion*, New Series 2, no. 3 (1975), 400–21, 403–4. Chantraine, *Dictionnaire étymologique*, on the other hand, tells us that any semantic connection between the two words is impossible, remarking with a surprisingly forceful paralipsis that "it is not even necessary to evoke the name of the belly, Gk. *huderos*, Skr., *udàram*" (vol. IV, 1162; translation mine). The argument is that *husteron*, "later," is a comparative form (from *ud* + *-tero*; the Sanskrit equivalent is *uttara*), while *hustera*, far from being a feminine form of the same word, must derive from a

different root entirely: *udara*, in Sanskrit the interior part, the belly. However, Karl Brugmann, *A Comparative Grammar of the Indogermanic Languages* (New York: Westermann, 1891), in a discussion of the development of the comparative form *-tero*, links the development of the Indo-European *-t-mmo-* to *-tero* with *-mmo-* to *-ero*, and illustrates this by juxtaposing *ud* + *-tero* (as the root of *husteron*, later) with *ud* + *-ero* (as the root of *huderos*, belly), thereby suggesting an earlier relation between the root of the two words (171). *Ud-* in Sanskrit is a prefix denoting up and out, also a flowing out, as a spring, while *uda-* and *udan* unequivocally indicate water, as in the Greek *hudōr*. The liquid movement from interior to exterior that lies buried in the Indo-European root of both terms distinctly echoes Irigaray's feminist analysis of fluid mechanics, not to mention an archaic connection between springing forth from the earth and biological birth. The resonances with Cavarero's reading of the feminine in antiquity that seeks to revalue natality and its relation to futurity over against a masculine metaphysics dominated by death (Cavarero, *In Spite*) are also undeniable.

87. *Met.* V.22 1022b32–33, Apostle's translation.

88. *Met.* I.1 980a22–27.

89. For instance at *Met.* IX.8, 1050a34–1050b1.

90. Heidegger, "*Phusis*," 226.

91. Ibid., 227.

92. Heidegger, *Aristotle's "Metaphysics"* θ 1–3, 94.

93. Ibid., 95.

94. *Met.* IX.2 1046b5–8, Apostle's translation, modified.

95. *Met.* IX.2 1046b23–24, Apostle's translation, modified.

96. *Phys.* II.8 198b12–14. From the context it seems he has in mind Empedocles and Anaxagoras as proponents of this theory.

97. *Met.* IX.2 1046b18, Apostle's translation.

98. *Met.*IX.5 1048a11–14, Apostle's translation, modified.

99. Heidegger, *Aristotle's "Metaphysics"* θ 1–3, 121–22.

100. Ibid., 117–18.

101. "The primary contrariety is that of possession and privation" (*Met.* X.4 1055a34–35). Also, "one of the contraries is sufficient to produce the change by its absence or presence" (*Phys.* I.7 191a6–7).

102. *Met.* IX.5 1048a6–8.

103. Heidegger, *Aristotle's "Metaphysics"* θ 1–3, 126.

104. Blair, in "The Meaning of 'Energeia' and 'Entelecheia,'" reminds us that although for every sense of *energeia* there is a corresponding usage of *entelecheia*. In *Met.* IX *energeia* is used sixty times but *entelecheia* only four times. In this section I will therefore restrict my discussion to *energeia*, without forgetting that *entelecheia* as holding the end within, being at the end, or being at perfection haunts and is intertwined with its signification.

105. *Met.* IX.6 1048a38–b7.

106. "It is true that a certain variety is to be observed among the ends at which the arts and sciences aim; in some cases the activity of practicing the art is itself the end, whereas in others the end is some product over and above the mere exercise of the art; and in the arts whose ends are certain things

beside the practice of the arts themselves, these products are by nature superior to the activities" (*Eth. Nic.* I.1 1094a3–6).

107. *Met.* IX.8 1049b25–29, second clause, Apostle's translation.

108. *Met.* IX.6 1048a35–38.

109. *Tim.* 52b. See ch. 3.

110. *GA* IV.10 778a5–9.

111. Giorgio Agamben, "On Potentiality" in *Potentialities*, ed. and trans. Daniel Heller-Roazen (Stanford, CA: Stanford University Press, 1999), 182.

112. Heidegger, "*Phusis*," 230.

113. Ibid., 183.

114. Ibid., 184.

CODA. MATTERS ARISING: FROM THE ALEATORY FEMININE
TO ALEATORY FEMINISM

1. "Now this is matter, and it is like the female which desires the male and the ugly which desires the beautiful" (*Phys.* I.9 192a23–24).

2. This is nicely formulated at *De Cael.* III.2 300a20–27.

3. Irigaray, *This Sex*, 76.

4. Althusser, *Philosophy of the Encounter*, especially "The Underground Current of the Materialism of the Encounter" (163–207).

5. I am writing this Coda in the wake of Walter Brogan's lecture series on Aristotle's *Politics* at the Collegium Phaenomenologicum, Città di Castello, Italy, July 2012, and my understanding of this text is newly indebted to his searching insights. The question of the role of *agon* and the potential scope of diversity given by this text are where his analysis and mine part ways. Brogan's analysis is strongly aligned with that of Arlene Saxonhouse in *Fear of Diversity: The Birth of Political Science in Ancient Greek Thought* (Chicago: University of Chicago Press, 1992), and my position here applies equally to her analysis. I am not convinced, in light of the discourse on the unsuitability of women and natural slaves for political life in the early books of the *Politics*, that the multitude, to which Aristotle refers as constituting the *polis* and ruling by turns, can be any more diverse than any group of elite males, exemplified by the range of characters present at Plato's Symposium—a doctor, a legal expert, a comedian, a tragedian, a general, a philosopher, and so on. Furthermore, the interests of the subaltern (who appear simply in the guise of the poor in the *Politics*) must always for Aristotle be balanced with those of the rich, otherwise the *polis* will be degraded and perverted, if not destroyed. Such a rapprochement between classes was of course a central tenet of European fascism. This modern political outcome of Aristotle's ethical injunction of maintaining the mean remains an irreducible and inescapable aspect of his politics.

6. This argument is offered in a polemic against Plato's *Republic* at Aristotle, *Pol.* II.2 1261a14–24.

7. For organismic analogies in the *Politics* see, for example, I.2 1253a20–22; I.5 1254a36–1254b9; III.4 1277a4–11; IV.4 1290b25–40; for the degenerate regime as a diseased, disproportionate, or deformed body, see V.3

1302b34–1303a4 ("sometimes this happens also through chance occurrences
[*tuchas*]"); V.9 1309b21–30; VI.6 1320b33–39.
    8. See *Pol.* II.12 1274a13; V.6 1306b6.
    9. *Met.* XII.10 1075a14–23, Apostle's translation.
    10. See Long, *Ethics of Ontology* and Aristotle *On the Nature of Truth*;
Baracchi, *Aristotle's Ethics as First Philosophy*.
    11. Reiner Schürmann, *Broken Hegemonies*, trans. Reginald Lilly
(Bloomington: Indiana University Press, 2003). In *Philosophy in the Tragic
Age of the Greeks*, Friedrich Nietzsche finds this movement at work at the
very dawn of Greek philosophy, in Thales's insight that all things are water:
"because contained in it, if only embryonically, is the thought, 'all things are
one.'" Trans. Marianne Cowan (Washington, DC: Regnery, 1962), 39.
    12. Donna Haraway, "Situated Knowledges: The Science Question in
Feminism and the Privilege of Partial Perspective," *Feminist Studies* 14, no.
3 (1988): 575–99.
    13. Long, *Aristotle on the Nature of Truth*, 7 and passim.
    14. For a clear and comprehensive exposition of these notions see Manuel
De Landa, "Nonorganic Life," in *Incorporations*, ed. Crary and Kwinter.
    15. In *PA* I.1 Aristotle gives a particularly clear exposition of his overall
methodology in this specific context.
    16. James G. Lennox, "Teleology" in *Keywords in Evolutionary Biology*,
ed. Evelyn Fox Keller and Elizabeth Lloyd (Cambridge, MA: Harvard University Press, 1992), 329. Lennox provides a clear, uncontroversial, and well-supported account of Darwin's teleologism.
    17. Gilbert Simondon, *L'individu et sa genèse physico-biologique* (Grenoble: J. Millon, 1995). A summary of this text is available in English as Gilbert
Simondon, "The Genesis of the Individual," in *Incorporations*, ed. Crary
and Kwinter, 297–319. See also Arne De Boever, Alex Murray, Jon Roffe,
and Ashley Woodward, eds., *Gilbert Simondon: Being and Technology*
(Edinburgh: Edinburgh University Press, 2012).
    18. Carl Zimmer, "Tending the Body's Microbial Garden," *New York
Times*, June 19, 2012, D1.
    19. Derrida, "Autoimmunity: Real and Symbolic Suicides." For an incisive
biopolitical discussion of the concept of immunity in modernity, its poetic,
political, and juridical history, and its emergence as a biological concept, see
Ed Cohen, *A Body Worth Defending* (Durham, NC: Duke University Press,
2009).
    20. According to evolutionary biologist Lynn Margulis, bacteria such as
spirochetes (some of which causes syphilis and lyme disease) may have thus
ended up being incorporated into our very physiologies as cilia and sperm
tails. See Dorion Sagan, "Metametazoa: Biology and Multiplicity," in *Incorporations*, ed. Crary and Kwinter, 362–85.
    21. Ibid., 377.
    22. Georges Canguilhem, *The Normal and the Pathological*, trans. Carolyn R. Fawcett and Robert S. Cohen (New York: Zone Books, 1991), originally published as *Essai sur quelques problèmes concernant le normal et le
pathologique* (1943), republished with the title *Le normal et le pathologique*,

augmenté de Nouvelles réflexions concernant le normal et le pathologique (1966).

23. *Phys.* II.8 198b29–33.

24. Theophrastus, *Theophrastus "On First Principles" (known as his "Metaphysics"),* ed. and trans. Dimitri Gutas (Leiden: Brill, 2010), 10a25–28; 11a14–16.

25. See Richard McKirahan, *Philosophy Before Socrates,* 2nd ed. (Indianapolis, IN: Hackett, 2010), especially ch. 16, "Fifth Century Atomism: Leucippus and Democritus," 303–42.

26. Lucretius, *On the Nature of Things,* trans. Martin Ferguson Smith (Indianapolis, IN: Hackett, 2001) V.791–2.

27. Ibid., V.836–49.

28. Ibid., I.58–61.

29. This is not, however, to claim that Lucretius advocates any sort of explicit feminist politics, or even that his work is particularly sympathetic to actual women. Georgia S. Nugent, in " 'Mater' Matters: The Female in Lucretius' *De Rerum Natura,*" *Colby Quarterly* 30, no. 3 (September 1994): 179–205, shows convincingly that while Lucretian matter certainly has positive, generative feminine qualities, the feminine is also associated in the poem with decay, stench, stifling romantic love, mortality, and void and is therefore thoroughly ambivalent: both celebrated *and* repudiated. See also Elizabeth Asmis, "Lucretius' Venus and Stoic Zeus," *Hermes* 110, no. 4 (1982): 458–70; and for positions seeking to reclaim Lucretius for feminism, see Don Fowler, "The Feminine Principle: Gender in the *De Rerum Natura*" in *Lucretius on Atomic Motion: A Commentary on "De Rerum Natura", Book Two, Lines 1–332* (Oxford: Oxford University Press, 2002), 444–52, and Barbara Clayton, "Lucretius' Erotic Mother: Maternity as a Poetic Construct in *De Rerum Natura,*" *Helios* 26 (1999): 69–84. I thank Brooke Holmes for alerting me to these lively debates.

30. Giordano Bruno, *Cause, Principle and Unity, and Essays on Magic,* ed. Richard J. Blackwell and Robert de Lucca (Cambridge: Cambridge University Press, 1998).

31. These tropes are definitively investigated in Hannah Fenichel Pitkin, *Fortune is a Woman: Gender and Politics in the Thought of Niccolò Machiavelli,* 2nd ed. (Chicago: University of Chicago Press, 1999).

32. Friedrich Nietzsche, *The Birth of Tragedy* in *The Birth of Tragedy and Case of Wagner,* trans. Walter Kaufmann (New York: Random House, 1967), esp. section 8.

33. Irigaray undertakes an extended reading of Dionysus in *Marine Lover of Friedrich Nietzsche,* in which he appears as a masculine, phallic appropriation of feminine powers: "The power of the mother and the goddess of love gives way to the nurses and female servants of the phallic cult" (141). It seems to me rather that Dionysus's androgyny and gender transgression point to an element of performativity in gender that may function as a nascent critique of an Irigarayan philosophy of sexual difference.

34. Johann Wolfgang von Goethe, "The Spiral Tendency," in *Goethe's Botanical Writings,* trans. Bertha Mueller (Woodbridge, CT: Ox Bow Press, 1989), 130.

35. Goethe, "On the Spiral Tendency in Plants" in *Botanical Writings*, 140.

36. Ibid., 145.

37. Epicurus, Vatican Saying 52, in *The Essential Epicurus*, trans. Eugene O'Connor (Buffalo, NY: Prometheus, 1993). See also Fragment 1, "Peace of mind (*ataraxia*) and freedom from bodily pain are static pleasures; joy and gladness, however are regarded as active emotions, in accordance with their motility."

38. Beauvoir, *The Second Sex*, see in particular part 3, "Myths." For Lacan's elaboration of this "psychical fantasy of woman," see Jacques Lacan, *The Ethics of Psychoanalysis, 1959–1960*, ed. Jacques-Alain Miller, trans. Dennis Porter (New York: W. W. Norton, 1997), especially ch. 11, "Courtly Love as Anamorphosis," and Drucilla Cornell's discussion in *Beyond Accommodation*, ch. 1, "The Maternal and the Feminine: Social Reality, Fantasy, and Ethical Relation." For Luce Irigaray's extended investigation of this dynamic in various texts of the history of Western philosophy from Plato to Freud see *Speculum of the Other Woman*.

39. A programmatic statement, no doubt, but attested to repeatedly by numerous works of feminist philosophy since *The Second Sex*.

40. "Sexual difference is one of the major philosophical issues, if not the issue, of our age." Irigaray, *An Ethics*, 5.

41. For a precise, comprehensive, and politically incisive survey and analysis of organismic analogies in social and political life in a modern and postcolonial frame see Pheng Cheah, *Spectral Nationality* (New York: Columbia University Press, 2003), esp. part 1.

42. Althusser, *Philosophy of the Encounter*, 167–68.

43. Pheng Cheah, "Non-Dialectical Materialism," in *New Materialisms: Ontology, Agency, and Politics*, ed. Diana Coole and Samantha Frost (Durham, NC: Duke University Press, 2010), 71.

44. Étienne Balibar, "Eschatology versus Teleology: The Suspended Dialogue between Derrida and Althusser," in *Derrida and the Time of the Political*, ed. Pheng Cheah and Suzanne Guerlac (Durham, NC: Duke University Press, 2009).

45. Jacques Derrida, *Specters of Marx*, trans. Peggy Kamuf (New York: Routledge, 2006), 227n2. This footnote also includes a suggestive and remarkable equivalence between historical materialism and the figure of the automaton on the part of Benjamin, in which the latter has, in an age of mechanical reproduction, obviously come to signify something vastly different from its range of meanings in antiquity.

46. Cited in Balibar, "Eschatology versus Teleology," 69.

47. Althusser, *Philosophy of the Encounter*, 174.

48. Ibid. 172. I will refrain from commenting here on Althusser's own psychotic break, prior to these writings, in which he killed his wife by strangulation.

49. See De Landa, "Nonorganic Life," in which he describes the work of economist Robert Crosby, ecologist C. S. Holling, and chaos theorists Stuart Kauffman and Christopher Langton, 158–59.

50. Cheah, "Non-Dialectical Materialism," 80.

51. Ibid. 81.

52. Rosalyn Diprose, in "Women's Bodies Giving Time for Hospitality," *Hypatia* 24, no. 2 (2009): 142–63, mounts an important feminist critique of women's hospitality as exploitable and exploited by state policy in the Australian context: put to the work of national security, public health, and unlimited and unlegislated economic production.

53. Sara Ahmed's *The Promise of Happiness* (Durham, NC: Duke University Press, 2010), for example, closes with a call for a "politics of the hap," of a relation to happenstance that "might embrace what happens, but . . . also works toward a world in which things can happen in alternative ways" (223). The notion of happenstance as something that resists mastery, that one could "choose not to master," is in turn derived from Jean-Luc Nancy, *The Sense of the World*, trans. Jeffrey S. Librett (Minneapolis: University of Minnesota Press, 1997), 151, cited on 219.

54. Haraway, "Situated Knowledges," 593; Heraclitus, B123 DK.

55. Bruno Latour, *We Have Never Been Modern* (Cambridge, MA: Harvard University Press, 1993), 142ff. The political ecological ramifications of a materialist stance are also explored at length in Latour's other works, including *Pandora's Hope: Essays on the Reality of Science Studies* (Cambridge, MA: Harvard University Press, 1999) and *Politics of Nature: How to Bring the Sciences into Democracy* (Cambridge, MA: Harvard University Press, 2004).

56. See Jane Bennett, *Vibrant Matter* (Durham, NC: Duke University Press, 2007); William Connolly, *A World of Becoming* (Durham, NC: Duke University Press, 2011); Félix Guattari, *The Three Ecologies* (New York: Continuum, 2000); Karen Barad, *Meeting the Universe Halfway* (Durham, NC: Duke University Press, 2007).

57. Irigaray, *Marine Lover*, 91.

58. Irigaray, *This Sex*, 209.

59. Ibid., 30.

60. It is true that the late Heidegger's notion of nearness (*Nähe*) itself draws near to Irigarayan proximity, a conjunction that is explored in Krzysztof Ziarek, "Proximities: Irigaray and Heidegger on Difference," *Continental Philosophy Review* 33, no. 2 (2000): 133–58. Rebecca Hill, *The Interval*, also investigates the topology of proximity and interval in the context of thinking through sexual difference.

61. I developed this notion of interruptivity, and the argument more generally, in "The Interruptive Feminine: Aleatory Time and Feminist Politics," in *Undutiful Daughters: New Directions in Feminist Thought and Practice*, ed. Henriette Gunkel, Chrysanthi Nigianni, and Fanny Söderbäck (New York: Palgrave Macmillan, 2012).

62. See Lisa Baraitser, *Maternal Encounters: The Ethics of Interruption* (London: Routledge, 2009) for a compelling account of maternal experience that interprets its interruptions as uniquely generative and transformative.

63. Anna Watkins Fisher, in "We are Parasites: On the Politics of Imposition," *Art & Education*, June 28, 2011, accessed August 13, 2012, http://

www.artandeducation.net/paper/we-are-parasites-on-the-politics-of-impo-
sition/, and in "Like a Girl's Name: The Adolescent Drag of Amber Hawk
Swanson, Kate Gilmore, and Ann Liv Young," TDR (The Drama Review)
56, no. 1 (Spring 2012): 48–76, develops a notion of "parasitical feminism"
in feminist performance art practice that shares many features of aleatory or
interruptive feminism.

64. The closing statements given by members of Pussy Riot at their trial
at Moscow Khamovniki District Court on August 8, 2012, are exemplary in
this regard. Transcriptions may be found in Pussy Riot! A Punk Prayer for
Freedom: Letters from Prison, Songs, Poems, and Courtroom Statements,
Plus Tributes to the Punk Band that Shook the World (New York: The Feminist Press, 2013).

WORKS BY ARISTOTLE AND PLATO

Aristotle. *De Anima*. Translated by W. S. Hett. In Aristotle, *On the Soul. Parva Naturalia. On Breath*. Cambridge, MA: Harvard University Press, 2000.

———. *De Caelo*. Translated by W. K. C. Guthrie. Cambridge, MA: Harvard University Press, 1953.

———. *De Generatione et Corruptione*. Translated by E. S. Forster. In Aristotle, *On Sophistical Refutations. On Coming-to-Be and Passing-Away. On the Cosmos*. Cambridge, MA: Harvard University Press, 1992.

———. *Aristotle's De Motu Animalium*. Translated and edited by Martha Craven Nussbaum. Princeton, NJ: Princeton University Press, 1978.

———. *Generation of Animals*. Translated by A. L. Peck. Cambridge, MA: Harvard University Press, 1942.

———. *History of Animals*. Vol. 1 [Books I–III]. Translated by A. L. Peck. Cambridge, MA: Harvard University Press, 1965.

———. *History of Animals*. Vol. 2 [Books IV–VI]. Translated by A. L. Peck. Cambridge, MA: Harvard University Press, 2006.

———. *History of Animals*. Vol. 3 [Books VII–X]. Translated by D. M. Balme. Cambridge, MA: Harvard University Press, 1991.

———. *Historia Animalium*. Vol. 1 [Books I–X]. Translated by D. M. Balme. Cambridge: Cambridge University Press, 2002.

———. *Metaphysics*. Books I–IX. Translated by Hugh Tredennick. Cambridge, MA: Harvard University Press, 1989.

———. *Metaphysics*. Books X–XIV. Translated by Hugh Tredennick. In Aristotle, *Metaphysics X–XIV. Oeconomica. Magna Moralia*. Cambridge, MA: Harvard University Press, 1977.

———. *Aristotle's Metaphysics*. Translated with commentaries and glossary by Hippocrates G. Apostle. Grinnell, IA: Peripatetic Press, 1979.

———. *Metaphysics*. Translated by Richard Hope. Ann Arbor: University of Michigan Press, 1960.

———. *Meteorologica*. Translated by H. D. P. Lee. Cambridge, MA: Harvard University Press, 1987.

———. *Nicomachean Ethics*. Translated by H. Rackham. Cambridge, MA: Harvard University Press, 2003.

———. "On Memory and Recollection," *Parva Naturalia*. Translated by W. S. Hett. In Aristotle, *On the Soul. Parva Naturalia. On Breath*. Cambridge, MA: Harvard University Press, 2000.

———. "On Prophecy in Sleep," *Parva Naturalia*. Translated by W. S. Hett. In Aristotle, *On the Soul. Parva Naturalia. On Breath*. Cambridge, MA: Harvard University Press, 2000.

———. *On Sophistical Refutations*. Translated by E. S. Forster. In Aristotle, *On Sophistical Refutations. On Coming-to-Be and Passing-Away. On the Cosmos*. Cambridge, MA: Harvard University Press, 1992.

———. *Parts of Animals*. Translated by A. L. Peck. In Aristotle, *Parts of Animals. Movement of Animals. Progression of Animals*. Cambridge, MA: Harvard University Press, 2006.

———. *De Partibus Animalium I and De Generatione Animalium I (with passages from II. 1–3)*. Translated by D. M. Balme. Oxford: Clarendon Press, 1992.

———. *Aristotle's Physics*. Translated with commentaries and glossary by Hippocrates G. Apostle. Bloomington: Indiana University Press, 1969.

———. *Aristotle's Physics*. Translated by Richard Hope. Lincoln: University of Nebraska Press, 1961.

———. *Aristotle's Physics: A Guided Study*. Translated by Joe Sachs. New Brunswick, NJ and London: Rutgers University Press, 1995.

———. *Physics*. Vol. 1 [Books I–IV]. Translated by Philip H. Wicksteed and Francis M. Cornford. Cambridge, MA: Harvard University Press, 1957.

———. *Physics*. Vol. 2 [Books V–VII]. Translated by Philip H. Wicksteed and Francis M. Cornford. Cambridge, MA: Harvard University Press, 2000.

———. *Poetics*. Translated by S. Halliwell. In Aristotle, *Poetics*. Longinus, *On the Sublime*. Demetrius, *On Style*. Cambridge, MA: Harvard University Press, 2005.

———. *The Politics*. Translated by Carnes Lord. Chicago: University of Chicago Press, 1985.

———. *Posterior Analytics*. Translated by Hugh Tredennick. In Aristotle, *Posterior Analytics. Topica*. Cambridge, MA: Harvard University Press, 1960.

———. *Prior Analytics*. Translated by Hugh Tredennick. In Aristotle, *The*

Categories. On Interpretation. Prior Analytics. Cambridge, MA: Harvard University Press, 1996.

———. *Rhetoric.* Translated by J. H. Freese. Cambridge, MA: Harvard University Press, 1926.

———. *Topica.* Translated by E. S. Forster. In Aristotle, *Posterior Analytics. Topica.* Cambridge, MA: Harvard University Press, 1960.

Plato. *Laws.* Vol. 1 [Books I–VI]. Translated by R. G. Bury. Cambridge, MA: Harvard University Press, 1994.

———. *Laws.* Vol. 2 [Books VII–XII]. Translated by R. G. Bury. Cambridge, MA: Harvard University Press, 1984.

———. *Phaedrus.* Translated by Alexander Nehemas and Paul Woodruff. In *Plato: Complete Works*, edited by John M. Cooper. Indianapolis, IN: Hackett, 1997.

———. *Republic.* Vol. 1 [Books I–V]. Translated by Chris Emlyn-Jones and William Preddy. Cambridge, MA: Harvard University Press, 2013.

———. *Republic.* Vol. 2 [Books VI–X]. Translated by Chris Emlyn-Jones and William Preddy. Cambridge, MA: Harvard University Press, 2013.

———. *Symposium.* Translated by Seth Bernadete. Chicago: University of Chicago Press, 1993.

———. *Theaetetus.* Translated by Harold North Fowler. In Plato, *Theaetetus. Sophist.* Cambridge, MA: Harvard University Press, 1921.

———. *Timaeus.* In *Timaeus and Critias*, translated by Desmond Lee. New York: Penguin, 1977.

———. *Timaeus.* Translated by R. G. Bury. In Plato, *Timaeus. Critias. Cleitophon. Menexenus. Epistles.* Cambridge, MA: Harvard University Press, 1989.

———. *Timaeus.* In *Gorgias and Timaeus*, translated by B. Jowett. Mineola, NY: Dover Publications, 2003.

———. *Plato's Timaeus.* Translated by Peter Kalkavage. Newburyport, MA: Focus Publishing, R. Pullins, 2001.

———. *Timaeus.* Translated by Donald J. Zeyl. Indianapolis, IN: Hackett, 2000.

OTHER WORKS

Aeschylus. *Eumenides.* Translated by Alan H. Sommerstein. In Aeschylus, *Oresteia: Agamemnon, Libation-Bearers, Eumenides.* Cambridge, MA: Harvard University Press, 2008.

Agamben, Giorgio. "On Potentiality." In *Potentialities*, edited and translated by Daniel Heller-Roazen, 177–84. Stanford, CA: Stanford University Press, 1999.

Ahmed, Sara. *The Promise of Happiness*. Durham, NC: Duke University Press, 2010.

Althusser, Louis. *Philosophy of the Encounter: Later Writings, 1978–1987.* Edited by François Matheron and Oliver Corpet, translated by G. M. Goshgarian. London: Verso, 2006.

———. *Reading Capital.* Translated by Ben Brewster. London and New York: Verso, 1979.

Anzaldúa, Gloria. *Borderlands/La frontera: The new mestiza.* 2nd ed. San Francisco: Aunt Lute Books, 1999.

Aquinas, Thomas. *Commentary on Aristotle's Physics.* Translated by Richard J. Blackwell, Richard J. Spath, and W. Edmund Thirlkel. New Haven, CT: Yale University Press, 1963.

Asmis, Elizabeth. "Lucretius' Venus and Stoic Zeus." *Hermes* 110, no. 4 (1982): 458–70.

Balibar, Étienne. "Eschatology versus Teleology: The Suspended Dialogue between Derrida and Althusser." In *Derrida and the Time of the Political,* edited by Pheng Cheah and Suzanne Guerlac, 57–73. Durham, NC: Duke University Press, 2009.

Balme, D. M. "The Place of Biology in Aristotle's Philosophy." In *Philosophical Issues in Aristotle's Biology,* edited by Allan Gotthelf and James Lennox, 9–20. Cambridge: Cambridge University Press, 1987.

———. "Teleology and Necessity." In *Philosophical Issues in Aristotle's Biology,* edited by Allan Gotthelf and James Lennox, 275–86. Cambridge: Cambridge University Press, 1987.

Baracchi, Claudia. *Aristotle's Ethics as First Philosophy.* New York: Cambridge University Press, 2008.

Barad, Karen. *Meeting the Universe Halfway.* Durham, NC: Duke University Press, 2007.

Baraitser, Lisa. *Maternal Encounters: The Ethics of Interruption.* London: Routledge, 2009.

Beauvoir, Simone de. *The Second Sex.* Translated by Constance Borde and Sheila Malovany-Chevallier. New York: Alfred A. Knopf, 2009.

Bennett, Jane. *Vibrant Matter.* Durham, NC: Duke University Press, 2007.

Berryman, Sylvia. "Aristotle on *Pneuma* and Animal Self-Motion." *Oxford Studies in Ancient Philosophy* 23 (2002): 85–97.

Bianchi, Emanuela. "The Interruptive Feminine: Aleatory Time and Feminist Politics." In *Undutiful Daughters: New Directions in Feminist Thought and Practice,* edited by Henriette Gunkel, Chrysanthi Nigianni, and Fanny Söderbäck, 35–47. New York: Palgrave Macmillan, 2012.

Bigwood, Carol. *Earth Muse: Feminism, Nature, and Art.* Philadelphia: Temple University Press, 1993.

Blair, George A. "The Meaning of 'Energeia' and 'Entelecheia' in Aristotle." *International Philosophical Quarterly* 7 (1967): 101–17.

Bloom, Harold. *The Anxiety of Influence.* New York: Oxford University Press, 1973.

———. *A Map of Misreading.* Oxford: Oxford University Press, 2003.

Boethius. *Consolation of Philosophy.* Translated by V. E. Watts. London: Penguin Books, 1969.

Boisacq, Émile. *Dictionnaire étymologique de la langue grecque.* Heidelberg: Carl Winter's Universitätsbuchhandlung, 1923.

Bos, A. P. *On the Elements: Aristotle's Early Cosmology.* Assen: Van Gorcum, 1972.

Brague, Rémi. "Aristotle's Definition of Motion and its Ontological Implications." *Graduate Faculty Philosophy Journal* 13, no. 2 (1990): 1–22.

Braidotti, Rosi. *Nomadic Subjects.* New York: Columbia University Press, 1994.

Bréal, Michel. "Étymologies grecques." *Memoires de la Societé de linguistique de Paris* 10 (1898): 402–7.

Brogan, Walter. *Heidegger and Aristotle: The Twofoldness of Being.* Albany: State University of New York Press, 2005.

———. "Heidegger's Interpretation of Aristotle on the Privative Character of Force and the Twofoldness of Being." In *Interrogating the Tradition: Hermeneutics and the History of Philosophy*, edited by Charles E. Scott and John Sallis, 111–30. Albany: State University of New York Press, 2000.

Brugmann, Karl. *A Comparative Grammar of the Indogermanic Languages.* New York: Westermann, 1891.

Bruno, Giordano. *Cause, Principle and Unity, and Essays on Magic.* Edited by Richard J. Blackwell and Robert de Lucca. Cambridge: Cambridge University Press, 1998.

Butler, Judith. *Bodies That Matter.* New York: Routledge, 1993.

———. *Gender Trouble.* New York: Routledge, 1990.

———. *Undoing Gender.* New York: Routledge, 2004.

Canguilhem, Georges. *The Normal and the Pathological.* Translated by Carolyn R. Fawcett and Robert S. Cohen. New York: Zone Books, 1991.

Caputi, Jane. "On the Lap of Necessity: A Mythic Reading of Teresa Brennan's Energetics Philosophy." *Hypatia* 16, no. 2 (2001): 1–26.

Casey, Edward S. *The Fate of Place: A Philosophical History.* Berkeley: University of California Press, 1997.

Cavarero, Adriana. *In Spite of Plato: A Feminist Rewriting of Ancient Philosophy.* Translated by Serena Anderlini-D'Onofrio and Áine O'Healy. New York: Routledge, 1995.

Chanter, Tina. *Ethics of Eros: Irigaray's Rewriting of the Philosophers*. New York: Routledge, 1995.

Chantraine, Pierre. *Dictionnaire étymologique de la langue grecque*. Paris: Éditions Klincksieck, 1968.

Cheah, Pheng. "Non-Dialectical Materialism." In *New Materialisms: Ontology, Agency, and Politics*, edited by Diana Coole and Samantha Frost, 70–91. Durham, NC: Duke University Press, 2010.

———. *Spectral Nationality*. New York: Columbia University Press, 2003.

Cherniss, Harold F. *Aristotle's Criticism of Plato and the Academy*. Baltimore, MD: Johns Hopkins University Press, 1994.

Clayton, Barbara. "Lucretius' Erotic Mother: Maternity as a Poetic Construct in *De Rerum Natura*." *Helios* 26 (1999): 69–84.

Cohen, Ed. *A Body Worth Defending*. Durham, NC: Duke University Press, 2009.

Colebrook, Claire. "Dynamic Potentiality: The Body that Stands Alone." In *Rewriting Difference: Irigaray and "The Greeks,"* edited by Elena Tzelepis and Athena Athanasiou, 177–90. Albany: State University of New York Press, 2010.

Connolly, William. *A World of Becoming*. Durham, NC: Duke University Press, 2011.

Cooper, John M. "Hypothetical Necessity and Natural Teleology." In *Philosophical Issues in Aristotle's Biology*, edited by Allan Gotthelf and James Lennox, 243–74. Cambridge: Cambridge University Press, 1987.

Cornell, Drucilla. *Beyond Accommodation: Ethical Feminism, Deconstruction, and the Law*. New York: Routledge, 1991.

Dean-Jones, Lesley. "Aristotle's Understanding of Plato's Receptacle and Its Significance for Aristotle's Theory of Familial Resemblance." In *Reason and Necessity: Essays on Plato's "Timaeus"*, edited by M. R. Wright, 101–12. London: Duckworth, 2000.

De Boever, Arne, Alex Murray, Jon Roffe, and Ashley Woodward, eds. *Gilbert Simondon: Being and Technology*. Edinburgh: Edinburg University Press, 2012.

De Landa, Manuel. "Nonorganic Life." In *Incorporations*, edited by Jonathan Crary and Sanford Kwinter, 129–67. New York: Zone, 1992.

Deleuze, Gilles. *The Logic of Sense*. Translated by Mark Lester with Charles Stivale, edited by Constantin V. Boundas. New York: Columbia University Press, 1990.

Derrida, Jacques. "Autoimmunity: Real and Symbolic Suicides: A Dialogue with Jacques Derrida." Translated by Pascale-Anne Brault and Michael Naas. In *Philosophy in a Time of Terror: Dialogues with Jürgen*

Habermas and Jacques Derrida, by Giovanna Borradori, 85–136. Chicago: University of Chicago Press, 2004.

———. "Chora." Translated by Ian McCloud. In *Chora L Works: Jacques Derrida and Peter Eisenman*, edited by Jeffrey Kipnis and Thomas Leeser, 15–32. New York: The Monacelli Press, 1997.

———. "The Double Session." In *Dissemination*, translated by Barbara Johnson, 173–285. Chicago: University of Chicago Press, 1981.

———. "Freud and the Scene of Writing." In *Writing and Difference*, translated by Alan Bass, 196–231. London: Routledge & Kegan Paul, 1978.

———. "*Geschlecht*: Sexual Difference, Ontological Difference." *Research in Phenomenology* 13 (1983): 65–83.

———. "My Chances/*Mès Chances*: A Rendezvous with Some Epicurean Stereophonies." In *Taking Chances: Derrida, Psychoanalysis, Literature*, edited by Joseph H. Smith and William Kerry, 1–32. Baltimore, MD: Johns Hopkins University Press, 1984.

———. "*Ousia* and *Grammē*: Note on a Note from *Being and Time*." In *Margins of Philosophy*, translated by Alan Bass, 29–67. Chicago: University of Chicago Press, 1982.

———. "Plato's Pharmacy." In *Dissemination*, translated by Barbara Johnson, 61–171. Chicago: University of Chicago Press, 1981.

———. *Rogues: Two Essays on Reason*. Translated by Pascale-Anne Brault and Michael Naas. Stanford, CA: Stanford University Press, 2005.

———. *Specters of Marx*. Translated by Peggy Kamuf. New York: Routledge, 2006.

Descartes, René. "Meditations on First Philosophy." In *Discourse on Method and Meditations*, translated by E. S. Haldane and G. R. T. Ross, 53–121. Mineola, NY: Dover Publications, 2003.

Deslauriers, Marguerite. "Sex Difference and Essence in Aristotle's *Metaphysics* and Biology." In *Feminist Interpretations of Aristotle*, edited by Cynthia Freeland, 138–67. University Park: Pennsylvania State University Press, 1998.

Diprose, Rosalyn. "Women's Bodies Giving Time for Hospitality." *Hypatia* 24, no. 2 (2009): 142–63.

duBois, Page. *Sowing the Body: Psychoanalysis and Ancient Representations of Women*. Chicago: University of Chicago Press, 1988.

Dudley, John. *Aristotle's Concept of Chance: Accidents, Cause, Necessity, and Determinism*. Albany: State University of New York Press, 2012.

El-Bizri, Nader. "'*Qui Etes-vous Chōra?*' Receiving Plato's *Timaeus*." *Existentia* 11 (2001): 473–90.

Empedocles. *The Poem of Empedocles*. Edited by Brad Inwood. Toronto: University of Toronto Press, 2001.

Epicurus. *The Essential Epicurus.* Translated by Eugene O'Connor. Buffalo, NY: Prometheus, 1993.

Fausto-Sterling, Anne. *Sexing the Body.* New York: Basic Books, 2000.

Ferrarin, Alfredo. *Hegel and Aristotle.* Cambridge: Cambridge University Press, 2001.

Fisher, Anna Watkins. "Like a Girl's Name: The Adolescent Drag of Amber Hawk Swanson, Kate Gilmore, and Ann Liv Young." *TDR (The Drama Review)* 56, no. 1 (Spring 2012): 48–76.

———. "We are Parasites: On the Politics of Imposition." *Art & Education,* June 28, 2011. Accessed August 13, 2012. http://www.artandeducation. net/paper/we-are-parasites-on-the-politics-of-imposition/.

Foster, Hal. *Compulsive Beauty.* Cambridge, MA: MIT Press, 1993.

Fowler, Don. "The Feminine Principle: Gender in the *De Rerum Natura.*" In *Lucretius on Atomic Motion: A Commentary on "De Rerum Natura," Book Two, Lines 1–332, 444–52.* Oxford: Oxford University Press, 2002.

Freeland, Cynthia A. "Accidental Causes and Real Explanations." In *Aristotle's Physics: A Collection of Essays,* edited by Lindsay Judson, 49–72. Oxford: Clarendon Press, 1991.

———. "Aristotle on Perception, Appetition, and Self-Motion." In *Self-Motion: From Aristotle to Newton,* edited by Mary Louise Gill and James G. Lennox, 35–63. Princeton, NJ: Princeton University Press, 1994.

———. "Aristotle on Possibilities and Capacities." *Ancient Philosophy* 6 (1986): 69–89.

———, ed. *Feminist Interpretations of Aristotle.* University Park: Pennsylvania State University Press, 1998.

———. "Nourishing Speculation: A Feminist Reading of Aristotelian Science." In *Engendering Origins: Critical Feminist Readings in Plato and Aristotle,* edited by Bat-Ami Bar On, 145–87. Albany: State University of New York Press, 1994.

Freud, Sigmund. *Beyond The Pleasure Principle.* Translated by James Strachey. In Vol. 18, *The Standard Edition of the Complete Psychological Works of Sigmund Freud,* 1–64. London: Hogarth Press and the Institute of Psycho-Analysis, 1955.

———. *The Ego and the Id.* Translated by Joan Riviere, edited by James Strachey. New York: W. W. Norton, 1960.

———. *Introductory Lectures on Psychoanalysis.* Translated and edited by James Strachey. New York: W. W. Norton, 1977.

———. "A Note upon the Mystic Writing Pad." Translated by James Strachey. In Vol. 5, *Collected Papers,* 175–80. London: The Hogarth Press and the Institute of Psycho-Analysis, 1953.

————. "The Uncanny." Translated by Joan Riviere. In Vol. 4, *Collected Papers*, 368–407. London: The Hogarth Press and the Institute of Psycho-Analysis, 1953.

Frisk, Hjalmar. *Griechisches etymologisches Wörterbuch*. Heidelberg: Carl Winter Universitätsverlag, 1970.

Furley, David. "Self-Movers." In *Self-Motion: From Aristotle to Newton*, edited by Mary Louise Gill and James G. Lennox, 3–14. Princeton, NJ: Princeton University Press, 1994.

Furth, Montgomery. *Substance, Form and Psyche: An Aristotelian Metaphysics*. Cambridge: Cambridge University Press, 1988.

Fuss, Diana. *Essentially Speaking: Feminism, Nature and Difference*. New York: Routledge, 1989.

Fuss, Diana J. "'Essentially Speaking': Luce Irigaray's Language of Essence." *Hypatia* 3, no. 3 (1989): 62–80.

Galen. *On the Usefulness of the Parts of the Body (De Usu Partium)*. Translated by Margaret Tallmadge May. Ithaca, NY: Cornell University Press, 1968.

Gallop, Jane. *Thinking Through the Body*. New York: Columbia University Press, 1988.

Gelber, Jessica. "Form and Inheritance in Aristotle's Embryology." *Oxford Studies in Ancient Philosophy* 39 (2010): 183–212.

Genova, Judith. "Feminist Dialectics: Plato and Dualism." In *Engendering Origins: Critical Feminist Readings in Plato and Aristotle*, edited by Bat-Ami Bar On, 41–52. Albany: State University of New York Press, 1994.

Gill, Mary Louise. "Aristotle on Self-Motion." In *Self-Motion: From Aristotle to Newton*, edited by Mary Louise Gill and James G. Lennox, 15–34. Princeton, NJ: Princeton University Press, 1994.

Glazebrook, Trish. *Heidegger's Philosophy of Science*. New York: Fordham University Press, 2000.

Goethe, Johann Wolfgang von. "On the Spiral Tendency in Plants." In *Goethe's Botanical Writings*, translated by Bertha Mueller, 131–45. Woodbridge, CT: Ox Bow Press, 1989.

————. "The Spiral Tendency." In *Goethe's Botanical Writings*, translated by Bertha Mueller, 127–30. Woodbridge, CT: Ox Bow Press, 1989.

Gotthelf, Allan. Introduction to *Historia Animalium*, by Aristotle, 1–48. Vol. 1 [Books I–X]. Cambridge: Cambridge University Press, 2002.

Graham, D. W. "Aristotle's Definition of Motion." *Ancient Philosophy* 8 (1988): 209–15.

Grandsaignes d'Hauterive, R. *Dictionnaire des racines des langues européennes*. Paris: Librairie Larousse, 1949.

Graybeal, Jean. *Language and "the Feminine" in Nietzsche and Heidegger.* Bloomington: Indiana University Press, 1990.

Green, Judith M. "Aristotle on Necessary Verticality, Body Heat and Gendered Proper Places in the Polis: A Feminist Critique." *Hypatia* 7, no. 1 (1992): 70–96.

Groot, Jean de. "*Dunamis* and the Science of Mechanics: Aristotle on Animal Motion." *Journal of the History of Philosophy* 46, no. 1 (2008): 43–68.

Grosz, Elizabeth. *The Nick of Time.* Durham, NC: Duke University Press, 2004.

———. "Notes Towards a Corporeal Feminism." *Australian Feminist Studies* 5 (1987): 1–16.

———. *Time Travels.* Durham, NC: Duke University Press, 2005.

———. *Volatile Bodies.* Bloomington: Indiana University Press, 1994.

———. "Women, *Chora*, Dwelling." In *Space, Time, and Perversion: Essays on the Politics of Bodies*, 111–24. New York: Routledge, 1995.

Guattari, Félix. *The Three Ecologies.* Translated by Ian Pindar and Paul Sutton. New York: Continuum, 2000.

Happ, Heinz. *Hyle: Studien zum aristotelischen Materie-Begriff.* Berlin: Walter de Gruyter, 1971.

Haraway, Donna. "Situated Knowledges: The Science Question in Feminism and the Privilege of Partial Perspective." *Feminist Studies* 14, no. 3 (1988): 575–99.

Hegel, G. W. F. *Lectures on the History of Philosophy: Plato and the Platonists.* Vol. 2. Translated by E. S. Haldane and Frances H. Simson. Lincoln: University of Nebraska Press, 1995.

———. *The Phenomenology of Spirit.* Translated by A. V. Miller. Oxford: Oxford University Press, 1977.

Heidegger, Martin. "The Anaximander Fragment." In *Early Greek Thinking*, translated by David Farrell Krell and Frank A. Capuzzi, 13–58. San Francisco: Harper & Row, 1984.

———. *Aristotle's "Metaphysics" θ 1–3: On the Essence and Actuality of Force.* Translated by Walter Brogan and Peter Warnek. Bloomington: Indiana University Press, 1995.

———. *Being and Time.* Translated by Joan Stambaugh. Albany: State University of New York Press, 1996.

———. *Country Path Conversations.* Translated by Bret W. Davis. Bloomington: Indiana University Press, 2010.

———. *The Essence of Human Freedom.* Translated by Ted Sadler. London: Continuum, 2002.

———. "Logos (Heraclitus Fragment B 50)." In *Early Greek Thinking*, translated by David Farrell Krell and Frank A. Capuzzi, 59–78. San Francisco: Harper & Row, 1984.

———. "On the Essence and Concept of Φύσις in Aristotle's *Physics B*, 1." Translated by Thomas Sheehan. In *Pathmarks*, edited by William McNeill, 183–230. Cambridge and New York: Cambridge University Press, 1998.

———. "On the Essence of Truth." Translated by John Sallis. In *Pathmarks*, edited by William McNeill, 136–54. Cambridge and New York: Cambridge University Press, 1998.

———. *Phenomenological Interpretations of Aristotle*. Translated by Richard Rojcewicz. Bloomington: Indiana University Press, 2001.

———. "Vom Wesen und Begriff der Φύσις: Aristoteles, Physik B, I." In *Wegmarken*, vol. 9 of *Gesamtausgabe*, 239–302. Frankfurt a. M.: Vittorio Klostermann, 1976.

Henry, Devin M. "How Sexist Is Aristotle's Developmental Biology?" *Phronesis* 52, no. 3 (2007): 251–69.

Heraclitus. *Fragments*. Translated by T. M. Robinson. Toronto: University of Toronto Press, 1987.

Hesiod. *Theogony*. Translated by Glenn W. Most. In Hesiod, *Theogony. Works and Days. Testimonia*. Cambridge, MA: Harvard University Press, 2006.

———. *Works and Days*. Translated by Glenn W. Most. In Hesiod, *Theogony. Works and Days. Testimonia*. Cambridge, MA: Harvard University Press, 2006.

Hill, Rebecca. *The Interval: Relation and Becoming in Irigaray, Aristotle, and Bergson*. New York: Fordham University Press, 2012.

Hofmann, J. B. *Etymologisches Wörterbuch des Griechischen*. München: Verlag Von R. Oldenbourg, 1949.

Holland, Nancy J. and Patricia Huntington, eds. *Feminist Interpretations of Martin Heidegger*. University Park: Pennsylvania State University Press, 2001.

Holmes, Brooke. *The Symptom and the Subject*. Princeton, NJ: Princeton University Press, 2010.

Homer. *Iliad*. Vol. 1 [Books I–XII]. Translated by A. T. Murray, revised by William F. Wyatt. Cambridge, MA: Harvard University Press, 1999.

———. *Iliad*. Vol. 1 [Books XIII–XXIV]. Translated by A. T. Murray, revised by William F. Wyatt. Cambridge, MA: Harvard University Press, 1999.

Homeric Hymn to Demeter. In *Homeric Hymns. Homeric Apocrypha.*

Lives of Homer, translated by Martin L. West. Cambridge, MA: Harvard University Press, 2003.

Huntington, Patricia J. *Ecstatic Subjects, Utopia, and Recognition: Kristeva, Heidegger, Irigaray*. Albany: State University of New York Press, 1998.

Irigaray, Luce. *An Ethics of Sexual Difference*. Translated by Carolyn Burke and Gillian C. Gill. Ithaca, NY: Cornell University Press, 1993.

———. *The Forgetting of Air in Martin Heidegger*. Translated by Mary Beth Mader. Austin: University of Texas Press, 1999.

———. *The Marine Lover of Friedrich Nietzsche*. Translated by Gillian C. Gill. New York: Columbia University Press, 1991.

———. "The Return." In *Rewriting Difference: Irigaray and "The Greeks"*, edited by Elena Tzelepis and Athena Athanasiou, 259–72. New York: State University of New York Press, 2010.

———. *Speculum of the Other Woman*. Translated by Gillian C. Gill. Ithaca, NY: Cornell University Press, 1985.

———. *This Sex Which Is Not One*. Translated by Catherine Porter. Ithaca, NY: Cornell University Press, 1985.

Jarry, Alfred. *Exploits and Opinions of Doctor Faustroll, Pataphysician*. Translated by Simon Watson Taylor. Boston, MA: Exact Change, 1996.

Judson, Lindsay. "Heavenly Motion and the Unmoved Mover." In *Self-Motion: From Aristotle to Newton*, edited by Mary Louise Gill and James G. Lennox, 155–71. Princeton, NJ: Princeton University Press, 1994.

Keyt, David. "Aristotle on Plato's Receptacle." *American Journal of Philology* 82 (1961): 291–300.

Kirk, G. S., J. E. Raven, and M. Schofield. *The Presocratic Philosophers*. 2nd ed. Cambridge: Cambridge University Press, 1983.

Kosman, Aryeh. "Aristotle's Prime Mover." In *Self-Motion: From Aristotle to Newton*, edited by Mary Louise Gill and James G. Lennox, 135–54. Princeton, NJ: Princeton University Press, 1994.

———. "Male and Female in Aristotle's *Generation of Animals*." Unpublished paper.

Kosman, L. A. "Aristotle's Definition of Motion." *Phronesis* 14 (1969): 40–62.

Kostman, James. "Aristotle's Definition of Change." *History of Philosophy Quarterly* 4, no. 1 (1987): 3–16.

Kraus, Cynthia. "Naked Sex in Exile: On the Paradox of the 'Sex Question' in Feminism and Science." *The Science and Politics of the Search for Sex Differences: A Special Issue of the National Women's Studies Association Journal* 12, no. 3 (2000); 151–77.

Krell, David Farrell. "Female Parts in *Timaeus*." *Arion*, New Series 2, no. 3 (1975): 400–21.

Kristeva, Julia. *Revolution in Poetic Language*. Translated by Margaret Waller. New York: Columbia University Press, 1984.

———. "Women's Time." Translated by Alice Jardine and Harry Blake. In *The Kristeva Reader*, edited by Toril Moi, 187–213. Oxford: Blackwell, 1991.

Kuenzli, Rudolf E. "Surrealism and Misogyny." In *Surrealism and Women*, edited by Mary Ann Caws, Rudolf Kuenzli, and Gwen Raaberg, 17–26. Cambridge, MA: MIT Press, 1991.

Lacan, Jacques. *Écrits: A Selection*. Translated by Alan Sheridan. New York and London: W. W. Norton, 1977.

———. *The Ethics of Psychoanalysis, 1959–1960*. Edited by Jacques-Alain Miller, translated by Dennis Porter. The Seminar of Jacques Lacan, Book 7. New York: W. W. Norton, 1997.

———. *The Four Fundamental Concepts of Psychoanalysis*. Translated by Alan Sheridan. London and New York: W. W. Norton, 1981.

———. *On Feminine Sexuality: The Limits of Love and Knowledge*. Translated by Bruce Fink, edited by Jacques-Alain Miller. The Seminar of Jacques Lacan, Book 20. New York and London: W. W. Norton, 1998.

Lange, Lynda. "Woman is Not a Rational Animal: On Aristotle's Biology of Reproduction." In *Discovering Reality: Feminist Perspectives on Epistemology, Metaphysics, Methodology, and Philosophy of Science*, edited by Sandra Harding and Merrill B. Hintikka, 1–15. Dordrecht, Holland: D. Reidel Publishing Company, 1983.

Lang, Helen S. *The Order of Nature in Aristotle's Physics*. Cambridge: Cambridge University Press, 1998.

Laqueur, Thomas. *Making Sex: Body and Gender from the Greeks to Freud*. Cambridge, MA: Harvard University Press, 1990.

Latour, Bruno. *Pandora's Hope: Essays on the Reality of Science Studies*. Cambridge, MA: Harvard University Press, 1999.

———. *Politics of Nature: How to Bring the Sciences into Democracy*. Translated by Catherine Porter. Cambridge, MA: Harvard University Press, 2004.

———. *We Have Never Been Modern*. Translated by Catherine Porter. Cambridge, MA: Harvard University Press, 1993.

Lennox, James. "Teleology, Chance and Aristotle's Theory of Spontaneous Generation." *Journal of the History of Philosophy* 20, no. 3 (1982): 219–33.

Lennox, James G. "Teleology." In *Keywords in Evolutionary Biology*, edited by Evelyn Fox Keller and Elizabeth Lloyd, 324–33. Cambridge, MA: Harvard University Press, 1992.

Liddell, Henry George and Robert Scott. *A Greek-English Lexicon*. Revised and augmented throughout by Sir Henry Stuart Jones with the assistance of Roderick McKenzie. Oxford: Clarendon Press, 1940. Perseus Digital Library. Accessed June 18, 2012. http://tinyurl.com/greek-engl-lexicon.

Lloyd, Genevieve. *The Man of Reason: "Male" and "Female" in Western Philosophy*. Minneapolis: University of Minnesota Press, 1984.

Long, Christopher P. *Aristotle On the Nature of Truth*. New York: Cambridge University Press, 2011.

———. *The Ethics of Ontology: Rethinking an Aristotelian Legacy*. Albany: State University of New York Press, 2004.

Lucretius. *De Rerum Natura*. Translated by W. H. D. Rouse. Cambridge, MA: Harvard University Press, 1975.

———. *On the Nature of Things*. Translated by Martin Ferguson Smith. Indianapolis, IN: Hackett, 2001.

Martin, Emily. "The Egg and the Sperm: How Science Has Constructed a Romance Based on Stereotypical Male-Female Roles." *Signs* 16, no. 3 (Spring, 1991): 485–501.

Mayhew, Robert. *The Female in Aristotle's Biology*. Chicago: University of Chicago Press, 2004.

McKirahan, Richard. *Philosophy Before Socrates*. 2nd ed. Indianapolis, IN: Hackett, 2010.

Mendell, Henry. "Topoi on Topos: The Development of Aristotle's Concept of Place." *Phronesis* 32, no. 2 (1987): 206–31.

Menn, Stephen. "The Origins of Aristotle's Concept of Ἐνέργεια: Ἐνέργεια and Δύναμις" *Ancient Philosophy* 14, no.1 (1994): 73–114.

Merleau-Ponty, Maurice. "The Intertwining—The Chiasm." In *The Visible and the Invisible*, edited by Claude Lefort, translated by Alphonso Lingis, page numbers. Evanston, IL: Northwestern University Press, 1973.

Morrow, Glenn R. "Necessity and Persuasion in Plato's *Timaeus*." *Philosophical Review* 59 (1950): 147–63.

Moss, Jessica. *Aristotle on the Apparent Good: Perception, Thought, and Desire*. Oxford: Oxford University Press, 2012.

Murphy, Susan. "Heron of Alexandria's 'On Automaton-making.'" *History of Technology* 17 (1995): 1–44.

Nagel, Ernest. *Teleology Revisited and Other Essays in the Philosophy and History of Science*. New York: Columbia University Press, 1979.

Nancy, Jean-Luc. *Being Singular Plural*. Translated by Robert D. Richardson and Anne E. O'Byrne. Stanford, CA: Stanford University Press, 2000.

———. *The Sense of the World*. Translated by Jeffrey S. Librett. Minneapolis: University of Minnesota Press, 1997.

Nielsen, Karen M. "Private Parts of Animals: Aristotle on the Teleology of Sexual Difference." *Phronesis* 53, no. 4–5 (2008): 373–405.

Nietzsche, Friedrich. *The Birth of Tragedy*. In *The Birth of Tragedy and The Case of Wagner*, translated by Walter Kaufmann, 15–144. New York: Random House, 1967.

———. *Philosophy in the Tragic Age of the Greeks*. Translated by Marianne Cowan. Washington, DC: Regnery, 1962.

Nugent, Georgia S. "'Mater' Matters: The Female in Lucretius' *De Rerum Natura*." *Colby Quarterly* 30, no. 3 (Sept. 1994): 179–205.

Nussbaum, Martha C. *The Fragility of Goodness: Luck and Ethics in Greek Tragedy and Philosophy*. Cambridge: Cambridge University Press, 1986.

———. "The Role of *Phantasia* in Aristotle's Explanation of Action." In *Aristotle's De Motu Animalium*, by Aristotle, translated and edited by Martha Craven Nussbaum, 221–69. Princeton, NJ: Princeton University Press, 1978.

Ortega, Mariana. "Exiled Space, In-Between Space: Existential Spatiality in Ana Mendieta's *Siluetas* Series." *Philosophy and Geography* 7, no. 1 (2004): 25–41.

Ortner, Sherry B. "Is Female to Male as Nature is to Culture?" In *Woman, Culture, and Society*, edited by Michelle Zimbalist Rosaldo and Louise Lamphere, 67–87. Stanford, CA: Stanford University Press, 1974.

Pahl, Katrin. *Tropes of Transport: Hegel and Emotion*. Evanston, IL: Northwestern University Press, 2012.

Parisi, Luciana. "Event and Evolution." *The Southern Journal of Philosophy* 48, Spindel Supplement (2010): 147–64.

Partridge, Eric. *Origins: An Etymological Dictionary of Modern English*. New York: Routledge, 2009.

Peck, A. L. Introduction to *Generation of Animals*, by Aristotle, xxxviii–lxx. Cambridge, MA: Harvard University Press, 1942.

Philoponus. *On Aristotle's Physics 2*. Translated by A. R. Lacey. London: Duckworth, 1993.

Pitkin, Hannah Fenichel. *Fortune Is a Woman: Gender and Politics in the Thought of Niccolò Machiavelli*. 2nd ed. Chicago: University of Chicago Press, 1999.

Pokorny, Julius. *Indogermanisches etymologisches Wörterbuch*. Bern: Francke Verlag, 1959.

Protevi, John. *Time and Exteriority: Aristotle, Heidegger and Derrida*. London: Associated University Presses, 1994.

Pussy Riot! A Punk Prayer for Freedom: Letters from Prison, Songs, Poems, and Courtroom Statements, Plus Tributes to the Punk Band that Shook the World. New York: The Feminist Press, 2013.

Roller, Lynn E. *In Search of God the Mother: The Cult of Anatolian Cybele.* Berkeley: University of California Press, 1999.

Rubin, Gayle. "The Traffic in Women: Notes on the 'Political Economy' of Sex." In *Toward an Anthropology of Women,* edited by Rayna Reiter, 157–210. New York: Monthly Review Press, 1975.

Russell, Bertrand. *History of Western Philosophy.* New York: Simon & Schuster, 1945.

Sagan, Dorion. "Metametazoa: Biology and Multiplicity." In *Incorporations,* edited by Jonathan Crary and Sanford Kwinter, 362–85. New York: Zone, 1992.

Salamon, Gayle. "The Bodily Ego and the Contested Domain of the Material." *differences: A Journal of Feminist Cultural Studies* 15, no. 3 (2004): 95–122.

———. "Sameness, Alterity, Flesh: Luce Irigaray and the Place of Sexual Undecidability." In *Rewriting Difference: Irigaray and "The Greeks,"* edited by Elena Tzelepis and Athena Athanasiou, 191–201. Albany: State University of New York Press, 2010.

Sallis, John. *Being and Logos.* Bloomington: Indiana University Press, 1996.

———. *Chorology: On Beginning in Plato's "Timaeus".* Bloomington: Indiana University Press, 1999.

———. "Reception." In *Interrogating the Tradition: Hermeneutics and the History of Philosophy,* edited by Charles E. Scott and John Sallis, 87–93. Albany: State University of New York Press, 2000.

Sauvé Meyer, Susan. "Aristotle, Teleology, and Reduction." *The Philosophical Review* 101, no. 4 (1992): 791–825.

———. "Self-Movement and External Causation." In *Self-Motion: From Aristotle to Newton,* edited by Mary Louise Gill and James G. Lennox, 65–80. Princeton, NJ: Princeton University Press, 1994.

Saxonhouse, Arlene. *Fear of Diversity: The Birth of Political Science in Ancient Greek Thought.* Chicago, University of Chicago Press, 1992.

Schürmann, Reiner. *Broken Hegemonies.* Translated by Reginald Lilly. Bloomington: Indiana University Press, 2003.

Sedgwick, Eve Kosofsky. "Paranoid Reading and Reparative Reading, Or You're So Paranoid, You Probably Think This Essay Is About You." In *Touching Feeling,* 123–51. Durham, NC: Duke University Press, 2003.

Serres, Michel. *The Birth of Physics.* Manchester: Clinamen Press, 2000.

Sihvola, Juha. "Aristotle on Sex and Love." In *The Sleep of Reason: Erotic*

Experience and Sexual Ethics in Ancient Greece and Rome, edited by Martha C. Nussbaum and Juha Sihvola, 200–21. Chicago: University of Chicago Press, 2002.

Silverman, Kaja. *Male Subjectivity at the Margins*. New York: Routledge, 1992.

Simondon, Gilbert. "The Genesis of the Individual." Translated by Mark Cohen and Sanford Kwinter. In *Incorporations*, edited by Jonathan Crary and Sanford Kwinter, 296–319. New York: Zone, 1992.

———. *L'individu et sa genèse physico-biologique*. Grenoble: J. Millon, 1995.

Simplicius. *On Aristotle's Physics 2*. Translated by Barrie Fleet. London: Duckworth, 1997.

———. *On Aristotle's Physics 3*. Translated by J. O. Urmson, notes by Peter Lautner. Ithaca, NY: Cornell University Press, 2002.

Solmsen, Friedrich. *Aristotle's System of the Physical World: A Comparison with his Predecessors*. Ithaca, NY: Cornell University Press, 1960.

Sophocles. *Electra*. Translated by Hugh Lloyd-Jones. In Sophocles, *Ajax. Electra. Oedipus Tyrannus*. Cambridge, MA: Harvard University Press, 1994.

Sorabji, Richard. *Matter, Space and Motion: Theories in Antiquity and Their Sequel*. Ithaca, NY: Cornell University Press, 1988.

Shields, Christopher. "Mind and Motion in Aristotle." In *Self-Motion: From Aristotle to Newton*, edited by Mary Louise Gill and James G. Lennox, 117–34. Princeton, NJ: Princeton University Press, 1994.

Spivak, Gayatri Chakravorty. "Feminism and Deconstruction, Again: Negotiations." In *Outside in the Teaching Machine*, 121–40. New York: Routledge, 1993.

Theophrastus. *Theophrastus "On First Principles" (known as his "Metaphysics")*. Edited and translated with introduction, commentaries, and glossary by Dimitri Gutas. Leiden: Brill, 2010.

Thucydides. *The Peleponnesian War*. Translated by Richard Crawley. London: J. M. Dent, 1910.

Tress, Daryl McGowan. "The Metaphysical Science of Aristotle's *Generation of Animals* and its Feminist Critics." *Review of Metaphysics* 46 (1992): 307–41.

Tuana, Nancy. "The Weaker Seed." *Hypatia* 3, no. 1 (1988): 35–59.

Tzelepis, Elena and Athena Athanasiou, eds. *Rewriting Difference: Irigaray and "The Greeks."* Albany, NY: State University of New York Press, 2010.

Urbanas, Alban. *La notion d'accident chez Aristote*. Paris: Les Belles Lettres, 1988.

———. "On the Alleged Impossibility of a Science of Accidents in Aristotle." *Graduate Faculty Philosophy Journal* 13, no. 2 (1990): 55–78.

Valpy, F. E. J. *Etymology of the Words of the Greek Language.* London: Longman, Green, Longman and Roberts, 1860.

Waterlow, Sarah. *Nature, Change, and Agency in Aristotle's* Physics. Oxford: Clarendon Press, 1982.

———. *Passage and Possibility.* Oxford: Clarendon Press, 1982.

Watkins, Calvert. *The American Heritage Dictionary of Indo-European Roots.* Boston, MA: Houghton Mifflin Harcourt, 2000.

Wedin, Michael. "Aristotle on the Mind's Self-Motion." In *Self-Motion: From Aristotle to Newton*, edited by Mary Louise Gill and James G. Lennox, 81–116. Princeton, NJ: Princeton University Press, 1994.

Weinstein, Jami. "A Requiem to Sexual Difference: A Response to Luciana Parisi's 'Event and Evolution.'" *Southern Journal of Philosophy* 48, Spindel Supplement (2010): 165–87.

Whitford, Margaret. *Luce Irigaray: Philosophy in the Feminine.* London: Routledge, 1991.

Witmore, Michael. "We Have Never Not Been Inhuman." *postmedieval: a journal of medieval cultural studies* 1 (Spring/Summer 2010): 208–14.

Witt, Charlotte. "Form, Normativity, and Gender in Aristotle: A Feminist Perspective." In *Feminist Interpretations of Aristotle*, edited by Cynthia Freeland, 118–37. University Park: Pennsylvania State University Press, 1998.

———. *Ways of Being: Potentiality and Actuality in Aristotle's Metaphysics.* Ithaca, NY: Cornell University Press, 2003.

Wolkstein, Dianne. *Innana: Queen of Heaven and Earth.* New York: Harper & Row, 1983.

Young, Iris. "'Throwing Like a Girl': Twenty Years Later." In *Body and Flesh: A Philosophical Reader*, edited by Donn Welton, 286–290. Malden, MA: Blackwell, 1998.

Young, Iris Marion. *On Female Body Experience: "Throwing Like a Girl" and Other Essays.* Oxford: Oxford University Press, 2005.

Ziarek, Krzysztof. "Proximities: Irigaray and Heidegger on Difference." *Continental Philosophy Review* 33, no. 2 (2000): 133–58.

Zimmer, Carl. "Tending the Body's Microbial Garden." *New York Times*, June 19, 2012, D1.

Aquinas, Thomas, 73, 74, 177, 257n82
archai, 29, 30
archē, 33, 68, 75, 86, 149–50, 155, 156,
  157, 173, 175, 192, 195, 197, 198,
  201, 203, 206, 277n102, 281n72;
  and *archē kinēseōs*, 35, 46, 47, 50,
  59, 66, 67, 133, 146, 156, 159, 162,
  176, 192, 197, 206, 259n91
Aristophanes, 71, 121, 267n25
atomism, 17, 48, 52, 57, 66, 89, 160–
  61, 162, 195, 225, 231, 252n67
autoimmunity, 144
automaton, 28, 43–46, 48, 51, 66,
  168; and animal motion, 170;
  contradictory aspects of, 73; and
  Darwinism, 81; distinguished
  from *tuchē*, 73–74; etymology of,
  68–72; externality *vs.* internality
  of, 73–76, 257–58n82; literary
  references to, 69–72; as mechanism,
  67–68, 72, 75, 113, 173; as against
  nature, 73–74; and necessity, 52;
  psychoanalytic aspects of, 71–72,
  79; as self-moving, 67, 68, 70,
  79, 80–81, 113; and spontaneous
  generation, 67

Bacchae (Euripides), 233
Bachofen, J. J., 107, 233
Balibar, Étiennne, 235
Balme, David M., 59, 254n23, 256n59,
  258n88
Baracchi, Claudia, 227
Barad, Karen, 239
Barthélémy Saint-Hilaire, Jules, 73,
  257n82
bastard reasoning, 12, 22, 98, 103, 109,
  118, 171, 180, 220, 265n79
Beauvoir, Simone de, 121, 234, 258n89
becoming: and *automaton*, 80; and
  contraries, 202; and *dunamis/*
  matter relation, 188–90, 210;
  and the feminine, 102, 222; and
  materialism, 57; in Plato's *Timaeus*,
  86, 87, 90, 94, 96, 98, 99, 100,
  109, 110, 114, 260n108. *See also*
  coming-to-be
being, 40, 157, 168, 251n52, 267n9;
  modalities of, 183–84; and motion,
  177–80, 182; in Plato's *Timaeus*,
  96, 99, 100; twofoldness of, 24,
  178, 186, 194, 198, 212, 216, 240
Benjamin, Walter, 236, 288n45
Bennett, Jane, 239
Bergson, Henri, 224, 266n4
bia, 10, 52, 53, 54, 56, 65, 143, 162,
  165, 168

Bigwood, Carol, 198–99, 240, 280n48
bin Laden, Osama, 239
biology, 1–2; and aleatory phenomena,
  49, 57, 60, 67; and animal motion,
  169–76; contemporary, 229–30;
  and feminist critique, 57; and
  Goethe's work, 233; and necessity,
  49, 57–67, 162, 254n23; and *polis*,
  174, 175, 176; and respiration,
  60; and sex/gender distinction,
  30–31, 35. *See also* embryonic
  development; sexual reproduction
Bloom, Harold, 115, 161
body: hierarchical, 62–63, 166;
  maternal, 101–2; mechanical, 173;
  Platonic universe as, 87, 165–66;
  and *polis*, 174, 175; political, 225
Boethius, 247n3
Bosch, Hieronymus, 276n100
Brague, Rémi, 177, 178, 179
Braidotti, Rosi, 224, 241
Bréal, Michel, 70
Brogan, Walter, 178, 194, 278n5, 285n5
Bury, R. G., 91
Butler, Judith, 93, 101, 102, 104, 105,
  106, 250n33, 261–62n25, 265n79,
  267n18, 270n65

Cage, John, 161
Canguilhem, Georges, 230
Casey, Edward, 121, 128, 130, 136,
  267n20, 269n42
castration, 24, 26, 77, 212–13, 217, 218,
  221
Categories (Aristotle), 35, 40
causation: and aleatory phenomena,
  9–10, 28, 39–50, 66, 73–74; errant,
  10, 47, 55; external *vs.* internal,
  73–76; and first causes, 29–30; and
  motion, 145, 192; and multiplicity,
  39, 40, 46, 48, 49, 66; and
  necessity, 52, 162, 214; physicalist
  account of, 30, 31–32, 49, 248–
  49n17; in Plato's *Timaeus*, 88–89;
  plurality in, 30, 39, 40, 46, 65–66,
  133; and sexual reproduction, 27,
  36–39, 47; and teleology, 195. *See
  also* four causes
Cavarero, Adriana, 85, 107, 210,
  283n83, 284n86
chance: and *automaton*, 43–46, 51,
  73; and biology, 49, 57; and
  causation, 43–46, 49; female state
  associated with, 28; and material
  indeterminacy, 66; and motion,
  143; and sexual reproduction, 39.
  See also tuchē

and femininity, 156, 189, 201–3;
Heidegger on, 213; and heredity,
207–10; and impassivity, 198–200;
and *logos*, 213–18; and masculinity,
186; and matter, 156, 166, 186–91;
and motion, 156, 166, 174, 177,
180; and passivity, 186, 197–200;
and prime mover, 151–53, 156;
and receptacle/*chōra*, 90, 111; and
sexual difference, 184–86, 191–97;
and sexual reproduction, 75, 82,
175, 176, 192, 200–210; as source
of change, 191–97, 279n24

earth, element of. *See* four elements
ecliptic, sun's path on, 7, 23, 88, 141,
151, 157–60, 274n52
efficient cause. *See* motive cause
ejaculation, female, 276n98
ekmageion, 22, 90–94, 96, 98, 104, 111
ekstasis, 150, 158, 162, 168, 282–83n80
Electra (Sophocles), 53–54
Eleatics, 41, 177, 180
elements. *See* four elements
embryonic development, 61, 67, 75–76,
173, 193, 201, 204–6, 255n41
Empedocles, 17, 49, 57, 64, 214, 231,
281n55
encounter, concept of the, 226, 232,
234, 236–37, 238, 241
energeia, 183–84, 208, 212, 218–22,
284n104; as actuality, 24, 63, 75,
78, 85, 90, 153, 178, 183, 186,
200, 202, 203, 206, 208, 219,
220; contrasted with *dunamis*,
16, 183–86, 203, 218, 220, 221;
distinguished from motion, 181,
277n108; as prior to *dunamis*, 188,
219–20; and sexual difference,
184–86
entelecheia, 15, 24, 78, 90, 145, 153,
184, 218, 277n108, 284n104; as
actuality, 166, 177–82; first, 192;
as form, 187
entelechy, 33, 84, 153. *See also* actuality
(entelecheia); teleology; *telos*
Epicurus, 66, 160, 162, 225, 231
epistemology: and accident, 43; and first
causes, 30; and formal cause, 34, 35
eros, 122–25, 136, 146, 155, 156,
261n20, 268–69nn32–33. *See also*
desire
errancy, mimetic, 105
errant cause, in Plato's *Timaeus*, 10, 55,
89, 96, 106, 107, 260–61n17
essence: and accident, 42–43; and *logos*,
34–36

essentialism, 104, 105, 134, 224, 241
eternality, 43, 50, 55–56; and Plato's
Timaeus, 88, 90, 111
ethics: and sexual difference, 120–21,
136, 138–39; and *telos* as limit, 29
Eumenides (Aeschylus), 54
Euripides, 233
event, concept of the, 28, 248n10
Evenus, 53
explanation, in relation to cause, 30,
249n18, 251n55
externality *vs.* internality: and accident,
252n64; and alterity, 193; and
automaton, 73–76, 257–58n82; and
causation, 73–76; and *dunamis*,
192, 203; and female state, 83, 84;
and place, 129, 130; and receptacle/
chōra, 98; and sexual difference,
192

fact, in relation to value, 27
"falling together," 7, 11, 20, 22, 28,
66, 79, 84, 98, 116, 129, 130, 141,
143, 160. *See also* coincidence;
sumptōma
Fausto-Sterling, Anne, 271n65
feminine symptom, 3–4, 6, 14, 16, 20,
83–84; and aleatory phenomena,
3–4, 28, 46, 51, 57, 84, 85, 143,
169; and biological necessity,
60–62; and *dunamis/energeia*
relation, 184–85; and *dunamis/*
matter relation, 190–91; and
feminist politics, 241; and heredity,
209–10; and motion, 148, 151, 169;
and phallic masculinity, 176; and
place, 114, 116, 130; and Platonic
cosmos, 96, 98; and practical good,
172; and sexual reproduction, 38,
39, 60–61, 210
femininity: and *adunamia*, 186, 202,
209–13; as archaic, 107, 210; and
atomism, 232; and becoming, 102,
111, 222; and *clinamen*, 161–62,
209; and cold, 133, 202, 209; and
dancing, 181–82; and desire, 107,
127; downwardness associated
with, 84, 141, 144, 163, 164, 167;
and *dunamis*, 156, 189, 201–3;
and *ekmageion*, 91–93, 98; and
embryonic development, 75–76;
and errant cause, 10, 96, 106, 107;
and exclusion, 106; and finitude,
168; and fluidity, 62, 92–93; and
heredity, 81; and indeterminacy,
82–83, 84, 102; and irrationality,
27; and lability, 103–6, 222; and